Technology-Enhanced Language Learning

Technology-Enhanced Language Learning

Michael D. Bush, Editor

and

Robert M. Terry, Associate Editor

In Conjunction with the American Council
on the Teaching of
Foreign
Languages

National Textbook Company
a division of NTC/CONTEMPORARY PUBLISHING GROUP
Lincolnwood, Illinois USA

ISBN: 0-8442-9396-2

Published by National Textbook Company,
a division of NTC/Contemporary Publishing Group, Inc.,
4255 West Touhy Avenue,
Lincolnwood (Chicago), Illinois 60646-1975 U.S.A.

8 9 VP 0 9 8 7 6 5 4 3

Contents

Foreword

Few human enterprises match the difficulty of learning a second language past childhood. After having already learned a first language with apparent ease, an adult wishing to learn a second faces a psychologically challenging proposition—that of becoming once again a beginner at communicating. With the ideas and thoughts of an adult, the learner is saddled with a communicative ability that is not much more than that of an infant. The challenge of this endeavor has led the language-teaching profession as well as individual learners over the years to seek solutions in diverse and fascinating places. It is therefore no surprise that technology of all sorts has been the target of a significant level of interest to all parties.

Flint Smith captured this interest in two volumes of the ACTFL Foreign Language Education Series in the mid to late 1980s at a very early stage in the development of technology. Where he and the authors in those volumes spoke of *Computer-Aided Language Learning,* or CALL, we speak of *Technology-Enhanced Language Learning,* or TELL. The difference stems from the fact that the computer component has at the same time become less visible and more ubiquitous. The change in emphasis from *computer* to *technology* places direct importance on the media of communication made possible by the computer, which itself often remains unseen, rather than on the computer itself. For example, it is possible to observe present technological evolution and conclude from different perspectives that on the one hand the computer is becoming a television, or on the other that the television is becoming a computer. Furthermore, the computer makes possible the Internet, that intriguing network of networks that enables communications of all sorts that have only recently become imaginable.

Despite this difference between those volumes of 1987 and 1989 and the present, an incredible number of the ideas presented then are not outdated, despite the mind-boggling changes in technology that have taken place over the past seven or eight years. These changes have not only continued to accelerate, but also there is no doubt that they will continue to accelerate, at least into the foreseeable future. Some of the ideas presented then were more imagined than real, but they are interesting as much for what did not actually happen as for what did. The main difference today is that changes, although not yet widespread in education, are not only more imminent than ever, but now it also seems likely that the changes that actually come about will be more drastic than those anticipated by many futurists of the 1980s.

Accelerating, drastic, and mind-boggling changes? The mood that evokes such descriptions provoked within us a sense of urgency that led us to undertake this volume of articles. Our purpose was primarily to show how we can use technology today, but we did not want to forget to stimulate imaginations toward the possibilities of the future. One cannot imagine what is conceivable for the future without a clear understanding of what is possible today.

I am very grateful to Ed Scebold, the Executive Director of ACTFL, as well as to Connie Knop and the ACTFL Publications Committee she chairs for the opportunity to undertake such a project within the purview of the ACTFL Foreign Language Education Series. I am not aware of a better forum for the dissemination of ideas that are so important for the future of language learning and teaching. Their proposal for me to share responsibilities with an associate editor, Bob Terry, allayed my fears of going through the sort of extraordinary, hard-work effort I watched Flint Smith experience as editor of the volumes I mentioned above when he was a Distinguished Visiting Professor with us at the Air Force Academy.

Can there be a better coworker than Bob Terry? I don't see how. He has been incredibly supportive, encouraging, and, above all, efficient. It is through the pace that he has set that we have been able to come very close to meeting the development schedule we set months ago and to enable ACTFL and NTC to return the volume to its normal publication schedule. He mastered the vagaries of FTP and file conversion problems so we could exchange manuscripts in record time, and it often seemed that no sooner did I make a file ready for him to review, he sent back an E-mail with comments and suggestions for the authors or for the volume. Thanks, Bob!

The work of the Volume Advisory Committee has enabled us to go about this volume in what is a new and, I think, interesting way. I wish to thank Jerry Ervin, Mary Ann Hansen, David Herren, Jerry Larson, Mary Ann Lyman-Hager, Gunther Mueller, Jim Noblitt, Sue Otto, Jim Pusack, Bob Terry, and Donna Van Handle for their work in reviewing the excellent proposals we received. The Epilogue documents the process we used to select authors for the volume, but nothing of that effort would have been possible without the willingness of this illustrious group to carefully review, comment, and judge each of the proposals.

The authors were selected from among a terrific group of people who put together what was for the most part an impressive collection of twenty-three initial proposals. They responded well to suggestions and time pressures, putting forth a noteworthy effort to make this volume as complete and as valuable as possible for its readers.

The Advisory Committee and authors together make up an interesting collection of people. In this group are researchers, scholars, teachers, and administrators; each individual fits into one or more of these categories but many fit into all. All use technology in their work and some are pioneers in finding new ways technology can be used. But foremost, all are professionals who represent the best of the foreign language education profession. I appreciate their contributions.

I am extremely grateful for the opportunity to have spent my foreign language education career working within two wonderful organizations, the United States Air Force Academy and Brigham Young University (BYU). In addition to the generous support for my research I receive from BYU, I continue to enjoy a fruitful association with the Air Force Academy. A NeXT machine I have on loan from them has been extremely beneficial in setting up the means to communicate and exchange files during every phase of content development for the volume. Furthermore, the skills and devotion to duty of administrators and colleagues of both institutions have made my association with them a truly joyful experience. I also appreciate and have a great deal of respect for my associates at our small multimedia-development company, Alpine Media of Orem, Utah. Thanks to all of these organizations I have had at my disposal resources and capabilities of which most people can only dream.

I would also like to pay tribute to the late Professor Richard S. Beal. In the course on the United Nations I took from him at Brigham Young University in 1971, he conveyed to me the philosophy that the computer did not have to remain a tool controlled solely by the "computer priesthood" who ministered behind the glass walls where resided the large mainframe of the day. His investigation of voting in the UN General Assembly, which he presented to us in class, inspired me to dust off my FORTRAN textbook that had lain untouched since my introductory course a couple of years earlier and to begin programming for the first time on "real" problems rather than on assignments in my long-past computer class. Following my demonstration to him of an unsolicited program I wrote for the class, Professor Beal hired me to work for him on his research. Through the ensuing close association, he taught me well and led me to conclude twenty-five years ago this fall that the computer would become an important tool for individuals.

Finally, I would like to express appreciation for my wife and family. Perhaps too often during my work over the years Annie has been a "computer widow" and my children "computer orphans." Their support has certainly been vital to everything I have undertaken.

Michael D. Bush
September 7, 1996
Provo, Utah

Introduction

Technology-Enhanced Language Learning

Michael D. Bush

Brigham Young University

*Information Superhighway. Information Revolution. Information Age.
Internet. World Wide Web. Cybersphere. Fibersphere. Infosphere.*

Anyone who has access to any form of media has heard some or all of these
terms. No matter where we turn, we are barraged with evidence that digital
technology is affecting virtually every aspect of our lives. For example, 1994
saw a computer market that surpassed television sales for the first time ever.
Not even the wildest dreamers of the early days of the computer industry
would have predicted that such a possibility could become reality as quickly
as it did. It is clear that some sectors of our society have experienced phe-
nomenal growth in the implementation of digital technologies.

Yet, what has been the impact of technology on teaching and learning
in the language classroom? It seems clear that there are significant numbers
of classrooms around the country where technology has had no impact at all.
Is there potential waiting to be fulfilled? And let's consider the developers
who have been striving to put these technologies to work for language learners. Are they "technology nuts," eager to adopt any new thing that comes
along, but who have missed the mark concerning what is important to the
profession? Or are they pioneers who have blazed trails that others will
follow? Is the foreign language learning profession poised on an exciting
threshold of tremendous development, or will it continue to go slow in finding
interesting and exciting ways that technology can help solve the language-
learning problem?

To understand the state of technology in language learning today, one
needs to consider the historical setting of the past fifteen or so years. In 1980
Solveig Olsen published an article in the *Modern Language Journal* that
provided a foreshadowing of an answer to the first question above on
technology's impact. Moreover, it is quite interesting to consider the findings
of her survey as a prediction of what seems to have in fact happened.

In 1978 and 1979, Olsen surveyed foreign language departments in 1,810 four-year colleges. Of the 602 that returned the survey, 527 indicated that computer-assisted instruction was not in use and would not be considered in the near future. When asked about the potential for using computers in language learning, many were suspicious:

"My advice is to stay out. Computers can now teach computer language, not a living language."

To the question of whether their department would introduce computer-assisted instruction by 1980, department chairs responded with comments such as

- "I hope not."
- "Forget it!"
- "CAI is a waste of time, energy, and money that should be used to buy library books."
- "Don't do it. It is a very stupid idea. Language is a living thing. You must really be desperate to think of anything so dumb."

Some apparently felt that the computer would replace the teacher:

- "Somehow it does not fit into our concept of a liberal arts college where *human* communication is paramount."
- "A waste of time; you are dehumanizing language instruction. It will be held against you when you argue the humanistic nature of language studies."

In contrast with the negative attitudes of this group, other sectors of our society were of a different mind. Computer sales jumped from 724,000 in 1980 to 2.8 million units in 1982. In January 1983 *Time* picked the computer as the "Machine of the Year," replacing their traditional "Man of the Year" for 1982:

"Time's Man of the Year for 1982, the greatest influence for good or evil, is not a man at all. It is a machine: the computer" (Friedrich 1983).

This event most certainly raised anxiety to serious levels for many of the members of Olsen's survey group. Furthermore, their worst fears continued to come true before their eyes and at a pace they probably could not comprehend.

Consider for example the fact that in 1994 there were 48.5 million PCs sold, representing startling growth in the number of machines installed during the period since the survey was conducted. Although quite impressive by the sheer numbers, the increases are overwhelming when considering the computing power that was sold in 1994. Although there were about 67 times more computers sold that year than fourteen years previously, most of those units were roughly 128 times more powerful than the computers of 1980. This means that there was 8,576 times more computing power sold in 1994 than in 1980!

In addition, the advances show no sign of slowing. Moore's Law says that computing power doubles roughly every two years, and there is no end in sight. These advances are making possible some very interesting technological capabilities, putting us on the threshold of another significant development that will perhaps eclipse developments to date. We are witnessing the convergence of computers, communications technologies, and media into a totally new, synergistic *something* that promises to be infinitely more important than any of the technologies by themselves. The visions of the most visionary of the computer pioneers of the 1970s doubtless did not include the things that in fact are becoming possible.

To place the potential impact of these technologies in perspective for education in general, consider the following recommendations made in a recently completed study by the RAND Corporation for the White House Office of Science and Technology Policy and the Office of Technology of the U.S. Department of Education (Glennan and Melmed 1996). This study took an in-depth look at the role that technology is playing and probably should be playing in public schools today and concluded:

- Educational technology has significant potential for improving students' learning.

- Extensive use of technology in schools has the potential to promote significant school restructuring and expand the time and motivation for student learning.

- The growth in use of technology by schools is strong; schools are adding equipment and developing connections to the national information infrastructure at a high rate. However, many schools still lack significant access to technology.

- Data from a study by the IEA in 1992 suggested that the availability of technology in schools serving poor, minority, and special needs populations did not appear to lag substantially behind the averages of schools taken as a whole. However, to the extent that technology enables learning outside the school, large disparities in the access of students of different classes and ethnicity to technology is a matter of concern.

- Some schools and school districts have moved rapidly to a fairly ubiquitous use of technology, and their experiences should provide guidance to others that are following.

- The costs of ubiquitous use of technology are modest in the context of overall budgets for public elementary education, but moving to such use requires significant and potentially painful restructuring of budgets.

- When technology is deeply infused in a school's operations, teachers tend to assume new roles and require new skills. There is a strong consensus among the experts we consulted that neither the initial preparation of teachers nor the current strategies for continued professional development have been effective in developing these skills.

- While there has been a rapid expansion in home education software, the market for school-based content software has been modest and comparatively stagnant. Quality content software for middle and secondary schools is not broadly available. However, this market is likely to evolve rapidly. [See <http://www.rand.org/publications/MR/MR682/ed_ch5.html# RTFToC1>.]

The changes that these conclusions portend for public schools should give rise to great reflection on the part of all foreign language educators. Ready or not, it appears that technology will play an ever-increasing role in each of our institutions. It therefore behooves foreign language education professionals to better understand technology and its potential for foreign language learning. From curricular objectives to lesson planning, from pedagogical considerations to capabilities of hardware and software combinations, and from teacher training to software applicability, there will be no aspect of foreign language learning that will not be influenced by the technological revolution.

Returning to our second question above, where are we today with respect to the implementation of technology for language learning? In 1987 and 1989 ACTFL published two volumes in the Foreign Language Education Series as a result of its commission to Flint Smith (Smith 1989; Smith 1987). Covering the impact of technology on foreign language education at that time, these volumes became two of the best sellers ever in the ACTFL Foreign Language Education Series. But as illustrated above, seven years is a very long time, given the speed with which technology is developing. Things that were interesting but too expensive for widespread implementation at that time are now becoming commonplace today. Things that were only marginally imaginable are now becoming possible.

Given the incredible changes that have taken place and that will continue to unfold in our classrooms, it is necessary to once again address how technology can benefit language learners.

Volume Overview

So how do we make sense of imminent technological change and the status of technology implementation in foreign language learning? The main purpose of this volume is to explore new technologies from the perspective of the foreign language teaching professional. Gunther Mueller, a member of the Volume Advisory Committee, proposed the following graphic to help define the specific topics that authors needed to cover. As illustrated, the areas to be addressed fall within the intersection of issues related to the Learner, the Teacher, the Technology, and the Curriculum and converge at educational and learning Outcomes.

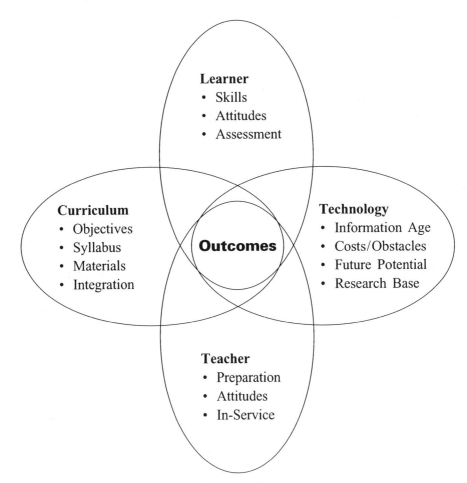

It was not possible to present every specific issue implied by this diagram; nevertheless, volume authors were challenged to address areas such as

- electronic technologies and ways their impact can benefit each of the four language skills;
- appropriate pedagogical strategies for technology in language learning;
- specific, noteworthy, technology-based applications for language learning;
- teacher education issues;
- technology implementation strategies to maximize positive impact on language-learning outcomes; and
- the potential for using technology to learn about the language-learning process itself.

Coverage of all possible topics was not exhaustive, but as the reader will see, the list of areas of concern discussed by the authors was extensive throughout the volume's nine chapters.

Chapter Overviews

In Chapter 1, "Taking Control of Multimedia," Pusack and Otto provide an excellent introduction to interactive technologies. After demonstrating how pedagogy must govern the ways new media are used, they go on to discuss how specific attributes can help both teachers and learners. They provide several excellent examples of actual applications and how they have been used to support sound language teaching pedagogy.

Chiquito, Meskill, and Renjilian-Burgy, in Chapter 2, "Multiple, Mixed, Malleable Media," contrast the dynamic nature of language with the static media that have traditionally been used in its teaching. They discuss specific projects and products and show how they can enrich the language-learning experiences of students. The authors have done extensive surveys of existing applications and provide this excellent overview of developments in the application of technology to individual language learning—from interactive videodisc to newer digital interactive multimedia technologies and network-based applications.

In Chapters 3 and 4, "Teaching Listening: How Technology Can Help" and "Hypermedia Technology for Teaching Reading," Joiner and Martínez-Lage each provide excellent theoretical underpinnings for how technology can support receptive skill learning. In Chapter 3, Joiner moves from more conventional approaches for teaching listening to multimedia technologies and provides an overview of how various technologies can be brought to bear on this particular skill, supporting her affirmations with actual research. In addition to the excellent overview in Chapter 4 of the reading process itself, Martínez-Lage also shows how she was able to create a hypermedia application from Laura Esquivel's best-selling novel, *Como agua para chocolate* (*Like Water for Chocolate*). She provides an overview of the development process as well as a glimpse at student results from using the application.

Teaching the productive skills with technology presents much more of a challenge than does teaching the receptive skills. In Chapter 5, "Computer-Mediated Communication: Technology for Improving Speaking and Writing," Beauvois reports on actual experiences using the computer in this mode. She thus provides empirical evidence for the efficacy of new approaches that combine technology-based communication and teacher-based instruction to address many important objectives for teaching speaking and writing.

Scinicariello, in Chapter 6, "Uniting Teachers, Learners, and Machines: Language Laboratories and Other Choices," provides an excellent overview of where the language laboratory is today and where it needs to go in the future. She points out that although language laboratories have experienced change in previous years, those of the past are almost insignificant with respect to the changes that are now taking place. Her discussion provides valuable insights into the restructuring that she says will need to take place. Not leaving things there, her advice pertaining to possible steps and potential pitfalls will be valuable to anyone involved with establishing, directing, or using language laboratories now or in the future.

As illustrated in Chapter 7, "Learning Language and Culture with Internet Technologies," Internet technologies such as E-mail and the World Wide Web are making an incredible entrée onto the education scene. In this chapter, Lafford and Lafford discuss activities using on-line technologies that students at various proficiency levels can perform as individuals or in small groups. They provide numerous examples of applications and show how they can be used with students.

Although there might be a great deal of interest among teachers for the use of technology in their language classes, unless they know how to use technology in the instructional programs they devise, it seems obvious to conclude that students will not benefit. In Chapter 8, "Meeting the Technology Challenge: Introducing Teachers to Language-Learning Technology," Kassen and Higgins point out how new technologies, more than ever before, dictate a serious need for teacher education. They also provide a specific example of a training program they have devised to address this problem.

Chapter 9, the final chapter of the volume, is entitled "Implementing Technology for Language Learning." With the goal of outlining reasonable expectations, Bush puts technology for foreign language education in the much broader contexts of technology in society and technology in education in general. Pointing out how foreign language students are not benefiting from the new learning tools becoming available, he illustrates how, without the profession's devising a coherent model for implementation, students will continue to miss out on the potential that technology has to offer for addressing language-learning problems. He also gives examples of how the situation can be turned around and places the potential for change within an overall societal context for technology in learning.

Conclusion

As illustrated by each of the chapters in this volume, technology for language learning can be an effective force for improving foreign language instruction. Furthermore, it is much more powerful and affordable today than ever before, and there is evidence that this situation will only continue to improve. Unfortunately, despite the incredible advances of recent years, not very many students benefit from its potential today. It is hoped that this volume will help change that.

REFERENCES

Friedrich, Otto. 1983. "The Computer Moves In." *Time,* January 3, pp. 14–24
Glennan, Thomas K., and Arthur Melmed. 1996. *Fostering the Use of Educational Technology: Elements of a National Strategy.* MR-682-OSTP. Santa Monica, CA: RAND Corporation. Also available at <http://www.rand.org/publications/MR/MR682/contents.html>.
Olsen, Solveig. 1980. "Foreign Language Departments and Computer-Assisted Instruction: A Survey." *Modern Language Journal* 64,3:341–49.
Smith, Wm. Flint, ed. 1989. *Modern Technology in Foreign Language Education: Applications and Projects.* ACTFL Foreign Language Education Series. Lincolnwood, IL: National Textbook Company.
———, ed. 1987. *Modern Media in Foreign Language Education: Theory and Implementation.* ACTFL Foreign Language Education Series. Lincolnwood, IL: National Textbook Company.

1

Taking Control of Multimedia

James P. Pusack and Sue K. Otto
University of Iowa

Introduction

Multimedia can be viewed as a way of managing and presenting the kinds of media we increasingly need for effective language teaching, as we develop new insights into language acquisition and expand our curricular goals. From the simplest drawing to the most demanding historical documentary, media provide grist for the language teacher's mill. Yet effective pedagogy and acquisition require control—control that computers can provide. In this chapter we look at control from several points of view. First, we consider the kinds of control computers can exercise over the media of instruction—both for teachers and for learners. Second, we explore how teachers can take control of multimedia in the classroom. Third, we introduce later chapters in this volume by outlining the ways that individual learners can interact with

James P. Pusack is Associate Professor of German and a former Director of PICS (the Project for International Communication Studies) at the University of Iowa. With Sue Otto, he co-authored a computer software package for foreign language instruction, DASHER, which is now widely used on several microcomputer platforms. In addition to contributing numerous articles, talks, and workshops in the field of computer-assisted language instruction, he has been engaged in the development of multimedia templates for the teaching of culture via authentic foreign video under a grant from FIPSE.

Dr. Sue K. Otto is Director of the Language Media Center, Adjunct Professor of Spanish, and Co-Director of the Project for International Communication Studies (PICS) at the University of Iowa. She was recently the Principal Investigator of "Building Cultural Fluency: A Multimedia Architecture," a federally funded grant project with the primary objective of full-scale integration of multimedia in a culture-based curriculum for intermediate language study in French and German. A Past Chair of the Executive Board of CALICO (The Computer Assisted Language Instruction Consortium) and Past President and Past Executive Director of the International Association for Learning Laboratories (IALL), Dr. Otto is a noted authority on the use of new technologies in the language laboratory and on computer-assisted instruction. She holds a Ph.D. in Spanish language and stylistics, and she has many years of experience in the development and programming of foreign language computer-assisted instruction. She teaches courses on foreign language instructional technology and has published articles and given papers and workshops on the use of media for language instruction.

multimedia. Fourth, we offer some perspectives on controlling factors that affect our ability as teachers to develop multimedia courseware. And finally, we sketch the various hardware and support issues that institutions must face when they choose to implement multimedia.

Interacting with Multimedia

Terms, Terms, Terms

To come to terms with current technology for teaching and learning, educators must decipher confusing terminology and a host of acronyms. They are confronted with complex hardware puzzles unlike any they have encountered in the past. Those who venture into this arena soon find that it is not for the fainthearted, not only because of the constant and inexorable evolution in the technologies themselves, but because of the ever-present challenge to determine how best to exploit new technologies to improve language education.

In the 1970s, the phenomenon of computer-assisted instruction (CAI) promised to revolutionize and individualize education. Due to the limitations of early computers, however, CAI or CALL (computer-assisted language learning) found limited acceptance among language professionals. But as computing has moved into graphical user interfaces and integrated media in the 1980s and 1990s, there has been a resurgence of interest in computer applications for student and teacher alike. Multimedia has captured our attention with its promise of multifaceted, multisensory experiences. Although one might say that multimedia represents education's most recent technological bandwagon—competing for this dubious honor with the Internet—it certainly constitutes the most compelling one to emerge in the past three decades in light of its promise to enhance the ways that language learners interact with the texts, sounds, and images of a foreign culture (Otto and Pusack 1993).

Simply defined, the term *multimedia* refers to the capacity to access and control via computer a full range of familiar media: text, motion video, photo images, sound, and graphics. At this writing, all media-related technology is moving toward what has been called the "digitalization of everything" in a unified environment. Related concepts that often arise in discussing the topic of multimedia are the terms *hypertext* and *hypermedia*. *Hypertext* describes the concept of a network of different documents cross-referenced via *hyperlinks,* which are words or phrases in one document that point to another text with more information related to that word or phrase. *Hypermedia,* a term derived by blending the terms *multimedia* and *hypertext,* is characterized by links to other media documents—audio, video, graphics, or text. The strength of multimedia software is in the synergy derived from presenting content using a variety of modalities that can reinforce each other and that are linked together in meaningful ways to provide an in-depth learning experience.

Hardware and the Digitalization of Everything

Before the emergence of multimedia, the field of media-enhanced computing was divided into interactive video and interactive audio. Without a lengthy discussion of all the Byzantine hardware configurations that came and went, involving such components as gigantic 15-inch floppy disks and computer boards with octopus tentacles attached to $1,200 VCRs, suffice it to say that we went through an early period of interactive audio and video based largely on traditional linear cassette technologies and various forms of randomly accessible analog recordings. On the audio side, the commercial success of digital audio compact discs set the stage for computer-based interactions with audio. Interactive audio is commonly based on digital audio texts stored on CD-ROM or on servers with massive hard drives. The focus for interactive audio is on listening comprehension practice and pronunciation tutoring. Certainly we can expect the traditional audiocassette-based language laboratory to disappear from the market in favor of computer-based digital audio technologies. For a decade or more we have stood at the threshold of speech input and recognition in interactive computer software. While speech input poses few problems for today's multimedia workstation, recognition of that speech to provide intelligent conversational interactions has proved to be too great a challenge for current technologies.

On the interactive video side, videodisc (a nondigital medium) became the standard format of choice and represents the present mature technology. The two primary variants currently seen in computer-controlled videodisc delivery environments are:

- two-screen configurations (a workstation with computer monitor and a separate video monitor); and
- one-screen configurations using video overlay technology in which the computer contains additional hardware that digitizes the video image from the videodisc and displays it on the computer monitor.

Barcode readers attached to videodisc players are a popular and less expensive alternative to computers for controlling videodisc. In fact, barcode-based interactive video represents the format that has found the most favor with commercial publishers of language materials. This variant of interactive video allows all the functions of videodisc playback control (searching to a frame or chapter, playing a specific videoclip, playing video without audio, etc.), but of course does not provide any of the other interactive or display capabilities we associate with computer-assisted language learning. The primary advantage of videodisc over existing digital technologies is in the high quality of the video images presented. However, videodiscs have remained expensive to produce and have limited storage capacity (generally a half-hour per side). In light of current technological advances, it is clear that videodisc is a format of the present and the past, not of the future.

The convergence of interactive audio, interactive video, traditional forms of CALL, and hypertext has resulted in what we know as multimedia. Because of the massive amounts of storage space needed for digital audio and video data, multimedia applications are now commonly distributed on CD-ROM. The CD-ROM format has established a foothold in the educational publishing marketplace to an extent that never occurred with other nonprint media formats. Likewise, it is unusual to find a computer system in an educational setting without a CD-ROM drive. However, we are at an interesting moment in this digital evolution of multimedia technology in which one critical component—video—still does not have an affordable, compact, high-quality digital alternative to analog forms. Current popular computer-based forms of digital video (such as Apple Computer's QuickTime) require massive storage capacity and are limited in their playback performance by slow access times from CD-ROM drives and servers. The video image is characteristically small, grainy, and jerky, and the sound is regularly out-of-synch with the video, a real liability for language learning.

A new consumer standard for digital media—DVD—looms on the horizon as a viable replacement for videodisc in the delivery of multimedia. DVD stands for *digital videodisc* or *digital versatile disc;* the format will store 4.7 gigabytes (4.7 billion bytes) of digital information on a single-sided, single-layer disc the same size as current CD-ROMs, which have a capacity of 650 megabytes. Employing a standard for compressing video and audio called MPEG-2, a DVD will be able to deliver a full-length, full-screen, full-motion film per side. Future plans include 9.4 gigabyte double-layer discs as well as double-sided, double-layer discs that will store 18.8 gigabytes, nearly thirty times the capacity of today's CD-ROMs. DVD has been adopted not only by all the major media-related corporations, including Toshiba, Sony, Philips, Time Warner, Pioneer, JVC, Hitachi, and Mitsubishi, but also by computer companies such as Microsoft, IBM, and Compaq. Because of this widespread support, the DVD format should occupy a stable niche in the near future while providing an acceptable storage and delivery mechanism for multimedia applications that rely heavily on motion video (Myslewski 1996). We live in exciting times in multimedia technology, which is both a curse and a blessing as we strive to strike a balance between what is available and what we have.

Educational Trends and the *Standards for Foreign Language Learning*

Technological details—daunting and unavoidable as they are—should not overshadow the more important issue of identifying the significant benefits of multimedia for language instruction. A brief survey of current models and trends in education, specifically language education, provides a logical point of departure in assessing the value of new technologies for languages. We are in an era of language education in which the emphasis is placed on process rather than product, on function over form. Current thinking has oriented our profession toward a more holistic approach to language education that moves beyond learning the forms of the language to attaining communicative competency and developing cross-cultural insights and strategies for effective communication with other peoples. In order to prepare students to function well in the language and culture, we have come to rely increasingly on the richness and depth of authentic materials for all levels of language learning, using them as a basis to build skills through authentic language experiences. Performance-based assessment is favored over assessment of factual knowledge and discrete skills. Collaborative group work is valued as an effective learning strategy. The concept of students as lifelong learners influences us to broaden language curricula with an eye toward development of critical thinking skills in a multidisciplinary context. We have begun to favor student-directed, student-centered learning models over teacher-dominated instruction. And we are making greater efforts to reach all language-learning populations—learners with disabilities, adult learners, learners in remote locations—and to accommodate different learner styles and strategies.

The five major goals outlined in the recently published *Standards for Foreign Language Learning* (*Standards,* 1996) encapsulate all these trends in our profession:

* communicate in languages other than English
* gain knowledge and understanding of other cultures
* connect with other disciplines and acquire information
* develop insight into the nature of language and culture
* participate in multilingual communities at home and around the world.

While the *Standards* do not extensively address technology, multimedia complements this philosophy of language learning through its potential to help learners reach all of the goals described, to amplify and enhance their learning experiences.

Dimensions of Multimedia

Several central attributes of multimedia instruction, particularly video-centered multimedia, warrant close examination in terms of their value for language learning:

• the combination of media types;
• the dimension of control, and
• aspects of help and guidance in interactivity.

In discussing these attributes, the close match between the technology and current trends as reflected in the *Standards* becomes very apparent.

Multiple Media

Various familiar information types have long been exploited by language teachers: printed texts, photos, slides, drawings, audio, and moving pictures. The primary defining characteristic of multimedia rests in the convergence of these media in a single interactive presentation environment, the computer. It has become an educational commonplace, bordering on cliché, to claim that learning is maximized when a combination of different modalities is used: we retain 10 percent of what we read; 20 percent of what we see; 30 percent of what we see and hear; and 70 percent of what we see, hear, and do (Rühlmann 1995:59). As we discover more about learner styles, however, it is just as important to consider that students may have personal modes or combinations of modes that work best for them as individuals, and we must never assume that specific media will be put to the same use or effect by all students. A multimedia environment has the potential to help students confront and comprehend material more effectively by offering alternative or redundant presentation modes to match learner preferences or needs.

Motivation can be an important effect of multimedia learning. Students can be much more intellectually engaged by interacting with complex mediated programs that present language and culture in context than they ever were studying paradigms and performing repetitive drills. They are motivated both by authentic experiences with the language and by the prospect of gaining skills that might have a practical application for them, that might prepare them better to live and work in the world (O'Malley and Chamot 1993:105). The appeal of multimedia is immediately obvious. Demonstrating multimedia language-learning materials to educated adults, for example, a group of university alumni, invariably evokes the welcome response, "I wish I'd had this when I was learning languages!" Nevertheless, the glitzy bells and whistles that seem so attractive to the casual observer are no substitute for solid pedagogical design and content.

Language is experienced in the real world in many ways—orally and written, formally and informally, actively and passively, with and without visual context. In full realization of this, important goals for language learners extend well beyond merely acquiring knowledge of the formal aspects of the language. Students should be prepared to handle the complex reality of a foreign language and culture not only at a rudimentary survival level but at a level that allows them to read, listen, write, and speak in a competent and informed fashion. To do this they must confront authentic documents, sounds, images, and ideas from the foreign culture. The allure of authentic video materials lies in the fact that students can observe real language in its full context, tapping a wealth of extralinguistic information to support learners in interpreting and comprehending not only the language but the culture as well. Students need extensive help as they encounter authentic materials, however, because little benefit (and great frustration) can be derived from the inherent difficulty of authentic language unless tasks are appropriate to the learners' linguistic level and familiarity with the culture. Cognitive psychology informs us that it takes knowledge to build knowledge; learners bootstrap themselves into new knowledge by using their existing knowledge and skills (Reeves 1992; O'Malley and Chamot 1993; Johnston and Milne 1995; McFarland 1995). Multimedia programs constitute the ideal response to this assumption because they can bridge students into learning through multiple interconnected support systems.

Further support for the potential of multimedia technology to enhance language learning can be found in the cognitive model of situated learning environments or contextualized learning experiences, which prepare students to apply what they have learned in an appropriate context. As Reeves (1992:50) describes it:

> A major concern for education and training is the degree to which learning transfers to external situations in which the application of knowledge, skills, and attitudes is appropriate. . . . [T]he way in which knowledge, skills, and attitudes are initially learned plays an important role in the degree to which these abilities can be used in other contexts. . . . In traditional instruction, information is presented in encapsulated formats, and it is largely left up to the student to generate any possible connections between conditions (such as a problem) and actions (such as the use of knowledge as a tool to solve the problem). There

is ample evidence that students who are quite adept at "regurgitating" memorized information rarely retrieve that same information when confronted with novel conditions that warrant its application.

This certainly reinforces the desirability of the simulations and task-based activities so well supported by multimedia. A case in point is the multimedia simulation *À la rencontre de Philippe*, whose basic task challenges students' language skills and their critical problem-solving skills. Beyond the direct interactions with the computer program, the context stimulates a variety of creative oral and written class-based activities: reconstructing and comparing multiple paths, creating new messages for the characters, "photographing" nonverbal cues for class critique. One of the most exciting outcomes from the implementation of this program is that students, who frequently work collaboratively in pairs or small groups, become so engaged and motivated by the tasks that they naturally focus on content rather than on form—they make authentic use of the language (Furstenberg 1992).

Control

Another defining attribute of multimedia resides in the dimension of control afforded the teacher and the learner, control over the lesson materials selected and the order in which they are accessed as well as control over the pace of progress through materials. In examining this issue, the double-edged nature of control emerges, especially as it concerns students and their ability to make the best choices for their own learning. For instance, a student using the recently published CD entitled *Le Louvre* may take a firsthand tour through the Louvre and discover a wealth of magnificently illustrated information about the Louvre buildings and salons, its collections, art history with period background music appropriate to the art works, and principles of artistic composition all narrated in clear accessible French. This rosy scenario of the empowered learner exploring a multimedia microcosm can rather quickly degenerate into just another episode of "Lost in Hyperspace," with the learner wandering through divergent pathways that never lead to any clear vision of the reality being explored. The research literature, as reported by Reeves (1993) and Hannafin and Sullivan (1995), indicates that students are often not the best judges of appropriate strategies for effective learning. While the research indicates that students' attitudes and motivation tend to be better if they have control over their learning and that some students do learn more if given the opportunity to control the amount and sequence of their work, the studies suggest that students who are of low ability, who have insufficient background knowledge, or who are confronted with very complex instructional tasks learn less than they do under more prescriptive program control.

This would seem to support the notion that in free-form multimedia environments, many learners will benefit from having at least some clearly defined tasks to perform while interacting with the materials.

Multimedia interfaces, especially those typically found in task-oriented lessons, provide a level of control that reduces anxiety and provides flexibility and efficiency in the playback of media and in the pacing of activities. For instance, in video-centered multimedia, students can watch the video as many times as they wish—starting, stopping, and replaying as necessary to cope with information overload. Moreover, they can choose which help features they need to access as they work to comprehend the material. This kind of control is quite different from that allowed by complex environments in which broader choices concerning selection of materials and of the sequence of presentation are determined by the learner. In the context of preparing students to be autonomous lifelong learners, however, we do need to teach them strategies and techniques for coping with complex systems and structures and for reflecting on and controlling their own learning progress.

From the teacher's perspective, enhanced control over media in the classroom setting can result in fundamental changes in both presentation content and classroom dynamic. Computer-controlled media have enormous advantages over traditional linear forms in the capability to navigate precisely in a video text, to control the mode of playback (such as video without audio and audio without video) for specific activity types, and to move easily between various media for a multifaceted presentation. For example, Project FLAME at the University of Michigan developed the Teacher's Partner, a multimedia workstation, in order to facilitate classroom instruction by presenting authentic native-speaker conversations. Johnston and Milne (1995) describe the impact of this technology in several critical areas: communicative talk, teacher talk, and assistance in complex teacher tasks. They observed that the Teacher's Partner encouraged more communicative language use: "The discourse of teacher and students was characterized less by talk about language or by drill and repetition, and more by direct interaction: either talk about the culture or talk in the TL [target language] about nonlanguage topics" (Johnston and Milne 1995:326). Although the amount of teacher talk in class did not decline with the use of the Teacher's Partner, focus of the teacher speech shifted from a central to a supportive role: "[T]he teacher talk is not dominating the classroom verbal activity, rather it is facilitating the students' attempts to become more independent speakers" (Johnston and Milne 1995:327). In spite of the enhanced presentation ability available to the instructor in conducting complex communicative discussions, Johnston and Milne (1995:328) point out that manipulating a complicated multimedia workstation adds its own demands on the teacher and that improvements in the computer hardware and its user interface are needed for more efficient use of the technology in the classroom.

Interactivity

A third defining characteristic of multimedia is its interactivity, which has many aspects including navigation and user interface design, lesson architecture, task formats and student input, help support systems, and recordkeeping. Issues of control and interactivity in multimedia instruction urgently require more attention from researchers to inform development. Luskin (1996:84) advocates the study of media psychology so that developers understand the cognitive impact that their design choices have on learners:

> The digital explosion, so far, has primarily been a technology drama. Consumer electronics companies, regional Bell operating companies . . . and other telecommunications firms, computer makers, print publishers, media conglomerates and budding software developers continue to invest literally hundreds of millions of dollars in the technology—the "how." To the present, very little has been carefully invested in the "why" of interacted [*sic*] program creation. We must now seize the opportunity to explore the "why" and to create a new discipline within which to structure our converging research.

The domain of navigation and user interface design covers a lot of terrain, from making sure the student can figure out how to move easily from place to place (without getting lost or confused), to understanding the use of icons, screen layout, and color, to framing the presentation of information to suit our pedagogical goals. For foreign language multimedia software developers, Gay and Mazur (1989) offer some of the best general design advice: begin with an epistemological analysis of the knowledge—analyzing the competencies, the underlying methodological theories and the conceptual structure—and then build a framework for interactions and activities that reflect this analysis. Too often software developers focus on the surface issues of look and feel without enough reflection on the match between interaction and desired learning outcomes.

Typically, interactions with the principal texts that comprise a foreign language multimedia program are supported by various kinds of contextualized links built into the environment: lexical help in the form of glossaries and illustrative images and video clips; hyperlinked annotations with cultural, grammatical, or other context-sensitive information; connections to other external resources on related topics. Too little is still understood about what actually helps students learn. The scant research that has been conducted in the area of help features for language learning has yielded some interesting results, cautioning that we cannot always assume that more media means better language learning. For example, Davey, Jones, and Fox (1995:42), who tracked student usage patterns in Danish language-learning software, suggest that there may be such a thing as too much help:

> The findings of the Guardian Angel project suggested that an over-generous supply of 'Help' information to language learners in IT [instructional technology] environments might cause problems. Indeed, some learners try to get the Help system to do as much of the work as possible, thus limiting their opportunities for supposedly productive practice and rendering themselves essentially passive. While it may be a good idea to avoid causing the learner stress, it is also possible that interactive effort needs to be required from the learner. This effort, in the context of language learning, may lie more in an active involvement in the learning process than in clicking 'buttons' or 'hotspots' on the screen.

Certainly many existing multimedia products feature predominately point-and-click interactions that require very little overt production or synthesis on the part of the student. However, we must not assume that no learning is going on, especially for the student who is making a good-faith effort to engage intellectually in the activities. But the repertoire of multimedia-based activity types clearly needs to include open-ended responses from students to balance and expand on more passive exercise formats.

In an experiment on the effectiveness of learning vocabulary with CALL materials, Greifnieder (1995) tested whether hearing the words as they were seen (text plus a pictorial representation) improved retention levels. Results indicated that audio support had no positive effect on retention of the words, suggesting to the researcher that visual perceptions dominated audio input in processing and retaining information. Complementary findings emerge in Chun and Plass's study (1996) of the effects of multimedia annotations—text, pictures, and motion video—on vocabulary acquisition. Their data showed that recall of vocabulary words with visual annotations (text + picture and text + video) was better than words with text-only annotations. Interestingly, annotations illustrated with static pictures proved more effective than annotations using motion video sequences, a result that the researchers speculated could be attributable to the generally unfixed, transient nature of motion sequences and possibly to some extent to the poorer image quality of the digital movies used in the experiment. They noted that when multiple annotations were available, students accessed them all, suggesting "that the availability of multiple types of annotations for words and ease of look-up may encourage more active behavior and that looking up a word more than once reinforces learning of that word" (Chun and Plass 1996:193).

Many language professionals engaged in CALL development have conspicuously failed to conduct research on their work. In their defense, this is due, at least in part, to the fact that this kind of research is quite difficult to conduct because of the multiplicity of uncontrollable variables, which leads to research on very narrow issues that do not provide developers with broad, generalizable guidance. The topics of the studies cited above represent the mere tip of the iceberg in investigating how students interact with multimedia and to what effect. Much more research needs to be done, not only to influence future development but also to validate CALL as a field of scholarship.

A Rationale for Foreign Language Multimedia

Theories of Language Learning

Multimedia is a technology, a device, one tool in a larger array of techniques for language teaching. There is no reason to believe that, if used systematically, multimedia could not occupy the exalted position of an approach or even a method on the same level, say, as small-group work or Total Physical Response. Alternatively, experience has shown that well-constructed multimedia components can play a useful role in a wide variety of approaches to language instruction. In this case, design and integration of computer-based activities must be driven by the more encompassing tenets of the overall approach. The realities of our current instructional delivery environments dictate that multimedia usage will continue to emerge within both top-down (methodologically driven) settings and bottom-up (opportunistically driven) settings. For those aspects of technology that are evolving most quickly, it will always be necessary to develop prototypes and conduct instructional experiments that demonstrate just what capabilities and features can be of significant use to students and teachers.

At the same time, our field functions within a larger research-based and theory-oriented framework. As Larsen-Freeman and Long (1991:288) already noted at the start of the decade, "there are at least forty 'theories,' 'models,' 'perspectives,' 'metaphors,' 'hypotheses' and 'theoretical claims' in the SLA [second-language acquisition] literature." In the context of this chapter on multimedia, it is important to clarify just how muddled the relationship between SLA theory and multimedia really is and must be. While SLA insights will stimulate and challenge developers of foreign language multimedia, the converse is also true: Multimedia offers some serious challenges to assumptions made in SLA research and theory.

The first point to make is that there are doubtless some areas of SLA theory (and research) that bear little direct relevance to CALL. For example, issues related to acquiring the speaking skill in naturalistic settings will continue to be peripheral. In instructed settings, too, a role for technology may be minimal as long as technology can only assist indirectly in teaching speaking (e.g., by providing conversational stimuli or by improving pronunciation). As will be demonstrated in this section, however, technology can fill many of the roles of the teacher in setting up environments and preconditions for speaking, in simulating speaking through writing, and so forth.

The second and larger point is that there are remarkably few areas of SLA theory and research that do not impact on the development and use of multimedia in foreign language teaching. At the same time, it is striking how seldom theorists and methodologists have reflected on the changes that multimedia has made or could make to their assumptions about the way instruction is delivered. A clear example of this is the familiar distinction between naturalistic language acquisition and instructed (classroom) acquisition. Most of the studies on instructed language acquisition deal only with traditional in-class, technology-free settings, which are usually contrasted with second-language settings where learning occurs in uninstructed situations in the target culture. Little or no attention has been paid to the way multimedia can replicate a subset of target-culture learning settings within the instructed foreign language setting.

In surveying the current panoply of issues in SLA theory and its correlated research, a few topics come to the fore as most germane to the application of multimedia in foreign language instruction:

- the overall value of instruction
- the role of grammar instruction
- the usefulness of error correction
- the impact of instruction on the development of accurate speech.

Unfortunately, while some of these tablets have been brought down from the mountain over the past two decades (beginning with Krashen in the mid-1970s), many have been recalled for further engraving. What is more striking here is the serious mismatch between what multimedia-based instructional materials can offer and the locus of theoretical debate. For example, the discussion of the value of error correction and negative input focuses primarily on spoken in-class performance. It is difficult to draw any interesting conclusions from this debate about the value of error correction in computer-based grammar tutorials, practice programs, listening comprehension training, cross-cultural skill development, or any other promising area of work with multimedia. While developers should certainly take steps to eschew discrete-point pounding on grammar paradigms, we lack adequate guidance from theory and research on how the computer's enormous power should respond to student input in a corrective or tutorial fashion.

On the other hand, tentative theoretical insights about the potential of instruction to impact the rate of acquisition and the value of comprehensible input should encourage us to develop testable materials and teaching environments using multimedia. To the extent that computer-based materials can selectively improve upon the familiar classroom setting by removing affective barriers, providing new error-correction modalities, offering new settings for the negotiation of meaning, and enhancing naturalistic experiences such as television viewing via the dimension of control, work with multimedia will parallel and hopefully correspond to the best insights of SLA theory and research.

Approaches, Skills, and Populations

In another context, we discussed in depth the ways that instructional technology can be shaped by and can shape various approaches to language learning (Pusack and Otto 1991). Here we would like to reiterate and reinforce our message that leaders in the field of language-teaching methodology need to forge alliances with technology-oriented colleagues to create exemplary materials. Only in this way will the best potential uses of multimedia be discovered and be brought to our students.

Other chapters in this volume treat specific language skills in depth: listening (chapter 3), reading (chapter 4), and writing (chapter 5). Many of the insights of those chapters can be applied to the kinds of classroom interaction we describe in this chapter. Our focus here will be how multimedia interactions can help prepare and deliver communicative language practice in the classroom.

In addition to viewing the potential of multimedia from the vantage points of various approaches and skills, it is also important to consider the impact this technology can have on various learner populations. In a review of how technology can affect young language learners; various school-age learners; learners with differing aptitudes, styles, and attitudes; students at risk; and students with learning disabilities, we conclude:

> Computers and powerful telecommunications technologies can and are being exploited to promote positive education reform: by creating student-centered instructional contexts that focus on building critical thinking skills; by presenting authentic, challenging tasks that engage students in meaningful learning experiences that are appropriate to individual students' level and needs; by facilitating collaborative learning activities that encourage all students to participate and contribute; and by linking students from different places and cultures to enhance learning and intercultural understanding (Otto and Pusack 1996:181).

Roles and Settings

Used effectively, multimedia will challenge traditional definitions and assumptions about the role of the student, the teacher, and the print textbook in language study. The basis for such a challenge is anchored in the prospect that multimedia can provide self-contained instructional experiences in a way that non-interactive media cannot. While we have certainly come a long way methodologically from the grammar-translation approach, our operational model of the textbook as the font of knowledge has not been discarded. As long as the printed page was viewed as the repository of arcane information and the exemplification of the target language and culture, the tendency was to assume that inexperienced language learners needed the teacher's exegesis to guide them through the material. Over the past decades, the most ambitious authors have attempted to overcome the shortcomings of their textbooks with elaborate color layouts, workbooks, answer keys, and even electronic ancillaries of various types. Yet until computers could deliver sophisticated interactions with multiple media, the old teacher-fronted classroom-plus-textbook model did not face serious challenge.

As early as the late 1960s, serious projects were under way to provide learners with keyboard-based grammar practice that embodied corrective feedback (see Adams, Morrison, and Reddy 1968). In the three decades since those experiments, what changes have been wrought? First, computers have become more available. Second, the nature of the displays has become less text-oriented and more image-oriented. And third, integration of sound via audio and video documents has been accomplished. Dozens of modest changes have brought us almost imperceptibly from the first clunky teletypes without benefit of umlauts and upside-down question marks to full-motion movies and even live video via the Web. The gradual nature of these changes has masked what can perhaps now, in the late 1990s, be viewed as a fundamental challenge to the textbook and thus also to the dynamics of the teacher/textbook/classroom model of instruction. Of course, the pioneers of technology were probably claiming such a revolution before the first "Wrong, try again!" message had scrolled off the back of the machine and onto the floor.

What changes have led to a paradigm shift in traditional classroom roles? The answer to this question lies in three factors: first and foremost, the heightened ability of multimedia computers to portray the target language and culture accurately; second, the capability of providing learners with control over the media and feedback concerning their actions; and third, theoretical and methodological advances that put input and intake of language at center stage in the language-acquisition process. As long as the goals of language teaching were focused on the production of sentences illustrating selected grammar paradigms, computers could replicate in-class or homework experiences, but not advance beyond them. Today's classroom learning is increasingly devoted to the extremely difficult task of constructing truly communicative experiences for language learners who have just a few communicative acts in their repertoire. This means that within the traditional fifty-minute class period, no matter what the chosen approach, the organizational demands on the instructor are extremely high. Of course, lesson plans and classroom scenarios vary widely. But if we can take a peek into what might be a typical classroom on many campuses, the instructor will

- present or review the needed lexical, syntactic, pragmatic, and cultural building blocks of a conversation while keeping focus on their meaningful use;
- provide a modest amount of oral or written familiarization with the more difficult components;
- move efficiently into a carefully crafted set of activities that involve truly communicative exchanges of information among members of the class; and finally
- execute a brief but critical reflection on the new forms and structures just used.

All this might constitute the hectic scenario for just one third of a typical class session.

This scenario is not meant to be prescriptive, but rather to provide an abstract outline of key components of a typical class period in a communicative language-teaching environment. Assuming that the components are valuable, even if their sequencing and implementation differ widely from teacher to teacher, where does multimedia fit in and what justifies the claim of an incipient paradigm shift in classroom roles? The answer lies partly in the time constraints caused by the mandate to implement communicative experiences for classroom language learners, partly in the nature of the classroom activities themselves, and partly in what, by implication, *cannot* be accomplished in the classroom.

Even the most experienced practitioner of communicative approaches to language learning will agree that it is no mean feat to establish communicative situations among a dozen or two students who drop in from a native-language environment with varying degrees of motivation, preparation, and sleep deprivation, to name just a few of the factors at work in classroom dynamics. What appears in a lesson plan as a 20-minute activity can easily inflate to more than a half-hour's intensive pursuit of an elusive goal. Under these conditions, it is safe to assume that shortcuts must often be taken and that planned steps may fall by the wayside, especially when classes are large. Even where the master teacher's lesson plan is not devastated by late arrivals, faulty equipment, sluggish responses, or even fascinating learner responses that deserve special recognition, that same master teacher will doubtless concede that there is never enough time for communicative activities.

This analysis postulates two things about today's language-learning classrooms: a need for radical improvements in teaching efficiency and a chasm between our ends and our means of achieving them. Higgs (1991:50) succinctly draws attention to this sobering state of affairs: "It would seem . . . that in spite of our best efforts we have not yet discovered a pedagogy that routinely produces second language users who are both fluent and accurate in their production of the target language. It may in fact be impossible to do so under the instructional conditions that we typically face." It is clear that multimedia—lacking as it does any sophisticated underlying mechanism for understanding language or engaging in human-to-machine conversation— cannot somehow replace traditional classrooms and instructors. It is equally clear, however, that many of the stages necessary to effective language acquisition can benefit from multimedia support, both in the classroom and outside it. What are the underlying resources necessary to make radical changes and to harmonize our means with our ends?

Classroom Use of Multimedia

A Classroom Multimedia Database

Multimedia as a massive storehouse of recorded realia makes a great deal of sense in the classroom setting. In its simplest form, this approach could mean scanning the illustrations contained in textbooks and workbooks. Without the constraints of the printed page, such imageware can be colorized, annotated, labeled, and randomized in such a way that classroom presentations can access them efficiently and flexibly. The same holds true for the audio components of the course. In like fashion, comprehensive databases of target-culture images can be searched and recalled in ways that enhance rather than constrain the instructor's lesson plan. Ultimately, one would hope for archives of relevant video materials. The ideal media database of images, animations, sounds, text, and video will also be indexed properly for lexical, phonological, syntactic, pragmatic, and cultural content. Otto (1983) describes the design of such a database.

While all this may seem utopian, if we survey the extensive set of materials that already accompany our first- and second-year textbooks, we realize that the elements of the needed database are present, but in their most inconvenient form. A typical college-level elementary textbook contains several thousand lexical items for active mastery, not all of which lend themselves easily to visualization through specially drawn sketches and/or photographs. Taking a look at a first-year German textbook that stresses the use of media may begin to illustrate the scope of the archive required. We can conduct such an experiment into media database construction using the third edition of McGraw-Hill's elementary textbook *Kontakte*, by Terrell, Tschirner, Nikolai, and Genzmer (1996). The authors and publishers have assembled an extensive set of graphics, audio recordings, and videoclips in traditional formats. *Kontakte* introduces roughly five thousand vocabulary items, of which one thousand have been selected by the authors for visual treatment, using commissioned artist's sketches: objects, locations, country names, qualities, physical actions, greetings, college subjects, and so forth. (The remaining lexical material is introduced through dialogues and readings.) For purposes of contextualization, these items have been grouped into seventy-two composite "vocabulary displays." In order to expand the range of visualization to sentence-length narrative content, fifteen short illustrated narratives have been included, each with ten to twelve panels corresponding to a single sentence in present or past tense. The image database for this textbook thus consists of 1,150 distinct items.

Kontakte also employs short dialogues that have been recorded by native-speaker actors of various ages and dialects. These twenty-eight dialogues consist of 236 lines of spoken text suitable for manipulation via multimedia.

The twenty-seven video clips that accompany the textbook on videocassette or videodisc should also be included here. This anthology, entitled *Blickkontakte* (Pusack and Tschirner 1996), comprises about 58 minutes of authentic video footage selected and organized to reflect the topics of the textbook. They range in length from about half a minute to about five minutes, with an average duration of 130 seconds. The authors of the accompanying guide have further indexed these segments into 125 shorter clips relevant to classroom instruction; these constituent clips range in length from one second to 151 seconds, with an average duration of 3.8 seconds. The video has not been indexed on a frame-by-frame basis for lexical, structural, or cultural content, so this possibility will be omitted here.

The quantity of available materials is summarized in the following chart:

Medium	Whole	Components
Images	87	1150
Dialogues	28	236
Video Clips	27	125
Total	142	1511

Additional items could be added in the form of photographs, copies of realia, supplementary dialogues from the student workbook, and the like. As multimedia databases go, a corpus of under two thousand items is not large. Yet, from an instructor's point of view, managing these materials is a large portion of one's daily effort, especially when the materials are not intended just for just casual inspection, but rather for intensive and exhaustive study by all students.

Aside from the essential task of indexing the materials, a few additional steps are needed to make it usable. First, if students are expected to learn the spelling of the words, each item in a vocabulary display must be labeled with text large enough to be read in the classroom. On the other hand, if interactive work of either a receptive or a productive nature is needed, then unlabeled versions are also required. This effectively doubles the size of the database or requires programming some interactive form of labeling on the original images. Third, a mechanism for clearly isolating images from their composite displays is needed so that items can be accessed in random order. This can usually be accomplished by presenting "clips" or segments of the original displays or by using labels to mark specific items in a larger display. Finally, the textbook's black-and-white illustrations typically can often benefit from judicious colorization, in order to make the objects more recognizable and visually interesting. Some further problems arise in converting images intended for high-resolution printed pages into the lower resolution typical of many computer displays; greater memory requirements for high-resolution images also play a role here, as well as concerns about the choice of a color palette. None of the steps described here is technically difficult, although it should be evident that more effort is involved than simply scanning in the images. Comparable concerns arise for the management of audio and video recordings, which must at least be indexed so that all of the components can be accessed directly. Excluding the video footage, the resulting materials amount to about 300 megabytes of microcomputer disk space or less than half a CD-ROM format. The video footage requires another disc in videodisc or CD-ROM. In the foreseeable future, the entire media database and accompanying software will fit easily on DVD.

This rather detailed glimpse of a media archive for elementary language study serves to indicate the scope and scale of such an enterprise. While the typical textbook publisher has already invested heavily in multiple forms of media—and has thus financed the underlying corpus of materials through traditional textbook sales—taking the next step to putting a fully indexed, random-access multimedia database in the hands of teachers is a task of significant magnitude. Finally, the stored and indexed media immediately become accessible not only to teachers for classroom presentation, but also to a wide array of software packages for manipulation, including practice programs involving comprehension-building activities, randomized presentation and recycling of items, individualized diagnostics, and feedback.

To demonstrate the value of our multimedia database, we need only examine more closely the four representative stages of classroom interaction that were described above:

- presentation of new material;
- familiarization;
- communicative exchange;
- reflection.

How can multimedia-driven instruction make the time-consuming progression through these stages more efficient, effective, and individualized?

1. Presentation

Establishing a meaningful context for communicative activities is not difficult in the early weeks of instruction in a new foreign language. New class members get to know each other, the campus environment can be described, the elements of the classroom serve as objects for manipulation. As the months pass, however, the relative poverty of new material, both lexically and syntactically, begins to place a burden on the instructor. Picture files and realia, even native speakers as the ultimate realia, are required to support the continuous infusion of culturally authentic plasma into the classroom. Even when textbook publishers have provided extensive ancillaries in the form of slides or overhead transparencies by the dozen, the cumbersome nature of these devices makes itself felt. Given the database that we have assembled above, evoking needed contexts in order to set up a classroom activity should no longer place great demands on the instructor's time and resources.

One of the most powerful forms of context-building can be found in carefully crafted activities centered on a short segment of authentic video. Multimedia templates can provide simple interactions for in-class or preclass use. Such interactions might include the following formats, which were developed at the University of Iowa in conjunction with a FIPSE-funded project devoted to the teaching of culture:

- Categories: Categorize statements according to specified classifications (e.g., true/false; French/U.S. or German/U.S.; matching names of characters to statements by or about them, etc.) based on a video clip.
- Chart Maker: Complete a chart based on information gleaned from watching a video clip.

- Checklist: Mark statements or words that apply to a specific video segment or subject.
- Object Matcher: Drag objects to appropriate locations on a graphic or special location on the exercise screen.
- Sequencer: Reorder scrambled descriptive statements about a video clip.
- Text Mover: Move text from a list to a graphic or special location on the exercise screen.

During in-class work with these activities, initial viewing of the video clip is often followed by small-group deliberation about the assigned task. A selected student then enters his or her group's responses, which are checked by the computer and modified during whole-class discussion. In this way, the presentation phase of a communicative activity expands to become a thematically relevant exercise in listening and cultural comprehension. Using the example of a third-semester French class working with a video version of a song by Francis Cabrel, Lyman-Hager (1995:182–87) describes a comparable set of listening, reading, and writing activities in what she calls "multitasking, multilevel, multimedia software."

2. Familiarization

Most instructors hope to move quickly from the context-building or scene-setting phase of their lesson to truly communicative exchanges. Inexperienced instructors, in fact, do so immediately. What is normally required for communicative exchange, however, is a sequence of both receptive and productive activities that are precommunicative. Put simply, if you have never actually uttered the words *Frühstück, Kühlschrank, Quark,* or *Brötchen,* you are going to have a hard time in German class telling your small-group partners what goes on at breakfast time. The role for multimedia in this phase of instruction should be to set up meaning-bearing tasks that stop just short of true communication, in order to help learners bind words and phrases to their meaning. It should be clear that for many of the things we are trying to teach at the early stages of language study, visual or aural definitions and reinforcements (rather than translation) are the optimal vehicle. Given the appropriate database of visual materials described above, the step to more interactive modes of presentation is not a great one. At its most rudimentary, this could mean simply the random display of items linked to a binary task: Which of the following items would you eat for breakfast? Which ones would Germans eat for breakfast? Media databases can provide either prompts for each step of a task or responses to learner contributions, confirming (or refuting) the meaning of what has been said. At the ambitious end of the scale, multimedia presentation of a wide range of realia can help approximate a complete target-culture environment. Such simulations are already available.

None of this is especially radical on a small scale. For decades, instructors have lugged in magazine photos of dogs, houses, cars, and cheese; course supervisors have fostered the ongoing compilation of archives for this purpose. What multimedia offers is a way to retrieve and present such materials efficiently, including real-time, in-class searching in response to the dynamics of student-to-student and student-to-teacher interaction. The more the instructor can use indexed multimedia to adapt to student contributions, even in the familiarization phase of a lesson plan, the less the instructor will tend to dominate the class session.

Beyond the kinds of tasks suggested above, multimedia in this phase of instruction can also offer various forms of assistance and elaboration through playback controls, textual annotations, or access to supporting media, as described in the previous section. The conclusions drawn by Larsen-Freeman and Long (1991:139) regarding the value of input modification in second-language acquisition strongly support the relevance of multimedia in building various language skills:

> There appears to be substantial evidence of beneficial effects for various kinds of adjustments on comprehension, with elaborative, or 'interactional structure,' modifications being successful, and having the added advantage of providing learners with continued access to the very linguistic items they have yet to acquire. Elaborative or 'interactional structure,' adjustments would therefore seem educationally more appropriate than what is commonly offered in current commercially produced materials.

It should be noted that these beneficial effects have been observed mainly in conversational, rather than media-based settings, so that research into this issue is still desirable.

Lee and VanPatten (1995:102) refer to precommunicative techniques of the kind described here as "processing instruction." They place a high value on this phase as an initial step toward acquisition:

> The results of the research so far are clear: processing instruction has a significant impact on learners' developing linguistic systems, and that impact is observable in both comprehension and production of target items. The same cannot be said of traditional approaches to grammar instruction. What is especially exciting is that . . . processing subjects never once produced the grammatical item during the experiment; their instruction was confined to structured input activities. Yet, they were able to produce the grammatical items *after* instruction as well as, if not better than, the subjects in the traditional groups could (Lee and VanPatten 1995:103).

The multimedia interactions we have described in this section offer significant opportunities for instructors to implement the kind of processing lessons described by Lee and VanPatten.

3. Communication

For the purposes of this chapter, we are laboring under the assumption that multimedia does not encompass a communicative exchange of information that a third party would classify as conversation-like. Although research in artificial intelligence will continue to advance the capabilities to handle natural language, and these capabilities will be brought to bear on various kinds of simulations, we still do not anticipate the arrival of simulated conversation partners anytime soon. If such partners are to respond like native speakers to junky input (i.e., our students' interlanguage), the advent of such tools is even more difficult to foresee. Another form of computer-based conversation, computer-mediated communication via the Internet or local area networks, also lies beyond the scope of this chapter.

This state of the technology means that when person-to-person speech is the agenda, multimedia can only play a somewhat peripheral role. Our shorthand for this is *stimulation,* not *simulation.* We have already outlined how multimedia databases and tasks can familiarize language learners with the components needed for a communicative task. It is likewise possible to draw on multimedia to set up the actual tasks that pairs or small groups of students will engage in. Lee and VanPatten (1995:167) stress the need for careful structuring in this phase of classroom activity:

> Although free conversation between instructor and learners can often serve as an interesting and useful oral communication activity, we have seen that pair and group tasks that involve the sharing of information provide many more opportunities for learners to develop communicative skills such as strategic competence. These tasks need to be carefully constructed, with attention paid to the level of the learners and the linguistic demands that can be placed on them.

In contrast to other sections of this chapter, we prefer to be cautious in our claims for major enhancements via multimedia over current practice. A well-constructed handout and/or a good videoclip with introductory statements by the instructor can probably contextualize and structure communicative tasks quite well, especially in classroom settings where only a single computer is available to a large group of students. Little is gained by diverting the conversational focus to an extraneous presentation device, although it is interesting to have the multimedia workstation remain at the students' disposal as a tool or information resource during the accomplishment of a larger task.

At the conclusion of a conversational activity, however, it may be fruitful to return to the multimedia display—under the control of either the teacher or the students—to collate, display, and analyze the results of pair or small-group work. This could amount to recording viewpoints in text, averaging opinion data for multiple-choice or Likert-scale responses, or even manipulating the media database to support follow-up presentations. Unfortunately, we have not seen much software that has been designed explicitly for the purpose of codifying the results of small-group work.

4. Reflection

The term *focus on form* is customarily used to describe instructional techniques that establish the salience of lexical or syntactic components of input in the interest of fostering or accelerating acquisition (see Ellis 1991:639–641 and Long 1991:316). Given a fully prepared and executed lesson that has successfully engaged students in the meaningful production of new material, and given that the learner is developmentally ready to utilize this kind of information, a focus on formal aspects of language can be viewed as an effective tool. If these assumptions are correct, multimedia can play the same role as a facilitator or organizer of information as it plays in the initial presentation phase. Given the strengths of multimedia in the display of audio and video information, however, it may be appropriate to extend the original concept beyond lexicon and syntax to reflection on those aspects of pragmatic and cultural learning where "rules," that is, transferable generalizations, are appropriate. If this approach is taken, the ability of multimedia directly to access examples of language use in context and to highlight salient features should strongly influence the way we follow up on communicative activities.

   In the reflection phase of in-class work, the multimedia interaction formats listed for phase 1 can prove useful, especially when items are devised for which no single correct answer is required. Two additional formats were designed specifically to prompt students to reflect on what they have seen and heard:

- Observer: Record observations about video scenes and develop a generalization or a summary statement about the culture.
- Opinions: Evaluate or rate statements on a value scale; students may compare their responses with those of other groups (e.g., responses from formal polls or from other students).

   Both of these interaction types rely on open-ended responses that are best handled in the classroom setting where both original insights and misconceptions can be dealt with sensitively. Computer evaluation of such responses is not productive.

This examination of four typical phases of work with multimedia in the communication-oriented language classroom has pointed up major opportunities for radically altering the efficiency level at which students and teachers can function. Having said all of this, we feel adequately prepared and even compelled to ask whether revamping the in-class lesson plan via multimedia marks the culmination of the natural progression toward full-scale multimedia integration. If many of these techniques work in the classroom, why not use the technology to take them out of the classroom? The answer to this question will also lead us one step closer to our definition of optimal roles for the teacher and the textbook.

Only phase 3, the actual communicative setting and student-to-student interaction, requires in-class delivery, for obvious reasons. We need to reconsider the other three phases and ask, in fact, how the delivery of preparation, familiarization, and follow-up can not only be accomplished outside the classroom, but possibly be accomplished better. In phases 1 and 2, clearly, the presentation of new materials preparatory to conversation should actually work more effectively in an individualized setting. Without noting the potential role for multimedia, Lee and VanPatten (1995:103) come close to this conclusion in their discussion of processing instruction:

> We also encourage instructors and materials developers to examine the possible use of structure-input activities for use outside the classroom. Instead of drills and other mechanical practices, homework would be an ideal opportunity for learners to obtain additional structured input activities for building up their linguistic systems.

The capability of the computer to direct the flow of multimedia sounds and images based on individual learner requirements must mean that stronger learners can work more quickly, while weaker learners can receive adequate repetition and amplification to prepare themselves for the ensuing in-class conversation. In phase 4, the follow-up or reflection, the degree of adaptability to out-of-class delivery will depend on whether the results of the communicative task form the basis for appreciation and analysis, or whether prepackaged multimedia elements can be used to illustrate structures, cultural differences, and the like.

Just a few years ago, when instructional computing was in its infancy and teachers felt threatened by what the machines might do, an adage was coined: "The teacher who can be replaced by a computer should be replaced by a computer." In the light of this discussion, we propose a more useful adage: "The teaching technique that can be replaced by a computer should be replaced by a computer." To make this adage work, we need to apply a single criterion systematically to each technique or lesson component: What aspects of the communicative situation make it impossible or at least undesirable to transfer this aspect of language instruction to multimedia delivery in an individualized setting? If the answer is "none," then the technique seems a valid candidate for export to the lab or the home.

The Teacher's Role

Lyman-Hager (1994:220) describes the classroom configuration and the role of the teacher within it under optimum conditions for in-class multimedia usage:

> The classroom itself is transformed into a grouping of individual learners into "pods" of 6 to 8 learners seated together at a table. Several computer workstations are available per table, and learners work collaboratively in groups of 2 or 3 to create messages which can be shared interactively with learners seated at other tables, as well as with the teacher who operates the multimedia computer from a podium but also circulates among groups of learners. . . . Thus, computer and video technology is available when needed but does not interfere with the primary communicative and interactive functions of human speakers in the classroom; rather, the technology supports, encourages, and enhances this "human" communication. All computers are linked together by a local area network, which is, in turn, linked to the campus classroom server and E-mail functions. Projection devices which fit directly on top of high-intensity overhead projectors display video and computer output onto large screens, where the attention of the whole class focuses on the output of an individual in the class or one of the small groups' work. Otherwise, students work together on various selected tasks set forth by the teacher on the smaller, networked personal computers.

In this setting, there is no diminishment of the role of the teacher. And even under the most ideal conditions, with students dutifully preparing for class via multimedia on an almost daily basis, there will still be a need for the teacher's day-by-day judgment about whether the students' preparatory work has built a solid foundation for a particular communicative activity. The teacher will have an enhanced role, not so much as a routinized presenter of content, but as what has been called a facilitator. Perhaps we can replace this infelicitous word with a suite of metaphors that together approximate the role of the teacher in the multimedia-based curriculum:

- the choreographer—designing the economical and artful movement of the learner through steps and scenes in the ballet of acquisition;
- the doctor, diagnostician, or midwife—examining, prescribing, or assisting the natural processes that give life to new language; or

- the coach—guiding each learner to the most appropriate practice and best possible performance given his or her own skills.

The list can easily be extended to other metaphors: the cook, the playwright, the building contractor, even the general (but avoiding the drill sergeant). What is common to all of these metaphors is the image of the teacher as one who directs students to opportunities both inside and outside the classroom, with the guiding assumption that classroom interaction is the privileged place for real communication, while multimedia technology can deliver nearly all the rest.

The Textbook's Role

Where is the textbook in this picture? What are *its* metaphors? In a previous era, especially in students' minds, it was the Bible. In the multimedia era the following list springs to mind: dinosaur or at least endangered species, crib sheet, Michelin guide, installation manual, security blanket, Dead Sea scroll. The worst of these images evoke the non-interactive, non-diagnostic, non-personalized aspects of a single document produced for mass consumption. We have a soft spot for print and paper and predict that the textbook's lasting metaphor will be the Baedeker, the quick and knowledgeable guidebook with plenty of hot tips on the best bed and breakfast and kind words of support for the timid traveler on new terrain.

Classroom Multimedia Present and Future

This section has described classroom uses of multimedia that may seem futuristic to some, while they are everyday practice to others. This gulf cannot be accounted for in terms of who has more resources available. On most campuses where multimedia usage has become widespread and effective, the process has been a gradual one. Often, progress has depended on the availability of video or software from a publisher. Grant funding may have become available because a farsighted administrator made modest investments in a few workstations at the right moment. Commitment of tenured faculty to work in multimedia alongside their regular scholarship may have tipped the scales. An important point to make here is that classroom multimedia can often be a good beginning because it involves teachers directly and it does not require the installation of multiple student workstations. Even the purchase of an inexpensive videodisc player with a bar-code reader can convert a VCR classroom to one equipped with an interactive teacher workstation. Such a workstation can provide most of the features of control described above. Once the advantages of one level of interactivity are established and demonstrated, the path to future developments becomes more clear.

Individual Use of Multimedia

The ancient history of foreign language multimedia—dating back to the late 1960s and early 1970s—reveals that today's courseware did not derive from visual and audio media (such as slide-tape programs), but rather from an attempt to conduct paper-based programmed learning on a machine not much different from a typewriter. The focus was on responding differentially to individual student input or "branching" based either on analysis of student answers (program control) or student decisions (learner control). With the addition of various media to the original keyboard-input/text-output configuration, the goal has remained largely the same: to enhance individual student productivity via work in the language laboratory and at home. Viewed in this context, it is not difficult to see why most developers of multimedia have been focused primarily on individual use of materials rather than in-class use.

Most of the available examples of good courseware for foreign language multimedia—and most of the subsequent chapters of this volume—reflect the profession's emphasis on out-of-class multimedia usage. In drawing the distinction between two settings (in-class vs. out-of-class, teacher vs. student, class vs. individual), false dichotomies should be avoided. The previous section called attention to possibilities for individualized work with multimedia in the classroom setting. Likewise, in the language laboratory setting there is a growing need for facilities that permit small-group use of multimedia. It is also difficult to uphold models of multimedia usage that assign particular language skills to particular locales, e.g., speaking to the classroom and listening to the lab. In the future, teachers will come to recognize that interactive multimedia makes the classroom more like a laboratory and the laboratory more like a classroom. As more and more of the teacher's content-delivery function is embodied in pedagogically sound courseware, it will become increasingly difficult to draw lines between the two venues.

We defer to the authors of subsequent chapters to illustrate the many uses of multimedia in small-group and individual settings on behalf of various language skills. Nevertheless, it may useful at this point to offer a brief overview. While language teachers tend to survey available and potential applications skill by skill, designers of instructional technology categorize applications according to the nature of the student's interaction with the content. Four categories seem adequate to cover the range of available courseware:

- tutorials and practice;
- simulations;
- exploration;
- tools.

Given the versatility of today's courseware-development tools and the multiplicity of instructional goals in our field, it should not be surprising that the lines separating these categories may often be blurred. In most cases, however, it is relatively easy to recognize the underlying instructional relationships in a piece of courseware, as illustrated below.

Tutorials and Practice

Into this category we place all language-teaching software whose approach is to explain and/or practice language skills in a systematic fashion. Pejorative terms are usually invoked here: *flashcard* or *drill-and-kill.* These terms do little justice to the kinds of interactions that sophisticated multimedia can bring to the fundamental need of learners to practice the target language. We have also chosen to merge once-distinct categories by linking the terms *tutorial* and *practice.* Given our current understanding of how language acquisition is most likely to occur, we project few instances where courseware would engage solely in cognitively oriented presentation of linguistic content without significant opportunities for meaningful and contextualized practice. A good example of a tutorial with a relatively modest amount of embedded practice can be found in the pronunciation tutors, such as the *Pronunciation Tutor* program, published by HyperGlot for various languages. These packages explain the articulation of vowels and consonants, work to establish aural recognition of sounds via minimal pairs, and offer sufficient lists of words for practice on individual morphemes and sentence-level intonation. Computer control over the multimedia elements (sound, illustrations of tongue and lip positions) is a valuable replacement for what can be accomplished in a classroom or via print or tape media.

The lion's share of this category is comprised of courseware that in one way or another attempts to build specific skills (grammar, listening, culture, vocabulary) by systematic practice. Most of the software that accompanies elementary or intermediate textbooks falls here. Today's multimedia practice materials generally follow the insights of textbook developers in setting up situational contexts for structural or lexical practice, in avoiding paradigm practice, in personalizing student responses, and in subordinating formal practice to the comprehension of meaning. For this reason, practice on grammatical forms is likely to follow, rather than precede, the presentation of listening-comprehension materials using a short video clip.

The most distinctive characteristic of tutorial/practice courseware is its *task* orientation. While students may be invited to watch an engaging soap opera or view scenes common to the experience of a tourist, they are still expected to accomplish specific tasks as learners: to generate questions, to identify cultural differences, to check off lists of geographic features, to create titles for newspaper articles, and the like. In sum, they are expected to do things that learners do, usually in a sequence that teachers find most productive. This distinguishes practice courseware from simulations and exploration.

Another distinguishing characteristic of practice courseware lies in the design of reactions to students' answers. Most practice programs set up a narrow linguistic or cultural frame in which just a few responses are reasonable. Students who produce reasonable responses receive helpful feedback, be it by a markup of their syntactic or spelling errors, a grammatical analysis of their errors, or an indication of which choices in a listening task were correct. The limited domain of acceptable responses in such instructional frames is what gives practice programs their power. The computer's diagnosis of error, if properly designed, has tutorial impact and advances the learner's understanding of the content.

When multimedia is mated with well-designed practice, the results can produce very effective learning situations. The series of templates described in the previous section, for example, have allowed faculty at the University of Iowa to create French and German modules aimed at improving students' listening comprehension and cultural fluency. Second-year French at Iowa, for example, is based on a variety of materials that contribute to the treatment of broad themes. No textbook is used. Currently, the third-semester course concentrates on daily life in France and social issues and uses as its core video text a short feature film entitled *D'après Maria*. Used as the text for a whole month during the semester, this video (along with its accompanying ToolBook template lesson) shows many important aspects of daily French life and presents a context for confronting the issue of racism in France. In the fourth semester, the organizing theme is the geography of France and regional life and culture. The *Autour de Paris* and *France-Régions* videodiscs constitute the core video texts, providing a variety of perspectives—thematic and visual—on Paris and on a number of different regions and locations in France.

Although various discrete tasks must be accomplished by the individual learner in the language laboratory—ranging from simply watching a videoclip to reacting personally to a cultural stereotype—the learner also has access to lexical aids, cultural background information, and video playback controls. Thus, within the defined task, which is obligatory, the learner has a wide array of tools and choices that affect the flow of the lesson. Questions can be answered before, after, or during the viewing of a videoclip. Definitions of words may be viewed only as needed. Background information can be called up when a need for it is perceived by the student. The dynamics involved in these task-embedded choices changes somewhat when several students gather around a multimedia workstation to work through an assigned segment of video, but the results may be equally effective. Given the cost of multimedia workstations and the goal of building student-to-student communication, many instructors make a point of encouraging small-group practice in the language laboratory when students' schedules permit it. Task-oriented courseware is one of the best ways to structure such group sessions.

Simulations

"Simulation, that's where students actually do something, right?" These are the memorable words of a colleague who sometimes likes to affect unfamiliarity with instructional computing. No one will dispute that a student who logs 183 minutes in the language laboratory working on a tutorial or practice program is "doing something." What this quotation is driving at is that simulations allow the student to do something *as if* in the target culture. Students become, for a short time, tourists or native speakers or spies or government officials of the target culture or country. Good examples are *Montevidisco* (from Brigham Young University) and *À la rencontre de Phillippe* (from Massachusetts Institute of Technology). In both cases the language learner becomes a participant in the situation and plays a role in its outcome. Whether it is a visit to a fictional Spanish-speaking town or assisting a young Frenchman find an apartment in Paris, the learner is engaged in a longer-term activity (often lasting several days or weeks) that requires the application of cultural knowledge, listening comprehension, and sometimes even language production.

Designers of simulations strive for maximum creativity at making the learner's experience relatively realistic while still providing various mechanisms that help the learner cope with gaps in his or her knowledge. The learner will have a computer phrasebook, a notebook, a surrogate who models correct speech, or a map of the subway system. In many simulations there are rewards for accomplishing the goals and there may be penalties for looking up too many words or acting inappropriately.

In contrast to practice courseware, where the tasks are well defined and brief and the contexts may change frequently, simulations offer an extended experience in which students may take on a new identity and pursue an encompassing goal or objective. The intent of the designers is to create a highly motivating setting where a complex mix of language skills can be brought to bear on a real-life problem. Students take different paths, possibly discovering different parts of the simulated world, but always with the underlying mindset that they are *using* their language skills, not *practicing* them.

Simulations for language learning cannot yet respond well to student output. While students may record statements or responses for later playback, today's computers are not able to convert these oral responses to text. The analysis of typed input has fewer technical problems, but it is safe to say that the parsing and understanding of typed student speech has a long way to go before it will play a major role in language instruction. The problem is exacerbated by the fact that language learners produce ill-formed sentences and language teachers do not welcome software that tolerates such sentences. For this reason, most simulations are driven by variants of a multiple-choice format derived either from the keyboard or from mouse clicks handled by the graphical user interface.

It is reasonable to expect advances in foreign language simulations that allow limited input in a well-defined range of syntax (commands, subject-verb-object statements) for a narrow lexical domain (foods, means of travel). In the future the most imaginative developers of simulations will provide us with breakthrough courseware that can offer a change of pace to practice software by giving students broad goals with small amounts of typed production rather than narrow tasks with large amounts of typed production.

Exploration

Many of the multimedia resources currently available to us correspond well to the ideal of student as explorer and self-directed learner. The critical issue here is the extent to which students can choose pathways that are productive for research and are able to synthesize the information that they encounter. We have identified several models that represent a continuum of levels of guidance and overt instructional intent found in current multimedia software designed for exploration.

Vi-Conte (the University of Calgary and the University of Guelph), a videodisc-based package intended to teach French listening comprehension and aspects of French Canadian culture, is an example of software that allows exploration but includes extensive pedagogical treatments as well as suggested pathways and tasks for students. The centerpiece of this program is a video entitled *CRAC!*, an award-winning animated short feature that follows the history of Quebec through the life of a rocking chair. To support the primary video, the disc includes comprehension exercises, cultural notes, slides of paintings by traditional and contemporary Canadian artists, photos of modern-day Montreal and Quebec, and a presentation of a French Canadian legend (*La chasse-galerie*), using still images accompanied by two narrations, one in standard Canadian French and the other in colloquial Quebec speech.

The student may explore any of the materials in any order; but there is a clearly identifiable pedagogical framework evident in the interface, which divides presentations and exercises into beginning, intermediate, and advanced levels. The accompanying print guide suggests dozens of activities for observation of details, analysis of content, and expansion on topics suggested by the materials.

The *Le Louvre* CD, described earlier in the chapter, allows the user free rein over navigation and choice of interactions. Although it has none of the overt pedagogical treatments found in *Vi-Conte*, the content is intuitively and consistently organized, with logical pathways strongly suggested by the interface.

Of course, the World Wide Web constitutes the quintessential multimedia exploratory setting, in which a student working individually can search for and explore materials that match personal interests, with virtually no restrictions in subject matter or geographic location of the source of information. The open nature of the Web makes it the most challenging kind of environment for students, requiring them to employ problem-solving and critical-thinking skills to derive real benefit from interactions with it.

Clearly, we want our students to develop fundamental problem-solving and critical-thinking skills and be experienced and efficient in exploiting the reference tools of the information age. Using the rapidly growing array of resources like those just described, we can teach our students to be competent explorers, giving them guidance with clearly defined tasks at first, then shifting to more independent projects as they learn how to interact effectively with complex information databases.

Tools

Most of the literature about multimedia emphasizes its role in teaching—how teachers use multimedia to enhance in-class presentations and activities and how students benefit from multimedia programs. We must not forget, however, the important role that multimedia can play as a tool for student creators. Just as word processors have become the common, essential medium for student writing, multimedia software, such as *HyperStudio,* which allows integration of text, graphics, sounds, and still and moving images in a single document, will soon become the common, essential medium for student presentations, compositions, and research papers and projects. Interestingly enough, our local junior high students have ready access to this kind of multimedia software for their schoolwork, while most university students do not.

Perhaps the most convincing evidence that these tools are a sure part of our educational future can be found in the Fair Use Guidelines for Educational Multimedia, currently under development by the Consortium of College and University Media Centers working with educators, librarians, and copyright holders. (See Website <http://www.dl.kent.edu/Fairuse.htm> for the current version of these guidelines.) There are specific provisions for fair use of copyrighted materials that have been embedded in student-produced multi-media programs. The guidelines state that students may display the programs for academic purposes and retain them for their personal portfolios for later use in applying for jobs or graduate school. Certainly, it seems inevitable that our students will be creating multimedia documents as part of their language-learning coursework, thus empowering them as well as their instructors.

Developing a Multimedia-Based Curriculum

Levels of Investment

Those who design and develop language curricula must carefully gauge the level of investment they can afford to make in order to obtain the benefits of multimedia. The decision to implement available packages (if any), develop selected multimedia materials on a modest scale over a number of semesters, or to engage in a full-scale research project to create new software from scratch depends on many factors that lie outside the control of the individual instructor or program director. In this section we outline a few of these factors. For further discussion of implementation projects, development projects, and research projects, see Pusack (1987). For an overview of research results relevant to instructional technologies, see Pusack and Otto (1995).

Integrated Packages

Implementation of any commercial software package requires substantial rethinking of the syllabus, installation of hardware, and staff training. Some of the most impressive stand-alone packages, such as *A la rencontre de Philippe* (Furstenberg and Malone 1993), may prove unwieldy if one tries simply to shoehorn them into an existing program without rebuilding the course from the inside out around the multimedia core. For this reason, multimedia packages comprised of anthology-like sets of material may permit more selective usage and adaptation to existing curricular goals. The under-lying issue may be whether it is more suitable to adapt the materials to the curriculum or the curriculum to the materials. In either case, however, think-ing of multimedia as an add-on, a fringe benefit, or a cosmetic change will seldom bring success.

In view of these concerns, the profession's best hope for serious progress with multimedia will continue to be commercial textbook publishers. While we have envisioned the long-term role of the print textbook as that of a friendly Baedeker guiding the learner through a multimedia landscape, the transition to this state of bliss will not come overnight and will not be accomplished in isolation from textbook publishers. The needed investment in multimedia in terms of design, materials, interaction, and delivery to students is so great that only those with a guaranteed annual revenue stream will find the resources. As things stand today, the financial mechanisms that will guarantee progress are not yet in place.

Selecting the Right Media

One of the greatest stumbling blocks to wider use of multimedia is access. For those who cannot rely on a textbook publisher to provide at least the original images and video/audio footage, major tasks lie ahead in either creating or obtaining media documents. Most instructors are familiar with the trade-offs between specially created (or home-brew) media and repurposed authentic media imported from the target culture.

Specially created materials have the advantage of accurately reflecting the curriculum, isolating elements that are of primary interest, and otherwise simplifying the complexity of reality as conveyed by photographs, recordings, and videos. At the earliest stages of language acquisition via multimedia, some use of pedagogically designed materials is probably unavoidable and doubtless more efficient for teaching purposes than recorded realia. At their best, such materials strive to reflect accurately and representatively the target language and culture. Still photos or video portrayals of objects, scenes, and situations taken in the target culture are ideal for these purposes. When sketches are commissioned, dialogues recorded, or videos shot to curricular specifications, however, dangers arise in the form of inaccurate renditions, nonnative pronunciation, and culturally inauthentic behaviors. Even when valiant efforts have been made to avoid such pitfalls, scripted media inevitably give rise to some criticisms. The most well-known cases in foreign-language multimedia range from obvious problems when culturally determined objects (doorknobs, food items, clothing) are mistakenly employed in multilingual packages to blunders in the regional hairstyle of a flight attendant or inappropriate behaviors by low-budget or nonnative actors. Many problems are solved by the use of semiscripted scenes played by experienced actors filmed in the target setting, with corresponding increases in the cost of production. Although such materials do not emanate from the target culture, they can achieve a high level of linguistic and cultural authenticity.

The alternative to pedagogically designed media can be found in media that are not only quasi-authentic in language and content, but also authentically derived from the target culture. In other words, learners are exposed to materials that were originally produced in the target culture for a communicative purpose involving members of the target culture. At the University of Iowa we have engaged in a long-term project, PICS (Project for International Communication Studies) to make available video materials produced by native speakers for native speakers. We have done this in the full knowledge that this solution, too, has its trade-offs. Authentic images and speech have levels of richness and complexity that challenge even the instructor, not to mention the learner. While avoiding most criticisms about authenticity of cultural content, we risk exposing our students to frustrating moments of incomprehensible input. The solutions to these problems lie in careful selection of materials, appropriate segmentation of longer documents, adequate preparation, and use of highly interactive tasks aided by the kinds of tools that only computer-based multimedia can provide (see "Interacting with Multimedia," above).

The drawbacks of using authentic materials must be recognized, especially in matching available footage to curricular sequences, but the advantages are manifold. They lie in the motivational effects, in the richness of the material (not least of all for the instructor who must experience the documents semester after semester), and in the head start that is gained by students who begin to confront difficult authentic material from the earliest days of language study. Without such early training, many students are ill-prepared to view authentic materials when they suddenly crop up in later semesters.

Access to Materials

A few lucky souls will obtain major grants or publisher subventions to design and create complex multimedia packages. We have already outlined some of the issues related to working with well-integrated textbook-based media. Most textbook publishers will welcome experiments by their adopters, but still require explicit permission. The risk here lies in the chance that multimedia developed at high cost can never be distributed to other campuses because of unforeseen rights problems. These dangers also apply to some of the major video-based courses whose creators have understandably chosen to reserve multimedia rights for themselves. Over the next few years, we will probably continue to witness the frustration of well-intentioned multimedia developers who have created excellent materials on an experimental basis, but who cannot obtain permission to digitize or distribute full-fledged multimedia packages based on footage created for these courses.

When we turn to authentic media, the issues are aligned somewhat differently. First, there are the problems of quantity, quality, and fit. As foreign TV networks continue to churn out massive amounts of authentic material, much of it available via satellite, we confront the problem of selecting the right material. Often, what may reach us through the convenience of broadcasting may not be the most useful genre of video (e.g., the nightly news). Typically, the relationship between image and text in commercial video lacks the reinforcement and redundancy that we might find ideal for language acquisition.

The second and greater hurdle as we race into the era of digitized video is that of copyright for broadcast programming. By now, most teachers have probably gotten the news that their selfless commitment to bettering society is not matched by a selfless disavowal of copyright by intellectual rights holders, who are entitled to earn fair revenue for their efforts. The fair use doctrine as defined in the U.S. permits some experimental use of broadcast media for educational purposes, but such opportunities can never serve as the basis for a multimedia curriculum. By definition, serious multimedia development is not spontaneous. The planned investment around a piece of video footage anticipates months of development followed by at least several years of repeated use, possibly at several sites. This does not constitute fair use as defined by existing copyright laws and guidelines. Some improvements can be anticipated in the legal use of broadcast video for short-term student projects. In some cases, such as the Deutsche Welle programs currently available via satellite, permissions may be easy to obtain. In other cases, such as news and feature films, rights may be either impossible or prohibitively expensive. Even when networks agree in principle to grant licenses, they often find they do not themselves have nonbroadcast rights (i.e., to make or sell videocassettes, videodiscs, or CD-ROM versions of their programming). And just when you least expect it, when all video rights seem to be cleared, a small piece of background music will rear its ugly head and delay a project for months. Music rights, however, can ultimately be cleared, for a price, if titles and performers are known. The experience of PICS at the University of Iowa has shown that national networks will grant licenses for instructional use on a highly selective basis at relatively low cost, but the effort to negotiate and obtain such rights can be great; in practice, it is seldom worth the network's time from a purely economic point of view. As we move from traditional media formats such as videotape and videodisc to digital media, new issues are emerging that make obtaining video rights even more difficult. Two main issues concern most rights holders: the easy proliferation of illegal copies and the ability to edit digital documents without specialized hardware.

Multimedia Authoring Tools

The art of creating computer-based instructional materials encompasses such activities as designing, writing, authoring, testing, evaluating, and documenting. The key component in this process is the vehicle used to make the computer do one's bidding. Over the past three decades, the tools available for creating courseware have evolved greatly, from early experiments with general-purpose programming languages (e.g., BASIC and Pascal) to authoring languages that included commands specifically designed to meet instructional needs, to the current generation of authoring systems for multimedia (Holmes 1983; Otto and Pusack 1985; Barker 1987). The increasing complexity of instructional software, especially the demands of the graphical user interface, have encouraged academic courseware developers to exploit the powerful new authoring tools, rather than creating all new interactions in a state-of-the-art programming language like C++. At the same time, the companies that produce these tools have found a ready market in the education and training fields for sophisticated and reliable authoring software with built-in functions for computer-storing and managing information and questions, displaying text and graphics, controlling time-based media such as audio and video, getting and judging student input, providing feedback, keeping performance records, and branching according to student progress.

Most authoring tools provide built-in control of multimedia elements. A very high degree of control over the complex elements that make up a multimedia courseware package is provided by object-oriented authoring systems. Familiar examples of this approach are *HyperCard* and *ToolBook*. While these tools are not designed explicitly for language study, their capabilities in the control of multimedia make them popular choices for those developing lessons built on videodisc or digitized video such as QuickTime.

Another development in tools for courseware creation are icon-driven authoring systems. *IconAuthor* for Windows and *Authorware* for both Windows and Macintosh illustrate this visually oriented model of authoring. This approach grew out of the concept of structured programming and the development of the mouse and display hardware that invites the use of graphic icons to facilitate interaction. Instead of lines or frames of code, the author builds a flow chart representation of the interaction, using a library of icons in the language. Each icon has underlying programming code to perform a function or activity, but the author is insulated from it. Operations are conceptualized as building blocks; lesson content is created with a series of editing utilities; and additional control information is elicited via menus and option screens associated with the icons. The author's role is to design the process, use the editing tools within the system to create the materials for the interaction, and "program" the structure, using the building-block icons. In this kind of software-development setting, the courseware developer automatically focuses on program design and flow.

Although general purpose authoring systems offer the developer a great deal of power, most foreign language instructors have found the learning curve for these tools very steep. In addition, many of the features of such authoring systems have not reflected the pedagogical needs of foreign language teachers, who have specialized concerns in the display of text, interaction with documents, handling of student responses, and the like. The need to reconcile demands for authoring power with ease of use has led to the emergence of specialized foreign language authoring systems whose purpose is to provide a relatively wide range of interesting interactions in a relatively convenient and easy-to-learn package. Some foreign language authoring systems have come to be dubbed "templates," because they are designed to guide the author in the production of a predetermined activity or set of activities. No programming or layout expertise is required of the subject-matter expert, and learning time is generally measured in hours. Typically, the author is led through the process of lesson writing by a series of prompts and menus. As foreign language authoring tools have evolved, however, the distinction between authoring systems and authoring templates has lost much of its meaning. Authoring systems may have narrow template-like formats, while templates may have a wide range of options and layouts.

MacLang, a foreign language authoring system for the Macintosh (Frommer 1987), can serve as a good example of a menu-driven tool that allows teachers to create exercises in a number of predetermined formats, including vocabulary flashcard, fill-in-the-blanks, paragraph (cloze), multiple-choice, and jumble. Exercises may be prepared in any Roman-alphabet language, as well as such non-Roman alphabets as Russian and Greek. More than one correct answer may be programmed and authors program anticipated wrong answers and appropriate feedback for them. Additional features include random- and reverse-order presentation of items, specialized help for each exercise, variable number of tries allowed, and support for videodisc. Other published multimedia authoring systems designed for foreign language study include *WinCalis* from Duke University, *Dasher* from the University of Iowa, and *Libra* from Southwest Texas State University. Burston and Fischer (1996) have assembled an excellent compendium of authoring systems of interest to potential foreign language courseware developers.

With any authoring system, the courseware developer can easily produce simple lessons or activities in the prescribed formats in a short time. Ease of use is by no means synonymous with simplicity or lack of sophistication.

Often the operations performed by these tools are powerful, complex, and polished—a better product than might be programmed by a subject-matter specialist working with more generic tools. By nature, however, authoring systems are shaped by the instructional design preferences of their developer. Often, the lesson author must accept the system's basic functions as provided, since there may be little or no latitude for modification.

Finally, it is important to note that even the most flexible authoring system may still require multimedia developers to work with an additional set of tools to create and/or edit media documents. This is because authoring tools focus their efforts on devising convenient pedagogical interactions, rather than on becoming a universal software package that can meet every need. Just as an authoring system is unlikely to have all the features of a full-scale word processor (nor would you expect it to), it will seldom have the most powerful features for editing audio, designing graphics, or processing video. Thus, teachers with ambitious plans for multimedia development often find themselves invited to learn a whole suite of software packages: *SoundEdit Pro* (for audio processing), *Photoshop* (for image manipulation), *Illustrator* (for graphics creation), *Pagemaker* (for page layout and documentation), *Premier* (for digital video editing and production), *Aftereffects* (for special effects), *Acrobat* (for delivery of documentation), and *Toast* (for CD-ROM mastering), to name just a few examples. Alternatively, they must recruit or hire a team of co-developers who can provide shared expertise of many kinds.

Delivering a Multimedia-Based Curriculum

Confronting Hardware Issues

Delivering a multimedia curriculum requires a significant investment in a technology infrastructure that begins with workstations in the media center to support independent and small-group work by students and extends to classroom presentation systems for use by instructors and students. Many considerations—platform options; software availability; resources (internal or external) for acquiring, maintaining and upgrading workstations; campus networks—complicate the development of a viable infrastructure for delivering multimedia. Regardless of the decisions planners make, every newly installed technology base becomes outdated all too quickly. The only comfort to be had in facing this fact is that software development never keeps pace with the hardware.

To run currently available multimedia software, hardware must be able to handle the full range of media: text, graphics, motion and still video, and audio. At this writing, a typical multimedia workstation—generically described—features the basic computer with a high-resolution monitor, a capacious hard drive and the more memory the better, a CD-ROM drive, sound capabilities (on the PC side this means installing a sound card) and, arguably, a videodisc player. A bar-code reader, microphone, and headphones are common additional peripherals. In the classroom setting, some means of projecting the computer screen is obligatory. Options include:

- a large multiscan monitor, which is expensive but does not require that the room be darkened;
- a high-resolution computer/video projector (usually mounted on the ceiling), which is also expensive and requires the room to be quite dark, but can display a much larger image; or
- an overhead projector LCD panel, which may be less expensive, usually has a poorer image quality, and requires a darkened room.

Computer and video sound sources must be amplified and piped to room speakers. If a projection device is used, AV blinds that eliminate outside light and dimmable ceiling lighting directed downward are recommended. This allows students to view the display and see their work, yet doesn't wash out the projected computer image. Because two-screen interactive videodisc applications are still common, wall-mounted TVs provide simultaneous viewing of videodisc images and projected computer video.

The final element in the general hardware equation is networking. Running instructional software on local area networks (LANs) can simplify many of the maintenance and recordkeeping tasks associated with using technology as an integral part of the curriculum. However, as multimedia software increasingly involves massive amounts of digital media data, as with digitized video, throughput problems arise related to regular LAN bandwidths (transmission capacity) and delays caused by contention: too many users want too much stuff. As Galbreath (1995) explains, multimedia information must flow across a network in a continuous stream, and current network architectures were simply not designed to handle delivery of data in that fashion. He does point out that emerging LAN technologies, including isoENET (isochronous Ethernet) and ATM (Asynchronous Transfer Mode), are breaking through the barriers to successful network-based delivery of multimedia.

Providing Support

Investments in hardware must be matched with investments in support. Delivering sophisticated multimedia-based teaching and learning is a very "high maintenance" proposition. Support takes a variety of forms:

- expertise to install and maintain hardware and software;
- training for faculty and students to use the hardware and software;
- assistance with problems users are having with the technology;
- support to allow faculty to learn about multimedia, revise their curricula, and develop their own materials.

In most settings the media center provides much of this support with professional and nonprofessional (i.e., student) staff.

Managing and maintaining current technology systems presents a much greater challenge to professional media center staff than the technologies of the past. With the exception of the VCR, everything has become increasingly computer-oriented (even audio language laboratory equipment), reflecting the evolution toward digital media. Complex computer systems and networks require expert support not only for installation, troubleshooting, and maintenance, but for collaborating in research and development activities as well. The media center's nonprofessional monitoring staff must know a great deal to solve student problems with multimedia hardware configurations and software applications. In the classroom environment, technical support is equally important for instructors trying to orchestrate activities centered on complicated multimedia materials. When something does not work, troubleshooting the problem often involves checking a whole list of variables or settings, which is difficult for the instructor who is focused on instruction, not hardware or software.

Training is especially important as we move beyond the era of the VCR, where the biggest challenges are turning on the power and putting the right side of the cassette in the slot. Students should be guided through hands-on sessions to introduce them to computer-based hardware and the software. This approach takes some of the mystery out of the hardware, encourages efficient and intelligent use of the software, and ideally provides some understanding of the pedagogical reasons for their use of the technology. Faculty and teaching assistants likewise need instruction in how to use the complex presentation systems in classrooms and understand the stunning potential of media to enhance language teaching and learning. The array of sophisticated equipment in an up-to-date presentation classroom can be tremendously intimidating to the teaching professional, who may still feel barely comfortable with an overhead projector, boom box, and VCR on a cart. Teacher education programs teach too little about technology, and, of course, the technology constantly changes. Teachers, therefore, need regular opportunities—workshops and hands-on demonstrations—to become familiar with new technology and how to use it.

Technology does not find its way into the curriculum by itself. Its potential will remain largely untapped without the time and expertise of language-teaching professionals who can make connections among technology, the most appropriate teaching practices, and curricular content. Certain support conditions will encourage the thoughtful integration of technology into language learning and teaching and the development of innovative, effective technological applications:

- sufficient release time to learn about technology and to revise the curriculum;
- an up-to-date workstation to experiment with applications and develop new ones;
- for major development projects, the collaboration of programming and design professionals to create new materials; and
- a reward system for salary increments, tenure, and promotion that recognizes work in technology-assisted language learning.

Conclusion

Multimedia has arrived. Lessons that demonstrate its viability have been designed by instructors and used by students on numerous campuses. The remaining technological hurdles (e.g., the transition from videodisc to digital videodisc) will affect the delivery but not the design of exciting interactions for all aspects of language learning. So what we can see and test today may get a bit faster, a bit smarter, and a bit more convenient to use, but it will not look or feel radically different from what developers have created or could create right now. For once, if anything, our pedagogy seems to be a year or two *ahead* of the technology.

In this chapter we have presented this state of affairs as a challenge. Given the high degree of control and interactivity that multimedia provides over critical elements of foreign language instruction, what will we make of it? Will we use multimedia to redefine the nature of instructed second-language acquisition? Will we find the theoretical insights, the classroom techniques, and the resources to make optimum use of multimedia? Our best prediction is that it will take an unprecedented amount of collaboration among institutions, administrators, researchers, faculty members, professional staff, and publishers to take control of multimedia, but it can be done.

REFERENCES

Adams, E. N., H. W. Morrison, and J. M. Reddy. 1968. "Conversation with a
    Computer as a Technique of Language Instruction." *The Modern Language Journal*
    52:3–16.
Barker, Philip. 1987. *Author Languages for CAL*. London: Macmillan Education.
Burston, Jack, and Robert Fischer. 1996. "A Panel Discussion on Multimedia/
    Hypermedia Authoring Systems: Design and Use," in Frank L. Borchardt et al.,
    eds., CALICO '96 Annual Symposium: Proceedings of the Computer-Assisted
    Language Instruction Consortium 1996 Annual Symposium "Distance Learning."
    Durham, NC: Duke University.
Chun, Dorothy M., and Jan L. Plass. 1996. "Effects of Multimedia Annotations on
    Vocabulary Acquisition." *The Modern Language Journal* 80,2:183–98.
Davey, Denise, Kirsten Gade Jones, and Jeremy Fox. 1995. "Multimedia for Language
    Learning: Some Course Design Issues." *Computer Assisted Language Learning*,
    8,1:31–44.
Ellis, Rod. *1991. The Study of Second Language Acquisition*. New York: Oxford
    University Press.
Frommer, Judith. 1987. "Foreign Language Authoring Systems: Judith Frommer's
    MacLang Spoken Here." *Journal of Educational Techniques and Technologies*
    20,1:19–25.
Furstenberg, Gilberte. 1992. "Making the Connection I: Interactive Videodisc
    Technology in the Language Lab and Interactivities in the Classroom. *À la
    rencontre de Philippe*: A Case Study," pp. 209–18 in Iwao Shinjo, Karen Landahl,
    Mary MacDonald, Keigo Noda, Shuji Ozeki, Tadashi Shiozawa, and Masatoshi
    Sugiura, eds., *Proceedings of The Second International Conference on Foreign
    Language Education and Technology*. Kasugai, Aichi: Language Laboratory
    Association of Japan and International Association for Learning Laboratories.
Furstenberg, Gilberte, and Stuart A. Malone. 1993. *À la rencontre de Philippe*: New
    Haven: Yale University Press.
Galbreath, Jeremy. 1995. "Multimedia on the Network: Has Its Time Come?"
    Educational Technology, 35,4:44–51.
Gay, Geri, and Joan Mazur. 1989. "Conceptualizing a Hypermedia Design for Language
    Learning." *Journal of Research on Computing in Education*, 22,2:119–26.
Greifnieder, Ute. 1995. "The Influence of Audio Support on the Effectiveness of
    CALL." *ReCALL* 7,2:29–35.
Hannafin, Robert D., and Howard J. Sullivan. 1995. "Learner Control in Full and Lean
    CAI Programs." *Educational Technology Research and Development* 43,1:19–30.
Higgs, Theodore V. 1991. "Research on the Role of Grammar and Accuracy in
    Classroom-Based Foreign Language Acquisition, " pp. 46–53 in Barbara F. Freed,
    ed., *Foreign Language Acquisition Research and the Classroom*. Lexington, MA:
    D. C. Heath and Company.
Holmes, Glyn. 1983. "Creating CAL Courseware: Some Possibilities." *System* 2,1:21–
    32.
Johnston, Jerome, and Lynda Milne. 1995. "Scaffolding Second Language
    Communicative Discourse with Teacher-Controlled Multimedia." *Foreign Language
    Annals* 28,3:315–29.
Larsen-Freeman, Diane, and Michael H. Long. 1991. *An Introduction to Second
    Language Acquisition Research*. New York: Longman.
Lee, James F., and Bill VanPatten. 1995. *Making Communicative Language Teaching
    Happen*. New York: McGraw-Hill.

Long, Michael. 1991. "The Design and Psycholinguistic Motivation of Research on Foreign Language Learning," pp. 309–20 in Barbara F. Freed, ed., *Foreign Language Acquisition Research and the Classroom.* Lexington, MA: D. C. Heath and Company.

Luskin, Bernard J. 1996. "Toward an Understanding of Media Psychology." *T.H.E. Journal,* 23,7:82–84.

Lyman-Hager, Mary Ann. 1994. "Video and Interactive Multimedia Technologies in French for the 1990s." *The French Review* 68,2:209–28.

————. 1995. "Multitasking, Multilevel, Multimedia Software for Intermediate Level French Language Instruction: Ça continue . . ." *Foreign Language Annals* 28,2:179–92.

McFarland, Ronald D. 1995. "Ten Design Points for the Human Interface to Instructional Multimedia." *T.H.E. Journal,* 22,7:67–69.

Myslewski, Rik. 1996. "We Have Seen the Future and It's Huge." *MacUser* (March) 12,3:25.

O'Malley, J. Michael, and Anna Uhl Chamot. 1993. "Learner Characteristics in Second-Language Acquisition," pp. 96–123 in Alice Omaggio Hadley, ed., *Research in Language Learning: Principle, Processes, and Prospects.* Lincolnwood, IL: National Textbook Company.

Otto, Sue K. 1983. "Videodisc Image Retrieval for Language Teaching." *System,* 11,1:47–52.

Otto, Sue K., and James P. Pusack. 1985. "Tools for Creating Foreign Language CAI," pages 96–108 in Patricia B. Westphal, ed., *Meeting the Call for Excellence in the Foreign Language Classroom: Selected Papers from the 1985 Central States Conference.* Lincolnwood, IL: National Textbook Company.

————. 1993. "An Introduction to Foreign Language Multimedia: The Ten Most Frequently Asked Questions," pp. 55–72 in William Hatfield, ed., *Visions and Reality in Foreign Language Teaching: Where We Are, Where We Are Going.* Lincolnwood, IL: National Textbook Company.

————. 1996. "Technological Choices to Meet the Challenges," pp. 141–86 in Barbara H. Wing, ed., *Foreign Languages for All: Challenges and Choices.* Lincolnwood, IL: National Textbook Company.

Pusack, James P. 1987. "Problems and Prospects in Foreign Language Computing," pp. 13–39 in Wm. Flint Smith, ed., *Modern Media in Foreign Language Education: Theory and Implementation.* Lincolnwood, IL: National Textbook Company.

Pusack, James P., and Sue K. Otto. 1991. "Dear Wilga, Dear Alice, Dear Tracy, Dear Earl: Four Letters on Methodology and Technology," pp. 80–103 in Ellen S. Silber, ed., *Critical Issues in Foreign Language Instruction.* New York: Garland.

————. 1995. "Instructional Technologies," pp. 23–41 in Vicki Galloway and Carol Herron, eds., *Research within Reach II: Research-Guided Responses to the Concerns of Foreign Language Teachers.* Valdosta, GA: Southern Conference on Language Teaching.

Pusack, James P., and Erwin Tschirner. 1996. *Blickkontakte: Video Guide to Accompany Kontakte.* New York: McGraw-Hill.

Reeves, Thomas C. 1992. "Evaluating Interactive Multimedia." *Educational Technology* 32,5:47–53.

————. 1993. "Pseudoscience in Computer-Based Instruction: The Case of Learner Control Research." *Journal of Computer-Based Instruction* 20,2:39–46.

Rühlmann, Felicitas. 1995. "Towards Replacement of the Teaching Process: The Emulation of the Teaching Process with CAL and Its Implications for the Design of a Multimedia CAL Tutorial." *Computer Assisted Language Learning,* 8,1:45–61.

Standards for Foreign Language Learning: Preparing for the 21st Century. 1996. Yonkers, NY: National Standards in Foreign Language Education Project.

Terrell, Tracy D., Erwin Tschirner, Brigitte Nikolai, and Herman Genzmer. 1996. *Kontakte: A Communicative Approach.* 3rd edition. New York: McGraw-Hill.

2

Multiple, Mixed, Malleable Media*

Ana B. Chiquito
University of Bergen, Norway

Carla Meskill
University at Albany State University of New York

Joy Renjilian-Burgy
Wellesley College

Introduction

As the presence of computers in instructional contexts rapidly expands, language professionals are being called upon to make decisions concerning what software products they will integrate into their teaching and learning practices. This decision-making process is not as easy as administrators and software vendors would make it out to be. In the brief history of technology

Ana Beatriz Chiquito is Associate Professor, Spanish and Literature in the Department of Spanish and Latin-American Studies, University of Bergen, Norway. She has worked as a video and multimedia producer and has authored electronic and printed materials for teaching Spanish. Her research and publications focus on theoretical and applied Spanish linguistics and the use of educational technology in second-language learning and teaching. Currently she is a Visiting Research Engineer at the Center for Educational Computing Initiatives (CECI) of the Massachusetts Institute of Technology.

Carla Meskill is Assistant Professor, Department of Educational Theory and Practice, University at Albany State University of New York. She directs the Center for Electronic Language Learning and Research. Her area of specialization is in computer-assisted language learning, the design and evaluation of multimedia in language classrooms. Her research interests involve design and integration processes of technologies use, especially as they relate to second-language acquisition strategies and interpersonal interaction.

Joy Renjilian-Burgy is a faculty member at Wellesley College. She is also a Visiting Scholar at the Center for Educational Computing Initiatives at the Massachusetts Institute of Technology. She is co-author of the CD-ROM *Juntos* (1996) as well as the author of the Video Guide to accompany the video series *Mosaico cultural* (1994). She was a member of the Advisory Board for the telecourse *Destinos,* and co-edited the intermediate-level literary reader, *Album: Cuentos des mundo hispánico.* On the state, regional, and national level, she is Past President of the Massachusetts Foreign Language Association, Chair of the 1992 Northeast Conference on the Teaching of Foreign Languages, and has been a member of the Executive Council of ACTFL.

in education, we have learned that in spite of the rhetoric, computers in general, and software products in particular, offer no magic panacea for instructional needs. On the contrary, it is the ways in which products are *used* and the *context* of this use that determine the ultimate efficacy of instructional technologies in language teaching and learning. Indeed, without careful consideration and crafting, machines and software tend to be used poorly or not at all.

There are numerous issues that must be considered as regards the "fit" and logistics of software adaptation in the foreign language curriculum and the everyday stream of instructional events. The recent proliferation of commercially available products adds to the complexity of this decision-making process. With such a wide range of quality in foreign language software products, assessing what is "good" software—software that can complement students' learning styles and your teaching style and agenda—is no simple matter. In this chapter, we offer some guidelines, or some "lenses" with which and through which you might examine computer-assisted language learning (CALL) products while understanding the future directions multimedia design and development are taking.

Background

In its fifteen-year history, the notion of "multiple media" on the screen of a personal computer has traversed vast conceptual territory. Our understandings of the computer as a language-learning tool have gone from grandiose visions of a technology that could transform language learning and teaching to more sober expectations about what we can accomplish with technology. Over time, the initial excitement that was sparked by the many possibilities that the medium represented has been toned down by the hard realities of instructional contexts in which we practice our craft. Nonetheless, we have come a long way both practically and conceptually regarding the nature of teaching with technology and our expectations of just what it is computers can do.

"The medium is not the message in a digital world. It is an embodiment of it." These are the words of Nicolas Negroponte from his book *Being Digital*. Media are now fast becoming digital, that is, changeable, no longer static. A major implication of this development is that learners can learn by *doing* rather than by interacting with preprogrammed instructional sequences. For example, software programs now commonly integrate tools such as word processors, paint programs, and image editors. Learners can manipulate information that is in, and can take on, multiple forms and formats. They can, in effect, recreate the material they see on the screen. This material—be it video, audio, text, or graphics—can be used, changed, read, and reconstructed by language learners. This aspect of newer digital technologies is exemplified in several of the newly released products in which, for example, the use of electronic notebooks and electronic portfolios allows students to transform the content within an application.

Such developments suggest that our quest for "the" best medium for a given purpose may not be getting us the answers we need as practitioners. It is, rather, the implications of manipulating multiple forms of target language material by our students—the trend in many new software products—that are deserving of our critical attention.

From Static to Malleable Media

Traditionally, foreign language instruction adhered to the McLuhanesque idea that a given medium was static—that a single medium had its own form, function, set of conventions, and, therefore, meaning. For instruction, this was very much a reality back when fluid, combined media were merely a futuristic notion. It is for this reason that the print medium, unlike other mediums, has remained the mainstay of instruction. Unlike static mediums, print can easily be adapted to the content and specific needs of a learning situation.

"Modern" instructional media have been constraining in that both authors and users are locked into a given medium's forms and conventions. There is no better example of this than the language laboratory where analog audio was, by virtue of its technological attributes, designed to be "listened to" and later "responded to" in very limited and limiting ways. Learners were cast in the role of "consumers" of aural input much as the audio medium was originally intended. We also used to think about computer screens as venues for the treatment of language-learning content that mirrored how content is treated in language textbooks. Content organization frameworks on the computer reflected what we were accustomed to seeing in books. Indeed, many software applications even *resemble* books, and forms of content presentation and the pervasive multiple-choice interface where students demonstrate a quantifiable mastery of targeted language continue to reflect the influence of the book. In CALL, we are now experiencing a shift away from static instructional content on computer screens to a more flexible, open-ended environment in which *tools* are becoming the metaphor for instructional technology.

Now, the random-access of digitized recordings, the possibilities of instant repetition and recording and, in the very near future, audio transmitted through networks, will allow for a high degree of manipulation and melding with other media by teachers and students alike. Digitization allows content to move fluidly between media in a generic form. A text in digital form is not only a text; it can also become speech. A clip of audio can be interpreted by the computer and become a text. Video can easily and quickly become a collection of stills, or a collection of stills or graphics can become a movie. Teachers and students can change, mutate, and tailor any of these media as part of the instructional process.

Videotape has likewise been traditionally cast in the same role as a consumable medium, but digitization now transforms our relationship with it. Where we were once limited to thinking about video as something that came to us via broadcast, we now, through digitization, have the capability to exercise a tremendous amount of control over its presentation, to change it, extract from it, recombine it with other media, and transport it.

What are the instructional implications of these mixed and mixable media? In this chapter, our approach in tackling this question is to (1) study this aspect as it is manifest in current multimedia applications; (2) suggest ways available media and available tools complement language teaching and learning; and (3) provide examples of how these tools are actually used in teaching and learning other languages. We address these points by specifically examining existing tools that students and teachers can use to manipulate and recombine online materials in contemporary multimedia products.

Aesthetics versus Functionality

In recent years, software manufacturers have invested a great deal in the look and feel of their products' screens. It is now rare to find a product that does not boast refined and appealing illustrations, animations, and eye-catching graphical icons. The first thing we see when we examine a software product is its aesthetic side—surface features such as screen layout, color, animations, the overall visual "look" of instructional screens. This is perhaps the most problematic feature of foreign language software products in that visual quality is at once very important for motivational and navigational reasons but can act as a shroud for poorly conceived pedagogical design. Screen design is the first thing we truly *see* when we look at a product; it is also something we need to look beyond with a critical eye. A visually sophisticated and appealing screen may, for example, be nothing more than a form of traditional multiple-choice drill.

When looking at malleable media, the agenda is quite different. Screen layout, color, and navigation are important, but it is the *tools* with which teachers and students can manipulate available material that become the critical focus for classroom and laboratory activity. It is with these tools that learners become active users and creators of meaning. It is these tools that guide teacher development of tasks and activities that involve students in using the target language productively.

Tools

Random-access videodisc and digitization have brought several new possibilities for manipulating and recombining materials. Available material is no longer static; it is dynamic and changeable within and across media. Many multimedia applications take advantage of this fact by including tools that students and teachers can use in a variety of ways. This section presents and discusses the various types of functionality that can be incorporated into online learning with malleable materials: video, audio, text, and graphics. We will discuss four different categories of on-line tools that are specific to working with combined, malleable media for language learning. These are

- control tools
- linking tools
- indexing tools
- communications tools.

Control Tools

Basic tools available to students and teachers in many multimedia applications enable users to play, pause, and rewind audio and video sequences. Many software applications also include some kind of sliding bar users can manipulate to scan forward or back or find a spot in a video or audio sequence (Figure 2.1a, b, c, d).

Such tools present clear advantages over static media in that teachers and learners can tailor their interaction with material by controlling pace and sequencing. For example, the capacity to repeat a selected sequence instantaneously and as many times as desired is certainly powerful for learning languages. In addition to these basic tools, the medium also has a decision-point capacity—learners can be prompted to make decisions about the sequence of a video or audio storyline (Figure 2.2).

Another form of control over video and audio presentation is the facility to access subtitles in a variety of forms. These can be verbatim, by key word, translation, phonetic transcription, or any combination of these (Figure 2.3a, b, c, d).

Figure 2.1a.
¡Dime!: Students click on number of video clip to play.

Figure 2.1b.
Discovering French Interactive: Students click on video still to play and stop.

Figure 2.1c.
Ven Conmigo: Students control presentation, using a slider.

Figure 2.1d.
Operación Futuro: Students control video, using a slider and control button combination.

Figure 2.2.
Operación Futuro: Students are asked to make a decision.

Figure 2.3a.
Ven Conmigo:
Students can
toggle between
captions in two
languages.

Figure 2.3b.
Allez Viens:
Students can
toggle between
captions in two
languages.

Figure 2.3c.
Phillipe: Students have multiple options to tailor subtitles.

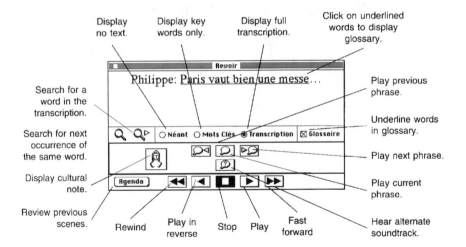

¿Y quién es tu amiga?

Figure 2.3 d.
¡Dime!: Students can display and hide subtitles.

Like subtitles, material in other forms can also be hidden, shown, moved, and tailored. For example, many applications allow access to catalogs of graphic images that can be cut, pasted, and melded with text, video, and audio materials (Figure 2.4a, b).

Graphics can, in many instances, be created, recombined, and reshaped. Paint programs are often an available tool in multimedia products. With these, learners can develop their own pictures as part of larger language-learning tasks. In the example shown in Figure 2.5, language learners select the physical attributes of a person and see them assembled on screen according to specifications made in the target language.

Figure 2.4a.
Juntos: Students search a catalog of graphic images.

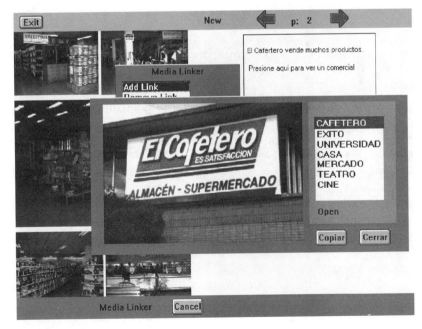

Figure 2.4b.
Operación Futuro: Students select media to illustrate their work.

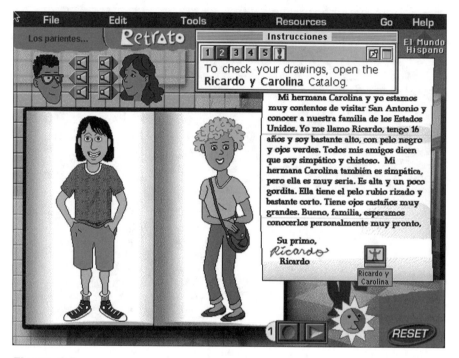

Figure 2.5.
Juntos: Students construct characters.

In terms of text-control tools, many applications now contain some facility for students to do word processing. Within these writing environments, learners can exercise total control over the target language while also enjoying access to "help" in a variety of forms: glossaries that can be text in combination with audio, video, and/or graphics; grammar help; catalogs of clips and images; prompts and cues, again in audio, video, graphics, text, or any combination of forms (Figure 2.6a, b, c).

These forms of control over available materials in a multimedia environment imply independent and collaborative creative language-learning processes. Use of these tools by students also suggests that they are exercising, and consequently developing, learning strategies.

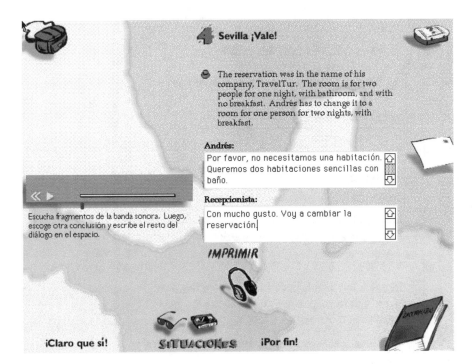

Figure 2.6a.
Travel Tur: Students compose with supporting language resources.

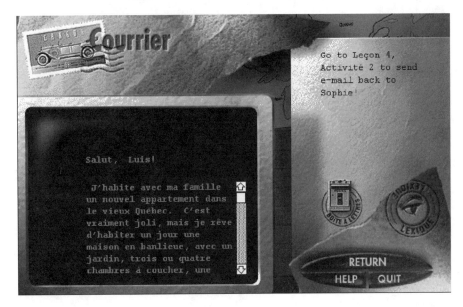

Figure 2.6b.
Vis-à-Vis: Students write a simulated E-mail message.

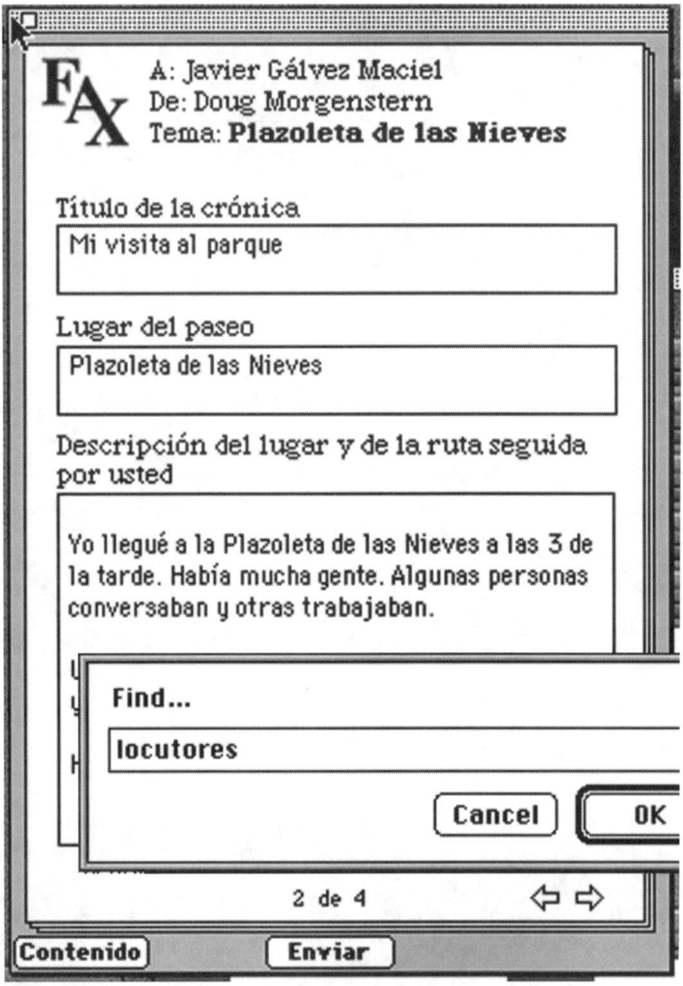

Figure 2.6c.
No Recuerdo: Students use writing templates and multiple utilities.

Linking Tools

In addition to controlling available materials, many applications permit learners to cut, paste, and incorporate material in different forms into their personal or collective online spaces. Combining or *linking* material in diverse forms is fast becoming a common feature; for example, cutting material in one form and pasting it into another environment where it becomes combined with material in another form. In Figure 2.7, video sequences can be linked with audio sequences.

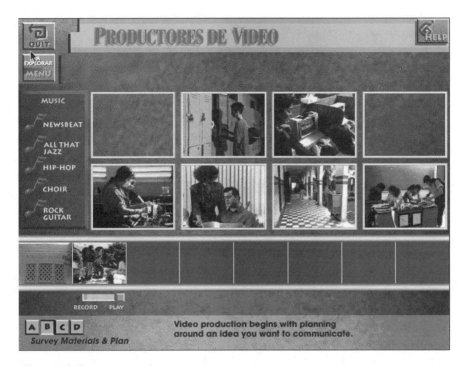

Figure 2.7.
¡Dime!: Students combine video with their own recordings.

Other kinds of linking can take place between video and text sequences or between graphics and text. Such linking opens up many possibilities for students to work with the target language in visual, aural, and textual forms (Figures 2.8 and 2.9a, b).

The capability of linking these various forms suggests that students can now work with target language material in fluid, creative, and therefore, potentially very meaningful ways. By assigning, supporting, and valuing the processes and outcomes of such activity, instructors can encourage interaction with the target language and culture that is student-centered and student-empowering (Figure 2.10).

Indexing Tools

Storage of audio and video in random-access media such as videodisc and CD-ROM implies that, like text, audio or video sequences can be treated as information. As such, one can use cataloging tools to store, index, search, and recombine video sequences. The *Multiple Functions Index* (MFI) is one example of a video cataloging tool that allows teachers and students to search

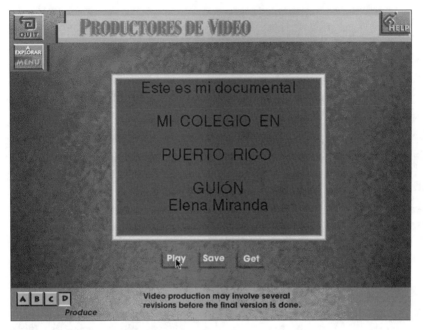

Figure 2.8.
¡Dime!: Students write text to accompany video sequences they select.

Figure 2.9a.
Juntos: Students combine text and graphics.

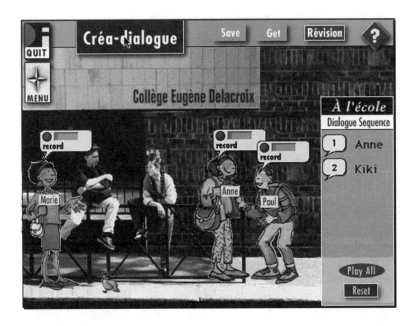

Figure 2.9 b.
Discovering French Interactive: Students combine graphics with audio.

Figure 2.10.
¡Dime!: Students assemble various media in their portfolios.

through the *À la rencontre de Philippe* videodisc (see Appendix). The MFI treats the video of *Philippe* as indexed information on which teachers can perform searches and select the video or audio sequences they want to use for their course. For example, users can search out all sequences on the videodisc that include a particular French grammatical structure or gesture. These can then be played back in any order (Figure 2.11).

Digitized video and audio make this kind of tool a powerful one in that increased speed, precision, and malleability expand the possibilities of student involvement with video material.

An example of a digital media cataloging tool comes from the application *Operación Futuro*. This tool works on a database of multimedia materials— videoclips, audioclips, photos, illustrations, and texts that are cataloged by semantic category. With this database a teacher can, for example, assign students to construct their own television commercials about a particular shop or product. By browsing or performing a key-word search, students can locate in the database the videoclips, audioclips, or photos they wish to incorporate into their commercials. (See also Figure 2.4b.) Access to these tools presents new forms of student control over, and interaction with, the target language. At the same time, these tools empower teachers to customize materials for their courses (Figure 2.12).

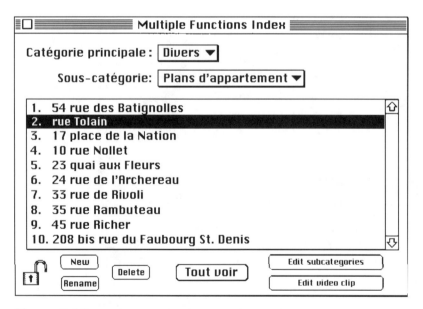

Figure 2.11.

À la rencontre de Phillipe: Students and teacher can perform sophisticated searches.

Figure 2.12.
Operación Futuro: Students create their own commercials.

Text indexing is commonly incorporated into multimedia products in the form of concordances, glossaries, dictionaries, encyclopedic entries, notes, and references. Teachers and learners can type in key words to access indexed text databases. Visual images (stills and graphics) can likewise be accessed, using tools such as the *Catálogos* features in *Juntos* (Figure 2.13).

Online Communications Tools

On-line communications tools with which students can communicate with one another are also becoming a popular feature within multimedia applications. Student exchanges can be in the form of notes posted to other students and/ or the teacher throughout an application (Figure 2.14).

Another example of student-written interaction is a running communications space. Any student can access this running commentary and add to the exchange while within the multimedia environment. Other students or the teacher can also participate in the interchange and contribute responses (Figure 2.15).

E-mail and programs that allow simultaneous communication, or "chat" modes, have also been integrated into language-learning applications (Figure 2.16).

Figure 2.13.
Juntos: Students search out images from a catalog.

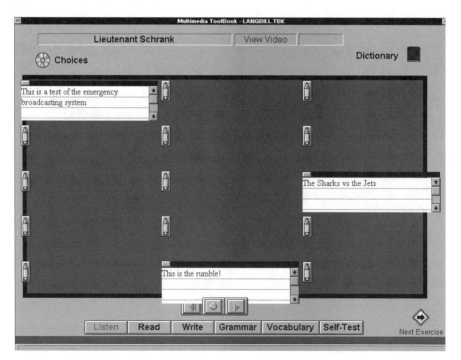

Figure 2.14.
MLLT: Students can leave comments for other students to read and respond to.

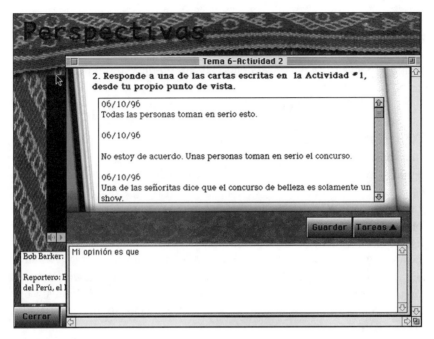

Figure 2.15.
Paradoja: Students engage in ongoing conversation about current issues.

Figure 2.16.
Operación Futuro: Students chat with one another about their work.

World Wide Web browsers and the increasing capabilities of the Internet have prompted the creation of useful tools to assist teachers in their classes. These tools can be as simple as a homepage with links to subjects being taught and writing spaces from which students can submit their assignments and on-line tests, or as complex as virtual workspaces ("whiteboards"), Multi-User Domains (MUDS), and shared applications where two or more students can collaborate on the same materials appearing on their screens at the same time from distant locations. Applications can now merge the local working space with the space provided by applications kept in remote machines. This process is seamless for the student and allows increased flexibility for the updating of materials.

It is now possible to download video or audio materials and create a table of contents that students can use the same day the materials are received. Publishers are and will be increasingly responsive to digital capabilities for accessing materials via the Internet. The day is fast approaching when a student in the U.S. will be able to see and hear a student in Taiwan through a computer screen, and the two students will be able to simultaneously use malleable media and accompanying tools to communicate about one another's language and culture.

Tools in Use

These *control, linking, indexing,* and *communications* tools and the digitized media that can be manipulated with them empower students to take control of their learning. They also open up many opportunities for creative integration on the part of teachers. The following are scenarios in which we see students and teachers using these different tools with multiple, malleable media for innovative language-learning activities.

"Trois Scènes" ["Three Scenes"]

Bob is a second-year university student of French. This semester his French course includes extensive use of multimedia, both in the classroom and for laboratory assignments. Bob's instructor assigns weekly tasks with the multimedia application *À la rencontre de Philippe,* an interactive video story in which learners help Philippe find an apartment in Paris. There are several subplots in this engaging story—Philippe's relationship with his aunt, problems with the plumber, his friends, and other characters, for example. Although there are numerous possibilities for using these multimedia materials, listening-comprehension practice in a problem-solving, decision-making environment is the major objective.

For this week, Bob's instructor has assigned a task with *Philippe* called *trois scènes*. In pairs, students are to choose three video sequences, still images, and text passages that illustrate the relationship between the two main characters in the story. Using a combination of tools—*control tools* for comprehension, review, and composition; *linking tools* to assemble the selected material; *indexing tools* to problem-solve and perform searches; and *communications tools* to collaborate with others to ensure no duplication—learners create a presentation of their *trois scènes*. Bob and his partner, Marlena, select and present three videoclips accompanied by supporting text and still images. They present and defend their rationale for their selections to the rest of the class the next day. Lively discussion ensues.

"Points of View"

Janice is in her third year of Spanish language study. Her course also makes use of multimedia for out-of-class assignments. She and her classmates spend 3 to 4 hours per week using an application called *No Recuerdo.* Students play the role of reporters in Bogotá, Colombia. Learners write for a newspaper about what they see, hear, and read concerning a scientist who has amnesia and has disappeared. Eventually students help him recover before a memory-loss epidemic spreads throughout the country.

For the "Points of View" assignment, Janice interrogates Colombians who may have valuable information. She uses a number of *control* and *linking tools* to get at and assemble information she needs to locate and assist the scientist. Janice has learned that it is critical for her to "read" her interviewees' personalities very carefully for, if she uses inappropriate forms of address, level of formality, or terminology, her interviewee will not cooperate and provide her with the information she needs. Today, after browsing through a database of possible informants, she is interviewing Clara. When she dives straight in asking about people Clara might know who can help her locate the scientist, she receives a warning: "You'd better make small talk with her for a while to put her at ease. Her hedging is a sign of discomfort." Janice proceeds accordingly and eventually uncovers the name of another character who might help her. Janice writes this name in her notebook with a note to start with this character when she logs on the next day.

"Travel Diary"

Rudy is in a first-year high school Spanish course. On Fridays, his instructor takes the class to the multimedia lab, where they engage in a variety of activities that complement the work they have been doing during the week. This week the class has been studying basic travel and geography vocabulary.

Today in the lab they are working in pairs with an application called *Operación Caribe*. Their assignment is to "travel" along the mighty Magdalena river, using a variety of *control tools*. As they navigate to and from various places, they select clips, stills, and text and use *linking tools* to copy them into their personal "Travel Diary." Once they have assembled what they decide is an illustrative collection of media segments, they use paint and word-processing tools to compose a final draft of their diary, then share it with the class for peer feedback and evaluation.

"Discuss It"

An integral part of Mary Shane's second-year Spanish class is the conversation that she continues with her students after they leave the classroom. Her students work with an application called *Paradoja* as homework. The application is a collection of video scenes on contemporary social topics in Latin America. Students use a variety of *control tools* to examine and understand differing perspectives on themes such as commercialism and indigenous cultures. Using an online *communications tool,* the *Tarea* (notebook), students compose their thoughts and commentary on these topics. This is a public notebook that Mary and others in the class read and respond to. There is, therefore, ongoing discussion of topics and issues throughout the week. On-line conversations, including particular aspects of language use and cultural queries, are brought back into the classroom for clarification and elaboration.

"Dramatizations"

The New Middle School has recently adopted the *¡Dime!* curriculum package for first-year Spanish. The text and workbooks form the basis for the majority of classroom and homework activity. The *¡Dime!* CD-ROM is used by students on an independent basis in a laboratory during study periods. As a unit review, students' assignment for this week is to create an original dramatization using the *control, linking,* and *indexing* tools available in the application. Using video sequences representative of the content they have studied for the week, learners take on the role of video characters in sequences they have selected and record their own dialogue to accompany characters' activity in the video. These "dramatizations" can be saved, edited, reviewed, and eventually presented to the rest of the class as a graded assignment.

"You're the Director"

Jasmine is studying French for the first time at her high school. One of her favorite language-learning activities is to play the role of director and create her own multimedia stories in French. Her course is based on the *Discovering*

French text and workbook. The stories she creates on the classroom's computer for her homework assignments are done with the *Discovering French Interactive* CD-ROM. The content of the multimedia application coincides with that of her course as a whole. She is familiar, therefore, with the kinds of language she needs to use in her stories, but has freedom and access to resources, using various *indexing tools* to let her creativity take off. Using available *control* and *linking* tools, Jasmine selects a series of pictures, records her version of what characters are saying to accompany these pictures, edits and revises the recordings and sequencing, and saves this work for her teacher and classmates to review and enjoy at a later time.

"Port It"

Ted Crandall is a French instructor. He believes very much in the value of developing his own original language-learning materials. Using *Super MacLang,* a multimedia authoring tool for creating language-learning materials, he develops online activities, exercises, and resources for his second-year students. His students can access these materials from terminals around the campus, including their dormitory rooms. They complete assignments such as video-based grammar exercises, then use *communications tools* to submit their work electronically to Ted. Ted can then detect weak or problem areas, provide tailored feedback, and update and revise his materials based on student performance and interest.

"Resource: The World"

A class of intermediate high school Spanish students is undertaking comparative cross-cultural studies of Spanish-speaking countries. Throughout the semester they have been using an engaging multimedia application called *Operación Futuro.* The application's core is an interactive story of a young Colombian couple planning to marry. The students' task is to collaborate with this couple to find solutions to several setbacks: money problems, job searches, college costs, doubts, and family relationships. To progress through the application, students need to familiarize themselves with local conditions, culture, and traditions. Extensive resources and *indexing tools* for doing so are available within the application and through *communications tools* that link students to the Internet.

This week, the class assignment is to compare the ways information is presented in four Spanish-language newspapers. *Operación Futuro* prompts learners to access today's editions of *El Tiempo* and *El Espectador* (Colombia), *La Jornada* (Mexico), and *La Vanguardia* (Spain) via the Internet. Their assignment is to locate and read the same lead story in the four papers and answer questions concerning the publication, its style, and its agenda. They are to compose a description citing the articles' similarities and differences and how this situation can relate to the Colombian couple's situation. In addition, expansion activities such as role-playing interviews of the main figures in the article and rewriting the article from a U.S. perspective are suggested. These written assignments are electronically submitted to the instructor, using *communications tools.*

Where Are We?—The Broader Context

When computer-assisted language learning (CALL) was in its early conceptual stages, software development and usage was still steered by the belief that foreign language learning was essentially language appreciation, not the attainment of communicative competence. Standardized tests assessed mastery of structures, vocabulary, and reading comprehension, not one's ability to use and understand the language productively. The trend was, logically at the time, to transfer existing foreign language textbooks to computer-based applications. Students could then essentially use the computer to turn pages of the textbook, fill in the blanks in workbook drills, and choose multiple-choice answers to questions. Within this usage paradigm, there was widespread belief that computers could, in and of themselves, work magic and, in effect, "teach." The available analogy for computer-assisted instruction was both the language textbook and independent work in the language laboratory; students would work with the language independently and thereby acquire skills in stand-alone dialogue with the medium. We now realize, however, that only a small percentage of foreign language students have the motivation, perseverance, and skills to undertake the amount of independent study envisioned within this paradigm. We also realize the limited and limiting results of the online workbook analogy.

Current perspectives on language learning recognize that drill and practice is necessary but not sufficient. It is also becoming widely recognized that if we are preparing students to use language productively in their lives and in their work, if we wish for them to truly acquire skills that they can use, foreign language courses must promote such competencies, not a contrived level of syntactic mastery. Indeed, the *Standards for Foreign Language Learning* (1996) are a reflection of this major shift in thinking as they emphasize communication, understanding other cultures, recognizing domain-specific perspectives of other nationalities, and one's ability to reflect on one's native culture by virtue of understanding a second one as the primary goals of instructional activities.

Technology, especially digital technology, can clearly play a complementary role in the implementation of these new ways of thinking about language acquisition in general and these language teaching guidelines in particular—digital media bring flexible representations of the target language and culture into learning environments and flexible tools with which to mix and tailor material. That role, however, is only complementary when learning with technologies is integrated into carefully crafted contexts of use, where tasks, off-line support, and valuing of online processes and outcomes are woven into larger classroom goals and processes.

Where Are We Going?—Materials Development

Because of the flexibility and mutability of the print medium, the textbook has been and continues to be the focal point of commercially packaged curricula. Over the years, in response to the growing accessibility of technologies in all learning contexts, publishers have been adding an increasingly diverse set of media to their language packages in order to make them more useful and attractive. Materials in several forms are available to teachers for activities in listening comprehension, writing, reading, speaking, and pronunciation. The most complete packages include a heavily annotated textbook for the instructor, teacher's guide, student textbook, activities/workbook, answer key, tape script, audiotapes/CDs, videotape and/or videodisc with workbook, software with a student guide, blackline masters, slides, and color transparencies. In coming years, other components such as access to publisher's homepages on the Internet, customized curricula, print-on-demand handouts and books will be changing the what and the how of language-learning materials development and distribution.

When developing these full-curriculum packages for language learning, the publishing industry has traditionally included audio, video, software, and picture materials as "add-ons" to an essentially textbook-centered package. "Other" materials are typically created after the fact around the core text of the coursebook. This curriculum design approach is on the brink of radical change. As we move quickly into a fully digitized world, the textbook may no longer be a sufficiently central, unifying object.

Digitization means that we can no longer approach the design of nonprint materials as if they were static. We have seen, for example, that in a multimedia environment, media elements can move fluidly from one form into another and that combined media and the tools for their combination of necessity bring us to reconsider language-learning materials in general and the ways students interact with them in particular. Multimedia products are now acquiring a character of their own. The products we have used as examples are striving for innovative uses of digitized media that can both mirror curriculum content and at the same time offer forms for interacting with it that are distinctive.

We still have a long way to go before new conventions are established that see the attributes of mobile media as the beginning point of design. Planning a language-learning materials package, for example, may start with a general framework for the product based on the simultaneous design of all media elements rather than on the design of the add-ons after the textbook or the video have been created. In other words, future design approaches will be based on the premise that media are no longer immutable, but dynamic, interchangeable, and mobile.

Technology represents possibilities to break from tradition in many respects. With these powerful tools, we can create new contexts, new approaches, and new ways of thinking about the craft of teaching languages. The combination of malleable media and powerful tools to manipulate them translates into active student participation and investment in the learning process, as well as a high degree of control and opportunity for creativity on the part of teachers. Technology presents an opportunity to reconceive the notion of what it is to learn another language and the best practices to meet that end.

NOTE

* Graphics were prepared by Ana B. Chiquito, Lestra Litchfield, and Luis Carlos, Center for Educational Computing Initiatives, Massachusetts Institute of Technology.

REFERENCES

Book

Negroponte, N. 1995. *Being Digital.* New York: Vintage Books.

Applications

Comprehensive descriptions of the applications cited and of other current applications are available at <http://ceci.mit.edu/doc/actfl>.

If you are interested in a particular application cited in this article, the publisher or developer will provide more information about it.

À la rencontre de Philippe
Publisher: Yale University Press, 1993
Author: Gilberte Furstenberg
Platform: Macintosh
Delivery medium: Laserdisc and diskettes.
Level: Intermediate-level college/university

Allez, Viens
Publisher: Holt, Rinehart and Winston, 1997
Platforms: Macintosh and PC
Delivery medium: CD-ROM
Level: Middle school, junior high, or high school

¡Dime! Interactive
Publisher: D. C. Heath and Company, 1995
Platform: Macintosh or Windows
Delivery medium: CD-ROM
Level: Middle school and high school.
Authors: Fabien Samaniego, M. C. Brown, P. Hamilton Carlin, S. E. Gorman, C. L.
Sparks

Discovering French Interactive
Publisher: D. C. Heath and Company, 1994
Platform: Macintosh or PC
Delivery medium: CD-ROM
Level: Middle school, junior high, or high school

Juntos Interactivo
Publisher: Prentice Hall, 1996
Platforms: Macintosh and PC
Delivery medium: CD-ROM
Level: Middle school, junior high, or high school
Authors: Authors: Ana B. Chiquito, M. González-Aguilar, Douglas Morgenstern, M.
Rivas-Rojas, Joy Renjilian-Burgy

Multimedia Language Learning Templates (MLLT)
Developer: Center for Electronic Language Learning and Research, State University
of New York at Albany
Platform: Windows, videodisc, and overlay/controller card

No Recuerdo
Developer: Massachusetts Institute of Technology (MIT). Major funding from the
Annenberg/CPB Project. Additional funding: National Endowment for the
Humanities, The Consortium for Language Teaching and Learning.
Level: Intermediate-level college/university
Platform: Macintosh.
Author: Douglas Morgenstern and J. Murray with Ana B. Chiquito, S. Felshin, S.
Malone.

Operación Futuro and *Operación Caribe*
Developer: University of Bergen, Norway, and Center for Educational Computing
Initiatives (CECI), Massachusetts Institute of Technology (MIT). Funding from
the Norwegian Research Council, University of Bergen and its Faculty of Arts,
Coltejer S.A., and Banco Ganadero.
Level: Intermediate-level college/university
Platforms: WindowsNT, Windows95, Xwindows.
Author: Ana B. Chiquito

Paradoja

Developer: Language Learning and Research Center (LLARC) and Spanish
Department, Massachusetts Institute of Technology (MIT) with funding from the
Consortium for Language Teaching and Learning and the Department of Foreign
Languages and Literatures at MIT.
Platform: Macintosh
Delivery medium: CD-ROM
Level: Intermediate- and advanced-levels college/university.
Authors: M. Ribas-Groeger, M. González-Aguilar and E. Lilienfeld.

Super MacLang

Publisher: Harvard University and Dartmouth College
Platform: Macintosh
Level: Generic
Author: Judith Frommer

Travel Tur

Publisher: Houghton Mifflin and Company
Platforms: Macintosh and Windows
Level: Beginning- and intermediate-levels Spanish college/university.

Ven Conmigo

Publisher: Holt, Rinehart and Winston, 1997
Platforms: Macintosh and PC
Delivery medium: CD-ROM
Level: Middle school, junior high, or high school

Vis-À-Vis

Publisher: McGraw-Hill, 1996
Platform: Macintosh
Delivery medium: CD-ROM
Level: Introductory-level college/university.

3

Teaching Listening: *How Technology Can Help*

Elizabeth Joiner
University of South Carolina

Listening: Past and Present

In 1926, Rankin found that listening accounts for roughly half of the time we spend using language, a finding that has been confirmed many times since (Coakley and Wolvin 1990:34). In Rankin's time, listening to language was more likely to take place in the presence of a speaker than to be mediated by technology. People conversed face to face, sat in lecture halls listening to an address, witnessed public debates and medicine shows, or attended live theater performances. Although the telephone existed, its use was not widespread, communication or information exchange at a distance being accomplished primarily through written media: newspapers, handbills, personal letters, and the like.

In the present era, referred to variously as the "information age" and the "postliterate age," the role of electronic media in communication is increasing almost daily. The telephone call has all but replaced the personal letter; tape pals, and even cyberpals, coexist with pen pals; newspapers are struggling to remain competitive with radio and television; classroom walls have been expanded via distance learning; commuters listen to audiobooks as they drive to work; live theater shares the entertainment stage with film and video; and the dusty roads traveled by Pony Express riders have been replaced by an information superhighway, capable of transmitting not only text but real-time audio and video as well. Furthermore, recording and playback equipment make it possible for us to store audio or video documents transmitted from

Elizabeth G. Joiner (Ph.D., The Ohio State University) is Professor of French at the University of South Carolina, where she serves as Academic Director of the Ted Mimms Foreign Language Learning Center. The co-author of three first-year textbooks as well as a video-based intermediate-level program, she has also published articles on listening comprehension, oral communication, teacher education, and the use of video in language teaching. In 1992, she was named a *Chevalier dans l'ordre des Palmes académiques.*

distant sources to listen to or view at our convenience. Every day we use technology that was unknown to Rankin and his contemporaries to overcome both distance and time, the limitations to human communication imposed by nature.

To see how presently available technology can facilitate second- or foreign-language listening comprehension, we might look inside a language-learning center at a medium-sized public university. In the audio-video laboratory, an ESL teacher is conducting a listening class. Although it at first appears that whole-class instruction is taking place, a closer look reveals that the instructor has paired students electronically so that they can converse as they complete their assignment. To do so, they will use a special feature of the Sony 9000 lab that allows them to mark up to four key places on the cassette tape and return to these marked passages almost as quickly as is the case with a compact disc.

Moving to the individualized learning section, we notice several students sitting in front of a large-screen monitor. They are watching the satellite news from China, picking up the sound via infrared headsets with individual volume control. In another area of the learning center, this same broadcast is being recorded for later viewing on small (13") monitors at individual stations. These stations, which consist of TV/VCR combination units, are also used for viewing films, television programs, and textbook-related instructional video housed in the learning center. In the center's computer area, Macintoshes and IBMs (and compatibles) stand ready to deliver a variety of interactive multimedia programs to students whose language ability ranges from elementary to advanced. Some are ancillary software-based programs that complement a set of materials adopted by one of the language departments; others are stand-alone programs whose place in the curriculum must be determined by teachers and/or students. These same computers provide access to the World Wide Web through the Netscape browser.

As we observe the students sitting in the audio-video lab or in front of computers and listening or viewing stations, we may assume that all are engaged in essentially the same activity. Yet to do so would be to ignore the fact that each medium has its own characteristics, as does each text and each student. No two listening experiences are totally analogous, and the fact that all the students in the learning center are wearing headphones and apparently focusing their attention on a sound source should not make us forget that there are many important "inside the head" and "outside the head" factors that contribute to comprehension (Samuels 1987).

In the sections that follow, we will see how these factors intersect in the act of listening. Beginning "outside the head," we will first examine characteristics of various media before considering procedures and strategies for teaching and learning that capitalize on the crucial "inside the head" factors. Finally, we will present some special listeners before concluding with a number of speculations as to how technology may be expected to assist listening instruction in the future.

Media Matters

Technology-mediated communication has become so much a part of our lives that we normally give little thought to how various electronic media differ among themselves or to how technology-aided communication differs from face-to-face communication. McLuhan (1964) used the terms *hot* and *cool* to divide media according to how much work the user has to do to encode messages presented by the physical stimuli. According to him, media that present sensory stimuli filled with data are *hot,* or complete, in contrast to *cool* media, which are incomplete, that is, characterized by sensory stimuli not filled with data. Relating media specifically to interaction among human beings, Purdy (1996) reminds us of the impact of media characteristics on communication, asserting that each medium "has qualities or characteristics that make it unique . . . and that affect in various ways the nature of the human communication that uses that medium."

In evaluating the effectiveness of a medium, a criterion that is often used is its ability to live up to the fullness of face-to-face communication, which is characterized by "presence," including immediacy and interactivity—feedback and response (Purdy 1996). As a participant in interactive communication, the listener functions as speaker and hearer, negotiating meaning with one or several interlocutors. In such an exchange there are opportunities to verify hunches, to ask questions, to interrupt, and to repair breakdown should it occur. Purdy goes on to point out that face-to-face communication has the potential for using all the senses (sight, sound, touch, taste, and smell) to clarify meaning, whereas mediated communication uses only some subset of the aforementioned sense channels. (The smell of burning toast that accompanies a horrified exclamation is not apparent on the other end of the telephone line, for example.) Other important clues to meaning that may be available to a listener in a face-to-face situation are lipreading (Kellerman 1990; Montgomery 1993), contextual clues, pragmatic markers, facial expression, and eye gaze direction (Montgomery 1993). In addition to these more obvious extralinguistic clues to meaning, the face-to-face condition facilitates the separation of speech sound from environmental noise spatially through binaural or "stereo" hearing (Montgomery 1993:316). Should noise nevertheless interfere with comprehension, the speaker-listener may turn down an overly loud television set or stereo or suggest moving to a quieter place or waiting until a train or parade has passed before resuming the conversation.

In reviewing the characteristics of face-to-face communication, we may make a number of observations. First, face-to-face communication is immediate. It takes place in the here and now. Second, it is interactive, including both response and feedback. Third, face-to-face communication is multisensory, relying as it does on extralinguistic as well as linguistic clues to meaning. Fourth, the speaker-listener has various means of obtaining help should communication be less than successful. Fifth and finally, the speaker-listener can make use of simple strategies to exert control over the situation. It will be important to keep these characteristics in mind as we consider how various audio and visual media, including computer-assisted multimedia, can be used in the development of foreign language listening comprehension skills. Other important criteria for the selection of audio-visual technology include convenience, availability, and cost.

Sound Advice

Of the media useful for the teaching of listening, audio has the longest history and is surely the least costly, the most convenient, and the most widely available. Shortwave radio broadcasts, audio magazines, and foreign music recorded on cassettes or compact discs can bring the target language into classrooms and learning centers or accompany students as they drive, jog, or shop. Lightweight cassette decks and compact disc players are easily transportable, and neither represents a great investment. Furthermore, most teachers and students are very familiar with audio technology and require little, if any, instruction in its use.

To understand how audio functions as a medium, let us reconsider the characteristics of face-to-face communication described above and examine what happens when a live conversation is recorded. Like all other sounds, the speech sounds emitted by a speaker-listener in the face-to-face situation are vibrations, or sound waves.[1] During recording, these sound waves will be transformed into electrical signals and transferred magnetically onto audiotape. In the case of digital media, signals representing sounds will be transformed into a string of electrical *ones* and *zeros*, the basic computer language. How much the recorded conversation resembles the original "live" conversation depends on a number of factors, including the skill of the person making the recording, the quality of the recording equipment, the quality of the tape or disc on which the conversation is recorded or stored, and the quality of the playback equipment. *Consumer Reports Audio-Video Buying*

Guide, published yearly, and a number of audiophile and stereophile publications provide evaluations of tape quality and compare various recording and playback devices from the standpoint of features and quality.

While tape is currently the medium of choice for recorded audio materials suitable for listening instruction, this situation may soon change as some publishers have already begun to offer an audio CD option to accompany textbooks. In addition to their random access capability (the possibility to access segments immediately), the digitized audio signal of compact discs normally has a wider dynamic range (the span between the softest and loudest sounds) and a greater frequency range (the span between the highest and lowest pitch) than audiotape and thus can come closer to delivering to listeners what Yang (1988:15) has termed *positive sound,* characterized by a "wide acoustic frequency band, wide dynamic range, good linearity, little distortion, even distribution of treble and bass and proper intermediate and low frequencies."

The quality of digitized audio used in computer-assisted language learning applications is discussed by Jones (1990:34), who, noting that the most important factor contributing to sound quality is the sample rate per second, concludes that "for most language learning programs, a rate of 11 kHz is recommended. A higher sample rate results in a higher quality recording, but it also requires more space for data storage." As data storage increases, it should be possible to avoid this unfortunate trade-off.[2]

The sounds of human speech are, of course, different from those of music, but there is some disagreement as to the range of speech sounds. Although it is sometimes stated that human speech occupies a rather narrow frequency band between 40 and 4,000 Hz (Pihlajamäki 1995), this belief is disputed by Tomatis (1991), who analyzed the sounds most characteristic of a number of languages and found that the preferred frequency bands of certain languages reach 12,000 Hz (12 kHz). The discrepancy between these points of view concerning the frequencies of human speech may result from the fact that a speech sound consists not only of a fundamental sound but also of a number of partials or harmonics that complete that sound. It is the harmonics or overtones that enable us to distinguish between voices and between closely related sounds (Handel 1989).

What happens when the listener's sound source does not adequately transmit the sounds of the language in question? Montgomery (1993:316) describes what occurs when he asks native speakers of English to transcribe a low-fidelity recording of a conversation among three speakers of their own language. He reports that in addition to having difficulty identifying the three speakers, the students will transcribe a number of words incorrectly. These errors typically involve acoustically similar sounds such as "b" and "v," low-intensity sounds such as "f," "ah," or unstressed "th," or sounds that contain high-frequency energy such as "s," "t," and "k." *Boaters* may be confused with *voters, fox* with *ox,* and *mark* with *mart.* As is the case with most monophonic recordings of spoken language, any noise (environmental or musical) recorded along with the conversation will be more difficult to separate from speech than is the case in a real-life situation, in which our two ears enable us to distinguish speech from other sounds "stereophonically."

In typical audio-only listening, we turn on the radio and have to cope immediately with rapid natural speech. Unlike participants in a face-to-face conversation, we are not able to use visual and kinesthetic clues to meaning nor are we able to control the aural message(s) by asking the speaker to slow down or clarify. In fact, the only feature that radio as a medium shares with face-to-face listening is *immediacy.* Interactivity is absent (except in the case of call-in shows); hearing is the only sense involved; the listener has no way of asking for help; the only control mechanism is the volume control; and strategy use will necessarily be more limited than in face-to-face interaction. Can we conclude, then, that audio is an unsatisfactory medium for teaching listening? Not at all, as we shall see in the following discussion.

Radio is a venerable medium, and over the years radio professionals have learned to compensate for lack of visual support in a number of ways. Working without the "visual safety net" provided by video, the best radio commentators have become excellent verbal communicators, choosing precise words, employing figurative language to evoke images in the minds of their listeners, and using intonation and expressive language to advantage. Creators of radio dramas, aware that meaningful sound is not confined to dialogue, add sound effects (dishes clattering, a thud when the corpse hits the floor), emotional sounds such as laughter, sobs, or screams, and music to set a mood or create suspense. Good audio can motivate and hold the attention of the listener, while providing rich verbal input. Further, technology, in the form of recording and playback equipment, adds control missing in the "live broadcast" condition by permitting pausing and relistening. Just as the reader circles back to review or retrieve, the listener can pause, rewind, and relisten to the fleeting auditory signal until the meaning becomes clear. In this way, the *immediacy* skill of listening can be made to resemble the *recursive* skill of reading.

While the technology for pausing and relistening to recorded audio is easily available, specialized equipment is required for controlling the audio signal by means of rate alteration. More than a decade ago, Harvey (1981) advocated allowing students access to both time-expanded and time-compressed speech so that they could determine their own optimal listening speed and build confidence as listeners. Indeed, listening to *time-expanded* (slowed) speech has been found to build confidence (Ko 1992), but its effect on comprehension has not been clearly established by research (Rader 1990; Griffiths 1992; Ko 1992). Listening to *time-compressed* (accelerated) speech is believed to increase concentration (Duker 1974; Ostermeier 1991). Normal speech typically falls within a range of 150 to 180 words per minute; the brain, however, can process information at a rate of about 400 to 800 words per minute (Pihlajamäki 1995). Because of this Speech-Thought-Time Differential, listeners are able to process their native language at higher than normal speeds (Duker 1974; Conrad 1989).

We have seen that technology provides valuable tools for manipulating audio material in such a way that it becomes more comprehensible. Other aids to comprehension, these nontechnological, may be present in the rhetorical organization of an audio passage and/or be provided in accompanying print documents. Each issue of the *Champs-Élysées* audio magazine,[3] an exemplary resource for teachers of French, begins with an advance organizer in the form of an overview of the contents of the program, and each text or song is briefly introduced by the *très sympathique* host Georges Lang, who provides transitions between various journalists. An accompanying booklet includes additional aids to comprehension in the form of a complete transcription of the oral text and numerous linguistic and cultural notes. Sensitive to user response, *Champs-Élysées* has modified its style somewhat over the years. In the original magazine, for example, music was played behind the news reports and other spoken material. Now, as a result of listener comments, music and text alternate with just a slight overlap of fade-out music at the beginning of the spoken text to provide an authentic feel. (We have seen earlier that monophonic recordings that combine several sound sources can be difficult to process.) Presently available only on audiocassette, *Champs-Élysées* will soon provide an audio CD option (Green 1996).

Changing Channels

Comparing audio and video, McLuhan (1964) characterized radio as a *hot,* or complete, medium. Television, on the other hand, he characterized as *cool,* or incomplete, because of the integrative work the viewer must do to create an image out of a visual signal that consists of a series of dots transmitted line by line. In contrast, foreign language specialists tend to think of television as being the more complete medium because of the extralinguistic and contextual clues to meaning provided by the visual image. As Noblitt (1990:43) put it: "It may sound odd to stress the visual elements in hearing, but comprehension is aided enormously by being able to see gestures, expressions, and elements of the surrounding environment." Lipreading, where possible, may also contribute to comprehension (Kellerman 1990; Montgomery 1993).

Video and film not only supply these important visual elements but also provide environmental and musical sounds as well as human speech on an audio sound track. Thus, though lacking smell, taste, and touch, video engages the senses of both sight and hearing, thereby approaching the face-to-face situation. Nevertheless, while video is capable of creating a feeling of immediacy or presence, Phillips (1991:344) notes as a characteristic of video ". . . the absence of opportunities to negotiate meaning as occurs with face-to-face communication."

Although linked, the audio and visual elements of a film or television program may, and most often do, function differently, and it is normally the visual that predominates. To illustrate this, let us consider the following scene from the beginning of "La Main dans le sac," (Cohen and Louchet 1983) a short video illustrating the French judicial system: *A young man is seen lurking near an automatic teller machine. Another man notices his suspicious behavior and decides to observe. A woman approaches the teller and withdraws money. The first man pushes her against the machine, snatches her purse, and begins to run. The second man starts after him. A chase ensues. The police arrive just as the thief has been wrestled to the ground. They handcuff the thief and force him into the squad car before setting off with sirens wailing.* In this crucial scene, there is no dialogue, the message being entirely carried by images supported by environmental and musical sounds.[4]

When sound and image exist together, their relationship is normally complementary rather than redundant. In other words, the same message is not often presented both visually and verbally except in pedagogical materials designed for young children or filmed demonstrations in which each step of a process (baking a cake, building a birdhouse) is illustrated on the screen. Phillips (1991) analyzed the relationship between the visual and the verbal in various types of oral texts (weather forecasts, advertisements, soft news and human interest stories, hard news, commentary, and editorials) present in German, French, and Spanish video newscasts. Items where the visual dominated included weather reports, advertisements, sports features, and business reports accompanied by charts. Even when visuals were present, however, they were not necessarily helpful. For example, in weather reports from South America, temperatures on the map were in Celsius but were given orally in Fahrenheit.

This observation has implications for selecting video materials for listening practice. It is important to choose those that provide sufficient clues for information processing and that do not present contradictory messages such as the one described by Phillips above. As Rubin (1990:315) has so aptly pointed out, "It is the selection that is critical, not just the use of video. . . ."

Unlike radio, television requires listeners to process simultaneously two types of stimuli, visual and auditory. Furthermore, visual stimuli include both images and text (a sign indicating that a certain establishment is a school, for example). How viewers process these various stimuli is a question that has intrigued a number of scholars. In comparing auditory and visual processing, Singer and Singer (1983:271) observe that: "One is a verbal-linguistic and perhaps more action-oriented processing system linked especially to the left hemisphere of the brain. The other coding system involves a more receptive, global, spatially oriented or imagery-focused process linked to the right half of the brain." Door (1986:29), pointing out the demands of processing the visual stimuli alone, observes that ". . . the television screen is usually full of more images than can be scanned in the time available before the scene or camera angle changes." This fact may explain why Long (1991), in a qualitative investigation, found that some students had difficulty in processing simultaneously the auditory and visual material of an authentic Spanish video and needed repeated viewings to take in the various stimuli present in the text.

In the previous decade, the processing of televised material by children was the subject of a number of interesting studies included in collections by Bryant and Anderson (1983) and Door (1986). Mielke (1983:260) reports on a study involving a chimpanzee trained to use sign language: "Features presented visually (e.g., the chimp brushing his teeth, eating pancakes at the breakfast table, and learning signs for various objects) . . . were recalled. More abstract scientific ideas buried in the audio track (issues of intelligence in humans and animals) . . . were not comprehended or recalled. What came across to the children was the idea that a chimp had been trained to do tricks, not the significance of symbolic language."

Two studies by Meringoff et al. (1983) found significant differences in recall when a narrative was presented to children through different media. In the first study, an African folktale was presented to two groups of children (twenty-four 6- to 7-year-olds and twenty-four 9- to 10-year-olds). The folktale was presented either as an animated televised film or read aloud from a picture book with illustrations shown to the children. Recall, which was examined on both a spontaneous and an aided basis, showed that children exposed to the televised story included more of the characters' actions in their verbal retellings and did more physical gesturing, while the children who were read the story in picture-book form recalled more figurative language and based their inferences more on textual content. The second study, built around an adventure story and involving preschool children, produced similar results, leading the researchers to conclude that ". . . when television and picture-book presentations were compared, preschoolers' memory for figurative language was increased dramatically by having a picture book read to them, as opposed to their language recall after watching the televised story" (Meringoff et al. 1983:176). This was true even though the two versions delivered the same narration and all of the book's content appeared in the film.

The results of the investigations described above raise several questions with respect to the process and outcomes of listening to video material. In these studies, video did not prove to be an effective means of producing verbal recall in young children acquiring their first language. Moreover, the study reported by Mielke revealed the primacy of visual over verbal recall, at least in the television viewing of the subjects of that study. While it would be unwise to generalize the results of studies of young children to other groups of listeners, such studies could serve as models for research into the processing of video materials by second- and foreign-language learners of various ages. Results of such research would provide important information on visual and verbal processing to guide teachers in their selection and use of televised material to develop listening skills.

The fact that television is primarily a visual medium is reflected in the relative importance accorded to sound and image by manufacturers of television equipment and associated recording and playback devices. Television sound, while comprehensible to native speakers with normal hearing, is not always of excellent quality. For example, in its 1995 ratings of eighteen 27-inch models, *Consumer Reports Audio-Video Buying Guide* gave an excellent audio rating to only two, although fully one-third were determined to have excellent picture quality. When television programs and films are videotaped and played back on a VCR, the sound is likewise often disappointing in quality. Some of the reasons for this loss of fidelity are given by Amyes (1990:18), who recommends the newer hi-fi videotape recorders that can deliver sound comparable to that of digital audio, for him the "ultimate sound quality."

The digital soundtrack of videodiscs (the image is analog) provides the listener with sound superior to that available on normal (not hi-fi) videocassettes. Is the difference important? There are some indications that this is the case. The developers of *Vidéo Vérité* (Joiner, Duménil, and Day 1994) and a number of native speakers transcribed the soundtrack of the televised interviews used in that instructional program. Some words that were incomprehensible to as many as nine native speakers who listened to the videotape and/or an audio recording of the video soundtrack became clear when the material was transferred to videodisc and played back on a videodisc player. Additionally, instructors using *Vidéo Vérité* at the University of South Carolina have reported that students comprehend the material with fewer listenings when the videodisc rather than the videocassette version is used for classroom viewing.

As is the case with audio, off-air broadcasts of televised material, while they provide the feeling of immediacy present in the face-to-face situation, lack interactivity and listener control. These can be compensated for when the material is recorded and played back on either a VCR or a videodisc player. The possibility of pausing and reviewing may be of particular importance in the instructional use of television with its ". . . remarkably 'cluttered' stimulus field, which holds viewer attention by piling up novelty through shifts of scene, content, mixtures of visual movement, music, sound effects and speech" (Singer and Singer 1983:272). Multiple opportunities for listening-viewing can help the listener process multiple sounds and images, and videodisc technology, which enables immediate access to video segments by means of barcodes and a laser barcode reader, is especially effective in compensating for the lack of interactivity and control present in live viewing.

In the preceding paragraph, we have seen that television, or at least American television, presents the listener with many stimuli that must be processed simultaneously. This being the case, adding yet another stimulus would seem unwise. Nevertheless, there is some evidence that the addition of a textual stimulus that duplicates the soundtrack helps, rather than hinders, comprehension. A character generator can be used to overlay on-screen captions (verbatim renderings of what is said on the soundtrack) onto materials recorded on videocassette or videodisc, thus enabling the listener to view, read, and listen simultaneously. Pusack and Otto (1995:31), after reviewing a number of recent studies of captioned video materials, note that ". . . all reported increases in listening comprehension and in vocabulary learning and control through the use of verbatim captioning of videotaped materials."

Two experimental studies, one in French and one in ESL, have reported interesting results on the use of captions in an interactive videodisc condition. Borrás and Lafayette (1994), whose subjects were fifth-semester college French students, concluded that allowing students to control the captions contributed not only to significantly higher performance on oral communication tasks but also to a significantly better attitude toward viewing authentic materials. It is their belief that a relatively high level of listening and reading skills (intermediate to advanced) may be necessary for students to profit maximally from the simultaneous activation of listening and reading skills required in the captioned condition. In a study involving ESL learners whose listening practice included captioned interactive video with results feedback, Smith and Shen (1992) found that these students had a significantly higher score on a treatment content-specific test but not on the TOEFL listening comprehension test when compared to the control group. The researchers concluded that using captioning for specific content will improve the comprehension of learners within that content but were unable to show that this improvement would transfer to other listening situations. Studies such as these two, while they evoke cautious optimism concerning the use of captioned video, also raise questions that will need to be addressed in further investigations.

Multimedia

The Borrás and Lafayette and Smith and Shen studies of captioned video used technology that is variously referred to as interactive video or interactive multimedia or computer-assisted multimedia. Nearly a decade ago, Douglas (1988:254) wrote enthusiastically of this technology that "the potential offered through the interfacing of the computer, videodisc, and audio recorder . . . is almost overpowering." Noblitt (1990:10) emphasizes learner control[5] when he defines multimedia as "a technique that combines images, sounds, and text with interactive control by the learner." The most obvious advantage of such computer-assisted multimedia applications is instantaneous random-access to any sentence or segment on the sound source, usually a CD-ROM or videodisc, and the ability to replay and relisten with ease to difficult passages. While this feature, in and of itself, is of considerable help to listeners, interactive multimedia programs facilitate listening in additional ways by adding text and providing a number of easily accessible online helps believed to contribute to the comprehension process. In the following analysis of selected multimedia programs, it will be helpful to keep in mind the benchmark of face-to-face listening with its characteristics of immediacy, interactivity, control, multisensory input, and the availability of various options for obtaining help. (A more comprehensive treatment of multimedia in language teaching can be found in Chapter 1 of this volume.)

Multimedia programs may be designed to promote two-way interactive (conversational) listening and/or one-way reactive (for information or entertainment) listening, two types of listening distinguished by Morley (1990). These distinct conditions make different demands on the listener. We have seen earlier that in face-to-face or conversational listening, the interlocutors have a number of means to repair breakdown in communication and, thus, a certain amount of control over the situation. At the same time, face-to-face interaction requires turn-taking skills and the ability to cope with unexpected changes of topic as well as the pauses, hesitations, and reformulations characteristic of spontaneous speech. The spectrum of oral texts to which we listen for entertainment and information (one-way listening) is so wide that generalizations about register and style are impossible. However, since listeners usually choose the film or play or television program that they wish to watch, they are normally able to make use of background knowledge and the typical rhetorical organization of the oral text to aid aural processing. The challenge of one-way, reactive listening is that listeners are required to process oral documents over which they have no control. Programs that simulate two-way interactive, or conversational, listening are prepared from carefully scripted video segments produced for that specific purpose. The basic material of programs that simulate one-way listening consists of foreign-language films or television programs recorded on videodisc and repurposed for instructional use. In order to see how multimedia can recreate and enhance the two types of listening situations identified by Morley, we will examine one example of each type.

The *Listening Tool* (Otto and Pusack 1992) software allows users to browse a variety of authentic French, German, or Spanish video documents (soap operas, morning shows, news and weather reports, interviews, and human interest stories) in an exploratory fashion typical of one-way reactive listening while at the same time providing them with instantaneous access to numerous online aids to comprehension.[6] At any point, the student can pause and replay a segment, request sentence-by-sentence play (in which there will be an automatic pause at the end of each sentence), call for key words or a transcription of the current sentence, repeat the current sentence, go back a certain number of sentences, or begin again at the first of the segment. In this manner, the rapidly delivered authentic text is brought under the control of the listener, who can instantly view the segment again, using the key words to guess at sentence meaning or the online transcription to segment the stream of speech into identifiable words.[7] While the *Listening Tool* is ideal for individualized learning, its features facilitate classroom listening activities as well.

A few interactive multimedia programs have been designed and scripted in such a way that the listener becomes an active participant in a simulated adventure. The basic assumption underlying these programs seems to reflect the functional-notional point of view that language is learned not linearly but "socially, purposefully and cumulatively in life experience" (Douglas 1988:257). One such simulated adventure is *Montevidisco* (Larson and Bush 1992). Filmed on location in Mexico, this program transports the listener-learner to a foreign environment, where he or she meets and interacts with foreign nationals in authentic situations and surroundings.

The user of *Montevidisco* assumes the role of a tourist visiting a medium-sized Mexican town. Like most tourists, the visitor will encounter a variety of situations and will need to cope with the accents of male and female native speakers of Spanish, ranging from cab drivers and bartenders to nurses, librarians, and priests. The visitor is not without resources, however. The program, which exists in a male and a female version, provides an *amiga* or *amigo,* depending on the gender of the user. While the language directed at the listener by the on-screen interlocutor is in dialogue form and usually ends with a question or suggestion, this helpful "friend," accessed by a mouse click, uses carefully articulated indirect discourse to tell the visitor what has just been said. Other aids to comprehension include an online dictionary and a transcription. With the help of as few or as many aids to comprehension as he or she wishes to use, the listener replies by clicking on one of four written "responses" to the interlocutor's questions and suggestions. Thus, selecting a written response replaces emitting a spoken response in the simulated conversations. While visiting *Montevidisco,* the student becomes alternately "speaker" and listener, engaging in dialogue with various representatives of the foreign culture in typical situations.

Montevidisco is a multiple-branching program that allows students to proceed in a variety of ways, depending on their choices. In fact, *Montevidisco* contains twenty-eight major sequences and provides 1,100 paths through the material (Gale 1983). In addition to presenting the listener-learner with the visual contextual clues to meaning present in real-life interactions, multiple-branching adventures such as *Montevidisco* could be expected to enhance listening comprehension in the following ways. The listener-learner in essence creates the story through choices, thus ensuring attention and increasing motivation to listen. The story literally will not advance without the active participation of the user. Furthermore, the fact that there are a number of ways to proceed through the program allows students to create several different adventures by going through the program a number of times, each time selecting different options. Additional comprehension practice is, thus, obtained without boredom. Finally, receiver apprehension, cited by some as contributing negatively to listening comprehension (Meyer 1984; Bacon 1989), should be alleviated by the learner's control over the material and by helps such as the *amigo/amiga.* A study comparing *Montevidisco* to an audiocassette program for teaching listening is currently under way at Brigham Young University (Larson 1996).

It is apparent that computer-assisted multimedia comes closer than the other audio and visual media to meeting the standard for listening embodied in face-to-face communication. Presence, interactivity, control, multisensory input, and multiple sources of assistance can be incorporated into this sophisticated technology. The resemblance to face-to-face listening is especially striking in the case of *Montevidisco,* which uses a speaker-listener turn-taking format. While the conversational partners are unable to negotiate meaning exactly as they would in a real-life situation, and the conversations are not actually spoken, the similarity to the real situation is far greater than is the case for most other materials available for listening instruction. The *Listening Tool,* too, bridges the gap between the learner's competence and authentic video materials in an effective and appealing manner by simulating one-way listening in an environment that encourages learners to risk and explore.

We have seen that interactive programs such as *Montevidisco* and the *Listening Tool* come closer than simpler audio and video technology to simulating the ideal face-to-face listening situation. In spite of their sophistication and power, however, computer-assisted multimedia programs may not be the best choice for every situation. Although less expensive than a few years ago, multimedia workstations are still costly when compared to other audio-visual equipment and they are somewhat cumbersome. A key factor in the decision to purchase multimedia programs for the development of listening-comprehension skills is faculty attitude toward computers in general and toward the use of computers as teaching devices in particular. Each medium should be evaluated according to acceptability to faculty and students as well as cost and ease of use. Whatever else may be said, the most effective medium for teaching listening is the medium that will be used the most frequently by students and instructors.

Sound Pedagogy

As we approach the end of the twentieth century, the possibilities for using technology to develop listening skills seem virtually limitless. Even simple, widely used audio-visual equipment can aid listening instruction by enabling us to

- bring additional voices into the classroom, thus exposing students to various accents, rates of speaking, and discourse levels;
- conserve our energy (and voices) by playing a tape three times rather than reading a passage aloud three times;
- arrange for different listening activities to take place simultaneously, as when several groups listen at the same time, each group using a separate tape player;
- separate the visual and verbal messages of video material, thus permitting sound-only or image-only viewing;
- edit texts, recording half a story on one tape and the other half on another in order to create an information-gap activity.

Furthermore, the pause, rewind/review (search), and fast-forward features of an audiocassette or compact disc player or video playback device can facilitate techniques such as the following:

- pause to let students write an answer or transcribe or simply process the aural text;
- pause to ask students to predict what might be coming up next;
- rewind to allow multiple listenings to the same passage;
- divide longer passages into manageable "paragraphs" by pausing at natural breaks;
- fast forward past material that is uninteresting or too difficult in an otherwise appropriate passage.

Going beyond the simple equipment used for the activities described above, computer-assisted multimedia programs designed to promote listening skills offer users multiple meaning sources including full-motion video, stills, written texts and graphics, and a variety of online helps such as dictionaries, comprehension hints, and maps, all of which can be accessed instantaneously through computer control.

With the wealth of possibilities available for teaching listening, it is unfortunate that there is no solid foundation in language-learning theory to guide us in making decisions as to which out of all possible activities should be implemented in order to attain a given objective or which of the available technological aids is best suited to enable that activity. In an ideal situation, there would be a widely accepted definition of the construct of listening, which would in turn facilitate research efforts into both the listening process and the pedagogy of listening. The effectiveness of various techniques and technologies could then be compared, using the results of valid and reliable standardized tests of listening, known by and readily available to foreign language professionals. The reality of the situation is that despite the fact that numerous definitions of listening have been proposed and even though very specific listening skills, subskills, and purposes have been delineated, there is presently no single agreed-upon definition of the construct. (For reviews of definitions, skills, and purposes of listening, see Richards 1983; Coakley and Wolvin 1986; Palmer et al. 1991.)

Given the important role of listening in language acquisition and the fact that listening is the most frequently used language skill, teachers of second and foreign languages can ill afford to postpone listening instruction while awaiting the perfect definition of the construct and the development of valid and reliable tests, nor have they done so. Indeed, a review of the literature related to language pedagogy over the past decade or so reveals an increasing interest in the teaching of listening and in listening as a process. During this period, several overviews of factors believed to be associated with second and/or foreign language listening skills were published (Byrnes 1984; Joiner 1986; Rost 1990; Dunkel 1991; Joiner 1991) and a number of practical guides (Lonergan 1984; Altman 1989; Joiner, Adkins, and Eyken 1989; Joiner 1990; Morley 1990) to the selection and use of audio and video in listening instruction also appeared. More recently, reviews of second-language listening-comprehension research by Swaffar and Bacon (1993) and by Rubin (1994) indicate a growing, though inadequate, body of knowledge related to the listening process, types of listening texts and tasks, and characteristics of listeners.

The renewed interest in listening reflected by the publications cited above is no doubt attributable to some extent to a number of trends, movements, and initiatives undertaken by professional organizations and leaders in the field of second and foreign language pedagogy. Some of these are related to theory; others are more pragmatic in nature. The comprehension approaches based on Krashen's (1981) theory of second language acquisition, the *ACTFL Proficiency Guidelines* (1988), the functional-notional approach sponsored by the Council of Europe, and the insights gained from transferring principles and practices of reading instruction to listening instruction have all provided different perspectives on listening and have served to inform a variety of instructional practices. In the following discussion, we will see how technology can be, or has been, used to develop various aspects of the listening skill brought to the forefront by the movements, trends, and initiatives cited above.

Comprehension Approaches

The comprehension-based approaches, which view listening as the key to language acquisition, have been particularly influential at the early stages of second/foreign language teaching. While approaches such as Asher's Total Physical Response (1986) and Terrell's Natural Approach (1982) make meaning clear through physical activity and interactions with a teacher and fellow students, Winitz' self-instructional *The Learnables* program,[8] now in existence for more than twenty years and available in nine languages, combines recorded audiocassettes with booklets of drawings that make the oral input comprehensible. Students associate sound and concept from the beginning and progress from words to phrases to sentences to narratives. Simple, inexpensive technology and a step-by-step format make *The Learnables* ideal for self-instruction, as their enduring popularity indicates. The program will, however, be incorporating more sophisticated technology in the fall of 1996, when the University of Missouri-Kansas City offers special sections of introductory Spanish and German, using as basic course material *The Learnables*

1 and *2* and *Basic Structures 1* and *2* delivered entirely by computer and audiocassette (Winitz 1996).

Like *The Learnables, The Rosetta Stone,*[9] a user friendly, CD-ROM-based program, follows a tutorial approach that associates sound and image from the beginning of language instruction. *The Rosetta Stone, Level I,* provides basic language instruction through a mixture of voice, photographic images, and text cues, plus a wide variety of learning and self-testing possibilities. In addition to listening-comprehension checks, the basic level of *The Rosetta Stone* offers listening-related options in the form of a dictation feature that teaches sound-symbol correspondence and a recording feature that allows students to listen and repeat. *The Rosetta Stone, Level II,* already available for ESL, will add motion video to the meaning sources outlined above, and an interface modification will allow students entering the program to choose the language skill they wish to develop. A student could, for example, choose to develop listening alone or listening plus another skill (Stoltzfus 1996).

Some proponents of comprehension-based instruction believe that narrative input is a logical sequel to simpler comprehensible input of the type embodied in *The Learnables* and *The Rosetta Stone.* For example, the episode hypothesis formulated by Oller (1983:12) states that a text will be easier to produce, understand, and recall to the extent that it is motivated and structured episodically. Thompson and Rubin (forthcoming) recommend increased use of texts with an episodic nature when teaching intermediate language learners, and Winitz uses simple illustrated stories as input in the intermediate level of *The Learnables* program.

Narrative input is also characteristic of *Vi-conte* (Mydlarski and Paramskas 1990), an interactive multimedia program based on *Crac!,* a prize-winning animated film by Frédéric Back.[10] Because *Crac!* relates the story of early French-Canadian settlers through a skillful combination of folk music and drawings, the developers of this program, who state specifically in the accompanying videoguide that it is based on comprehension theory, were able to add to the film a narrative sound track that replicates exactly the message of the colorful animated illustrations. For example, when viewers see the woodcutter using a saw, they hear the words *il sciait* ("he sawed") delivered in a clearly articulated French-Canadian accent. The two sound tracks of the videodisc allow the film to be viewed without, as well as with, the added soundtrack, a feature that can be used to familiarize students with the story schema before introducing the linguistic input. As is the case with *The Learnables* and *The Rosetta Stone,* the mutual association and reinforcement of sound (in this case, narrative text) and image is a major feature of *Vi-conte,* the episodic structure of which should also be expected to increase both understanding and recall. Other aspects of *Vi-conte* that can be used to teach aural comprehension are a sound-plus-picture dictionary, multiple-choice comprehension checks at two levels of difficulty, and a series of listening cloze exercises.

Real-World Listening

The simultaneous presentation of sound and image characteristic of the technology-mediated programs described in the previous section is appropriate for making input comprehensible; we have seen, however, that the relationship of sound and image in the video material that students are likely to encounter in the real world is more often one of counterpoint or complementarity than of duplication of message. This being the case, influential professional groups such as ACTFL and the Council of Europe have underscored the importance of including authentic materials in foreign language instruction. Their position with respect to real-world listening is echoed by another nonprofessional group to whom foreign language teachers should pay particular attention, namely students. A recent survey of intermediate students at thirteen universities revealed that the respondents ranked listening, ". . . defined as the ability to understand conversations, radio, TV, news broadcasts and films," second out of fourteen goals proposed by the questionnaire (Harlow and Muyskens 1994:145). Students and professional groups alike, then, seem to agree that simple or simplified listening texts should be supplemented, and eventually supplanted, by more complex and realistic authentic texts typical of real-world listening situations.

Listening Texts and Tasks

A very important contribution of technology to the teaching of listening is the simple fact of making authentic texts available for listening practice. Thanks to technology, teachers now have access to an abundance of authentic oral language materials available "live" from satellite broadcasts, shortwave radio, and the World Wide Web as well as recorded in the form of audio and video magazines and films and television programs on videocassette or videodisc. As Phillips (1991:344) has so aptly put it: "With advances in satellite transmission and video recordings, oral documents are now as readily available for foreign language learners as they have been for second language learners." (For an exhaustive inventory of audio and video resources for teaching ESL/EFL, see Gebhard et al. 1991.)

Technology can provide an array of texts and equipment for teaching listening. What technology cannot do is (a) select from among these texts those that are most suitable for a given group of learners working toward a specified listening goal and (b) design tasks that will bring together learners and text in a way that leads toward that goal. In this section, we will examine some theoretical positions with respect to texts and tasks as they relate to listening instruction.

The use of complex, unaltered texts in the teaching of listening has necessitated a rethinking of the relationship between text and task within the context of skill development. Over a decade ago, Richards (1983) made the important distinction between a listening test and a listening task and recommended simplifying the listening task rather than modifying the authentic text in early listening practice. Since that time, even though much has been written about listening tasks, the profession seems not to have reached total agreement concerning the use of the term. While some do not distinguish among terms such as *exercise, activity,* and *task,* using the three interchangeably to refer to what the listener does during and/or after viewing or listening, others are more precise in their use of the word. Nunan and Miller (1995:vi), for example, provide a definition that encompasses the text within the task when they state that: "the two essential ingredients in any listening task are some form of aural stimulus that provides a point of departure for the task and, second, a set of operations that the learners perform on the task." Similarly, Lund (1990) proposes two important task elements: listener function in reference to the text (the aspects of the text the listener attempts to process) and listener response (what the listener does to demonstrate comprehension).

The lack of total agreement on terminology among theorists should not overshadow the fact that the various definitions reflect a general consensus that listeners should be active, responding to the text in some kind of observable way. Several types of responses are implied by Swaffar and Bacon (1995:135) when they ask: "Should the listener recognize, replicate, or react to a text heard?" Recognition may, of course, be demonstrated by a variety of traditional exercises (matching, true-false, multiple-choice). Some members of the profession, however, influenced by the functional-notional approach and the ACTFL Proficiency Guidelines, recommend authentic, real-world responses to authentic texts. Such is the position of Lund (1990), who proposes that all aspects of listening instruction, including text, function, and response, should have a natural feel. While total authenticity is certainly the ideal way to bridge the gap between classroom and real-world listening, it is almost impossible to avoid a certain amount of artificiality in classroom listening practice. The guiding principle in task construction should probably be that, whether engaged in skill-getting or skill-using, learners should be actively interacting with an interesting and authentic oral document.

Listening Activities and Curricula

The consideration of text and task in the previous section should not cause us to overlook a key factor in the development of listening activities: the listener-learner. It is the successful interaction of text and task with learner characteristics, the putting it all together, that produces an effective listening experience, one that leads beyond the immediate comprehension objective to listening-skill development. In order to determine how text, task, and learner factors can best be integrated into listening activities and curricula, foreign language teachers have looked for guidance to reading theory, to the *ACTFL Proficiency Guidelines,* and to ESL teachers, whose experience in teaching listening is longer and broader than our own. In the following paragraphs, we will examine only a few of many possible examples that illustrate the contribution of each of these fields to foreign language listening instruction.

Shrum and Glisan (1994), capitalizing on the fact that recording technology has made the *immediacy* skill of listening resemble the *recursive* skill of reading, have used insights from reading instruction to create a six-phase model for teaching interactive listening that includes recognition, replication, and reaction. Following a prelistening activity designed to activate background knowledge, establish a purpose for listening, and focus prediction strategies, students listen once for the main idea(s), once for detail, and once to synthesize the main idea(s) and details. In the two final steps of the procedure, they recreate the text and react to it in some way.

Upon closer examination of the interactive model, we can see that its six steps actually can be grouped into three sequential stages: prelistening, during-listening, and postlistening. It is the first of these, the prelistening phase, that has been the most thoroughly researched. Studies using different types of advance organizers, some visual, others verbal (Mueller 1980; Eykyn 1992; Herron 1994; Berne 1995; Herron, Hanley, and Cole 1995), to prepare students for listening to audio or video texts have found that increased comprehension results when students are primed for listening or listening-viewing through an activity designed to help them anticipate the content of the upcoming oral text. Herron (1994), for example, found that the use of an advance organizer in the form of several brief sentences written on the board significantly increased the comprehension of second-semester French students whose course material was video-based. The results of Schmidt-Rinehart's 1994 study of topic familiarity as a factor in listening comprehension, in the absence of an advance organizer, led her to advocate the use of prelistening activities based on an assessment of the conceptual base that learners bring to the listening experience.

The results of the experiments summarized above are comparable to those of similar studies in reading that have established the important contribution of background knowledge to the top-down processing of texts. Consistent with reading theory, Glisan (1995) has identified four important factors (two "inside-the-head" and two "outside-the-head") that teachers should consider when planning listening instruction: the listener's background knowledge and prediction strategies and how to activate them, the listener's purpose for listening, the listening input (text type, text length, level of difficulty), and the treatment of new structures and vocabulary.

A different, though not incompatible, approach to bringing together text, task, and learner factors in listening instruction is advocated by Lund (1990) and Omaggio Hadley (1993), who use the *ACTFL Guidelines* as a point of departure for task design. While Omaggio Hadley arranges listening tasks in a hierarchical manner, categorizing those appropriate for the novice/interme-diate or advanced/superior levels, Lund proposes a taxonomy, the key elements of which are listener function and listener response, with listener function being the more important of the two. The functions of his function-response matrix for listening include identification, orientation, main idea comprehension, detail comprehension, full comprehension, and replication; the responses comprise doing, choosing, transferring, answering, condensing, extending, duplicating, modeling, and conversing. According to Lund (1990:113), "At least five elements are essential to the design of effective listening tasks: the function, the response, the text, the topic, and the method of presentation (prelistening activity, context, repetition, use of scripts, video, etc.)." The disappointing results of ACTFL's attempt to validate the listening guidelines (Dandonoli and Henning 1990) argue for caution in using the levels rigidly when planning exercises and curricula. Lund's taxonomy, however, goes beyond strict adherence to the Guideline levels by allowing flexibility in the integration of text, response, and function in the design of listening tasks.

Lund's taxonomy based on the *ACTFL Guidelines* and Shrum and Glisan's interactive model inspired by reading theory can serve to guide the creation of original listening activities that combine authentic texts and appropriate tasks in ways that engage learners in the act of listening. For those who prefer practice to theory and examples to models, *New Ways in Teaching Listening* (Nunan and Miller 1995), a practical handbook of classroom-tested techniques contributed by EFL and ESL teachers from throughout the world, offers an abundance of exercises, more than 50 percent of which require audiotaped or videotaped materials (a substantial number of them authentic). The activities included in *New Ways* are grouped into the following categories:

- Part I: cognitive strategies (listening for main ideas, listening for details, predicting);

- Part II: activities that focus on the interrelatedness of language skills (listening paired with other skills, especially speaking);
- Part III: authentic texts (listening to authentic data);
- Part IV: technology in the listening classroom (recorded telephone messages, etc.);
- Part V: listening for academic purposes;
- Part VI: affective aspects of the listening process (use of songs, relaxation techniques, etc.).

Each activity has a specific stated goal such as "Practice taking down phone messages" or "Focus on listening for expected words using authentic materials."

If listening skills are to be developed in any kind of systematic way, we must move beyond mere exercise goals to curricular goals. Lund's taxonomy, dealing as it does with goals, objectives, and planning, provides principles that can be used not only to create listening tasks but also to plan listening curricula. Additionally, Guntermann and Phillips (1982) furnish the curriculum planner with an extensive list of the functions of real-world listening. Guidelines based especially on ESL/EFL experience are offered by Richards (1983), who elaborates a model for a needs-based listening course, and Morley (1990), who discusses design principles and practices.

Independent Listening

A review of recent articles and books on technology-based listening instruction leads to the conclusion that most of such instruction is conducted in the classroom under the direction of the teacher. It is most often the teacher who selects the text and topic, manipulates the equipment (especially the important pause button), and conducts prelistening and postlistening activities. Although this process is efficient and may be effective, it has two major disadvantages: (1) everyone is required to listen at the same time to the same material, and (2) learners have little input into or control over their listening instruction.

In an attempt to compensate for the shortcomings of in-class listening, Morley (1990) advocates independent outside listening practice, as does Bacon (1989), who points out that even if half of each class were devoted to listening practice, foreign language students enrolled in university-level language courses would have only about nineteen hours of in-class listening per semester. Since Bacon's estimate of time devoted to listening is generous, it is evident that in-class listening alone cannot provide sufficient input either for language acquisition or the development of listening skills. Fortunately, in an age in which a plethora of live and recorded audio and video material is readily available, in which many students have portable and vehicular audio equipment, and in which videocassette players are present in many homes and dorm rooms as well as being accessible in learning laboratories, listening instruction does not have to be confined within classroom walls.

The decision to incorporate outside listening practice into the curriculum raises two important questions. The first is how complex and sophisticated authentic materials can be made accessible to novice or intermediate listeners working independently of the instructor. The second is how to integrate out-of-class listening into in-class activities so that independent work does not seem irrelevant to students.

The first challenge, that of providing adequate support to students listening on their own, can be met in a number of ways. In some cases, there are published materials that include outside listening practice guided by workbook exercises, although such materials are much more easily available for ESL than for FL instruction. More typical of the foreign language situation are authentic audio and video materials accompanied not by ready-made listening or viewing exercises in workbook form but by written support materials that can be used to guide listening practice. *Champs-Élysées* and its Spanish, German, and Italian counterparts and the videos in French, Spanish, and German distributed by PICS are representative of this tendency. Instructors who must create exercises of their own can use models such as those outlined in the preceding section to direct their efforts.

Although we tend to think that independent outside listening will be more difficult than teacher-guided in-class practice, this is not necessarily the case. The opportunity for the listener to control the technology, pausing and relistening as needed, can compensate, at least to some extent, for the absent teacher. Further support, both linguistic and moral, is made available when listeners work together in pairs or groups to complete outside listening assignments. Finally, when all students are assigned the same outside listening exercise, the teacher can conduct an in-class prelistening activity to prepare students for listening on their own. Such an activity could be designed to promote both top-down processing by activating background knowledge and bottom-up processing by presenting key vocabulary and structures.

Since students tend to think that instructional activities that take place in class are more important than out-of-class work, in-class prelistening activities serve the dual purpose of providing essential preparation for outside listening while at the same time underscoring the significance that the teacher attaches to such assignments. This is especially true when postlistening activities are also incorporated into classroom instruction. We have seen in the preceding section that postlistening activities can involve skills other than listening and that they can include responses that require students to make use of information in the oral text to accomplish real-world tasks.

While audio and video documents with accompanying support materials and exercises can be used effectively for outside listening, computer-assisted multimedia represents an almost ideal technological aid for such practice. We have seen earlier that control of oral documents on CD-ROM or videodisc is faster and more precise than is the case with taped materials. In addition, multimedia applications usually include a variety of online helps (dictionaries, key words, transcriptions, etc.) that the listener can access at will.

Even though multimedia provides students with a great deal of support for independent listening, it is up to the teacher to select and use multimedia applications to their best advantage. If conversational listening is the focus of the course, *Montevidisco* is an ideal choice for outside listening. On the other hand, if listening for information is the goal, the *Listening Tool* can help students comprehend a variety of news and weather reports. In the case of applications such as *Montevidisco* and the *Listening Tool,* prelistening should include an in-class demonstration of the features of the program so that students will be able to take full advantage of their options.

Like outside listening based on more traditional audio-visual materials, outside listening built around a multimedia application should be integrated into classroom practice. Students using *Montevidisco* could be asked, for example, to keep a daily travel diary of their adventures as tourists in that Mexican town (DeMyhrer 1996) or to relate their individual adventures to each other in classroom discussion. If students are assigned to use the *Listening Tool* to watch a news program, they can be asked to play the role of the television journalist and present a recapitulation of the news highlights or to write a news article based on the report. Lyman-Hager (1994) suggests additional techniques for incorporating video and interactive multimedia resources into instruction.

In addition to using existent multimedia materials, instructors can, if they wish to do so, use one of several authoring systems available for the Macintosh and IBM platforms to create exercises for out-of-class listening that are tailored to the particular needs of their students. Students could be provided with one or more advance organizers before listening to the text, allowed multiple listenings, each perhaps accompanied by a different exercise to complete, and offered a selection of postlistening tasks and comprehension checks. An example of a tailor-made program is provided by Brett (1995), who reports on numerous options incorporated into a multimedia-based resource for developing listening skills within the field of business English.

Strategic Listening

If, in conducting the prelistening phase of a listening activity, the instructor writes three sentences on the board and tells the students that these sentences constitute a summary, in chronological order, of the events that they will view in the upcoming video, he or she will be employing an advance organizer that has proved to be effective in enhancing comprehension (Herron 1994). If, following the listening experience, that same instructor goes on to conduct a brainstorming session in which students are encouraged to identify where in real life they can find similar written information that will help them prepare to view a foreign film or television program (*TV Guide,* film reviews, etc.), he or she is teaching students to employ prediction strategies to increase their comprehension of unfamiliar material.

One of the most positive developments in second and foreign language instruction in recent years is strategy training of the type described in the previous paragraph. Teaching learners about the learning process and encouraging them to participate in their own instruction liberates them from overdependence on the teacher and provides them with strategies to continue learning on their own whether in class, in a learning center, in their rooms, in their cars, or on the streets of a foreign country. Strategy training applied to language learning in general has been widely discussed in the professional literature (Wenden and Rubin 1987; Oxford 1990; Rubin 1995). In this section we will examine some of the strategies believed to be of importance to listening comprehension and see how they relate to technology-oriented instruction.

Most studies that have reported on listening strategies have dealt with strategy use rather than with strategy instruction *per se* and have relied heavily on self-reporting by learners. In her study of strategy use by advanced students of Italian, Laviosa (1991) conceptualized listening comprehension as a problem-solving process involving four stages: (1) a perceived problem sets into motion (2) a mental planning process that results in (3) the use of a particular strategy, which, if well chosen, will result in (4) a solution. She was able to identify three planning processes and seven strategies employed by her subjects in response to nine problem types. In an investigation involving students of Spanish, Bacon (1992) compared successful and less successful listeners with respect to a number of strategies and attitudinal factors and found that successful listeners used a greater range of strategies and used them in a more flexible manner. One especially interesting finding of Bacon's study involved the use of background knowledge by the two groups. Successful listeners were able to use background knowledge (personal, world, or discourse) effectively as one among a number of combined strategies; the unsuccessful listeners, on the other hand, were characterized by an overdependence on prior knowledge to the exclusion of other strategies. Vogely (1995), who investigated the relationship between perceived strategy use and listening recall of students enrolled in four levels of elementary and intermediate Spanish courses, found that the first-semester students (who perceived themselves to be the most strategic listeners) outperformed students in the second semester (who perceived themselves to be the least strategic listeners) on three different recall tasks. These and other studies of actual strategy use by learners have increased our knowledge of the listening process and of those factors that contribute to successful processing of oral texts. Most studies of strategy use conclude that effective language learners combine or "orchestrate" a number of strategies. (See Swaffar and Bacon 1993; Glisan 1995; and Thompson and Rubin, forthcoming, for a more complete review of studies of strategy use by listeners.)

Clearly students can, and sometimes do, apply strategies when listening to oral texts, but can they be taught to do so? To date, few studies have addressed this question, and the results of these few studies have been somewhat mixed. Results of the first longitudinal, classroom-based study of strategy instruction in listening have recently been reported by Thompson and Rubin (forthcoming), who begin their article with a detailed review of the literature relating to strategy training. In their own study, these researchers found that systematic training in the use of strategies resulted in improved listening comprehension of third-year students of Russian, who watched a variety of simulated authentic and authentic Russian texts over a two-year period. Students involved in this study were taught to apply the following strategies:

Metacognitive strategies (management techniques by which learners control their learning process):

a. *Planning,* e.g., deciding how many times to view a particular segment, whether to view it with the sound on or off, determining how to break up the segment into manageable portions;

b. *Defining goals,* e.g., deciding what exactly to listen for, determining how much needs to be understood;

c. *Monitoring,* e.g., assessing one's comprehension, identifying sources of difficulty, isolating problematic portions;

d. *Evaluating,* e.g., assessing the effectiveness of strategies used.

Cognitive strategies (responses to specific processing problems):

a. *Predicting content* based on visual clues, background knowledge, genre of the segment, information from the clip itself, logic of the story line, actions, and relationships;

    b. *Listening for the known,* e.g., cognates, familiar or partially familiar words and phrases;

    c. *Listening for redundancies,* e.g., repeated words and phrases;

    d. *Listening to tone of voice and intonation;*

    e. *Resourcing,* e.g., jotting down words and phrases to find out what they mean, or searching for background information.

In addition, students were taught specific cognitive strategies for each genre included in the video material. They were told to focus on the story line while watching *drama;* to pay attention to the question and answer sequence when watching an *interview;* and to consider the *who, what, where, when,* and *how* of *news broadcasts* (adapted from Thompson and Rubin, forthcoming).

In their discussion of the above experiment, the researchers explain that they used video rather than audio texts not only because they thought television-generation students would be more motivated by such texts, but also because they thought that video, which provides both audio and visual clues to meaning, would allow for a wider range of strategy application than audio alone. In this regard, however, several students commented that they sometimes elected to make use of only one channel at a time. For example, some stated that they preferred to begin with sound-off viewing in order to get a general idea of what the segment was about from the visual clues alone while others reported that turning the picture off was helpful when listening to news broadcasts for the second time because they found the visuals distracting. These observations by Thompson and Rubin parallel the findings of Long (1991) and suggest that we still have much to learn about the way students process video material.

Thompson and Rubin conclude the report on their study by recommending that more time should be devoted to listening both in and outside of language classrooms and that emphasis should be placed on the process of listening rather than on merely providing opportunities to listen or testing listening comprehension. This same philosophy has guided the creation and development of a fourth-semester oral communication course at the University of South Carolina. For six years now, students enrolled in this course have participated in a program of combined in and out-of-class listening consisting of in-class viewing of authentic video material from French television[11] and extensive outside viewing of a variety of authentic audio and video materials (both off-air and recorded) of their own choosing. Students, who develop listening strategies through in-class viewing practice, are encouraged to apply these same strategies to outside viewing and to report on both their use of listening strategies and their perceived degree of comprehension in a weekly journal.[12] (Among the options for outside viewing are several videodiscs accompanied by the *Listening Tool* software described earlier.) In written responses to the journal entries, instructors provide positive feedback while at the same time encouraging wider strategy use and perhaps suggesting different types of audio and video materials. Like Thompson and Rubin, instructors of this course have found that students are capable of analyzing and reporting on their listening strategies.

The strategy training procedure used in the oral communication course described above and that reported on by Thompson and Rubin (forthcoming) are representative of what Rubin (1996) has deemed the prevalent model of strategy instruction: Teachers are first taught about learner strategies and about how to teach learners to use them more effectively. They then present these strategies during a foreign or second language class. While this model has met with success, it requires a great deal of precious classroom time. An alternative or supplement to these opportunities made possible by technology is the *Language Learning Strategies Program*,[13] a computer-assisted multimedia application developed by Joan Rubin Associates.

The *Language Learning Strategies Program,* based on investigations into strategies used by expert learners as well as on research involving the development of higher-order cognitive skills, aims to increase students' participation in their own learning by enabling them to activate what they already know about grammar, vocabulary, and communication. Eight hours of instructional material recorded on videodisc provide students with the opportunity to develop strategies for reading and speaking as well as listening. The listening situations include listening both to the radio and to television, and the listening comprehension strategies include, among others: "use your knowledge of the world, listen for familiar names and places, and use key words to narrow predictions" (Rubin 1996:160–61). The main languages of the multimedia program are Russian, Korean, and Spanish; however, during the course of instruction, the learner is exposed to twenty different languages. Students are drawn into the plot as the four major characters ask questions and struggle through various situations. Intended for beginning language learners, the program was field tested both at the Defense Language Institute's San Francisco branch and the United States Air Force Academy, where learners reported such affective outcomes as high motivation and a high comfort level when interacting with the material (Rubin 1996:160).

Rubin (1996) observes that an important component of strategy instruction is the increase in students' awareness of the background knowledge they bring to the task. Here, the word *awareness* is crucial. Good native language listening skills can contribute to successful foreign language listening (Feyten 1991). However, without strategy training, or at least consciousness raising, students may fail to transfer their native language listening skills to foreign language listening situations simply because these strategies operate on an unconscious level. Strategy use, which enables listeners to compensate for their lack of automatic processing skills by drawing upon the strengths that they bring to the comprehension task, may be of particular importance when beginning and intermediate students attempt to comprehend the many authentic audio and video texts made possible by advances in technology. Glisan (1995), in fact, views strategy training as one of two elements crucial to the degree of success students experience when given a video task, the other being the selection of appropriate video materials.

Special Listeners

In the past, the makeup of foreign language classrooms has been rather predictable, a situation that is changing significantly as we approach a new century. Even though the majority of students presently enrolled in foreign language study in the United States are young people ranging in age from the early teens to the early twenties whose purpose for language study is to meet a college entrance or exit requirement, this fact should not prevent us from recognizing that in recent years the population of students engaged in foreign language learning has become more diverse in age, in ability, and in purpose for learning. The move toward a global economy and the many opportunities for faster, less expensive international travel and communication have resulted in increased interest in developing foreign language proficiency. Responding to this interest in foreign languages, schools have initiated FLES programs, and colleges and universities are now enrolling an increasing number of nontraditional students not only in special programs such as Elderhostel but also in regular course offerings, some taught in the evenings or on Saturday to accommodate working adults. Adding to the complexity of this diverse population of language learners are students with learning disabilities who are mainstreamed into regular language classes.

The implications for foreign language instruction of this increasingly varied population of language learners are myriad. In this section, however, we will limit our discussion to two groups of learners: adult learners, including the elderly, and those with listening-related learning disabilities, whether diagnosed or undiagnosed.

The Older Learner

It is not difficult to find examples of how changes in the student population will necessitate the adaptation of foreign language instruction and especially of listening instruction. In a recent letter to Dear Abby, a couple from Arkansas complained about the prevalence of overly loud background music on television that "drowns out the dialogue." Agreeing with them that this was a real problem, Abby, in replying, confessed to having had to become an expert lip-reader herself because of the extremely loud background music of one of her favorite shows (*The State,* Columbia, SC, Thursday May 9, 1996). Although the couple from Arkansas did not reveal their age, Abigail Van Buren is now in her seventies, and, given their mutual complaint, it is quite likely that both she and the two Arkansans have reached the time in life when they are beginning to experience some of the unfortunate results of the hearing loss that is an inevitable part of aging.

With age, comprehension is made more difficult by a number of factors, not all of which will be present in every individual. There is, however, almost always a progressive decrease in hearing acuity (sound perception/discrimination), which is often accompanied by a gradual slowing down of the central auditory processing structures. In addition to deficits in hearing *per se,* changes in memory and attention associated with aging may adversely affect concentration and recall, two important characteristics of successful listening. Yet another consistent finding in the field of audiology is that hearing loss is greater among elderly men than elderly women.

Studies comparing the hearing of younger and older listeners who share the same native language have revealed a number of interesting differences between the two groups, especially in the area of hearing sensitivity or acuity. Haber and Runstein (1989:21), for example, state that "some young people can hear as high as 23 kHz, but the ear's high-frequency response drops off with increased age, and few people over 60 years of age can hear above 8 kHz." While we have seen earlier that human speech is believed by some to fall within a range of 400 to 4,000 Hz (Pihlajamäki 1995), sound discrimination, that is, the ability to distinguish between voices and between different musical instruments playing the same tone, requires the ability to perceive the overtones or harmonics associated with the fundamental speech sound. This may explain why clinical audiologists so often hear the report from elderly clients that even when they can "hear," they often cannot "understand" what is being said even in their native language (McCarthy and Sapp 1993:334). Studies have found that not only are there differences in auditory acuity between the younger and older population in conditions of both quiet and noise but also that this difference is greater in noise than in quiet. In addition to the extreme difficulty experienced by older listeners when background noise is present, Blumberg et al. (cited in McCarthy and Sapp 1993) found that older listeners performed less well than younger listeners when the rate of the speaker increased, when the speech signal was filtered, or in a reverberant listening environment.

Given the factors outlined above, older learners studying foreign languages merit special attention, whether they are enrolled in regular college classes or in courses designed exclusively for adults. Great care, for example, should be given to the selection of audio and video materials and equipment to be used in the instruction of these learners. It is essential that equipment be of very high quality to offset losses in sound perception and that recorded materials meet that same high standard. Video, or at least material that provides visual support, may be a better choice than audio for older listeners because it allows input through two senses.

Other features of technology that might be expected to benefit older learners are the captioning of video material (to allow reading to support listening), rate alteration (to permit slower speech), and computer-assisted self-paced learning (to provide the listener with precise control over the oral text as well as infinite possibilities for repetition and review). Among multimedia programs, *The Rosetta Stone,* which combines image, sound, and text within a self-paced tutorial format, would seem to be a wise choice for older learners.

While technology alone can help compensate for impaired hearing, combining strategy training with technology can increase the effectiveness of both. Older listeners should receive instruction on how to enhance comprehension by making use of the extralinguistic clues present in video and should be encouraged to use multiple listenings to offset a slower processing rate. Other strategy training might be directed at teaching mature adults to activate and make efficient use of their strengths such as extensive world knowledge and, in many cases, a vocabulary larger than that of the younger generation. Some of the elderly may also need instruction in using equipment with which they are unfamiliar.

Learning Disorders

Research findings are increasingly supportive of the theory that learning disorders and perceptual difficulties are often interrelated. We have seen in the previous section that age-related auditory factors may negatively influence the communicative ability of older learners. Problems in auditory processing have also recently been implicated in learning disorders that have a negative impact on language acquisition by younger learners. An article in the January 29, 1996, issue of *Time* begins as follows: "At age 5, Keillan Lecky dreaded kindergarten. So many of the words her playmates gleefully shouted or conspiratorially whispered seemed to hover just out of reach, as elusive as a vanishing rainbow" (Nash 1996:62). The article goes on to describe the astonishing improvement in auditory skills made by Keillan and twenty-one other children in a special program for children of average intelligence who had difficulty distinguishing among phonemes. The program that helped Keillen and her classmates was a series of computer "games" incorporating a program that made hard consonants easier to hear by ". . . elongating them, spacing them farther apart and making them louder" (Nash 1996:63). The creators of this program believe that defective auditory processing is responsible not only for oral language disorders but for dyslexia as well, a theory that is controversial but not without support from others in the scientific community.

Twenty-five years ago, after more than twelve thousand case studies conducted over two decades had convinced him of a connection between dyslexia and deficient auditory processing, Alfred Tomatis, a French otolaryngologist and surgeon, published his findings in *Éducation et Dyslexie* (1971).[14] Eight years later, on this side of the Atlantic, Frank Vellutino proposed the same link in *Dyslexia: Theory and Research* (1979). More recently, teams of physicians at Beth Israel Hospital and Harvard Medical School have established a neurological basis for the connection between auditory processing and dyslexia and reported their findings in the *Proceedings of the National Academy of Sciences* (*Newsweek,* August 29, 1994).

Related to these findings is the linguistic deficit coding hypothesis proposed by Sparks and Ganschow (1991) and defended by them and their associates in a series of articles published since that time (Sparks and Ganschow 1991; Sparks, Ganschow, Javorsky, Pohlman, and Patton, 1992; Sparks and Ganschow 1993a, 1993b, 1995 to cite only a few). Using Vellutino's work to support their hypothesis, these specialists in learning disabilities contend that students of normal intelligence who meet with repeated failure in foreign language classes do so because of undiagnosed learning disabilities based on auditory factors.[15]

The linguistic deficit coding hypothesis has set off a veritable firestorm of professional controversy, since it may be seen to support the argument that there is a specific "foreign language learning disability" that could be used to excuse students from foreign language requirements. Attacking the hypothesis with a counter-hypothesis, several researchers in the foreign language field have argued that it is anxiety (Horwitz and Young 1991; Macintyre 1995) that explains the lack of success of otherwise successful students in foreign language classes. In a recent article, Ganschow and Sparks (1996) report on a study that examined the relationship between anxiety and native language skill and foreign language aptitude measures among 154 high school foreign language learners. They conclude that, although there is a strong association between high anxiety and success or failure in foreign language classes, this high anxiety is probably the consequence of low language aptitude rather than the primary cause of failure. Their results also lead them to maintain that poor phonological/orthographic skills, in particular, distinguish good from poor language learners.

A connection between native and second language auditory ability is assumed but viewed somewhat differently by Tomatis (1991), who believes that it is possible to become "deaf" to the sounds of languages other than one's own simply because of lack of exposure to these sounds over a period of years. His position is that this "deafness" can be remediated by using technology to retrain the ears to hear "missing" sounds. Tomatis, then, not only recognizes that phonological problems exist but also proposes a means for overcoming these impairments.

At the Centre Tomatis in Paris, clients wishing to learn a foreign language are given a placement test (if they already have some language background) and a diagnostic listening test. Analysis of the client's listening profile is used to design an individualized listening program including both musical and language sounds, the frequencies emphasized being those most characteristic of the foreign language to be studied. According to Tomatis, this program, mediated by a device called the Electronic Ear, prepares the way for more efficient foreign language learning by increasing the client's likelihood of perceiving the sounds of the foreign language accurately. Tomatis (1991:83) asserts that ". . . the Electronic Ear is . . . a 'tuning in' device. It does not teach grammar, syntax or vocabulary. It does make the acquisition of these things simpler and more lasting." Although no carefully designed studies have compared the Tomatis approach to foreign language learning to approaches involving other technologies, written evaluations are very positive,[16] and Tomatis counts many celebrities among his former clients. Gérard Depardieu, for example, completed a listening program designed by Tomatis in order to be able to understand directions in English when he began to act in English-language films. (A more complete account of Depardieu's experience *chez Tomatis* can be found in his 1994 biography by Paul Chutkow.)

The use of technological aids may be the key to accommodating the needs of an increasingly diverse population of foreign language learners. Specialized equipment such as the Electronic Ear, from which Depardieu benefited, and the multimedia program used to help Keillan and her schoolmates improve their auditory skills would seem to offer hope of remediation to the special listeners identified in this section. Moreover, there are several foreign language multimedia programs that, by reinforcing sound-symbol correspondence, could be expected to increase learners' phonological/orthographic skills, identified by Sparks, Ganschow, and their associates as a major factor in foreign language learning. These multimedia applications include *The Rosetta Stone,* which contains a dictation feature, and *DIAS* (Parker, Davis, Cannon, and Van Doren 1991), a dictation program that "speaks" the dictation, allows for text input by the student, and checks the student's answers while repeating any incorrect words or phrases. The effectiveness of these technological aids must, of course, be established through qualitative and quantitative research.

Listening: Present and Future

Using tools to help them transcend their limited powers, humans have advanced over the centuries from the Stone Age to the Industrial Revolution and beyond. The present age, characterized by diverse and ever more sophisticated possibilities for communication and information transfer, offers us an unprecedented array of tools for the teaching of listening, the most frequently used communication skill. In this chapter, we have seen how technology, and specifically electronic media, can be used to overcome the limitations to information exchange imposed by time and distance. Cable and satellite transmissions make available a variety of oral texts from distant countries, and equipment for recording and playback enables us and our students to store and manipulate oral documents at our convenience in ways that minimize the stress experienced when such texts are viewed or heard "live." Further, when recorded audio and video are interfaced with a computer, the resulting interactive multimedia program allows learners not only to manage their listening by controlling the fleeting stream of oral speech but also to maximize their comprehension by receiving messages through multifold channels of perception and in multiform modes of presentation (text, graphics, stills, full-motion video, music, and environmental and speech sounds).

With the twenty-first century on the horizon, we can expect technology to continue to improve and become more widely available and less costly in response to both the consumer and the instructional markets. Furthermore, as academic institutions increasingly embrace technology to support teaching, some of the inconveniences currently associated with the use of technology (shortage of equipment, lack of technical support, etc.) can be expected gradually to disappear. In this respect, several promising trends have already become apparent.

One of the most important technological advances in recent years and one that is sure to prevail is the move from analog to digital sound. As this trend continues, the oral texts to which we and our students listen will be increasingly delivered by audio CDs, videodiscs, CD-ROMs, or via digital satellites or the World Wide Web. Digital audiovisual technology will take a giant step forward in the fall of 1996 with the launching of the DVD (Digital Video Disc), a digital, CD-sized, high-capacity optical storage disc, which combines some of the best features of audio CDs, videodiscs, and CD-ROMs and surpasses all three in storage capacity. According to the May 1996 issue of

Popular Mechanics, a single-sided DVD disc will hold up to two hours and thirteen minutes of video and will have image quality superior to videodiscs and sound a step up from Dolby Pro Logic. DVD-ROM will provide even higher storage capacity for computer applications. The playback device for the DVD will be able to play audio CDs as well, and DVD-ROM is being designed to be backwardly compatible with CD-ROM.

In addition to having access to smaller, more sophisticated, and higher-quality equipment for sound delivery, teachers of listening are likely to benefit from a number of trends that seem to be emerging in the instructional use of interactive multimedia. Just a few years ago, multimedia development was confined to a few pioneering institutions, and multimedia applications were developed primarily, though not exclusively, in French, Spanish, or German. Learning centers that had only Macintosh computers were excluded from interactive applications that were developed for the IBM platform and vice versa, and those who chose to develop their own multimedia applications had to devote an enormous amount of time to projects that might not be recognized as "academic" by their colleagues.

Now, happily, the situation described above seems to be evolving toward one that will offer a greater choice in the selection of materials and that will reward multimedia authorship. With respect to increased choice, we might note the following developments. Level I of *The Rosetta Stone,* for a number of years available only in English, Russian, and the more commonly taught foreign languages, has now been expanded to include Japanese, Chinese, and Italian; *Montevidisco,* originally released for the IBM platform, will soon be available for the Macintosh as well; and a few recent programs such as the listening-based *Nouvelles Dimensions* (Petit and Noblitt 1995) have been released with both videodisc and CD-ROM versions. Other positive developments have to do with authoring. Recognizing the creativity, knowledge, and dedication necessary to develop multimedia applications, a few university foreign language departments have begun to include multimedia development in their criteria for tenure and promotion. Additionally, those instructors who do not wish to create entire multimedia applications but who nevertheless would like to provide their students with custom-made computer-assisted listening experiences can now obtain authoring templates that simplify the development task.

The future looks bright for the use of technology in the teaching of listening. Yet in order for us to make the most effective use of technology we need to increase considerably the small but growing body of research related to technology-mediated listening instruction. Little is understood about how vibrations in the air (live or recorded) become meanings in the mind, and both qualitative and quantitative studies are needed in order to respond to the many questions yet to be answered regarding both the listening process and listening instruction. Investigations into the functioning of the brain and ear in listening should be aided by technological advances in brain imaging that will help us observe the listening process more directly than has been possible in the past. Although the time-honored ways of transmitting the results of studies through scholarly presentations and papers will no doubt continue, scholar-teachers should also take advantage of the possibilities for a rapid exchange of ideas offered by electronic mail. The Listen-2 listserve initiated by members of the International Listening Association offers such a forum to its subscribers.[17]

Throughout this chapter we have seen that *text* and *technology* can combine powerfully in the teaching of listening. These two words, closely associated in listening instruction, are also etymologically related, both being derived from the Indo-European root *teks*. Interestingly, *teks* is also the ancestor of the word *architect,* and it is as an architect of learning that the teacher can best function in technology-oriented listening instruction. While today's technology provides not only a rich variety of oral documents and various equipment to display and manipulate them, technology cannot and should not replace the teacher, the architect or designer of learning. The teacher's important role in listening instruction becomes one of mediating between technology, oral texts, and language learners by choosing equipment of sufficiently high quality that students will be able to hear the sounds of the language accurately, selecting (or helping students select) appropriate texts, designing appropriate tasks for learners of various abilities and with diverse backgrounds, incorporating into classroom instruction listening strategies that students will be able to transfer to independent listening, and providing ample opportunities for listening both in and out of class. Integrating effective listening instruction into the curriculum may require some rethinking on the part of teachers more accustomed to dealing with materials consisting of words in print rather than of sound waves in the air. Even so, given the essential role of listening both in language acquisition and in communication, whatever retraining is required to enable us to use the wealth of technology presently at our disposal will be well worth the effort.

NOTES

1. Although we tend to think of spoken words as series of discrete sounds following each other in much the same way that we would transcribe them phonetically, this is not the case. A schematic representation of the production of a simple one-syllable word such as *bag,* for example, reveals so much overlapping that "hardly any part of the acoustic signal can be attributed to only one of the phonemes" (Handel 1989:147).

2. The standard sampling frequency for music recorded on compact discs is 44 kHz. The resulting frequency range for music CDs is 20 to 20,000 Hz (20 kHz).
3. To obtain additional information about *Champs-Élysées* and its German, Spanish, and Italian counterparts, call 1-800-824-0829. The *Champs-Élysées* home page address is <http://www.champs-elysees.com>.
4. This film is available from PICS, 270 International Center, University of Iowa, Iowa City, IA 52242-1802.
5. In a study of computer-based interactive videodisc instruction involving EFL students, Yeh (1994) found significant main effects for learner control, especially among those students with low strategy use.
6. These videodiscs and the *Listening Tool* software are available from PICS (address above).
7. In addition to the previously mentioned aids to comprehension, the prototype of the *Listening Tool* program included a slower, very clearly articulated soundtrack, but this feature is available only with the *Télédouzaine* videodisc.
8. Additional information concerning *The Learnables,* published by the International Linguistics Corporation, can be obtained by calling 1-800-237-1830.
9. More information concerning *The Rosetta Stone,* which exists in a number of languages, can be obtained from Fairfield Language Technologies, Harrisonburg, VA.
10. *Vi-conte* is distributed by PICS. See address above.
11. This authentic video material is one component of Joiner et al., *Vidéo Vérité.* Complete bibliographical information is provided in the references.
12. Guidelines with respect to the journal, or listening log, can be found in the *Vidéo Vérité Instructor's Resource Manual,* listed in the references.
13. The LLS Program is distributed by Joan Rubin Associates, 2011 Hermitage Avenue, Wheaton, MD 20902.
14. The North American distributor for *Education and Dyslexia,* the English-language translation of this book, is Les Éditions France-Québec, 3350 est, rue Rachel, Montréal, Québec H1W 1A7.
15. Sparks and Ganschow are not the first to make the connection between audition and foreign language learning. Nearly thirty years earlier, Pimsleur et al. (1964) had studied underachieving foreign language learners and found that otherwise very bright students nevertheless were sometimes poor foreign language students, their greatest problem area being listening.
16. During a sabbatical in Paris in 1995–1996, I was able to review evaluations of clients accumulated over the previous year and to interview clients enrolled in language instruction at that time.
17. To subscribe to Listen-2, send a message to the following address: listserv@bgu.edu. Your message should read as follows (omitting the quotation marks): "subscribe listen-2 first last [*first last* = your name].

REFERENCES

ACTFL Proficiency Guidelines. 1988. Yonkers, NY: American Council on the Teaching of Foreign Languages.
Altman, Rick. 1989. *The Video Connection.* Boston: Houghton Mifflin.
Amyes, Tim. 1990. *The Technique of Audio Post-production in Video and Film.* Boston: Focal Press.
Anderson, Daniel R., and Jennings Bryant. 1983. "Research on Children's Television Viewing: The State of the Art," pp. 331–53 in Jennings Bryant and Daniel R.

Anderson, eds., *Children's Understanding of Television: Research on Attention and Comprehension.* New York: Academic Press.

Asher, James J. 1986. *Learning Another Language through Actions: The Complete Teacher's Guidebook.* 3rd ed. Los Gatos, CA: Sky Oaks Productions.

Bacon, Susan. 1989. "Listening for Real in the Foreign Language Classroom." *Foreign Language Annals* 22:543–50.

——. 1992. "The Relationship between Gender, Comprehension, Processing Strategies, and Cognitive and Affective Response in Foreign Language Listening." *Modern Language Journal* 76:160–78.

Berne, Jane E. 1995. "How Does Varying Pre-listening Activities Affect Second-language Listening Comprehension." *Hispania* 78:316–29.

Borrás, Isabel, and Robert C. Lafayette. 1994. "Effects of Multimedia Courseware Subtitling on the Speaking Performance of College Students of French." *Modern Language Journal* 78:61–75.

Brett, Paul. 1995. "Multimedia for Listening Comprehension: The Design of a Multimedia Based Resource for Developing Listening Skills." *System* 23:77–85.

Bryant, Jennings, and Daniel R. Anderson, eds. 1983. *Children's Understanding of Television: Research on Attention and Comprehension.* New York: Academic Press.

Byrnes, Heidi. 1984. "The Role of Listening Comprehension: A Theoretical Base." *Foreign Language Annals* 17:317–29.

Chutkow, Paul. 1994. *Depardieu: A Biography.* New York: Alfred A. Knopf.

Coakley, Carolyn Gwynn, and Andrew D. Wolvin. 1986. "Listening in the Native Language," pp. 11–42 in Barbara H. Wing, ed., *Listening, Reading and Writing: Analysis and Application.* Middlebury VT: Northeast Conference on the Teaching of Foreign Languages Teaching.

——. 1990. "Listening Pedagogy and Androgogy: The State of the Art." *Journal of the International Listening Association* 4:33–61.

Cohen, Michèle, and Jean-Claude Louchet. 1983. "La Main dans le sac." Paris: CNDP (Ministère de l'Éducation Nationale).

Conrad, Linda. 1989. "The Effects of Time-compressed Speech on Native and ESL Listening." *Studies in Second Language Acquisition* 11,1:1–16.

Dandonoli, Patricia, and Grant Henning. 1990. "An Investigation of the Construct Validity of the ACTFL Proficiency Guidelines and Oral Interview Procedure." *Foreign Language Annals* 23:11–22.

DeMyhrer, Alicia. 1996. Personal communication.

Door, Aimée. 1986. *Television and Children: A Special Medium for a Special Audience.* Beverly Hills: SAGE Publications.

Douglas, Dan. 1988. "Testing Listening Comprehension in the Context of the ACTFL Proficiency Guidelines." *Studies in Second Language Acquisition* 10:245–61.

Duker, Samuel. 1974. *Time-compressed Speech: An Anthology and Bibliography in Three Volumes.* Metuchen, NJ: The Scarecrow Press, Inc.

Dunkel, Patricia. 1991. "Listening in the Native and Second/Foreign Language," *TESOL Quarterly* 25:431–57.

Eykyn, Lollie B. 1992. "The Effects of Listening Guides on the Comprehension of Authentic Texts by Novice Learners of French as a Second Language." Unpublished Ph.D. dissertation, University of South Carolina, Columbia.

Feyten, Carine. 1991. "The Power of Listening Ability: An Overlooked Dimension in Language Acquisition." *Modern Language Journal* 75:173–80.

Gale, L. E. 1983. "Montevidisco: An Anecdotal History of an Interactive Videodisc." *CALICO Journal* 1:42–46.

Ganschow, Richard, and Leonore Sparks. 1996. "Anxiety about Foreign Language Learning among High School Women." *Modern Language Journal* 80:199–212.

Gebhard, Jerry G., Deming Mei, Lian-Aik Wong, Darlene Huang, Melanie Boston, and Ivannia Jiminez. 1991. *Authentic Listening: Four Annotated Bibliographies (within an ESL Media and Materials Fair Context).* [EDRS: ED 340 220]

Glisan, Eileen W. 1995. "Listening," pp. 61–84 in Vicki Galloway and Carol Herron, eds., *Research Within Reach II,* Valdosta, GA: Southern Conference on Language Teaching.

Green, Wesley. 1996. Personal communication.

Griffiths, Roger. 1992. "Speech Rate and Listening Comprehension: Further Evidence of the Relationship." *TESOL Quarterly* 26:385–91.

Guntermann, Gail, and June K. Phillips. 1982. *Functional-Notional Concepts: Adapting the FL Textbook.* Washington, DC: Center for Applied Linguistics.

Haber, David M., and Robert E. Runstein. 1989. *Modern Recording Techniques.* Carmel, IN: SAMS.

Handel, Stephen. 1989. *Listening: An Introduction to the Perception of Auditory Events.* Cambridge, MA: MIT Press.

Harlow, Linda L., and Judith A. Muyskens. 1994. "Priorities for Intermediate-Level Language Instruction." *Modern Language Journal* 78:141–54.

Harvey, Thomas E. 1981. "Rate Alteration Technology and Its Place in the Language Laboratory." Paper presented at the International Foreign Language Education and Technology Conference, Tokyo, Japan. [EDRS: ED 218 974]

Herron, Carol. 1994. "An Investigation of the Effectiveness of Using an Advance Organizer to Introduce Video in the Foreign Language Classroom." *Modern Language Journal* 78:190–98.

Herron, Carol A., Julia E. B. Hanley, and Steven P. Cole. 1995. "A Comparison Study of Two Advance Organizers for Introducing Beginning Foreign Language Students to Video." *Modern Language Journal* 79:387–95.

Horwitz, Elaine, and Dolly Young. 1991. *From Theory and Research to Classroom Implications.* Englewood Cliffs, NJ: Prentice Hall.

Joiner, Elizabeth G. 1986. "Listening in the Foreign Language," pp. 43–70 in Barbara H. Wing, ed., *Listening, Reading, and Writing: Analysis and Application.* Middlebury, VT: Northeast Conference on the Teaching of Foreign Languages.

———. 1990. "Choosing and Using Videotexts." *Foreign Language Annals* 23:53–64.

———. 1991. "Teaching Listening: Ends and Means," pp. 194–214 in James E. Alatis, ed., *Linguistics and Language Pedagogy: The State of the Art, Georgetown University Round Table on Languages and Linguistics 1991.* Washington, D.C.: Georgetown University Press.

Joiner, Elizabeth G., Polly B. Adkins, and Lollie B. Eykyn. 1989. "Skimming and Scanning with *Champs-Élysées:* Using Authentic Materials to Improve Foreign Language Listening." *French Review,* 62:427–35.

Joiner, Elizabeth G., Annie Duménil, and James Day. 1994. *Vidéo Vérité.* Boston: Houghton Mifflin.

———. 1994. *Vidéo Vérité Instructor's Resource Manual.* Boston: Houghton Mifflin.

Jones, Randall L. 1990. "Interactive Audio and Computer-Assisted Language Learning," pp. 35–42 in Peter C. Patrikis, ed., *Multimedia and Language Learning: Technology in Higher Education.* [EDRS: ED 358 819]

Kellerman, Susan. 1990. "Lip Service: The Contribution of the Visual Modality to Speech Perception and Its Relevance to the Teaching and Testing of Foreign Language Comprehension." *Applied Linguistics* 11:272–80.

Ko, Peter. 1992. "The Effects of Rate-controlled Speech on Advanced Chinese EFL Learners' Short-term Listening Comprehension and Confidence." Unpublished Ph.D. dissertation, Florida State University, Tallahassee.

Krashen, Stephen D. 1981. *Second Language Acquisition and Second Language Learning.* New York: Pergamon.

Larson, Jerry. 1996. Personal Communication.

Larson, Jerry, and Charles Bush. 1992. *Montevidisco.* Provo, UT: Brigham Young University.

Laviosa, Flavia. 1991. "An Investigation of the Listening Strategies of Advanced Learners of Italian as a Second Language." Paper presented at the Conference on Bridging Theory and Practice in the Foreign Language Classroom, Baltimore, MD. [EDRS: ED 345 563]

Lonergan, Jack. 1984. *Video in Language Teaching.* Cambridge: Cambridge University Press.

Long, Donna R. 1991. "What Foreign Language Learners *Say* They Think About When Listening to Authentic Texts." Unpublished manuscript.

Lund, Randall J. 1990. "A Taxonomy for Teaching Second Language Listening." *Foreign Language Annals* 23:105–15.

Lyman-Hager, Mary Ann. 1994. "Video and Interactive Multimedia Techniques in French for the 1990s." *French Review* 68:209–28.

MacIntyre, Peter. 1995. "How Does Anxiety Affect Second Language Learning: A Reply to Sparks and Ganschow." *Modern Language Journal* 79:90–99.

McCarthy, Patricia A., and Julie V. Sapp. 1993. "Rehabilitative Considerations with the Geriatric Population," pp. 331–73 in Jerome G. Alpiner and Patricia A. McCarthy, eds., *Rehabilitative Audiology: Children and Adults.* Baltimore: Williams and Wilkins.

McLuhan, Marshall. 1964. *Understanding Media: The Extensions of Man.* New York: McGraw-Hill.

Meringoff, Laurene, Martha M. Vibbert, Cynthia A. Char, David E. Fernie, Gail S. Banker, and Howard Gardner. 1983. "How Is Children's Learning from Television Distinctive? Exploiting the Medium Methodologically," pp. 151–79 in Jennings Bryant and Daniel R. Anderson, eds. *Children's Understanding of Television: Research on Attention and Comprehension.* New York: Academic Press.

Meyer, Rene. 1984. "Listen My Children and You Shall Hear." *Foreign Language Annals* 17:343–44.

Mielke, Keith W. 1983. "Formative Research on Appeal and Comprehension in 3-2-1 CONTACT," pp. 241–63 in Jennings Bryant and Daniel R. Anderson, eds., *Children's Understanding of Television: Research on Attention and Comprehension.* New York: Academic Press.

Montgomery, Allen A. 1993. "Management of the Hearing-Impaired Adult," pp. 311–30 in Jerome G. Alpiner and Patricia A. McCarthy, eds., *Rehabilitative Audiology: Children and Adults.* Baltimore: Williams and Wilkins.

Morley, Joan. 1990. "Trends and Developments in Listening Practice: Theory and Practice," pp. 317–37 in James E. Alatis, ed., *Georgetown University Round Table on Languages and Linguistics 1990.* Washington, DC: Georgetown University Press.

Mueller, Gunther A. 1980. "Visual Contextual Clues and Listening Comprehension." *Modern Language Journal* 64:335–40.

Mydlarski, Donna, and Dana Paramskas. 1990. *Vi-conte.* Calgary, AB: University of Calgary.

Nash, J. Madeleine. 1996. "Zooming in on Dyslexia." *Time,* January 29:62–64.

Noblitt, James S. 1990. "Multimedia and Listening Comprehension," pp. 43–47 in Peter C. Patrikis, ed., *Multimedia and Language Learning: Technology in Higher Education.* [EDRS: ED 358 819]

Nunan, David, and Lindsay Miller, eds. 1995. *New Ways in Teaching Listening.* Alexandria, VA: TESOL.

Oller, John W. 1983. "Some Working Ideas for Language Teaching," pp. 3–19 in J. W. Oller and Patricia A. Richard-Amato, eds., *Methods That Work.* Rowley, MA: Newbury House.

Omaggio Hadley, Alice. 1993. *Teaching Language in Context: Proficiency-Oriented Instruction.* 2nd ed. Boston: Heinle and Heinle.

Ostermeier, Terry H. 1991. "Fast Talkers and Speeding Listeners: Television/Radio Commercials." *Journal of the International Listening Association* 5:22–35.

Otto, Sue, and James Pusack. 1992. *Listening Tool.* Iowa City, IA: PICS.

Oxford, Rebecca. 1990. *Language Learning Strategies: What Every Teacher Should Know.* New York: Newbury House/Harper and Row.

Petit, Bernard, and James Noblitt. 1995. *Nouvelles Dimensions.* Boston: Heinle and Heinle.

Palmer, Barbara C., Marilyn F. Sharp, Beverly Carter, and Yvette Roddenberry. 1991. "The Effects of Music and Structured Oral Directions on Auding and Reading Comprehension." *Journal of the International Listening Association* 5:7–21.

Parker, Richard, Robert Davis, Joanne Cannon, and Julie Van Doren. 1991. DIAS (Digital Interactive Audio System). Northampton, MA: Smith College Center for Foreign Languages and Cultures.

Phillips, June K. 1991. "An Analysis of Text in Video Newscasts," pp. 343–54 in James E. Alatis, ed., *Linguistics and Language Pedagogy: The State of the Art, Georgetown University Round Table on Languages and Linguistics 1991.* Washington, DC: Georgetown University Press.

Pihlajamäki, Klara. 1995. "Does Technology Help Organizations to Listen?" Svenska Institutet für Systemutveckling Publikation 95:15.

Pimsleur, Paul, D. Sundland, and R. McIntyre. 1964. "Underachievement in Foreign Language Learning." *International Review of Applied Linguistics* 2:113–50.

Purdy, Michael. 1996. "The Limits to Human Contact: How Communication Technology Mediates Relationships." Unpublished paper presented to the International Listening Association.

Pusack, James, and Sue K. Otto. 1995. "Instructional Technologies," pp. 23–41 in Vicki Galloway and Carol Herron, eds., *Research Within Reach II.* Valdosta, GA: Southern Conference on Language Teaching.

Rader, Karen E. 1990. *The Effects of Word Rate on the Listening Comprehension of Third-quarter University Spanish Students.* Unpublished Ph.D. dissertation, The Ohio State University, Columbus.

Richards, Jack. 1983. "Listening Comprehension: Approach, Design, Procedure." *TESOL Quarterly* 17:219–40.

Rost, Michael. 1990. *Listening in Language Learning.* London: Longman.

Rubin, Joan. 1990. "Improving Foreign Language Listening Comprehension," pp. 309–16 in J. E. Alatis, ed., *Georgetown University Round Table 1990.* Washington, DC: Georgetown University Press.

————. 1994. "A Review of Second Language Listening Comprehension Research." *Modern Language Journal* 78:199–221.

————. 1995. "Learning Processes and Learner Strategies," pp. 11–22 in Vicki Galloway and Carol Herron, eds., *Research within Reach II*. Valdosta, GA: Southern Conference on Language Teaching.

————. 1996. "Using Multimedia for Learner Strategy Instruction," pp. 158–63 in Rebecca Oxford, ed., *Language Learning Strategies Around the World*. Manoa: University of Hawaii Press.

Samuels, S. Jay. 1987. "Factors that Influence Listening and Reading Comprehension," in R. Horowitz and S. Jay Samuels, eds., *Comprehending Oral and Written Language*. San Diego, CA: Academic Press.

Schmidt-Rinehart, Barbara C. 1994. "The Effects of Topic Familiarity on Second Language Listening Comprehension," *Modern Language Journal* 78:179–89.

Shrum, Judith, and Eileen Glisan. 1994. *Teacher's Handbook: Contextualized Language Instruction*. Boston: Heinle and Heinle.

Singer, Jerome L., and Dorothy G. Singer. 1983. "Implications of Childhood Television Viewing for Cognition, Imagination and Emotion," pp. 265–95 in Jennings Bryant and Daniel R. Anderson, eds. *Children's Understanding of Television: Research on Attention and Comprehension*. New York: Academic Press.

Smith, Eric E., and Shen, Chung-Wei. 1992. "The Effects of Knowledge of Results Feedback of Captioning on Listening Comprehension of English as a Second Language in Interactive Videodisc Systems." [EDRS: ED 348 026]

Sparks, Richard L., and Leonore Ganschow. 1991. "Foreign Language Learning Differences: Affective or Native Language Aptitude Differences?" *Modern Language Journal* 75:3–16.

————. 1993a. "The Impact of Native Language Learning Problems on Foreign Language Learning: Case Study Illustrations of the Linguistic Coding Deficit Hypothesis." *Modern Language Journal* 77:58–74.

————. 1993b. "Searching for the Cognitive Locus of Foreign Language Learning Difficulties: Linking First and Second Language Learning." *Modern Language Journal* 77:289–302.

————. 1995. "A Strong Inference Approach to Causal Factors in Foreign Language Learning: A Response to MacIntyre." *Modern Language Journal* 79:235–44.

Sparks, Richard L., Leonore Ganschow, James Javorsky, Jane Pohlman, and John Patton. 1992. "Identifying Native Language Deficits in High and Low-risk Foreign Language Learners in High School." *Foreign Language Annals* 25:403–18.

Stoltzfus, Eugene. 1996. Personal communication.

Swaffar, Janet, and Susan Bacon. 1995. "Reading and Listening Comprehension: Perspectives on Research and Implications for Practice," pp. 124–55 in Alice Omaggio Hadley, ed., *Research in Language Learning: Principles, Processes and Prospects*. Lincolnwood, IL: National Textbook Company.

Terrell, Tracy. 1982. "The Natural Approach to Language Learning: An Update." *Modern Language Journal* 66:121–32.

The Editors of Consumer Reports Books with Dean Gallea. 1995. *Consumer Reports Audio/Video Buying Guide*. Yonkers, NY: Consumers Union.

Thompson, Irene, and Joan Rubin. Forthcoming. "Can Strategy Training Improve Listening Comprehension?" *Foreign Language Annals*.

Tomatis, A. A. 1971. *Éducation et dyslexie*. Paris: Editions E.S.F.

————. 1978. *Education and Dyslexia*. (Trans. Louise Guiney) Fribourg, Switzerland: AIAPP.

————. 1991. *The Conscious Ear*. (Trans. Stephen Lushington and Billie Thompson) Barrytown, NY: Station Hill Press.

"Report from Las Vegas." 1996. *Popular Mechanics.* May:25–28.

Vellutino, Frank. 1979. *Dyslexia: Theory and Research.* Cambridge, MA: MIT Press.

Vogely, Anita. 1995. "Perceived Strategy Use During Performance on Three Authentic Listening Comprehension Tasks." *Modern Language Journal* 79:41–56.

Wenden, Anita, and Joan Rubin, eds. 1987. *Learner Strategies in Language Learning.* Englewood Cliffs, NJ: Prentice Hall.

Winitz, Harris. 1996. Personal communication to the author.

Yang, Mei Ling. 1988. "On Principles of Tape Editing and Recording and Its Quality Assessment." [EDRS: ED 304 088]

Yeh, Shiou-Wen. 1994. "Effects of Learner Control and Advance Organizers on EFL Learning from Hypermedia-based CBIV Lessons." Unpublished Ph.D. dissertation, Purdue University.

4

Hypermedia Technology for Teaching Reading

Ana Martínez-Lage

Middlebury College
George Mason University

Introduction

This chapter examines the application of interactive hypermedia technology to the teaching of reading in a foreign language (FL). Research in the area of teaching reading skills has grown tremendously in the last decade, and, if nothing else, the results have demonstrated that reading in a foreign language entails much more than decoding words with the help of a dictionary. It is encouraging to see that in recent years, materials for the teaching of reading[1] are being developed following the recommendations given by Barnett (1989) and Swaffar, Arens, and Byrnes (1991), among others. The advances made by these and many other scholars toward a better understanding of FL reading must continue to guide methodological decisions made with respect to reading activities as well as to the texts that we select for our FL courses. At the same time, while the development of interactive technology applied to FL teaching is constantly growing (Borchardt and Johnson 1995), there is not yet a solid understanding of how this technology can be effectively used in the area of FL reading instruction. Readers of this chapter will not only find a review of how current hypermedia technology integrates up-to-date research into FL reading, but will also encounter specific guidelines for creating their own computer-based materials for teaching reading.

Ana Martínez-Lage, formerly Assistant Professor of Spanish (Foreign Language Pedagogy and Methodology) in the Department of Modern and Classical Languages at George Mason University, is now Assistant Professor in the Department of Spanish and Italian at Middlebury College. She teaches courses in Spanish language at all levels and has also created and taught a number of methodology courses for graduate students in the Spanish Language Summer School at Middlebury College. She has developed a variety of teaching materials at all levels of language instruction and has co-authored an introductory Spanish language textbook, *¡Tu Dirás!*, and a CD-ROM for beginning Spanish, *Mundos Hispanos*. She is currently the recipient of a two-year Mellon Grant for the development of computer-based teaching materials. Her research interests include the application of hypermedia technology to the teaching of reading.

Reading in a Foreign Language: Obstacles to the Process and Ways to Overcome Them[2]

Developing reading skills in a foreign language cannot be equated with the process of achieving literacy in the native language (L1). The adult FL learner brings along a linguistic system already in place and a knowledge of the world that together determine the way this person selects and processes new information. Most FL readers, overwhelmed by a page full of unfamiliar words, no matter what their L1 reading ability is, tend to approach texts written in a foreign language in a linear way, concentrating their attention mainly, if not exclusively, on the linear aspects of the text (letters and words) and perceiving them in an isolated manner as if they were not part of a larger unit: the sentence, the paragraph, the whole text. This text-driven approach to reading, also known as "bottom-up" (Barnett 1989:12), makes reading in a foreign language a matter of decoding words rather than a process of interacting intelligently with the text to make sense out of it.[3]

To better understand the factors that hinder reading comprehension and slow down reading ability in another language, we need to take a look at the characteristics that differentiate a successful FL reader from an unsuccessful one. A skilled reader interacts with the text, establishing significant connections between textual and extratextual elements. This kind of interaction allows him or her to integrate the different "textual subsystems (e. g., content, context, intent, language) into a larger metasystem of meaning" (Swaffar, Arens, and Byrnes, 1991:21). However, the unskilled reader perceives the text as a chain of isolated words, each of which has to be deciphered individually in order to move on with the reading. While the successful reader encodes, that is, creates meaning, the unskilled reader exclusively decodes, replicating "textual language without reference to reader or textual framework of meaning" (Swaffar et al. 1991:22).

Because FL learners, unless they are otherwise trained, perceive reading as a matter of vocabulary knowledge, they often experience what Clarke (1980) has defined as a "short-circuit," a phenomenon by which the ability to read that an individual possesses in his or her native language is completely deactivated due to a limited knowledge of the FL linguistic system. Lack of vocabulary knowledge usually results in an overuse of bilingual dictionaries that, if not handled properly, very often fail to provide the correct answers (Martínez-Lage 1995a). The following example illustrates how an inappropriate use of a Spanish-English dictionary can lead to clear misunderstanding. In a reading journal kept by a third-year Spanish student, we find the following: "What is the sentence: *Pero el día de hoy la niña se había lucido* (Esquivel 1989:148)? Is it in English today the child shines?"[4] The word *lucir* in Spanish means in fact 'to shine'; however, when the verb is used in the reflexive form (something the reader failed to recognize) it figuratively means 'to make a big mess,' which is very far from the meaning 'to shine' that the reader selected for it.

Looking up every other word slows down the reading process, and, consequently, readers not only forget what they have just read, but also fail to look forward in the text for contextual cues that will facilitate comprehension (LaBerge and Samuels 1974; McLaughlin 1987). Let us pause here for a minute to reflect upon who is in fact responsible for this ineffective approach to reading. On behalf of students it is my contention that FL instructors should consider themselves accountable, at least in part, for this FL reading behavior. Swaffar et al. have pointed out that "reading word for word—reading with a dominant focus on vocabulary or formal features rather than textual message—is an inadvertent by-product of second- and particularly foreign-language instruction" (1991:29). In most first- and second-year FL classes reading comprehension is tested in the target language according to the reader's ability to answer questions such as *who, what, when,* or *where.* This type of question encourages FL students to believe that comprehending is finding concrete answers instead of discovering the global meaning of the text. In other words, "since traditional comprehension checks generally focus on myriad text details, many students learn to answer not by understanding the text well, but by looking progressively through the text, following the questions as they go" (Barnett 1989:134). Phillips uses the made-up sentence "The gloopy malchicks scatted razdrazily to the mesto" to demonstrate that one can answer questions without understanding a word: "What is the sentence about? (*malchicks*); What are they like? (*They are gloopy*); Where did they go? (*To the mesto*)" (cited in Barnett:134). Along the same lines, when first-year Spanish students were asked in a pilot study to answer a question in Spanish, they could identify in the text the right word without understanding its meaning. This became clear when the same subjects were asked to answer the same question in English.[5]

It seems that while on the one hand, FL instructors may inadvertently encourage the use of ineffective reading styles, we, on the other hand, can teach L2 readers to abandon a purely text-driven approach by making them look at the text globally with an interactive perspective. Explicit instruction on the process of reading that integrates both textual and extratextual information will help students abandon a purely linear approach to reading. There is evidence in the literature (Barnett 1988a; Carrell 1985; Kern 1989) that supports that teaching students to use explicit reading strategies enhances their reading comprehension. By strategies, I refer to "the conscious or unconscious mental operation involved when readers purposefully approach a text to make sense of what they read" (Barnett 1989:77).

Research in FL reading has shown that students can read more successfully and overcome most of the difficulties they experience in understanding a foreign language text when they apply effective reading strategies. At the same time, a number of studies have provided empirical evidence that supports the positive effect of providing students with the necessary background knowledge on increasing the level of comprehension (Barnett 1988b; Bransford, Barry, and Shelton 1984; Carrell 1984a and b; Davis 1989; Floyd and Carrell 1987; Goldman and Reyes 1983; Hudson 1982; Johnson 1982; Lee 1986; Swaffar 1988). In addition, when students make predictions and anticipate content, they are better prepared to make intelligent guesses when they come across unfamiliar words and structures, as well as new passages in a story (Barnett 1989).[6]

Furthermore, if a reader is able to remember what has been previously read, knows how to look for key words, and contextualizes the information as it is read, the level of reading comprehension is also enhanced. When an interactive relationship between the text and the reader is established, reading becomes a creative act in which the reader is no longer a passive factor but an active one (Zamel 1992; Swaffar et al. 1991). An effective way to engage FL students in an active-interactive reading process is to have them write as they read. Writing about one's reading experience seems to facilitate reading comprehension and leads to the discovery of the different factors that intervene in the reading process (Edelsky 1986; Hudelson 1984; Martínez-Lage 1995a; Zamel 1992).[7]

Whole Texts in Foreign Language Intermediate Courses: Pedagogical Implications

FL students who, after completing the first two years of instruction, decide to continue with the study of the language, whether as majors, as minors, or out of interest, will have to take courses such as an introduction to literary analysis, surveys in literature, and culture and civilization, among others, in which they have to read and understand lengthy texts in the target language. Teachers in these classes often struggle with the fact that most of their students are not well prepared to carry out the required tasks of reading and analyzing a given text. This should not surprise us, since most of these students have not received explicit instruction on how to proceed when reading a complete text. In most cases, when we consider the textbooks used in first- and second-year language courses,[8] the reading experience has been limited for the most part to short excerpts, ads, cultural capsules, and the like. Shook, after conducting a survey on how textbooks introduce beginning learners to literary works, indicates that "college FL students typically receive very little exposure to literary works until their advanced levels of language study" (1996:201). This supports Knutson's observation (1993) that after completing the second year of language study the majority of FL students have had no exposure to long, whole texts and consequently have not received instruction on how to read them efficiently.

Reading whole texts without appropriate guidance can become a frustrating experience, a time-consuming endeavor that seldom results in a complete understanding of the text. A skilled reader, proficient in the target language, will be able to enjoy and obtain satisfaction from a short story, a novel, or a play assigned for a particular class. For unskilled readers, however, the same task of reading a whole text "can also present significant difficulties stemming from the students' lack of linguistic knowledge and/or cultural and literary context" (Knutson 1993:12). For these unprepared readers, what should have been a source of powerful cultural and linguistic input (Kramsch 1985) becomes "a three- to four-hour ordeal" (Crow:242, cited in Davis 1992). To ensure that reading FL texts is beneficial for all students alike, the role of instruction should be to make both intensive and extensive reading possible by reducing to a minimum the negative effects that arise from a limited knowledge of the language. According to Munby (1979), *intensive* reading requires the reader to pay close attention to the text in order to understand all its details, while in *extensive* reading, done mostly for pleasure, the reader does not have to process all the details: all he or she needs to do is to be able to comprehend the main ideas and the author's intent. Students need explicit FL reading instruction and practice with these two types of reading in order to advance in the development of their reading ability so that they can both enjoy what they read and learn from it. In other words, instruction should facilitate "the transition from learning to read to reading to learn" (Schulz 1981:43).

In addition to gradually incorporating longer, complete texts in first- and second-year language courses, I want to take a stand in encouraging the development of courses designed to guide students formally through the reading process of lengthy texts before they enter advanced-level courses such as introduction to literature.[9] In this regard, Knutson indicates that "it is in the interest of every academic foreign language program to develop a coherent approach to the teaching of reading across all levels, and it is particularly important to reconsider and reflect upon the transitional courses, in which relatively inexperienced students are first introduced to the experience of reading literature in the foreign language" (1993:22–23).

Davis, Lyman-Hager, and Hayden point out that "in order to understand what they are reading, foreign language students need much more than a dictionary in which to look up word meanings" (1992:22). Traditionally, foreign language readers (i.e., anthologies) have provided students with marginal glosses to help them decode lexical items. Davis, in a study that investigates whether these glosses improve understanding of a literary text, found that "subjects who received the vocabulary and guide either before or during reading recalled significantly more of the passage than those receiving no help" (1989:44). Moreover, Davis concludes that "the finding that presenting background information before reading enhances comprehension adds confirming evidence to previous L2 studies" (44).

Bernhardt (1991), in her Model for Second Language Reading, proposes six different components necessary for reading comprehension of any foreign language text:

- word recognition
- phonemic/graphemic decoding
- syntactic feature recognition
- intratextual perception
- prior knowledge
- metacognition

Along the same lines, Davis et al. point out that in order to fully understand a literary work, four components need to be present:

- decoding successfully the literal meaning of words and sentences;
- awareness of historical and cultural referents as well as understanding of the spatiotemporal context of the text;
- knowledge of the literary conventions relevant to the text;
- ability on the part of the reader to re-create or reconstruct the text (1992:359).

Davis indicates that the first three components "should be addressed in instruction" (359), something we fully endorse. Knutson, commenting on the role of reading instruction, points out that "instructors at the third-year level must enable students to master progressively more advanced reading tasks. . . . Ideally instructors should adopt an approach which is both informed by research on reading and comprehension and consistent with prior reading instruction" (1993:12).

In this regard, I strongly support the incorporation of whole texts early in language courses. Reading a full text has many advantages for the FL reader provided that the instructor knows how to supplement it to make the text accessible to the beginning and intermediate learners. While the length can initially discourage the reader, it can also help him or her in many ways. First of all, the reader will "develop familiarity with the author's style" (Knutson 1993:15). This familiarization will result in the construction of a particular background knowledge in the reader's mind that is specific for the text at hand. This background knowledge will facilitate comprehension because, as the reader moves along in the text, he or she will recognize lexical items, syntactical patterns, text structure, characters, behaviors, locations, figurative uses of the language, and so on. Also, once the reader is involved in the text, he or she will be able to make more accurate predictions about what lies ahead. In addition, when students are involved in reading a long text, they rapidly realize that they have to read for meaning because "the low profitability or inefficiency of word-for-word, linear reading, is more than evident to students faced with substantial amounts of text" (Knutson 1993:15). On the other hand, when we ask students to read short texts and incomplete passages by different authors, the background knowledge built for the first reading will serve as no help for the second one; the background building process will have to start all over again for each individual reading. One final advantage derives from reading a whole text: the reader's sense of accomplishment after completing a novel in a foreign language.[10]

Our own experience in the classroom demonstrates that students can read a full text that is of interest to them with the help of reading guides.[11] These guides provide students with directions for before, while, and after reading, which help them cope with the text, facilitating the comprehension of particularly complex passages[12] (Martínez-Lage 1995a and b). These reading guides are developed according to the following principles:

A. Before reading

- Always provide necessary background information before starting the reading. (In some cases, extra background information relevant to a particular passage of the text may be needed later on in the reading.)
- Ask specific questions to help students anticipate content.
- Have students recapitulate what they have learned/read so far.

B. While reading

- Point out difficult passages such as those containing abrupt changes in time and location.
- Solve ambiguities.
- Guide them with specific questions to guess the meaning of key words using the surrounding context.

- Clarify structures, text organization, vocabulary, and cultural references.

C. After reading
  - Provide a framework for the discussion of content, structure, and language use within a passage.
  - Lead students to state their own opinion about the reading.
  - Have students summarize the main ideas or give their own account of what happened.

In conjunction with these guides (See Appendix A for a *sample* reading guide), I ask that students keep a reading journal in which they record their own reading experience, raise questions about the texts, answer questions in the reading guides, and react to each passage individually. As I pointed out earlier, writing about reading makes the reader interact with the text and enhances reading comprehension (Martínez-Lage 1995a).

If we succeed in helping students get through a complete text in a foreign language while making their experience a satisfactory one, we may be at the same time building a bridge to another activity—free voluntary reading. According to Krashen (1993), this type of reading practice has proven very profitable in both L1 and FL reading development. Krashen has long advocated the incorporation of this type of reading, which he claims "is highly beneficial for language acquisition and literacy development, far more beneficial than direct instruction" (72). Along the same lines, he also supports the practice of sustained silent reading for FL students. In this kind of reading "students are given quiet time, usually five to fifteen minutes per day, for self-selected reading, and are not held accountable for what they read" (Pilgreen and Krashen 1993:21). The results of a study conducted with ESL high school students suggest that ". . . encouraging students to read for pleasure . . . can make major contributions to second-language literacy development" (23). While I can see the benefits of both free voluntary reading and sustained silent reading, I believe that students will not take advantage of these types of reading experiences unless they have received explicit instruction on the reading process in the ways that I have suggested here.

Hypermedia Annotations: From Research and Theory to Practical Application

In the previous sections I argued that FL readers can use all the help they can get from the instructor so that they can read a foreign language text, understand its meaning, and, ultimately, enjoy the experience. There are several ways in which FL teachers can deliver this help to their students. On the one hand, we can provide it in the form of printed worksheets that include glosses, pre-reading, while-reading, and post-reading activities such as the example included in Appendix A. There is, however, an important limitation embedded in this medium: it limits our options to supplying only textual information. Our other option is to take advantage of existing technology in order to attach different media (text, sound, and images) to a particular text. A number of authoring systems are available today that assist FL instructors in the preparation of computer-based course materials (Borchardt and Johnson 1995). More specifically, in the last few years, several authoring tools have been developed that enable foreign language educators to annotate texts, using different media to make them more accessible to the FL reader.[13]

The following sections illustrate the process of developing hypermedia annotations and discuss how these annotations incorporate current foreign language reading methodology. Examples will be taken from a project based on Laura Esquivel's best-selling novel *Como agua para chocolate* (*CAPC*) that has been annotated using *Guided Reading* (*GR*) (Herren 1996a), one of the authoring tools available for foreign language educators. The purpose of this project was to make a complete literary work accessible to intermediate-level Spanish students.

The Authoring Tool

After a successful experience in a fifth-semester Spanish class with the novel CAPC, the idea of using a hypermedia authoring system to annotate the text became possible thanks to a summer research grant.[14] After looking at several programs, I decided to use *GR* as the authoring tool.

According to the author, *GR* is

> a template, or electronic form, whose purpose is to assist the instructor in the preparation of media-based annotations of texts. It provides an easy means for the instructor to answer questions one time that she knows the students will ask over and again each semester about a text that forms part of the course. I am further hopeful that it will simultaneously engage the student in a way they may not otherwise be engaged. With very little practice, the instructor will be able to annotate any text in virtually any language using digital audio, interactive video, virtual reality, still graphics, and text. These annotations will provide support to the intermediate and beginning language students as they investigate short stories, poetry, or excerpts in the target language (Herren 1996b:23).

GR was selected for this project for several reasons, not least among which was its method of distribution and its cost. *GR* and all of the xMediaEngine templates[15] are distributed via anonymous ftp (File Transfer Protocol)[16] as "shareware," hence one has an opportunity to work with the program at no expense. Only when the software has been tested and one decides to continue using it does a small fee have to be paid to the author. This lowered the barriers to experimentation, since no real costs were involved during the development and experimental stage.

Besides the low cost and the convenient method of distribution, the following features make *GR* a highly suitable authoring tool to accomplish our task at hand:

- The program is designed in such a way that the process of producing simple annotations is nothing more than point and click, which significantly lowers barriers to entry for educators just beginning to investigate these technologies. Advanced features can be accessed by clicking a single button once the user has gained some experience. The program remains flexible even for really advanced users capable of scripting, allowing for possibilities far beyond those imagined by the designers.

- Annotations can consist of virtually every technology available: videodisc, audio compact disc, still images, digital video, recorded digital sound, fully styled text, and it is one of the first packages to directly support QuickTimeVR[17] and to make this exciting new technology accessible to educators.

- All windows that are designed to contain content are movable and resizable, providing the student user with much flexibility in arranging his or her working style.

- All primary authoring functions are located in a single menu.

- It includes a tracking mechanism so lessons can be monitored and easily refined over time.

- The program works in Arabic, Chinese, Cyrillic, Hebrew, Japanese, and any other language for which one has the appropriate typeface so that successful experiences in one language can be extended to colleagues in other languages.

- *GR* lessons can be linked to other lessons for even more three dimensionality in the annotation process; in addition, they can be linked to other types of lessons in the xMediaEngine series.

- The modular design results in modest resource requirements for delivery of lessons: virtually any color Macintosh with eight megabytes of RAM is suitable for delivery of the lessons to students. In addition, it will even compress still images or recorded digital sound automatically for saving even more disc space.

- The software's author is very responsive to suggestions for additional features.

There are a number of drawbacks associated with *GR* that have to be pointed out, which, nonetheless, do not diminish the advantages.

- Currently the program is only available for the Macintosh, though the author is working on a viewer for the Wintel[18] platform.
- While *GR* will import the primary text to be annotated, texts used as annotations themselves have to be either manually typed or copied and pasted into the program.
- It directly supports only still images in the PICT format and not GIF (Graphic Interchange Format) or JPEG (Joint Photographic Experts Group) as commonly found on the World Wide Web, though it is quite easy to convert images, using readily available utility software.

This authoring tool does not include a set of templates for developing traditional reading comprehension activities such as true/false, multiple-choice, cloze, and the like.[19] The instructor who engages in the task of annotating a text with *GR* can include, however, open-ended questions in the textual annotations to have students reflect about the reading and react to any particular part of it.

Text Appearance on the Screen

GR offers the capability of importing the primary text directly into the template, a great advantage when one is working with lengthy texts. Once the text is imported, *GR* lets us make the necessary adjustments so that its appearance on the screen reproduces the printed text as closely as possible. For instance, the *CAPC* pages on the screen correspond exactly to the pages in the paperback edition of the text. This is extremely important for two reasons: first, the original text remains as its author intended it to be; second, I expect users of the hypermedia-annotated version to always keep a copy of the original printed text with them. Moreover, I envision that some readers will perform part or most of their reading task from the printed book, and that they will use the electronic annotated version only when in need of help. If the electronic version of the text were different from the original, the task of finding a particular page could become unnecessarily convoluted.

During the process of developing the hypermedia annotations, I decided to avoid the use of font styles such as boldface, italics, underline, and so forth to prevent drawing readers' attention to a particular word, sentence, or paragraph in the text. The only visual indication that alerts the reader of the existence of an annotation occurs at the page level: when the student enters a page that has page-level annotations,[20] he or she will see a list of them right away in a window that appears to the right of the text. Figure 4.1 shows a sample of such a list.

On the other hand, glosses[21] will not be displayed until the reader double clicks on words, and sentence-level annotations[22] will not be announced until the reader highlights part of the text.

Upon entering the *CAPC* electronic version, students have access to a set of instructions (see Appendix B) that explain how the text has been annotated. Learners can freely explore these annotations according to their individual needs, which are, as we well know, different in each case. I believe that pointing out the words or sentences that have annotations will distract readers from the main task of reading the text. Because the extratextual information is not pinpointed and obstacles are not suggested by flagging text that may not be problematic, readers will investigate only those words and sentences for which they need confirmation and those that present a problem to them.

Figure 4.1.
Sample of page-level annotations list

Annotating the Text

Instructors can make a literary work or any other type of text readable and accessible to FL readers by using the following tools available in *GR:* page-level annotations (see note 19), sentence-level annotations,[23] and a glossary. Figure 4.2 illustrates the different media to which the instructor has access both at the sentence and at the page level while he or she annotates a text.

Keeping in mind the six components essential to reading comprehension proposed by Bernhardt (1991), as well as the four constituents outlined by Davis et al. (1992), the sections below describe the process of how *CAPC* has been annotated in order to assist students[24] in the following areas:

- prior knowledge
- word recognition
- syntactic feature recognition
- intratextual perception.

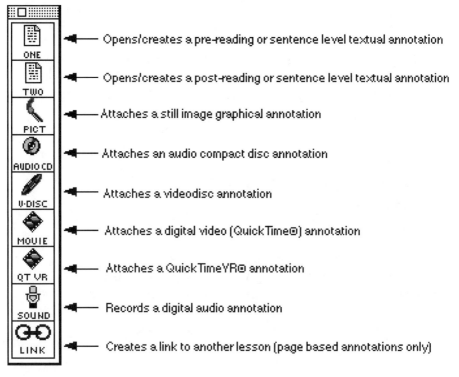

Figure 4.2.
Annotated version of the instructor palette

1. Prior Knowledge

Research results indicate that when a reader approaches a given text with the necessary background knowledge, comprehension is enhanced (see first section of this chapter). *GR* makes it possible for the instructor to provide students with background information that is appropriate for the target text by using a "pre-reading" text at the page level and other media available, such as digital sound and video, still images, videodisc, and so on.

The "pre-reading" text is a scrolling window in which one can include up to twelve pages of text. It is designed in such a way that it will always open up automatically, covering the target text as the student enters a page. The intent is to force the reader to go over any specific instructions or information that pertain to that particular page so that he or she can begin reading with the necessary prior knowledge. This window can be easily moved to another section of the screen or even be resized so that both the text and the pre-reading information are available simultaneously.

Our experience with *CAPC* in the classroom led us to the identification of several areas that were considered crucial for a better understanding of the novel. As a result, a pre-reading window was created and attached to the very first page, that is, the title page, which opens up as the reader first enters the novel.

The purpose of this pre-reading text is to provide students with the necessary background knowledge for this particular novel. Figure 4.3 shows the beginning part of the pre-reading window that lists the six areas covered in this annotation:

- location of the story
- historical period
- the narrator
- main and secondary characters
- general text structure
- general chapter structure (Appendix C includes part of this annotation).

This information could be further discussed in class with the instructor, who can then guide students in their investigation of the printed book by looking at its physical characteristics and reflecting in general terms about the formal features of the text.

Besides this general background knowledge window, other pre-reading texts have been attached to subsequent pages that supply students with specific prior knowledge. Sometimes readers are alerted to a change in time (see section on "Intratextual perception") so that they know what to expect when reading a particular page. In other instances, they are asked to pay attention

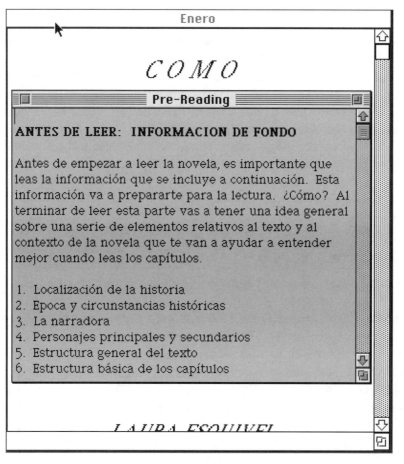

Figure 4.3.
Pre-reading window with general background information

to the use of a particular literary license such as hyperbole so that they are not flustered by Esquivel's style, which often eliminates the barriers between reality and fantasy.

In addition to using text for providing students with prior knowledge, *GR* gives instructors the advantage of accomplishing this same objective by attaching other media to the target text. In the *GR* version of *CAPC* still images have been added to help students visualize unfamiliar objects, and videodisc segments from the *CAPC* movie have been attached to facilitate students' anticipation of content (see section on "Role of visual input in enhancing reading comprehension" for a detailed explanation of how visuals have been incorporated in this project).

2. Word Recognition

The main purpose of the glossary and the sentence-level textual annotations ("text-one") is to assist students in the decoding of both literal and intended meaning of words and sentences. As the instructor selects "extract vocabulary" from the *GR* instructor menu, the program automatically extracts all the words in a given text and creates a list in the order in which they appear in the text. The instructor can then enter the glossary (see Figure 4.4 below) and type the appropriate glosses next to each word. *GR* also lets you record every word in the glossary so that when students double-click on them to see the gloss they can also hear how the word is pronounced. In addition, the software allows for manually glossing groups of words when necessary.[25]

Enero

Glossary

recetas - (sust. f.) falso cognado. *Recipes*.
remedios - (sust. m.) cognado.
caseros - (adj.) se refiere a algo que está hecho en casa, a la manera tradicional. Piensa en la diferencia entre "remedios caseros" y remedios comerciales.
TORTAS - torta - (sust. f.) *rolls, small bread loafs.*
NAVIDAD - (sust. f.) el día de Navidad es el 25 de diciembre, día en que, según la tradición cristiana, se celebra el nacimiento de Jesucristo. El término "navidad" se utiliza para designar el período de tiempo entre el 24 de diciembre y el 6 de enero, día de Reyes.
Lata - (sust. f.) *tin can.*
Sardinas - (sust. f.) cognado.
Chorizo - (sust. m.) *kind of sausage, sometimes hot and spicy.*
Cebolla - (sust. f.) *onion.*
Teleras - (sust. f.) un tipo de pan en forma redonda y/o alargada que se utiliza para hacer las tortas.
finamente - (adv.) se refiere a la manera en que hay que picar la cebolla. Piensa en uno de los significados del adjetivo *fine* en inglés.

• Record •   Clear/Clear all

Figure 4.4.
Sample of the glossary

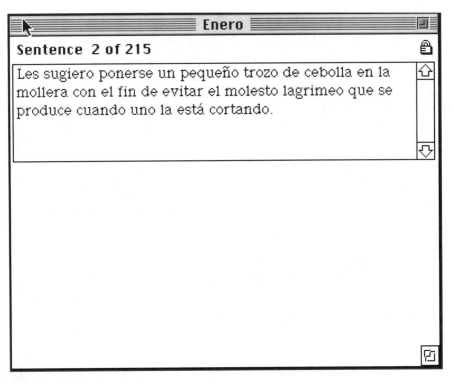

Figure 4.5.
Sample of sentence card

Similarly, when one selects "extract sentences" from the *GR* instructor menu, the program extracts automatically all the sentences and places each one of them on a separate card.[26] Once the sentences have been extracted, the instructor has access to the palette shown in Figure 4.2 (see page 133) to begin creating and attaching annotations to the sentence in question.

According to Chun and Plass, "in the process of reading comprehension in a second language (L2), one of the integral components, though not the only or most important component, is the ability to decode or understand individual vocabulary items in a text" (1996:183). In other words, unfamiliar vocabulary, although it is not the only aspect involved in reading comprehension, is one of the elements in the text that hinders it.

There are at least two reasons that justify the use of specific text-based glosses. First, while it is important that students learn adequate skills to acquire new vocabulary and that they practice strategies that will help them guess word meaning from context (Barnett 1989:126–27), it is also true that this guessing strategy is not always effective. Second, whereas learners need to be able to use both bilingual and monolingual dictionaries effectively, the use of figurative language and idioms in a text can make a regular bilingual dictionary useless in helping students find appropriate translations.

We can gloss a given word or group of words in several ways. Sometimes it may be more beneficial for reading purposes to provide a direct translation of a term instead of a definition in the target language so that the reader can quickly move on with the text. I also recommend using the glosses as a means for teaching more vocabulary in the target language, and I therefore encourage providing synonyms as well as explanations in L2. The glossary can also be used as a tool for practicing the strategy of guessing word meaning by asking the reader pertinent questions that will lead to the correct interpretation of a word or expression. Figure 4.6 illustrates how the glossary in *GR* appears on the screen when the reader double-clicks on words.

GR offers FL students the advantage of keeping a personal glossary of all the words that they look up after each reading session. When the student leaves the program, a dialogue box opens up automatically, asking the reader whether to print the glossary or to save it as a file. This facilitates the task

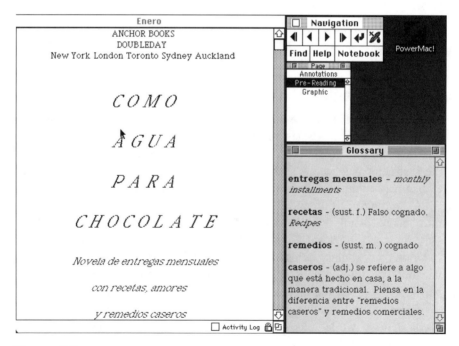

Figure 4.6.
Sample of glossary words looked up

of reviewing the vocabulary looked up during the session and makes it possible for the student to bring it to class in case some of the glosses need further explanation. A by-product of having the glosses appear on the screen in a separate window that can later be saved or printed for review purposes is that students will not write direct translations on top of the words in their text.

Someone could claim that by providing readers with these glosses we are not teaching them to use a bilingual dictionary effectively. This is indeed a legitimate criticism but, while I recognize the importance of knowing how to look up words in a dictionary, our main emphasis here is that FL readers keep reading after finding the correct meaning of a given word or expression. Teaching them to use a bilingual dictionary should be part of class instruction, and specific activities need to be designed for this (Barnett 1989:133–34). Finding the text-specific meaning for a word immediately allows the reader to continue with the task, avoiding, however, the slowing down that occurs when one stops reading to reach for the dictionary, looks up the word, and finally succeeds, or not, in finding the answer sought. According to Davis (1989) glosses, rather than distracting readers, ensure more fluent reading of the selection.

Blake (1981) refers to studies by Miller and Galdea to show that "having instantaneous access to lexical information, as one does through an interactive computer system, aids vocabulary development immensely" (cited in Lyman-Hager et al. 1993:94). In a recent study, Lyman-Hager et al.[27] investigated whether or not the ability of instantaneously accessing an online dictionary would produce greater vocabulary acquisition. They compared two groups of French students: one used a computerized version of *Une vie de boy*[28] that offered online help for the first 1,600 words; the other used the print text and had access to the accompanying glosses and audiotape. Their initial results showed that "students who worked with the computer program were better able to retain the vocabulary" (96).

Besides the glossary, which is appropriate for short definitions or direct translations of words and groups of words, *GR* offers the option of attaching a sentence-level annotation when a complete sentence calls for a lexical explanation. Instructors may be tempted to use this option to provide students with a complete translation of the sentence, something I strongly discourage, since it will defeat the purpose of discovering meaning through reading. Instead, one should try to clarify the meaning of the selected sentence by means of circumlocution and by adding any extra information needed so that the reader can fully understand it. Figure 4.7 shows what happens when the reader highlights a sentence or part of it in search of information (Appendix D includes the full text of the annotation).

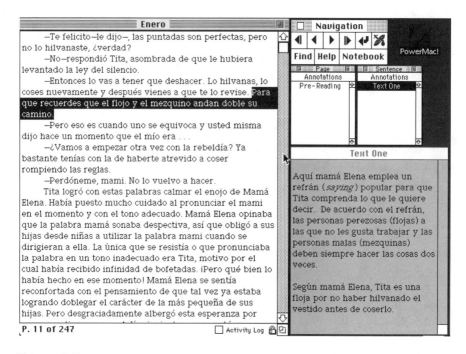

Figure 4.7.
Sample of "text-one" sentence-level annotation

The same way students can keep a personal file with the glossary words they look up, they can also save for future reference any information included in the textual sentence-level annotations by simply selecting it, then copying and pasting it in a separate file or in the *GR* notebook (see section "The notebook").

3. Syntactic Feature Recognition: Sentence Annotations

Research conducted on discourse markers indicates that function words are essential to identifying cohesion in texts (Swaffar et al. 1991:66). Cooper (1984), in a study that investigated the role of vocabulary and syntax in reading comprehension, asked his subjects to list all the unfamiliar words they encountered. According to Swaffar et al., "what is striking about the list he [Cooper] provides is that many are discursive connects such as *despite, nevertheless, consequently* or markers of macropropositional logic such as *contrast with, similarly, function as, characterize*" (67). Barnett, in a study with fourth-semester French students, found that readers who can follow cohesive ties and reference words obtain higher recall protocol scores (Barnett 1986). On the other hand, when the reader cannot assign meaning to these ties, comprehension is obviously obstructed: "The story is not linear and so I needed to re-read it in order to understand the main ideas. Also, the sentences include phrases like *a que, de que, para que, a que sí,* and these are impossible to understand."[29] This particular student pointed out in her journal the difficulty she was experiencing in providing meaning to a number of cohesive elements that appear frequently on the text. Her case is not an unusual one.

To assist the reader in comprehending the syntactical relationships among the words in a sentence, the instructor can use a text window ("text-two" in the *CAPC* annotation) at the sentence level. If a student needs clarification on the use of connectors or any other grammatical aspect in a given sentence, he or she can highlight that sentence and read the information provided by the instructor. Readers can, for further reference, keep this information by simply highlighting it, then copying and pasting it in another file or in the *GR* student notebook. Figure 4.8 illustrates how a "text-two" annotation appears on the screen (Appendix E includes the complete text for this annotation).

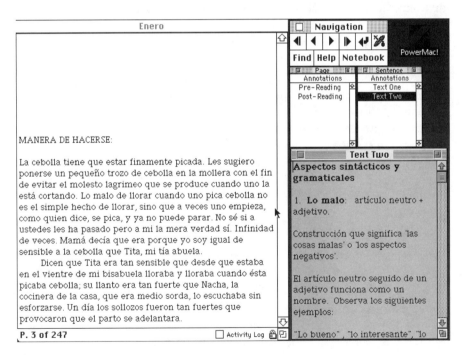

Figure 4.8.

Sample of "text-two" sentence-level annotation

4. Intratextual Perception

Some texts present a higher degree of difficulty than others when it comes to the way in which the different parts of the text relate to preceding and succeeding elements. In this respect a novel like *CAPC* is especially challenging. First of all, the novel is organized around the months of the year, starting in January and ending in December, "but [these] correspond to monthly installments rather than to actual time" (Francescato 1994:104). In addition, the author plays in a very peculiar way with the time sequence, moving back and forth from the present of the narrator to the past of the story, distorting the linearity of events by introducing numerous flashbacks. This treatment of time can cause a great deal of confusion to the unexperienced reader. Thus, to minimize the degree of difficulty that originates when one is confused about when things are happening, a text window can be inserted at either the page ("pre-reading") or the sentence level ("text-one") to help students make the necessary connections between different segments of a passage. Figure 4.9 illustrates the use of a pre-reading window to alert the reader to the fact that a flashback begins and to direct attention to the particular sentence in the text that initiates the time change (Appendix F includes the full annotation).

In *CAPC* it is not only the flashbacks that disrupt the linearity of the story. The different parts that make up a given recipe are interwoven sporadically throughout the chapter: a sentence here, a paragraph there. This, especially at the beginning, confounds the reader who looks for a linear development of events. To diminish the chaos that this particular text structure can create in the mind of the intermediate reader, students received general background information about the structure of the chapters in the pre-reading window at the beginning of the reading task (see section on "Prior knowledge"). I find it useful also to point out the transitions from one text type to another, namely the recipe and the narration, by using the "text-one" window at the sentence level.[30]

The Role of Visual Input in Enhancing Reading Comprehension

Does visual information in the form of still images and video enhance understanding of a foreign language text? Omaggio (1979) carried out a study in which she investigated the effect of different visual aids used as advance organizers. Her results showed that students who received a picture representing the beginning of the story scored significantly better than those receiving no such help. The overall conclusion from this study is that "the best visual context for subjects at relatively low proficiency levels is the one that provides enough background to aid them in finding an appropriate overall

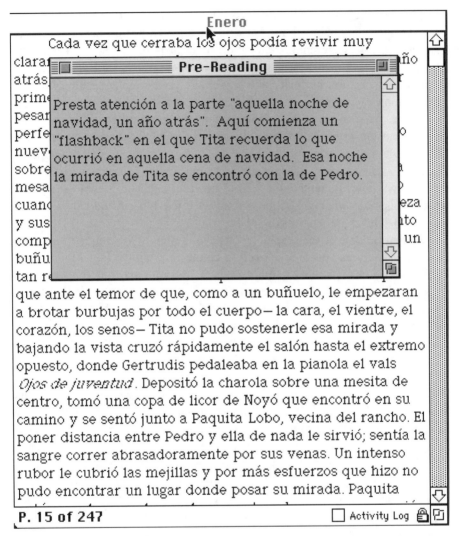

Figure 4.9.
Sample of pre-reading window

schema for comprehending the story" (1993:144). Hudson (1982) conducted a similar experiment in which he compared the effect of providing visual information versus vocabulary information. His results indicate that pictorial cues increased comprehension of the passage and that "induced schemata via picture cues can overcome the deficits of the lower-proficiency readers" (cited in Omaggio 1993:145).

These studies support the use of visual assistance during the pre-reading stage because they help to build background knowledge pertinent to the target text and facilitate the contextualization of what is being read. At the same time, visuals can also be used by instructors to "catch students' attention, capitalize on natural curiosity and encourage prediction by asking how the illustrations . . . might relate to the text" (Barnett 1989:117).

In the pre-reading window with general background information that is included at the beginning of the *GR* version of *CAPC* (see section on "Prior knowledge") there is a reference that indicates to students the geographical location where the story takes place. Through written instructions in the pre-reading window, students are asked to open an attached graphic annotation that consists of a map of Mexico and are instructed to locate Piedras Negras, the town where the story takes place.

So that the role of the graphic goes beyond merely looking at it, a journal writing activity has been developed in connection with it (see Figure 4.10). This activity ensures that the map serves its purpose and functions as a pre-reading aid. This visual annotation has a very precise goal: students become aware of the geographical location of the story they are about to read, and based on this information they can make some predictions about the content of the novel. (Appendix G includes the part of the general background pre-reading window related to the location of the story and the journal activity connected to it.)

Still images, besides helping students activate background knowledge and make predictions, serve another important purpose. They not only provide a concrete image for unfamiliar words but also seem to help learners remember new words more easily. In this regard, early research on L2 conducted by Kellogg and Howe (1971), reviewed by Chun and Plass, indicates that "foreign words associated with actual objects or imagery techniques are learned more easily than words without" (1996:183). Chun and Plass have recently investigated the effectiveness for vocabulary acquisition of using annotations with different media types such as video and pictures. They conducted three studies using *Cyberbuch,* "a hypermedia application for reading German texts that contains a variety of annotations for words in the form of text, pictures and video" (183). The goals of their investigations were:

- to assess the level of incidental vocabulary learning when the objective is reading comprehension;
- to evaluate the effectiveness of different types of annotations; and
- to examine the relationship between look-up behavior and performance in vocabulary tests.

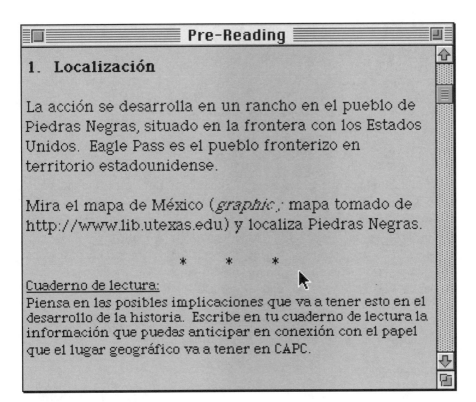

Figure 4.10.
Sample of reading journal activity

The results showed "a higher than expected rate of incidental learning of vocabulary" (194). With respect to the second goal of the study, "the significantly higher scores for words annotated with text + pictures than those with only text support previous studies revealing that visual imagery aids in the learning of foreign words" (194). The third issue examined showed "no overall correlation between the type of annotation looked up and performance on the vocabulary tests" (195) which, according to the authors, could be related to individual differences among learners' cognitive styles.

In *CAPC* there are numerous objects related to food, cooking, and daily life which, while being completely familiar to the Mexican reader, are unknown to those not acquainted with Mexican culture. As Francescato (1994) points out, "[t]ranslating this novel must have been quite a challenge for Carol Christensen and Thomas Christensen. The vocabulary is not easy even for native speakers" (103). For example, in the list of ingredients for the recipe in the first chapter we come across *chiles serranos* and *teleras,* among other things. Later in this same chapter we learn that Tita, the main character, is fed during the first months of her infancy mainly with tea and *atole.*[31] To illustrate these objects, readers have been provided with access to pictures of *chiles* and *atole.* They can also see a videodisc segment of the *CAPC* movie that has been selected and attached to the text so they can get an exact idea of what *teleras* are like. These visual aids ensure that students obtain an accurate visual representation of these unfamiliar objects.

Along with stills, I have selected videoclips from the movie based on the book to illustrate particular segments of the text. In some cases the videoclips help students visualize moments of the story in which a unique use of hyperbole can make a scene not only completely unbelievable but also incomprehensible for those unfamiliar with Latin American magical realism.[32] In other instances, the video is used as a way for students to reflect upon the differences and similarities between the novel and its adaptation to the screen (see Appendix H). Finally, at the end of each chapter, students may choose to watch the complete video segment that corresponds to the chapter they have just read. This way they can test their own understanding of the text against the images.

The Notebook

GR provides students with access to a notebook (see Figure 4.11), that they can use in a number of ways. They can take their own notes, write down questions for discussion in class, and paste into it any useful information they find in the annotations that they want to keep for further reference.

In Martínez-Lage (1995a), I examined the benefits for both the students and the instructor of having learners keep a journal in which they record their personal reading experience during the different stages of the reading process: before, while, and after reading. The inspiration for developing this activity came from Zamel (1992) and I have been using it effectively in my courses for several years. Students report on the progress of their reading, and through the journal they communicate with the instructor on an individual basis.

GR lets us investigate even further the possibilities of this reading journal activity. The text windows make it possible to insert directions for the use of the journal at different levels by using the pre-reading and post-reading windows at the page level, and the text-one and text-two windows at the sentence level respectively. (See Appendix I.) This way I can direct students' attention to specific parts of the text and have them react in writing to a number of issues both textual and extratextual. Students can write about vocabulary usage, sentence structure, chapter organization, or the content of

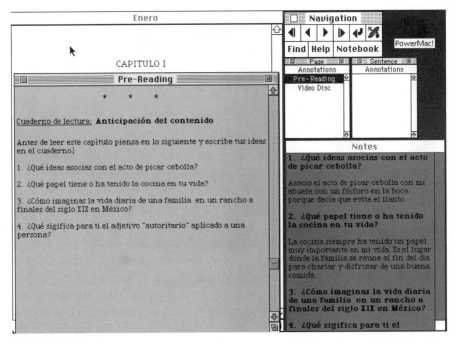

Figure 4.11.
Sample of notebook

a passage. They can react in writing to the visual aids (stills and video) and comment about the differences and similarities they perceive between the text and its adaptation to the big screen.

These journal entries or any other text written using the *GR* notebook can be printed and/or saved in a text file that can be turned in to the instructor for comments and corrections. Exchange of these files between students and instructors can also be carried out through E-mail, since saved text files can be easily sent using any E-mail package.

Empowering Students with Hypermedia Technology

Up to this point I have argued that FL instructors can use interactive hypermedia technology to make reading a more accessible and effective task for students. This technology, though presented this far from the perspective of the instructor as the developer, can also provide students with an opportunity to play an active role in the process of annotating a foreign language text. A number of institutions are experimenting in this area, getting students involved in using the *GR* template for annotating a text and to prepare class presentations. The following projects can be mentioned: one in Chinese directed by Clara Yu, one in German conducted by Michael Geisler, both at Middlebury College; and one in Spanish literature supervised by Douglas Cameron, at Ursinus College.[33]

The experience of having students annotate the work seems to produce very positive results in learners' attitudes toward the task. According to Cameron, "students like to work up passages for presentation on the templates. It makes them feel like they could become an authority on an issue by means of a close reading. . . . After they have prepared a few passages, they become confident about undertaking a paper on larger issues" (Cameron 1996).

The case of Geisler's project is particularly remarkable since it originated as a class project in which upper-level students enrolled in a German senior seminar developed a hypermedia-annotated version of Böll's *Katerina Blum* that ended up being used by intermediate-level students enrolled in German 202 in a subsequent semester. According to Geisler, "the project had come to its completion as soon as a viable interactive text had been created by the participants in the senior seminar. Demonstrating the project to others or actually using it in the classroom was only a potential secondary goal" (1996). Students at both levels seem to have benefited from this experience. The upper-level students, when they finally saw the project coming together, "began to develop a sense of ownership" and "were quite proud of what they had done" (Geisler 1996). The evaluations from the German 202 students revealed, with one exception,[34] that "the program had been extremely useful to them, with several of the respondents stressing the fact that they could not have gotten through the novel without it" (Geisler 1996).

According to Nunan (1988), what educators need to keep in mind in their effort to provide the right environment for the development of second language skills is "engaging learners in interesting and meaningful classroom experiences" (45). Since learning should always provide opportunities for growth and progress, "all learners should be exposed to new methods, materials and approaches from time to time" (Nunan 1988:46). The projects described above show how the incorporation of hypermedia technology can serve as an excellent tool to supply FL learners with such meaningful experiences. Within the context of this type of learning environment, students have a opportunity to gain a better understanding of the learning process, and in return, cultivate their autonomy as learners (Nunan 1988).

Summary: Advantages of Using Hypermedia Technology in Foreign Language Reading

The use of interactive hypermedia technology in the teaching of reading, as presented herein, brings a number of unquestionable benefits to both instructors and students. A tool such as *GR* lets both FL teachers and students prepare reading lessons that learners will explore individually outside of the classroom. This frees up classroom time that can be spent more effectively getting students involved in discussions based on aspects of the text other than sentence structure, vocabulary, idiomatic expressions, and the like. After students have worked individually with the annotated text, they come to class prepared to comment on the content and meaning of what they have read because they have a solid understanding of the assigned text.

Hypermedia-annotated reading lessons provide immediate access to textual, sound, and visual annotations. Lessons that include appropriate reading and writing activities, along with supporting information, can teach readers to cope more effectively with the difficulties that they typically encounter when deciphering a text in a foreign language. In return, this may encourage inexperienced readers to move away from an exclusive bottom-up reading process and toward an interactive approach that combines "top-down processing (understanding of schema, propositions) and bottom-up processing (recognizing or understanding individual vocabulary words)" (Chun and Plass 1996:195).

Reading and understanding a foreign language text require not just the decoding of words one by one, but going beyond the word level to discover the connections that the writer establishes among those words to create larger units of meaning. Readers of a hypermedia-annotated text like *CAPC* will no longer look at the text linearly but globally. To better understand a word, a sentence, or a passage, readers are given the opportunity to interact with the text and to explore the supporting information on their own. Working with the target text and the textual annotations, students learn both *about* the language and *with* the language in a contextualized way, and they become actively involved in the reading process. An authoring system such as *GR* offers the advantage of acknowledging the individual needs of the readers as they interact with a particular text since the hidden annotations, available to those who wish to consult them, will not distract the advanced reader with information that is not necessary.

Immediate access to online information attached to a text seems to have a positive effect on the learner. When the reader encounters an unfamiliar word, getting the appropriate meaning immediately allows him or her to continue reading without the distraction that opening up a bilingual dictionary usually implies, especially when the correct translation or meaning is not found.

Beyond immediate textual support, another clear advantage of hypermedia technology is that it gives students access to images. Visual information, in the form of still images, QuickTimeVR, digital video, or laser videodisc, attached to a word, a sentence, or a page lets the reader check one against the other in order to confirm or reject hypotheses made about the meaning of a word or a passage.

Another benefit associated with the use of this type of technology in the area of language learning is "the ability to track learners' choices as they are engaged in reading for meaning" (Lyman-Hager et al. 1993:93). *GR* includes a tracking device that lets instructors know what information students request while reading the text. The program will "record the date and time the student enters the lessons, when they request a gloss and whether or not the word is indeed glossed . . . , any text fragment that they request annotations for, and which annotations they actually view. It will then log the time the student exits the lesson" (Herren 1996b:29). This capability of the program is, according to Garret, "the *sine qua non* of research-oriented didactic software" (cited in Lyman-Hager et al. 1993:93) since it allows us to gather data for research purposes.

Technology alone is not what makes a difference in the teaching of reading; the use of the technology coupled with sound pedagogical principles is also necessary. Technology is nothing but a tool in the hands of the teacher. In this regard, F. Borchardt (1991), in a CALICO banquet address, pointed out that "by itself technology is value-neutral. It depends entirely on those who use it" (20). We can rest assured that computers will never replace teachers, but we cannot ignore the power that technology has to enhance both our teaching and the learning process of students. Consequently, we can expect that those who understand and recognize this power and who know how to use the technologies available will eventually supplant those who do not.[35]

Reading in a foreign language is not an easy task, especially for beginning- and intermediate-level students. It seems, however, that the use of hypermedia technology can not only facilitate FL reading in a number of ways but may also inspire FL students to make the transition from learning to read to reading to learn. I do not claim that by using a hypermedia-annotated text reading will become easier automatically. The process of creating and discovering meaning in a foreign language text will still take time and effort on the part of the reader. I strongly believe, however, that the time that students invest in reading a hypermedia-annotated text, as I have described herein, will not be wasted time as is so often the case when learners try to get through a foreign language text by themselves with just the help of a bilingual dictionary.

NOTES

1. The following are available in Spanish: P. Casals, *Las Aventuras de Héctor: El misterio de los traficantes de arte; El enigma de las monedas de oro,* adapted by B. Christensen, Heinle and Heinle, 1993; I. Allende, *Diez cuentos de Eva Luna,* edited by K. M. Taggart and R. D. Woods, McGraw-Hill, 1995; Lee, Binkowski, and Van Patten, *Ideas: Estrategias, lecturas actividades y composiciones.* McGraw-Hill, 1994; M. Muñoz, *El ladrón de la mente,* McGraw-Hill, 1995.

2. Parts of this section are based on the article "Benefits of Keeping a Reading Journal in the Development of Second Language Reading Ability" pp. 65–79 in Robert Terry, ed., *The Future Is Now. Dimension: Language '95.* Valdosta, GA: Southern Conference on Language Teaching, 1995.

3. The following journal entries, as well as the ones included in notes 6 and 7, were originally published in the article mentioned in note 2. They are reproduced here with the permission of the Southern Conference on Language Teaching. These two entries serve to illustrate an excessive focus on words commonly found among foreign language readers:

   "I feel as though I should know the meaning for every word, which is almost impossible. For the first reading assignment, I felt as though I was looking up every word just to make sure I had the correct interpretation."

   "When I don't understand something I look up every word and try to piece it all together to make sense. I'm having problems with the vocabulary, some of the words I have never seen. This usually throws me off with the rest."

4. The original was written in Spanish: "¿Qué es la frase 'Pero el día de hoy la niña se había lucido'? ¿Es en inglés 'today the child shines'?

5. Pilot study conducted with second-semester Spanish students at George Mason University and the College of Charleston. The text on which the questions were based was: *"Rosario era viuda, su marido había muerto hacía tres años, y tenía un hijo de cinco años. Ella era abogada y le gustaba mucho su trabajo."* ("Rosario was a widow, her husband had died three years ago and she had a five-year-old son. She was a lawyer and she really liked her job.") The question was: "What was Rosario's job?" When required to answer in Spanish one subject said: *"era abogada"* ("she was a lawyer"). When the same subject responded to the same question in English, the answer was "she was a nurse." The results of this pilot study are published in Martínez and Godev (1994).

6. These two journal entries illustrate the positive self-reported effect that training students to make predictions about a particular reading has in reading comprehension.

   "I would definitely have to say that my predictions made the story easier to understand this time around. I only hope that my predictions stay on target, so that I can continue to understand the story."

   "I understand the reading a lot more because I knew what to expect. Knowing what to expect is also a factor in being able to read easier."

7. The following journal entry shows the self-reported positive effect in overall reading ability of teaching students to read globally without stopping every time they run into an unfamiliar word.

   "I am understanding the book a lot better lately. The past sections have been easier to read. I have found that I can read a whole paragraph or even a whole page without looking in my dictionary. This makes me feel very accomplished! *Until we were told to try and read the whole thing without looking up every word I was spending hours on one page.* [I see it is true] about not having to understand every single word to comprehend the basic context." (Emphasis added.)

8. The following are just a sample of some commonly used textbooks in first-year Spanish: Knorre, Dorwick, Glass, and Villareal, *Puntos de partida,* McGraw-Hill, 1993; Terrell, Andrade, Egasse, and Muñoz, *Dos mundos,* McGraw-Hill, 1990; Higgs, Liskin-Gasparro, and Medley, *Entradas,* Heinle and Heinle, 1993; Van Patten, Lee, Ballman, and Dvorak, *¿Sabías qué . . .?* McGraw-Hill, 1992.

9. It is interesting to note that while most FL university and college programs have third-year courses in conversation and composition, very few include in their curriculum a course in teaching reading at this level. At George Mason University there is now a 300-level course within the Spanish program (*Developing Reading Skills*) required for all majors and minors. It is also a prerequisite for all literature courses. For further information on this course, see note 23.

10. These two journal entries were written by students enrolled in Spanish 300 at George Mason University after completing the reading of *Como agua para chocolate.*

    "I can read now much better than when I started this class. Before I took Spanish 300, I couldn't read anything, except sentences in the books for class. Now, I can even read books outside of class. I read a novel for my self-selected reading, and I was very surprised that I could read it. This was very special for me. Before we read *Como agua para chocolate,* I couldn't believe I could read a whole book written in Spanish."

    "My ability to read has greatly improved. Before class, I could read a little but that was very difficult. Now, it is easier to read things. I don't need to look up each word. I can use the context to guess the meaning of a word. I never thought I could read a novel in Spanish. I am very impressed."

11. I have developed reading guides for Ben Christensen's *Las aventuras de Héctor: El misterio de los traficantes de arte* and for Laura Esquivel's *Como agua para chocolate,* and I have used them in a fourth-semester Spanish class and in a fifth-semester Spanish class respectively.

12. Students' unsolicited responses to these guides seem to indicate that they benefit from this kind of help. At different points in the reading, students have spontaneously provided us with testimonials on the effectiveness of these reading guides. These come from students enrolled in Spanish 300:

    "I had problems with some of the vocabulary. Also, though I hate doing the worksheets, they help a lot."

    "The movie helped me understanding the scene between Mamá Elena and the revolutionary soldiers, and the worksheet helped me with the flashbacks, to see when they begin and when they end."

13. The following are some of the authoring systems available for developing hypermedia annotations of texts: Herren, *Guided Reading;* O. Foelsche et al., *Annotext Authoring;* T. Thibeault, *Smarttext;* Lyman-Hager et al., *GALT;* and Nisus Software, *Nisus Writer* (special thanks to Joe Kissell from Nisus Software for his assistance in translating this file for publication).

14. In the summer of 1996 we started working on the hypermedia annotation of this text, thanks to George Mason University, which funded the first steps of the project with a research summer grant. Our special thanks go also to Middlebury College, and in particular to D. Herren, for providing the technical support without which this project would have never been developed.

15. xMediaEngine is the application that runs all of the following Herren's templates: *Guided Reading, CDictation, QTDictation, VideoDictation, Guided Listening & Viewing,* and *Photo CD Catalogue.* It is xMediaEngine that controls all of the media such as the videodisc player, the CD-ROM drive, images, digital video, and so on.

16. All the templates mentioned in note 15 can be downloaded from the following address: ftp://ftp.flannet.middlebury.edu/pub/ (note that once connected, one needs to switch to the ht directory). Since xMediaEngine is the application that runs behind all the templates, those who wish to download any of the templates must also download xMediaEngine.

17. VR stands for virtual reality. QuickTimeVR is a system for user-controlled viewing of panoramic images and for manipulation of objects in three dimensions.

18. The term *Wintel* refers to computers that use Intel Corporation central processing units and are designed to run one or more of the three versions of the Windows program from Microsoft.

19. Instructors interested in using these types of reading comprehension activities can complement a *GR* annotation with lessons developed with other authoring tools. The following programs are available for the Macintosh platform: O. Foelsche et al. *SuperMacLang;* R. Fischer, *Libra;* Pierian Spring Software, *Digital Chisel.* For the Windows and DOS platform the following can be mentioned: R. Kunst and S. Scoville, *WinCALIS;* Asymetrix, *Multimedia Toolbook;* U.S. Air Force Academy, *Language Tool.*

20. The *GR* template lets one attach the following types of annotations to a page: a pre-reading text ("text-one") of up to 12 pages, a post-reading text ("text-two") of up to 12 pages, still images, digital video, recorded digital sound, audio compact disc, and QuickTimeVR.

21. When groups of words are annotated manually, readers can ask the program to show these groups. Under the student menu, the reader will select "show groups." They will then appear underlined in the text. Students can turn off this option at any time.

22. One can attach to a sentence the same types of annotations that can be attached to a page.

23. As the first two icons of Figure 4.2 illustrate, the software provides the instructor with two sets of textual annotations: one and two. At the page level, these are called "pre-reading" for text one and "post-reading" for text two. At the sentence level, the first textual annotation attached to a sentence is called "text-one" and the second textual annotation, "text-two." In the sentence-level annotations of *CAPC* I have chosen to use "text-one" to provide the reader with information related to the meaning of the sentence and "text-two" for grammar and syntax explanations.

24. The original target audience of this hypermedia version of *CAPC* were fifth-semester students enrolled in Spanish 300 who had completed four semesters of the language or demonstrated, after taking a placement test, appropriate knowledge of the language

for this level. The objective of this course is to provide students with the opportunity to develop their reading ability in Spanish. This is a transition course within the curriculum that students take before entering introduction to literature courses, culture and civilization courses, and so forth. The expectation is that students who have never before read a complete text in a foreign language will leave the class with the sense that they are able to do so. Among the goals of this course is that students gain in reading fluency, and that they increase their confidence in their reading ability while reading a complete novel that is of interest to them.

25. The instructor can highlight a group of words and then choose "gloss the selection" from the instructor menu. The selected group of words is then added to the glossary field.

26. It is also possible to combine two or more sentences on one card by selecting "combine sentences" from the instructor *GR* menu. This lets you create annotations at the paragraph level, if appropriate.

27. The template developed with *ToolBook* (Asymetrix) at Penn State with which the text used in this experiment was annotated was originally called *ClearText*. The template has since gone through several revisions and it is now called *GALT* (Glossary Authentic Language Texts).

28. This is a Francophone African text by Ferdinand Oyono.

29. The original was written in Spanish: *"La historia no es linear y entonces necesitaba releer para entender las ideas importantes. También las oraciones incluyen frases como 'a que,' 'de que,' 'para que,' 'a que si' y estas frases son imposibles de entender."*

30. When students are, for instance, reading the first chapter of *CAPC,* they can highlight the opening sentence: *La cebolla tiene que estar finamente picada* ("Take care to chop the onion fine." *Like Water for Chocolate,* p. 3) and have access to the following information in a text-one window: *Esta es la primera frase en el texto relacionada con la receta de las tortas de navidad. Hemos reunido aquí todas la referencias a la receta que aparecen en el capítulo.* ("This is the first sentence in the text related to the Christmas Rolls recipe. We have gathered here all the references to the recipe that appear in this chapter.") The rest of the annotation includes a paragraph from page 7, and another paragraph from page 13 of *CAPC.*

31. *Teleras* are Mexican bread rolls used for stuffing; *atole* is a beverage made of flour and water; and *chiles serranos,* obviously a particular kind of chile peppers, with whose physical appearance not everyone is familiar.

32. The birth of the main character, Tita, at the beginning of the story is a good example of how the author makes use of hyperbole. In the pre-reading text, students are asked to reflect about the use of hyperbole and are instructed to watch the video clip before they read the text. They are also told to write in their reading notebook about it.

33. I want to express my gratitude to Clara Yu, Michael Geisler, and Douglas Cameron for sharing with me their experience with *GR.* I am aware that there are other projects being developed at other institutions in which students are involved in the process of annotating texts. The only reason that no more projects are mentioned here is because specific information for them has not been made available to me.

34. The one student who dissented from the rest also indicated that he or she had never used the program.

35. Or as Ray Clifford (cited in Borchardt 1991:24) said, "computers will not replace teachers, but teachers who use computers will replace teachers who don't."

REFERENCES

Allende, Isabel. 1995. *Diez cuentos de Eva Luna,* edited by Keneth M. Taggart and Richard D. Woods. San Francisco: McGraw-Hill.

Asymetrix Corporation. 1994. *Multimedia ToolBook.* Belleview, WA.

Barnett, Marva A. 1986. "Syntactic and Lexical/Semantic Skill in Foreign Language Reading: Importance and Interaction." *Modern Language Journal* 70:343–49.

———. 1988a. "Teaching Reading Strategies: How Methodology Affects Language Course Articulation." *Foreign Language Annals* 21:109–19.

———. 1988b. "Reading Through Context." *Modern Language Journal* 72:150–59.

———. 1989. *More than Meets the Eye. Foreign Language Reading: Theory and Practice.* Washington, DC: Center for Applied Linguistics.

Bernhardt, Elizabeth B. 1991. *Reading Development in a Second Language. Theoretical, Empirical and Classroom Perspective.* Norwood, NJ: Ablex Publishing Corporation.

Blake, Robert J. 1981. "Second Language Reading on the Computer." *ADFL Bulletin* 24: 17–22.

Borchardt, Frank. 1991. "Press Any Key to Continue: Technology and Fantasy for the Rest of the 90s." *CALICO* 8:17–24.

Borchardt, Frank, and Eleanor Johnson, eds. 1995. *CALICO Resource Guide for Computing and Language Learning.* Durham, NC: Computer Assisted Language Instruction Consortium.

Bransford, John D., Barry S. Stein, and Thomas Shelton. 1984. "Learning from the Perspectives of the Comprehender," pp. 28–44 in J. Charles Alderson and Ann H. Urquhart, eds., *Reading in a Foreign Language.* New York: Longman.

Cameron, Douglas. 1996. Personal communication.

Carrell, Patricia. 1984a. "The Effects of Rhetorical Organization on ESL Readers." *TESOL Quarterly* 18:441–69.

———. 1984b. "Evidence of a Formal Schema in Second Language Comprehension." *Language Learning* 34:87–112.

———. 1985. "Facilitating ESL Reading by Teaching Text Structure." *TESOL Quarterly* 19:727–52.

Casals, Pablo. 1993a. *Las Aventuras de Héctor: El misterio de los traficantes de arte,* adapted by Ben Christensen. Boston: Heinle and Heinle Publishers.

———. 1993b. *Las Aventuras de Héctor: El enigma de las monedas de oro,* adapted by Ben Christensen. Boston: Heinle and Heinle Publishers.

Chun, Dorothy M., and Jan L. Plass. 1996. "Effects of Multimedia Annotations on Vocabulary Acquisition." *Modern Language Journal* 80:183–98.

Clarke, Mark A. 1980. "The Short Circuit Hypothesis of ESL Reading or When Language Competence Interferes with Reading Performance." *Modern Language Journal* 64:203–09.

Cooper, Malcolm. 1984. "Linguistic Competence of Practiced and Unpracticed Non-Native Readers of English," pp. 122–35 in J. Charles Anderson and Ann H. Urquhart, eds., *Reading in a Foreign Language.* Essex, NY: Longman.

Davis, James. 1989. "Facilitating Effects of Marginal Glosses on Foreign Language Reading." *Modern Language Journal* 73:41–48.

———. 1992. "Reading Literature in the Foreign Language: The Comprehension/ Response Connection." *The French Review* 65:359–70.

Davis, James, Mary-Ann Lyman-Hager, and Susan B. Hayden. 1992. "Assessing User Needs in Early Stages of Program Development: The Case of Foreign Language Reading." *CALICO* 9:21–26.

Edelsky, Carol. 1986. *Writing in a Bilingual Program: Había una vez.* Norwood, NJ: Ablex.

Esquivel, Laura. 1989. *Como agua para chocolate.* New York: Doubleday.

——. 1992. *Like Water for Chocolate.* Translated by Carol Christensen and Thomas Christensen. New York: Doubleday.

Fischer, Robert, and Michael Farris. *Libra.* San Marcos, TX: Southwest Texas University.

Foelsche, Otmar et al. *Annotext.* Hanover, NH: Dartmouth College

Foelsche, Otmar, and Judith Frommer. *SuperMacLang.* Hanover, NH: Dartmouth College and Cambridge, MA: Harvard University.

Floyd, Pamela, and Patricia Carrell. 1987. "Effects of ESL Reading of Teaching Cultural Content Schemata." *Language Learning* 37:89–108.

Francescato, Martha P. 1994. Review of *Como agua para chocolate* by Laura Esquivel. In *Review: Latin American Literature and Arts* 48:102–4.

Geisler, Michael. 1996. Personal communication.

Goldman, Susan R., and Maria Reyes. 1983. "Use of Prior Knowledge in Understanding Fables in First and Second Languages." Paper presented at the Annual Meeting of the American Educational Research Association, Montreal. [EDRS: ED 233 571]

Herren, David. 1996a. *Guided Reading: A Hypermedia Shell.* Middlebury, VT: Green Mountain Mac.

——. 1996b. *Guided Reading Documentation.* Middlebury, VT: Middlebury College.

Higgs, Theodore, Judith Liskin-Gasparro, and Frank Medley. 1993. *Entradas.* 2nd ed. Boston: Heinle and Heinle Publishers.

Hudelson, Sarah. 1984. "Kan you ret and rayt en Inglés: Children Become Literate in English as a Second Language." *TESOL Quarterly* 18:221–38.

Hudson, Thomas. 1982. "The Effects of Induced Schemata on the Short Circuit in L2 Reading: Non-decoding Factors in L2 Reading Performance." *Language Learning* 32:1–31.

Johnson, Patricia. 1982. "Effects on Reading Comprehension of Building Background Knowledge." *TESOL Quarterly* 16:503–15.

Kern, Richard G. 1989. "Second Language Reading Strategy Instruction: Its Effects on Comprehension and Word Inference Ability." *Modern Language Journal* 73:135–49.

Knorre, Marty, Thalia Dorwick, William Glass, and Hildebrando Villareal. 1994. *Puntos de partida.* 4th ed. San Francisco: McGraw-Hill.

Knutson, Elizabeth. 1993. "Teaching Whole Texts: Literature and Foreign Language Reading Instruction." *The French Review* 67:12–26.

Kramsch, C. 1985. "Literary Texts in the Classroom." *Modern Language Journal* 69:356–66.

Krashen, Stephen. 1993. "The Case for Free Voluntary Reading." *The Canadian Modern Language Review* 50:71–82.

Kunst, Richard, and Satsuki Scoville. n. d. *WinCALIS.* Durham, NC: Duke University.

LaBerge, David, and S. Jay Samuels. 1974. "Towards a Theory of Automatic Information Processing in Reading." *Cognitive Psychology* 6:293–323.

Lee, James. 1986. "Background Knowledge and L2 Reading." *Modern Language Journal* 70:350–54.

Lee, James, Alex Binkowski, and Bill Van Patten. 1994. *Ideas: Estrategias, lecturas actividades y composiciones.* San Francisco: McGraw-Hill.

Lyman-Hager, Mary-Ann, James Davis, Joanne Burnett, and Ronald Chennault. 1993. *"Une Vie de Boy:* Interactive Reading in French," pp. 93–97 in Frank Borchardt and Eleanor Johnson, eds., *CALICO Proceedings.* Durham, NC: Computer Assisted Language Instruction Consortium.

Lyman-Hager, Mary-Ann, Marilynne Stout, and Morris Weinstock. 1995. *Glossing Authentic Language Texts.* State College, PA: Education Technology Services, The Pennsylvania State University.

Martínez, Elizabeth, and Concepción B. Godev. 1994. "Should Reading Comprehension Be Tested in the Target or in the Native Language? A Pilot Study." [EDRS: ED 390 288]

Martínez-Lage, Ana. 1995a. "Benefits of Keeping a Reading Journal in the Development of Second Language Reading Ability," pp. 65–79 in Robert Terry, ed., *The Future is Now. Dimension: Language '95.* Valdosta, GA: Southern Conference on Language Teaching.

———. 1995b. "Making Sustained Reading Available to L2 Readers: A Reading Guide for *Like Water for Chocolate.*" [Paper presented at the 29th Annual ACTFL Meeting. Anaheim, CA November 18–20.]

McLaughlin, Barry. 1987. *Theories of Second Language Learning.* London: Edward Arnold.

Munby, John. 1979. "Teaching Intensive Reading Skills," pp. 142–58 in Ronald Mackay, Bruce Barkman, and Ronald R. Jordan, eds., *Reading in a Second Language: Hypothesis, Organization and Practice.* Rowley, MA: Newbury House.

Muñoz, Elías Miguel. 1995. *El ladrón de la mente.* San Francisco: McGraw-Hill.

Nisus Software. 1995. *Nisus Writer 4.1.* Solana Beach, CA.

Nunan, David. 1988. *The Learner-Centred Curriculum.* Cambridge: Cambridge University Press.

Omaggio, Alice. 1979. "Pictures and Second Language Comprehension: Do They Help?" *Foreign Language Annals* 12:107–16.

Omaggio Hadley, Alice. 1993. *Teaching Language in Context.* 2nd ed. Boston: Heinle and Heinle Publishers.

Pierian Spring Software. 1995. *Digital Chisel.* Portland, OR.

Pilgreen, Janice, and Stephen Krashen. 1993. "Sustained Silent Reading with ESL High School Students: Impact on Reading Comprehension, Reading Frequency, and Reading Enjoyment." *School Library Media Quarterly* 22:21–23.

Schulz, Renata A. 1981. "Literature and Readability: Bridging the Gap in Foreign Language Reading." *Modern Language Journal* 65:43–53.

Shook, David J. 1996. "Foreign Language Literature and the Beginning Learner-Reader." *Foreign Language Annals* 29:201–16.

Swaffar, Janet. 1988. "Readers, Texts, and Second Languages: The Interactive Process." *Modern Language Journal* 72:123–49.

Swaffar, Janet, Katherine M. Arens, and Heidi Byrnes. 1991. *Reading for Meaning: An Integrated Approach to Language Learning.* Englewood Cliffs, NJ: Prentice-Hall.

Terrell, Tracy, Magdalena Andrade, Jean Egasse, and Elías Miguel Muñoz. 1990. *Dos mundos.* 2nd ed. San Francisco: McGraw-Hill.

Thibeault, Thomas. n. d. *Smarttext.* Carbondale, IL: Southern Illinois University.

U.S. Air Force Academy. n. d. *Language Tool.* Colorado Springs, CO.

Van Patten, Bill, James Lee, Terry Ballman, and Tricia Dvorak. 1992. *¿Sabías qué . . . ?* San Francisco: McGraw-Hill.

Zamel, Vivian. 1992. "Writing One's Way into Reading." *TESOL Quarterly* 26:463–85.

Appendix A. Sample of a Reading-Guide

These instructions were given to students before reading chapter 2 of *CAPC*. (This is a translated version of the original guide, which was written in Spanish.)

A. Before reading

 1. Read the title and scan the first part of the chapter. Remember the action is circumscribed by the recipes. Tita and Nacha are making all the arrangements for the wedding banquet. Nacha does it because it is her job, but what about Tita? (You will find the answer to this question in the third paragraph of page 25.)

 2. Remember what you read in chapter 1. Make your predictions and write in your journal what you think is going to happen in this chapter.

B. Reading the text (Before you read all the pages, follow the instructions below.)

 1. As you know, the action develops in between the segments of the recipe. The narrator first explains how to prepare the dough for the cake. At the end of page 23 and on page 24, she tells the reader about the procedures they used to get the eggs they needed.

 2. On page 24 when Tita is cracking the eggs, she remembers something: *Asociaba los blanquillos con los testículos de los pollos a los que había capado un mes antes.*

 3. On page 28 we see that Nacha and Tita are alone in the kitchen. Pay attention to what Nacha tells Tita. Following, there is an explanation of why Nacha and Rosaura never got along. Write in your journal the reason for this.

 4. Later, on page 30, we see an example of how the smell of food can affect us: *En cuanto Tita abrió el frasco, el olor de los chabacanos la hizo remitirse a . . . .* What does this smell make her think of?

 5. On page 31, the narrator tells us about the wedding night sheet: *Era una sábana de seda blanca.* The color of the sheet will have a special effect on Tita. What happens to her?

C. After reading: Read again the whole text and then answer these questions in your journal.

 1. Identify the parts in the text where Mamá Elena treats Tita cruelly.

 2. Explain the effect that cracking the eggs had on Tita.

3. Can you tell how long ago the incident with Pedro happened?

4. What aspect of the Revolution is mentioned in this episode? Can you explain why?

5. Identify the different ways in which the color white is mentioned in the text. Explain why this happens and comment on the effect that this had on you.

Appendix B. Instructions for the Readers of the *GR* Version of *CAPC*

(This is a translated version of the original instructions, which were written in Spanish.)

To the reader:

In order to facilitate the task of reading Esquivel's work, the novel has been annotated the following way:

1. Page-level annotations that will guide the reader through:

   a. A "pre-reading" text

   b. A "post-reading" text

   c. Visual annotations in the form of graphics, pictures, and video.

2. Sentence-level annotations (individual sentences and combined sentences) that will help the reader to interpret meaning as well as the syntactical relationships of the different elements in a sentence. Sentence-level annotations include

   a. Text-one: information related to meaning

   b. Text-two: information related to grammar and syntax

   c. Visual annotations in the form of graphics, pictures, and video.

3. Word-level glosses (individual words and groups of words). The glossary includes

   a. Word definitions and explanations

   b. Synonyms

   c. Cognates

   d. Direct translations.

Appendix C. Partial Text of a "Pre-reading" Window with General Background Information

(The text of this pre-reading is a translated version of the original, which was written in Spanish.)

Before you begin reading Esquivel's text, it is important that you read the information included below. This information will prepare you for the task of reading the novel. It will help you build the necessary background knowledge related to both the text and the context, which will facilitate your understanding of the story.

1. Location
2. Historical period
3. The narrator
4. Main and secondary characters
5. General text structure
6. General chapter structure

(The full "pre-reading" window—about 1500 words—includes an explanation for each one of the six areas listed here.)

Appendix D. Sample of a "Text-One" Annotation

(This is a translated version of the original text-one annotation, which was written in Spanish.)

The annotated sentence is: *Para que recuerdes que el flojo y el mezquino andan doble su camino (CAPC,* p. 11). ("And remember that the lazy man and the stingy man end up walking their road twice" *Like Water for Chocolate,* p. 11.)

"Text-one": Mamá Elena uses a popular saying so that Tita understands what she is trying to say. According to the saying, lazy people and mean people always have to do things twice. According to Mamá Elena, Tita is lazy because she did not baste the dress before sewing it.

Appendix E. Sample of a "Text-Two" Annotation

(This is a translated version of the original "text-two" annotation, which was written in Spanish.)

Annotated sentence: *Lo malo de llorar cuando uno pica cebolla no es el simple hecho de llorar, sino que a veces uno empieza, como quien dice, se pica y ya no puede parar* (*CAPC*, p. 3). ("The trouble with crying over an onion is that once the chopping gets you started and the tears begin to well up, the next thing you know you just can't stop" *Like Water for Chocolate,* p. 3.)

"Text-two" annotation:

1. *Lo malo:* neuter article + adjective. This construction means 'the bad things, the negative aspects.' Generally speaking, the combination of the neuter article *lo* followed by an adjective functions as a noun. Look at the following examples: *Lo bueno* (the good thing), *lo interesante* (the interesting thing), *lo divertido* (the fun thing).

2. Pay attention to the use of the following connectors:
   - *sino que:* 'but' after a negative statement. A clause introduced by *sino (que)* corrects the information included in another one. In other words, it is not one thing but another. *Sino (que)* requires that there be a previous negative sentence. In this case, the negative sentence is *no es el simple hecho de llorar.* Other conjunctions with similar value are *pero, sin embargo, no obstante.* These, however, do not require the presence of a previous negative statement.
   - *como:* 'like, as,' in this sentence it is a modal conjunction. This sentence *como quien dice* is an idiomatic expression, and in this context means 'for instance.' *Como* has also other meanings, so look up other "text-two" annotations when you encounter *como* in a sentence.

Appendix F: A "Pre-reading" Text That Alerts the Reader of the Beginning of a Flashback

(This is a translated version of the original "pre-reading" annotation, which was written in Spanish.)

"Pre-reading": Pay attention to *aquella noche de navidad, un año atrás.* Here begins a flashback in which Tita remembers the events that took place at that Christmas dinner several years ago. That night, Tita's eyes met Pedro's.

(This "pre-reading" corresponds to page 15 of *CAPC*.)

Appendix G: "Pre-reading" Information about the Location of *CAPC* and Journal Activity to Explore Visual Aid

(This is a translated version of the original "pre-reading" annotation, which was written in Spanish.)

Location: The action takes place in a ranch in Piedras Negras, a town located on the border with the U.S. Eagle Pass is the border town in the U.S. territory. Look at the map and locate Piedras Negras (see graphic, map taken from <http://www.lib.utexas.edu>).

Reading notebook: Think about the possible implications that this location will have in the development of the story. Write in your journal the information you can anticipate in relation to the role this particular geographical location may play in the novel.

The following is a translated version of an actual journal response from a student, originally written in Spanish:

"The story takes place in a town that is located in the border with the U.S., and because of this we may see some war conflicts in the town of Piedras Negras, because this story takes place during the time of the Mexican Revolution."

Appendix H: "Pre-reading" Text and Journal Activity to Compare the Novel and the Movie Included in a "Post-reading" Text

(This is a translated version of the original "pre- and post-reading" annotations, which were written in Spanish.)

"Pre-reading" text: Look at the videodisc annotation. Keep in mind that the movie may not always follow the book and that there are some differences between the two media. First, watch the video, and then read this page. Remember that what you are going to see is at times different from what you will read.

"Post-reading text": Reading notebook. As I indicated in the "pre-reading" text, this is a good example that shows the differences that exist between the book and its adaptation to the screen. Now that you have read this page, answer the following questions in your reading journal:

1. What differences have you found between the movie and the book?

2. Why do you think these differences exist?

3. In what respects is the reader of a book different from the viewer of a movie?

(These "pre- and post-reading" texts correspond to page 6 of *CAPC*.)

Appendix I. Sample of a Reading Journal Used as a Pre-reading Activity

(This is a translated version of the original "pre-reading" annotation, which was written in Spanish.)

"Pre-reading": At the beginning of this chapter, the narrator, as you can see in the movie clip (see videodisc annotation), is reading a cookbook and is making comments as she reads the recipe. Later on in the book you will find information about the origin of this book and about how the narrator found it.

Reading journal: Anticipation of content. Before you read this chapter, think about the following and write the answers in your journal.

1. What comes to your mind when you think about chopping onions?
2. What is or has been the role of the kitchen in your life and that of your family?
3. How do you imagine daily life in a late 1900 Mexican ranch?
4. What does the adjective "authoritative" mean to you?

The following are translated versions of actual students' journal responses for the questions above. They were originally written in Spanish:

"When I think about chopping onions, I immediately think about crying. I have chopped onions, and I am very sensitive so I start crying immediately."

"The kitchen has played a relevant role in my life. At home, we cook Mexican food everyday. Part of the smell at home is the aroma from the dishes being cooked anytime of the day, and my house always smells good."

"I think about the house chores that the members of the family have to share. I also think about the parents' authority."

"The adjective authoritative refers to a person, generally a mother or father, to whom the children have to obey. Their authority cannot be questioned."

5

Computer-Mediated Communication (CMC): *Technology for Improving Speaking and Writing*

Margaret Healy Beauvois
University of Tennessee — Knoxville

Introduction

Recent studies on the benefits of computer-assisted writing (Pennington 1996a, 1996b; Selfe and Hilligoss 1994) have provided important insights into the role of computers in language learning. If it is true that "we can't tell people how to write . . . we can only put student writers into writing situations" (Kemp 1993), then the computer seems to provide an excellent opportunity to do just that. Equipped with a screen, a keyboard, and word processing software, students find themselves in a relatively stress-free writing situation in which correction and revision are made easy, and one that seems to encourage the flow of their thoughts (Carter 1989; Daiute 1986; Pennington 1996a; Faigley 1990, 1992; Hawisher and Selfe 1989; Kinneavy 1991; Slatin 1991; Vaché 1994).

In the areas of English as a second language (ESL) and foreign language writing, research, while less extensive, also supports the premise that computers facilitate the writing process. The title of Martha Pennington's forthcoming book, *The Computer and the Non-Native Writer: A Natural Partnership* (1996a), contends that writers and computers have a natural connection. This connection creates an atmosphere in which students seem to have less anxiety about writing and tend to write more fully because of the ease of revision

Margaret Healy Beauvois, Ph.D. in Foreign Language Education from the University of Texas, is Assistant Professor of French and Coordinator/Supervisor of First- and Second-Year Instruction in the Department of Romance and Asian Languages at the University of Tennessee-Knoxville. She is Chair of a campus-wide initiative to incorporate the use of computer networking into the curriculum across disciplines. Her area of research is computer-assisted communication and writing on a LAN.

and correction. Some data suggest that students express themselves more openly and perhaps better online in some instances than in the more traditional pen-and-paper mode (Lam and Pennington 1995; Pennington 1996b; Selfe and Hilligoss 1994).

The networked computer lab, because it goes a step further than the one student/one computer situation, offers new options in classroom instruction. The tremendous resources available on the Internet have transformed the way we look at information gathering in general and have enhanced our instructional possibilities. Within the broad context of networking, there are many avenues open to both learner and instructor.

One aspect of computer-mediated communication (CMC) that has stimulated some recent research is synchronous student-student-teacher interaction on a local area network (LAN)—communication that occurs in real time as opposed to asynchronous discourse in which there is a time lapse, e.g., E-mail. In synchronous LAN communication, individuals write messages to one another in the here and now within the time limits of a class period rather than by means of an online "phone" connection or asynchronous E-mail communication. Instead of a "worldwide" connection, students and teachers remain in the classroom, linked by a LAN, exchanging ideas with each other simultaneously in real time.

The result of this intense and heretofore unexplored communication option results in something more extensive than the "natural connection" mentioned by Martha Pennington. What happens in the shared writing environment in addition to the above mentioned advantages is the formation of a special linguistic community that is essentially different from the traditional classroom setting. I am referring to a new manifestation of the process of "scaffolding" and Vygotsky's theory of "ZPD" or the Zone of Proximal Development (Vygotsky 1978), which emphasize that development is based on the building of support systems for learning. In this networked computer environment, the scaffolding is the interaction on the LAN that forms the basis for real-time communication—electronic discussion—that supports the learners as they collaboratively construct knowledge. When teachers and classmates discuss ideas in what has been called a "conversation in slow motion," the process of production changes and allows for more time to think and compose. Because the thoughts of the other participants online become visible, it is possible for students to become guides for one another in this decentralized lab-classroom. What we see in the LAN community, which will be described more fully below, is an interactive situation that in social constructivist terms, occasions the creation of needed social structures that are so crucial to language learners as they progress along the continuum of interlanguage, somewhere between expression in the native language and competence in the target language, and as they struggle to overcome the affective, psychological, and linguistic difficulties of second-language acquisition.

Background on the Development of Electronic Networks for Interaction

The use of a local area network (LAN) in native-speaker English instruction began in the mid-1980s in the English department at Gallaudet University (Washington, DC) under the direction of Professor Trent Batson. Batson developed the idea of electronic networks for interaction (ENFIs) to provide the means by which deaf students might communicate with one another in English (instead of in American Sign Language) with the ultimate goal of developing their writing skills. By putting students on a LAN and having them converse with one another electronically, he hoped to improve their English expression and eventually their composition work in English. The Gallaudet experiment was very successful (Batson 1988; Day and Batson 1995). Batson found that not only the students' writing improved but also their confidence in class and their general ability to express themselves.

The concept of using ENFIs in English composition classes led to the eventual development of an academically oriented software package, the Daedalus package mentioned above, by a group of graduate students and faculty in the English department at the University of Texas at Austin (Butler 1992; Bump 1990; Faigley 1990; Kemp 1993; Peterson 1989). Today at UT-Austin over 30 percent of all English courses are taught in a LAN environment, from freshman composition to graduate-level courses.

Use of Synchronous CMC in ESL and Foreign Language Learning

Since the late 1980s, interest in implementing real-time CMC on a LAN in second-language learning has grown, especially in French, Portuguese, and ESL. Several research projects have demonstrated its effectiveness as a means to increase student communication in the target language (Kelm 1992; Beauvois 1992a, 1994, 1996b; Kern 1995). The process can be described as effectively bridging the gap between written and oral expression for the linguistically limited student whose oral skills are not adequate to allow for full expression of ideas in the target language. By slowing down the process of communication and allowing the students to reflect and compose a message (similar to an "utterance"), electronic interaction in the classroom encourages student use of the target language.

In the InterChange module (the computer conferencing component) of the Daedalus software, students log on to a LAN with their classmates, and instead of responding to the teacher's oral questions, they read the teacher's posted questions based on a text that has been assigned for that day's class work. They then respond by sending written messages to the teacher and to one another. The ensuing electronic discussion creates a radically different classroom interaction (Bump 1990), one that is lively, conversational, student-driven, and inclusive of all members of the class (Beauvois 1992b) in a way not possible in face-to-face discussion.

This type of interaction represents a decided departure from that of the traditional classroom because there is no turn-taking on a LAN, and all members of the session can participate at will. Teacher intervention is minimized. For better or worse, students are largely in control of the flow of the discussion. The reticent and fearful seem less inhibited in their communication because they do not feel "put on the spot," as students often state in their evaluations of the process (Beauvois 1994). The InterChange module also automatically saves a written record of the in-class discussion, which can be reread and studied at a later time. Both a chronological form and a sorted-by-sender form of each participant's individual contributions are saved and can form the bases for oral interaction at a future meeting of the class.

The hybrid nature of this exercise, which is neither traditional writing nor traditional conversation, becomes a means of communication that is completely new. Unlike asynchronous E-mail, this process involves writing and reading messages from classmates and instructor in real time. The slow-motion conversation is made possible by combining the LAN, the facilitating software, a text (literary, authentic document, or video), and a minimum of five to ten students. The instructor need not participate in the ongoing discussion (Kern 1995), but he or she usually chooses the text and provides the initial discussion questions.

As students compose and "send" their responses, an evolving exchange of ideas is created online by the participants and is limited only by the imagination of the group. Code switching (use of English) is rare in this setting (Beauvois 1992a, 1994; Kelm 1992). Students tend to express themselves in the target language at their own pace and with less anxiety than seems inherent in oral classroom discussion. In fact, instead of the silent masses that one frequently observes in university language classrooms, in LAN sessions all members of a class are busily deciphering and responding to an incredible variety of messages scrolling by on the computer monitors in front of them. Bursts of laughter occasionally interrupt the sound of steadily clicking keys as the students come across a humorous message. The mood is intense—eyes focused on the great amount of information appearing on the screen as students try to read, make sense of, think about, and then compose a response to the ongoing discussion of the text being studied.

The Daedalus software provides the means to control this seemingly chaotic expression of ideas in large classes by providing two kinds of "conferences": a main whole-class conference and smaller conferences composed of fewer students, usually five to eight participants. These small groups function independently from the main conference, and the messages sent can be seen only by those who have joined the small group. The instructor may direct each group of students to discuss a certain aspect of a text being studied for a limited period of time, perhaps 20 to 25 minutes.

At the end of that time, students terminate their individual conferences and return to the whole-class conference with the results of their more intense discussion of the topic. Having fewer participants in the smaller conferences allows students to explore a subject more deeply, perhaps, than in the main or larger conference in which there may be as many as twenty-five participants. By returning to the main conference for the final 20 minutes of the class period, all the students can benefit from the reports of the small groups' in-depth discussions of the topic.

At the end of a LAN session, the participants leave the class with either a downloaded or hard copy of the discussion, which can serve as the basis for the follow-up oral discussion by the class of the ideas generated online. The initial brainstorming phase, done on the LAN, has allowed students (with or without the input of the teacher) to thrash out their interpretation of a text. The oral phase can complete the process by putting the instructor in a position to clarify the students' grasp or lack of comprehension of the given text during a subsequent meeting of the class.

The LAN process allows for immediate clarification of the ideas presented in the text. Student misconceptions can be corrected in a way that is often not feasible in traditional class discussion. Instructors are sometimes unaware of confusion arising from a text in a second language, and students tend not to ask questions for fear of appearing stupid in front of their classmates (Beauvois 1992a, 1993). *Written* debate about text content, however, gives the instructor a concrete view of the comprehension of the topic. The instructor can then comment on what is accurate or inaccurate in the students' perceptions.

What is the instructor's role in this unconventional environment, since, as mentioned above, the LAN process tends to be student-driven and student-centered? The instructor's input is but another line on the computer monitor. His or her ability to control the flow of the discussion during the class period is minimal. He or she has the advantage, if desired, of posing the initial questions and requiring some student response, thus setting the tone of the discussion. However, the instructor may find that students do not always answer all questions asked in the course of the lab session.

A student interviewed on the subject of the instructor's importance in this type of online, real-time discussion reported that he answered the professor's posted questions during the session ". . . if I found them particularly interesting," but he added, "however, I tend to pay more attention to what my classmates are saying in general" (Beauvois 1992a).

In a few words, a LAN discussion is the students' "day in court." This process gives them the opportunity to "talk" to one another in the target language, which they seem to feel compelled to use (Beauvois 1994). The instructor becomes the facilitator, a guide whose role in such a session is to plan the type of questions that will stimulate a thorough exploration of the text at hand. That role will also open up other possible interpretations of the text.

In a more conventional classroom setting, when the instructor looks out at the faces in the class and tries to determine if a text has been absorbed or even understood, he or she can only guess at student awareness and comprehension. The finest lecturers in the world know only what they have tried to communicate to students, not what the students have actually understood.

One of the advantages of CMC is the possibility of reviewing the student's input with an eye to follow-up comment and correction. LAN discussion requires teachers to look at the learning process in a different light, that is, as learning in progress. Students in turn become responsible for their own learning in that the burden of delving into the text, negotiating for meaning, and coming to consensus lies with them in this initial phase of study.

Synchronous, real-time, electronic brainstorming can make classroom follow-up discussions more succinct, more tailored to the students' needs in regard to comprehension of the text (Gallupe, Bastianutti, and Cooper 1991). The LAN exercise allows increased student manipulation of a text and enhances the possibilities of teacher explanatory input. It stands to reason that giving students more opportunities to extract meaning from a text allows for creation of knowledge about that text. The interactive LAN environment, in which the participants are free to explore ideas and express themselves in the target language, provides an original opportunity for learning that may be less inhibiting than the traditional classroom setting. In the light of these data, two interesting questions emerge:

1. If writing more, and more frequently, leads to better writing in a second language (Pennington 1996a), does increased written communication on a LAN also lead to better overall student acquisition of a second language?

2. More specifically, since communication is critical in language learning (to say nothing of all other aspects of life), does synchronous, real-time, classroom CMC result in better **spoken** language—the main goal of today's language class?

Does Synchronous CMC Produce Better Language Acquisition? A Look at the "Natural Writing" Model

Martha Pennington (1996a) poses a thought-provoking model of the four stages associated with writing on computer. This model is directly applicable to the hybrid written/conversational communication process experienced in real time on a LAN. Using her description of computer writing as a means of examining the effects of real-time synchronous classroom communication on computers may help to clarify what the research in this innovative application of CMC is beginning to show. The following discussion will focus on the natural effects and the transformative effects of communicating on a LAN.

The Development of a Natural Communication Process on a LAN

In ESL and foreign language classrooms, students report that communication in the lab setting is easier than oral communication in the classroom, even for those without strong keyboarding skills (Beauvois 1996a; Beauvois and Eledge 1996; Cononelos and Oliva 1993; Kelm 1992; Kern 1995). The consequence of delaying output and allowing students the time necessary to respond to a question—time that is not possible in oral interaction—seems to have a very positive effect on student attitudes and performance. Students claim to be freer in their comments (sometimes too free, as "flaming," i.e., using inappropriate language, will attest to) and more willing to participate in class discussions (Beauvois 1993). Classroom performance anxiety seems to be endemic to second-language learning (Phillips 1991;Young 1992). LAN communication provides an anonymous, less pressured environment that tends to lower the affective filter, according to student exit interviews from two previous studies, statements echoed by most student evaluations of the process. (Beauvois 1992a, 1994):

> "In class, when the teacher asks a question and looks at you, and there is this big silence, and everyone is waiting, and you're sitting there . . . and finally,

you say something, anything! And then everyone gives this sigh of relief. But in the lab, you can take your time, write your answer, or whatever you want to say, and it doesn't get sent until you are ready to send it. And nobody is waiting and wishing you'd hurry up!"

"I never feel 'on the spot' in the lab like I do in class."

In a typical class period of 50 minutes, students will post from two hundred to three hundred messages to the ongoing "discussion." These messages often consist of several sentences. The rapidity of student-student-teacher interactions and the relative ease with which they are conducted contribute to the feeling of hybrid communication—somewhere between writing and speaking.

Increased Student Production in the Target Language

All previous studies on synchronous CMC in second-language classrooms attest to the fact that students participate more in the LAN environment than in the traditional setting. These studies show 100 percent participation in most cases (Beauvois 1992a, 1992b; Beauvois and Eledge 1996; Conolos and Oliva 1994; Kern 1995).

In his 1993 study, Kern (1995) found that students in a second-semester first-year French course produced "two to four times more sentences during the InterChange module sessions than they did T-units [turns of one complete sentence] during the oral discussions." Comparing student output in both LAN and oral environments, Kern found as well that there was a "dramatically higher level of direct student-to-student interaction in the InterChange discussion." Overall, his findings confirm previous studies attesting to the empowerment of students in the LAN environment (Beauvois 1992b, 1993, 1994) by providing them with more opportunities to express themselves in the target language in a relatively anxiety-free environment.

Communicating Differently

In synchronous CMC, there are many levels at which students communicate differently. This section will focus on the quantity and quality of individual student-student-teacher communication and the resulting spirit of classroom community.

As mentioned above, the instructor's role changes dramatically in this electronic environment. It is also true that the content of the discussion tends to be different because of student involvement and the lack of instructor control. From the following example taken from an ESL second-year literature class, the flow and movement of the discussion initiated by the instructor evolves as students clarify vocabulary and express their ideas. The instructor's presence is felt only minimally as the students carry the intellectual responsibility for the evolution of the discussion. In the following example, the reader should note that after posting the first question, the instructor does not intervene again until several students have already posted both questions and responses to one another. The following transcript entries are not edited for typos or misspellings and do reflect the varying linguistic skill levels of students. Although the students' errors may seem striking because written, they are not more numerous than mistakes in students' spoken target language. One might fear that students could see and remember these errors, but studies to date have not shown this to be true. In general the teacher does not interrupt the students' interactions during the normal course of such a discussion to correct errors, but he or she might rephrase the sentence to provide a more indirect correction. More extensive error correction is usually deferred to a follow-up session of the class in which the teacher may decide to focus on certain mistakes or patterns of error in the transcripts. At this later date he or she can comment on certain inaccuracies in form and vocabulary usage.

In this excerpt from a longer text, one can get a sense of the interactivity of LAN communication. Student names have been replaced by numbers.

InterChange Session on Eliot's "The Hollow Men"

Instructor: Below you will find some questions to consider about the poem for today. HOWEVER, if you have specific questions about vocabulary or basic comprehension of the text, you may begin by asking those questions.

Student #1: Does hollow mean empty?

Student #2: could you give me an explanation about the meaning of the different kingdoms ?

Student #3: Hollow means empty?

Student #4: Who does the poem talks about? I mean who are "we"? The reader and the poet?

Student #5 to students #1 and 3: yes hollow means empty.

Student #6: Why did he use several sections in the poem. What was his aim in doing so ?

Student #7: There is only a comparison between Life and Death?

Student #6: what are the meaning of the use of biblical references at the beginning first and after along in the text.???

Student #8 to Student #6: I think that in the first section the poet is talking about civilization. Does somebody has understood something else?

Student #9: Maybe he sees death as empty, without hope of an after life which makes it even more cruel.

Student # 10 to Student #4: "We" seems to represent the poet and all the members of his "family". I mean men like him.

Instructor to Student #2: Could the different kingdoms be those on earth and those in the after-life?

Instructor to Student #4: Perhaps he uses "we" in a general sense to represent all of humanity. What do you think?

Student # 2: for him there are several kingdom the one which are unreachable and the one are visible of human beings. Am i wrong?

Student #11: This doesn't sound very happy. I think Eliot was a christian, but in this poem he expresses in a way a very pessimistic point of view upon death and "after life". It is funny how many christians fear death. . .

Student #4: So if he uses "we" in a general sense it means that the whole humanity is empty; does that mean that man is nothing in the universe?

Student #1: Eliot thinks that the notion of conception is not done in relation with the emotions

Instructor to Student #1: what in the text leads you to think this about conception and emotion?

Student #1: in line 84 . . . .

Student #5 to Student #1: what do you mean by the notion of conception?

Instructor to Student #2: About the different kingdoms: Do you see a strange perspective in the sense that the poet can speak from the perspective of those in "death's dream kingdom"? If so, what can we infer from this perspective?

The discourse just cited represents thoughtful questions and comments on the text. It would be a rare occurrence in traditional foreign language courses for students to begin a discussion in the target language by asking and answering each others' questions over a text—except perhaps at the seminar level with a select group of upper-division or graduate students. In the vast majority of undergraduate courses, the instructor initiates all facets of instruction/discussion, and this is as it should be for a majority of classroom time. Complete student autonomy is not always desirable or effective in the learning of a second language.

By means of LAN technology, however, the instructor now has the additional option of encouraging student-student participation in a "natural" environment, one in which students control the flow of the discussion. In this way they can communicate with one another in the target language and practice the material presented in class in an autonomous manner. By means of their own electronic "polylogue," students progress in their acquisition of the language specifically through the following three-point process:

1. They define their own thoughts on the material being studied.
2. They test those theories, opinions, ideas on their peers and instructor by asking questions, responding to messages, or simply expressing an idea, waiting to see what the response of the group will be—risks they are not usually willing to make in a conventional conversational setting in a language classroom.
3. They construct knowledge through this process and learn.

What do students learn? The answer to this question lies to some extent in future carefully controlled studies designed to measure student progress, achievement, and long-term retention of material both quantitatively and qualitatively. However, a certain perception of achievement comes from observation of students' progress over the semester. Certainly the fact that students use only the target language (Beauvois 1992a; Kelm 1992; Kern 1995) in these discussions leads to the development of some linguistic skills.

A carryover from written to oral expression has been established in at least one study (Beauvois 1996b), which will be discussed later in this chapter. In addition, the fact that as students read the evolving conversation and participate in it, they are perceiving, judging, thinking critically, and refining their own knowledge of the subject. To carry on a discussion of a literary nature, they must use higher-order thinking skills. In poststudy evaluations of the process, student self-reports suggest a strong perception of linguistic improvement as a result of the intense practice of reading and writing in the target language (Beauvois 1994, 1996a). If the topic of discussion is based on a difficult text, the students have ample opportunity to explore the text in a "safe" environment with their peers in the target language. They then receive feedback from the instructor on their grasp of it.

Community Building

In a lower-division university language class, there can be as many as twenty-five to thirty students or more per section. Students frequently do not know many of their classmates. Generally, the "stars" of the class are quickly determined as well as those students who are not linguistically capable. (Students always seem aware of who is strong in the class and who is not.) But even when the teacher favors a small-group approach to diffuse competition and to allow for more student interaction, students tend to become familiar with only the four to six members of their group and not with the rest of the class. Typically, if the instructor asks a student to return papers to his or her classmates, the student will not know more than a handful of their names.

The difference in the LAN setting is that the student's name is posted with each message sent. The other students see the names on their screens and fit the names to the messages and information contained therein. The names then are associated with the faces when the class has its follow-up oral discussion. In some instances, during an animated discussion in the lab, a student, uncomfortable with the anonymity, will stand up in the middle of a lab session and ask out loud "Who is Jim?" or "Who is Sarah?" For some reason, the motivation to know who this person is and not just his or her name seems to be part of this type of communication. Students often comment in exit interviews that they get to know their classmates and their instructor better in the lab setting than in the classroom (Beauvois 1994). Perhaps an explanation for this phenomenon in CMC is the compelling force of the printed word. Students seem eager to match log-in names with faces and ideas.

The feeling of community developed in synchronous CMC classrooms is due in part to the fact that students do know each others' names. In addition to experiencing that personal component, they have also collaborated in a discussion that is of their own creation. They have expressed their opinions, thoughts, questions, and feelings on a given subject in response to one another, often with little teacher intervention. They have sometimes asked personal questions of each other that they might not have asked in oral classroom interaction. The sense of trust developed during these exchanges imparts a new dimension to student communication that is open and honest. Smith (1988) writes about the feeling of belonging that comes from establishing oneself as a member of a community. Bruffee described this process from a "social constructivist position which . . . assumes that entities we normally call reality, knowledge, thought, facts, texts, selves . . . are constructs generated by communities of like-minded peers. Social construction understands reality (and) knowledge . . . as community-generated and community maintained linguistic entities . . ." (Bruffee 1986:774, as cited in Butler 1992). In this electronic environment in which their thinking becomes visible, students to a great extent create their own learning environment. They become members of a community of speakers of a second language, a phenomenon of which they are aware as evidenced in their evaluations of the LAN experience (Beauvois 1994).

Examples of this type of community building are numerous, and the following examples are but two from an intermediate French course. In a second-year French course in which the family was discussed in both the lab and in the classroom, the difference in content was startling. In the traditional setting, students were reluctant to go beyond the most rudimentary description of their families. They talked in numbers—"I have three cousins on my mother's side" and "I have one dog, two brothers, three grandparents"—and in minimal descriptions, limited perhaps by their textbook vocabulary. On the LAN, the students discussed everything from divorce to sibling rivalry to growing up in an immigrant family to abortion (Beauvois 1996a). They seemed more willing to risk making mistakes and trying complex constructions than in the oral exercise on the same topic. What began as an teacher-instigated exercise based on recently studied vocabulary evolved into a very personal discussion about their lives. The students in the LAN class continued their discussion as they left the lab.

As an extension of the earlier discussion, the conversation took another turn, to family values and, eventually, to personal values. A question regarding youthful drinking and smoking elicited enough responses to constitute a "hot message" (Faigley 1992), i.e., one that engenders much response from the participants. The following excerpt gives an idea of the straightforward exchanges in which some students took a rather strong stand on issues such as drinking and smoking. It all began with a message from a male student, JF:

> **J.F.:** Est-ce que la biere est si mal? On doit boire avec l'idee de moderation. Fini.
>
> *[**J.F.:** Is beer so bad? One has to drink with the idea of moderation. That's all.]*

To which a female student replied:

> **L.R.:** J., mais les alcooliques boivent la bierre avec l'idee de moderation? Et j'aime ma cerveau, et toi?
>
> *[**L.R.:** J., but do alcoholics drink beer with the idea of moderation? And I love my brain, and you?]*

He responded rather defensively:

> **J.F.:** L. R., si vous aime votre cerveau, puis vous ne buvez pas! Je n'ai pas parle que on doit boire pour amusement.
>
> *[**J.F.:** L. R., if you love your brain, then you don't drink! I did not speak [say] that one must drink for amusement.]*

Followed by this comment from another male student:

> **L.V.:** K-J., Fumer et boire trop ce n'est pas une activite mur. c'est le cause de mauvaise sante!
>
> *[**L.V.:** K-J., To smoke or to drink too much this is not a mature activity. It's the cause of bad health!]*

Under this rubric of "communicating differently," the variance lies in the honest expression of feelings that the electronic medium seems to encourage. In most non-LAN classroom discussion, the normal reticence of students to single themselves out would be powerful. Having strong convictions or being in disagreement with one's peers on certain subjects (e.g., drinking on campus) would definitely inhibit an exchange like the one above, especially in a second language. The fact that students are more candid in their comments in these online discussions than in most classroom exchanges has not gone unnoticed (Peterson 1989; Beauvois 1992a; Bump 1990; Kelm 1992).

Collaborative Responses

In classes such as an ESL literature course at l'Université Paul Valéry in France, where there are a limited number of computers, students must come to consensus before sending a message. They then must identify themselves as one of the two members of a pair. In the class from which the following excerpt was taken, the students were working two or three to a computer. The text in question was Bernard Malamud's *The Magic Barrel.* This kind of immediate reporting after collaboration differs from pair or small-group work in the traditional classroom in that the process is much more interactive than would be possible in more typical group work in which only one group could speak at a given time. In the case of reporting online, the whole class can benefit from the immediate input and can refer to the recorded information at a later time.

The following collaborative responses in this short passage from the transcript appeared in the first three minutes of the discussion. Only the students' names have been changed. Once again, the transcript is unedited and reflects student errors.

Instructor: What do you think is Salzman's reward for being a matchmaker?

Pair #1 (Sylvie et Paul): We say: Using a matchmaker can be either positive or negative; in Finkle's case I'd rather consider it is a suitable way of finding a potential girlfriend.

Pair #2 (Christian et Michel): Salzman does not inspire any confidence as he does not listen to the wish of his clients; His behavior clearly shows that he does not care to know whether the couples he forms will be appropriate or not, he only wants to abuse people's credibility and loneliness to make profit

Pair #3 (Véronique et Vivienne): Is using a matchmaker a suitable way of finding a potential partner?

Pair #4 (Pierre et Marc): We don't think that using a matchmaker is the best way of finding a potential partner because you just wait your matchmaker to 'bring' you a suitable person so it's a passive behavior, whereas looking for by yourself implies that you make the effort and that you really care about the girl you find : you don't choose a girl as you choose any object in a catalogue. . .

Pair # 5 (Marie-Claire et Guy): According to us, Salzman is not a bad character, he only wants to please and to satisfy Finkle; We think he is a bit pitiable above all when we enter his house: it's a real ramshackle house ,and ,if we consider his wife more carefully, we realize that he may not be happy in life : in fact, he wants to do other people's bliss.

Three person team (Anne, Stéphanie, et Stéphane): Salzman's behavior inspires as much confidence as an immoral "business man." He only meets people for professional relationship, though people cannot join him. He pulls the strings.

The above examples help illustrate the different dynamic that one can expect in this new environment—students sharing with each other and with the rest of the class. It is up to the instructor to exploit the enhanced communicative opportunity and effectively use the LAN process as a step toward building oral communication skills. In the next section, we will consider the question of improved communication through LAN discourse.

Communicating Better

Does the idea of communicating differently necessarily lead us to the same conclusion as Stage 4 of Pennington's model, "Better Communication"? As in any study of innovative techniques of teaching and learning, one must tread cautiously before claiming that one method, approach, or exercise is better than another. We have examined the improvement in the quantity and, to some extent, the quality of honest discourse in CMC. We also looked at the social benefits of a LAN community. These findings tend to support the idea that students communicate with more awareness of their environment, with less anxiety, and with more depth in electronic media. "Conversation in slow motion" (Beauvois 1992b) allows the time to think and respond more fully to questions and comments on a text being studied. The freedom afforded to the students in this decentralized environment contributes to independence and responsibility in learning.

Initial studies of students using asynchronous CMC, such as E-mail (Underwood 1987; Warschauer 1995; Walthers 1994), have also demonstrated a definite motivational advantage. Students are willing and even eager to get online with native or nonnative speakers to communicate informally in the target language (Underwood 1987; Kelm 1992). Instructors experienced in the regular use of LAN communication would say that students do communicate better as a general rule in the computer lab, if *better* means using longer, more complete utterances, expressing less superficial ideas, and communicating generally more openly about any given subject. The product, in terms of length and breadth of T-units, of LAN communication at the first- and second-year levels has been shown to be definitely better. More research in this area will provide additional information as to how this initial phase of learning might affect the long-term retention of information.

Affective measures in both synchronous and asynchronous electronic communication have shown positive student and teacher response in this area of CMC (Beauvois 1994; Bump 1990; Kern 1995). There are also some indications from recent research that seem to support LAN discourse as more beneficial in preparing students for conversational exchange in the target language than in regular classroom interaction. The findings of a 1995 pilot study on the transfer of skills from writing to oral performance are of interest and are examined below.

In the spring of 1995, at the University of Tennessee, Knoxville, a study of fourth-semester French students taking a final required course, French 212, was conducted. Students were randomly assigned to four sections of the course in which six weeks of the semester were spent studying five lessons of *French in Action* and six weeks reading short stories from the reader *Les Aventures du Petit Nicolas*. There were two teachers, each having one LAN section and one traditional section. All sections followed the same curriculum.

The syllabus of French 212 requires three oral exams covering the material studied in the course. For these oral exams, students meet with their instructors, one on one, to answer questions related to the material as well as to their own lives. In this semester, the exams took place at mid-February, at the end of March, and at the beginning of May. The two instructors used the same oral exam questions in the LAN and traditional sections.

As part of their course work, two of the French 212 sections met once a week in the computer lab to use the Daedalus InterChange module for the specific purpose of answering questions over the chapters electronically. The other two sections discussed the same texts in the classroom in whole-group and small-group discussion. A T-test was done on the final averages of the three oral exam scores of the two groups to determine a difference in student grades. A significant difference in achievement was found in the group using the LAN (see Table 5.1 for a breakdown of the data). The oral scores of students who "discussed" the chapters in *French in Action* and *Nicolas'* short stories *only* electronically using the LAN and the InterChange module were

Table 5.1.

Pilot study on oral scores

Group	N	Mean	StdDev	T	ProbT
Control	46	84.15	12.63	2.20	0.03
IC	37	89.19	8.15		

superior to the scores of the students who discussed the texts orally in the traditional classroom setting.

This is an interesting first finding demonstrating the possible transfer of skills through written production on a LAN to oral expression in the target language. The results of this study seem to support the instructors' contention in their exit interviews that the CMC sections did a better job of improving students' oral performance in French than did the traditional classroom oral discussions.

All attempts were made to keep the treatment of the material in the four sections as equal as possible. The oral and computer exercises were carefully planned so that all four groups had the same preparation for their oral exams. However, it should be noted that just as each class has its own character and atmosphere, two sections of a course are never absolutely identical in their classroom activities, even with the same teacher.

The limitations in this pilot study lie in the relatively small number of subjects (N = 83 students in four sections). Further, the computer sections were limited to twenty students each throughout the semester, whereas the other sections were limited to twenty-four students. The smaller numbers in the LAN sections might have influenced student achievement. These limitations notwithstanding, the results of this study still suggest that the LAN process can be an effective step in improving students' production in the target language. (For a more complete report of this study see Beauvois 1996b.)

As in a description of Stage 4 of Pennington's model on writing, it can also be said of synchronous electronic discourse that it is typically more efficient in terms of time on task than classroom discourse for several reasons. Primarily, more is communicated in less time, and since the exchanges are from one to many instead of one to one, the overall result is a more extensive coverage of the topic or text. All students can and usually do participate (Beauvois 1993; Kelm 1992; Kern 1995), thereby providing greater usage of the target language by all members of a class. At the end of an InterChange session, all the ideas generated by the students and the professor can be saved and studied for the next class session. A continuity is thus created that cannot be duplicated in other than an electronic environment.

Conclusion

In elementary and intermediate language classes, providing a mid-step between the reading of a text and its eventual oral exploration in class is now an instructional option for the teacher. LAN discussion provides a bridge for the student between limited oral skills and expression of ideas because it slows down the communicative process. Yet the delay in student production to allow for thought and self-correction made possible by a LAN is not as slow as true written communication because of the context of the real-time environment. The classroom setting by its nature gives a sense of immediacy to the discussion, and the addition of the LAN technology promotes an interactive environment in which to process and express ideas in a low-stress setting.

As mentioned above, in addition to the linguistic benefits of the process just described, a scaffolding of sorts is built through this sharing of ideas on a common theme, as well as through the negotiation of meaning among students and instructor to build a more thorough comprehension of text. As students work through their affective and linguistic difficulties in this dynamic, interactive, and essentially social setting on a LAN, they become active constructors of knowledge. The instructor, as the more skilled "other," guides them through the "zone of proximal development," in which the learner goes from a level of actual, present development to a level of potential development with the aid of a more competent person and in collaboration with others (Vygotsky 1978). This "potential" level of development refers to what the learners can achieve given the optimum guidance, encouragement, and, in the case of language learning on a LAN, the freedom to practice and explore their linguistic skills with less of the inherent language learning anxiety.

This process is not suggested as a replacement for any activity, but rather as an innovative addition to the curriculum, as a means to enhance written and oral communication. Even with the limited research results available at present, it would seem that enough initial data exist to support a recommendation of this CMC activity as both linguistically and socially effective for the student and as a powerful tool for the instructor in the ongoing endeavor to enhance the language acquisition process.

REFERENCES

Batson, T. 1988. "The ENFI Project: A Networked Classroom Approach to Writing Instruction." *Academic Computing* 2:32–33.

Beauvois, Margaret H. 1992a. *Computer-Assisted Classroom Discourse in French Using Networked Computers.* Unpublished doctoral dissertation. The University of Texas at Austin.

———. 1992b. "Computer-Assisted Classroom Discussion in the Classroom: Conversation in Slow Motion." *Foreign Language Annals* 25:455–64.

————. 1993. "E-Talk: Empowering Students Through Electronic Discussion in the Foreign Language Classroom." *The Ram's Horn* 7:41–47.

————. 1994. "E-Talk: Attitudes and Motivation in Computer-Assisted Classroom Discussion." *Computers and the Humanities* 28:177–90.

————. 1996a. "Conversations in Slow Motion Revisited." Manuscript accepted for publication.

————. 1996b. "Write to Speak: The Effects of Electronic Communication on the Oral Achievement of Fourth-Semester French Students." Manuscript submitted for publication.

Beauvois, Margaret H., and J. Elledge. 1996. "Personality Types and Megabytes: Student Attitudes Toward Computer Mediated Communication (CMC) in the Language Classroom." *CALICO Journal* 13,2,3:27–45

Bump, J. 1990. "Radical Changes in Class Discussion Using Networked Computers." *Computers and the Humanities* 24:49–65.

Butler, Wayne M. 1992. *The Social Construction of Knowledge in an Electronic Discourse Community.* Unpublished doctoral dissertation, University of Texas.

Carter, L. 1989. "Telecommunications and Networked Personal Computers: Opening up the Classroom." Paper presented at The Conference on College Composition and Communication, Seattle, WA, March 17.

Cononelos, T., and M. Oliva. 1993. "Using Computer Networks to Enhance Foreign Language/Culture Education." *Foreign Language Annals,* 26:525–34.

Daedalus Integrated Writing Environment. The Daedalus Group, Inc., 1106 Clayton Lane, Suite 248W, Austin, TX 78723.

Daiute, C. 1986. "Physical and Cognitive Factors in Revising: Insights from Studies with Computers." *Research in the Teaching of English* 20:141–15.

Day, M., and T. Batson. 1995. "The Network-Based Writing Classroom: The ENFI Idea." *Computer Mediated Communication and the Online Classroom,* 2.

Faigley, L. 1990. "Subverting the Electronic Workbook: Teaching Writing Using Networked Computers," pp. 290–312 in Daiker and Morenberg, eds., *The Writing Teacher as Researcher: Essays in the Theory of Class-Based Writing.* Portsmouth, NH: Boynton/Cook Publishers.

————. 1992. *Fragments of Reality: Postmodernity and the Subject of Composition.* Pittsburgh: University of Pittsburgh Press.

Gallupe, R. B., L. M. Bastianutti, and W. H. Cooper. 1991. "Unblocking Brainstorms." *Journal of Applied Psychology* 76:137–42.

Hawisher, Gail, and Cynthia Selfe. 1989. *Critical Perspectives on Computers and Composition Instruction.* New York: Teachers College Press, Columbia University.

Kelm, O. R. 1992. "The Use of Synchronous Computer Networks in Second Language Instruction: A Preliminary Report." *Foreign Language Annals* 25:441–45.

Kemp, F. 1993. "The Daedalus Integrated Writing Environment." *Educators' Tech Exchange* Winter:24–30.

Kern, Richard G. 1995. "Restructuring Classroom Interaction with Networked Computers: Effects on Quantity and Characteristics of Language Production." *Modern Language Journal* 79,4:457–76.

Kinneavy, James L. 1991. "I Won't Teach Again without Computers." (Invited paper). Conference on College Communication and Composition, Boston, March.

Lam, F. S., and Martha C. Pennington. 1995. "The Computer vs. the Pen: A Comparative Study of Word Processing in a Hong Kong Secondary Classroom." *Computer Assisted Language Learning* 8,1:75–92.

Pennington, Martha C. 1996a. *The Computer and the Non-Native Writer: A Natural Partnership.* Cresskill, NJ: Hampton Press.

————. 1996b. "Writing the Natural Way on Computer." Forthcoming in *Computer-Assisted Language Learning.*

Peterson, N. 1989. "The Sounds of Silence: Listening for Difference in the Computer-Networked Collaborative Writing Classroom," pp. 6–8 in T. W. Batson, ed., *Proposal Abstracts from the 5th Computers and Writing Conference* at The University of Minnesota, Minneapolis, May 12–14. Washington, DC: Gallaudet University.

Phillips, Elaine. 1991. "Anxiety and Oral Competence: Classroom Dilemma." *The French Review* 65,1:1–14.

Selfe, Cynthia, and Susan Hilligoss. 1994. *Literacy and Computers.* New York: Modern Language Association of America.

Slatin, J. 1991. "Is There a Class in This Text? Creating Knowledge in the Electronic Classroom," pp. 27–51 in Edward Barrett, ed., *Socio-Media: Multi-Media, Hypermedia, and the Social Construction of Knowledge.* Cambridge, MA: MIT Press.

Smith, F. 1988. *Joining the Literacy Club: Further Essays in Foreign Language Education.* Portsmouth, NH: Heinemann.

Underwood, J. 1987. "Correo: Electronic Mail as Communicative Practice. Computers in Research and Teaching." *Hispania* 70:413–14.

Vygotsky, Lev. 1978. *Mind in Society: The Development of Higher Psychological Process.* Cambridge, MA: Harvard University Press.

Vaché, Jean. 1994. "Using Computers to Monitor Students' Performance in Essay Writing." *ASP: La Revue de l'Anglais Spécialité*, Université de Bordeaux II, June:45–57.

Walthers, J. B. 1994. "Anticipated Ongoing Interaction Versus Channel Effects on Relational Communication in Computer-Mediated Interaction." *Human Communication Research* 4:473–501.

Warschauer, Mark. 1995. *E-mail for English Teaching.* Alexandria, VA: TESOL.

Young, Dolly J. 1992. "Language Anxiety from the Foreign Language Specialist's Perspective: Interviews with Krashen, Omaggio Hadley, Terrell, and Rardin." *Foreign Language Annals* 25,2:157–72.

6

Uniting Teachers, Learners, and Machines: *Language Laboratories and Other Choices*

Sharon Guinn Scinicariello
Case Western Reserve University

Introduction

Was the first language-learning technology a clay tablet and a stylus with which the teacher could draw a picture? Who acquired the clay? Who stored the finished product for future use? Imagine early librarians rejecting such "nontext" duties, forcing teachers to organize the first language media centers, to buy a supply of clay, and to maintain a collection of finished images for classroom use. Soon they might decide to conduct their classes in the center to avoid transporting the tablets. Then the students would ask to be able to consult the tablets independently in order to practice and review between classes. The primitive language laboratory was born.

Language-learning technology is more complex than clay tablets, but the language laboratory has long been the traditional locus for the meeting of media, teachers, and students. Other chapters in this volume are concerned with the purpose of language-learning technology; this one focuses on its delivery. This focus is particularly appropriate now because modern society is emphasizing the need for technological literacy, while administrators are turning to technology in an attempt to increase both student learning and

Sharon Guinn Scinicariello (Ph.D., University of North Carolina-Chapel Hill) is the Senior Network Information Specialist in the Kelvin Smith Library and an Adjunct Assistant Professor in the Department of Modern Languages and Literatures at Case Western Reserve University, Cleveland, Ohio. A language laboratory director from 1982 to 1996, Scinicariello is a frequent presenter on both language laboratory issues and the applications of technology in the French curriculum. She is the co-author of "Television Technology in the Foreign Language Classroom" in the ACTFL volume *Modern Technology in Foreign Language Education: Applications and Projects.* Her current interests include the intersection of task- and content-based learning with educational technology, technology-enhanced special-purpose language learning, and applications of networked multimedia.

faculty productivity. After a long period of scarce funding, money is once more available for the creation and renovation of labs, but rapid technological changes and the evolution of language pedagogy have made it difficult to conceptualize and build labs that are both useful today and ready to adapt to the needs of tomorrow. Even the term *language lab* is obsolescent, a form of shorthand that represents a variety of entities responsible for delivering technology-based language instruction. New names like "language media center" or "learning resource center" attempt to reflect new goals and new technologies. In this period of opportunity and turmoil for the language lab, there is only one certainty: we know that all current technologies are converging into one digital environment, but we cannot know what form this will take. As institutions plan their language laboratories, they must consider both the future of technology-enhanced education and their own priorities and goals. There is no ideal language lab for the twenty-first century. This chapter is designed to help faculty, administrators, materials developers, and funding agencies consider the issues involved in the delivery of technology-based language instruction.

The Coming Digital Environment

Many language lab professionals working today remember when the premier language-learning technology was reel-to-reel audiotape. We have seen the conversion to cassettes and the invention of affordable VCRs and satellite antennas. These changes were important, but they posed few difficulties for the planners of language laboratories. The change from reels to cassettes did not alter the way audio was used in language instruction, but it significantly reduced storage, duplication, and repair problems. The advent of video did influence the materials and methods of language instruction, and language labs had to find space for both individual and group viewing. However, the technology itself did not change once it was introduced. Certainly one might have invested in formats other than the VHS that became a standard, but viewing stations established ten years ago can still be used today. Other technologies for distributing audio and video, for example, videodiscs and audio CDs, are used but have yet to replace tape.

On the other hand, computer technology changes so rapidly that by the time equipment is purchased and installed it is no longer state of the art. Although early attempts to use computers in foreign language education did not significantly alter foreign language curricula—probably because of the limitations of the hardware and the design of the software—multimedia CD-ROMs and networked computing have begun to inspire the same enthusiasm and change brought about by the availability of affordable video. The World Wide Web, which has particularly intrigued language teachers in the past year, is the current interface of choice for a "digital environment" predicted to have an enormous impact on all aspects of our lives. Like the Web, the digital environment assumes the convergence of all media into one platform.

Nicholas Negroponte (1995) plausibly describes this new environment in *Being Digital.* It is an environment in which data exist as digital "bits" of information that can be obtained and viewed in a variety of formats determined by the user of that information. For example, a foreign language learner might search in an information archive for greetings in the target language. One choice in the archive might represent a scene from a film in which a variety of people greet each other at a party. The learner can determine if these bits will be displayed as text, as audio, as video, or as a three-dimensional holographic simulation of the party in which he or she can participate. It is an environment in which the physical format and location of materials are no longer important, an environment in which individuals will have access to information whenever and wherever they want it—information that will be displayed in a form that they have chosen to meet their own needs. The digital environment is also an interactive environment in which individuals can become information providers as well as consumers. It is extremely difficult for individuals to become television broadcasters; it is relatively easy to create digital video archives.

The ultimate realization of this vision depends upon two factors: (1) that producers will create data in digital form using data bits and what Negroponte (1995:18) calls "bits-about-bits," that is, bits that contain descriptive information about the content of the data and possible formats for its display; and (2) that everyone will have access to a machine connected to a wealth of information archives. The dream of universal access is already being realized. Telephone and cable companies are racing to wire neighborhoods with fiber-optic cable in order to become network providers. Most colleges and universities have or are constructing campus-wide networks with Internet access; federal, state, and local government agencies are providing similar access to public schools. Community centers and libraries offer access to those who cannot or will not have access from the home.

Many of us already spend time in this new digital environment. We use our computers to find and retrieve information in a variety of formats without being consciously aware of the location of that information. We regularly distribute information to individuals and groups through electronic mail, discussion groups, and other Internet resources. We no longer have to travel to a Parisian movie theater to see previews of current films or travel across campus to work with others on a group project. We participate in international meetings from the comfort of our own homes.

   Although the digital environment is not yet fully realized, the concept is already affecting language laboratories in significant ways. Should new language labs assume the demise of analog media and be equipped only with computers? If everyone has a personal machine with which to access materials, does the lab as a collection of equipment cease to exist? What might be the structure and role of a "virtual" language lab?

Changing Goals and Methods of Language Instruction

The traditional audio language laboratory was closely tied to a specific instructional methodology. Stack (1971:3) could write as late as 1971 that "from the outset it should be understood that the only realistic purpose of the language laboratory is to provide a convenient means of hearing and responding to audiolingual drills." The physical characteristics of these early labs—usually rows of little booths often located in ill-lit basements—and the mindless mechanistic quality of the drills combined to discourage both teachers and students. When the audiolingual method lost favor with language teachers, many language laboratories were happily abandoned. But a fundamental change had taken place in foreign language instruction: the acquisition of listening and speaking skills emphasized by the audiolingual method had become an important goal. Writers like Dakin (1973) began to explore how the audio technology of the lab could be used to promote the acquisition of listening and speaking skills in conjunction with methodologies other than ALM. These efforts, combined with the adoption of new technologies, revitalized the lab (Bakker 1992:8).

   Because language labs almost did not survive their close association with the audiolingual method, directors and faculty have since shied away from a close association with any specific methodology or theory of language acquisition. Language lab directors recognize that their facilities serve "many different languages from many different cultures which are taught according to many different methods and goals" (Aoki 1990:3). Technology is used to deliver materials and to enhance whichever language-learning activities are used in a given course or program. However, at least two recent trends in education affect the design and use of language labs. The first is the current emphasis on cooperative or collaborative learning, an affirmation and expansion of language instruction's use of paired and small-group work. It is implemented in language laboratory design when the individual booths yield to more flexible workstations that can accommodate multiple simultaneous users. The second trend involves a fundamental change in the roles of teacher and learner. The teacher is no longer an authority imparting knowledge to the students but rather acts as guide or coach as the students work to achieve the course's instructional goals. An increased emphasis on the role of language teacher as facilitator may lead to more faculty involvement in the creation of technology-based materials and increased integration of these materials in classroom instruction.

The teacher-as-facilitator model adapts well to two relatively new emphases in language programs that also affect language laboratories: support for lifelong learning and distance education. Teachers facilitate lifelong learning by helping students acquire strategies for using authentic materials so that they can continue to learn after completing their formal instruction. Labs support this continuing education by providing materials for faculty, staff, and students who need or desire to enhance their language skills independently. Distance education may take many forms—from classrooms linked by videoconferencing to the reincarnation of correspondence courses using electronic mail. The language laboratory, as the delivery system for technology-based instruction, has an obvious role to play in this area.

If language labs are no longer tied to a specific instructional methodology, they are expected to support the goals of the language program and of the institution as a whole, and these goals have been changing. The traditional role of language in a liberal arts education—the liberation of individuals from the assumptions of their own culture through the study of another's language and literature—is challenged by students who, recognizing the reality of an economically, politically, and ecologically interdependent world, want their language study to be concretely useful. They want to be able to communicate from their first lessons. They do not want to wait for advanced literature courses to discuss the target culture. In fact, many students do not want to study literature at all. Special-purpose courses geared toward students' professional interests have become popular; they attract students who do not participate continuously in the language program. While traditional audio and video technologies support communicative goals, new computer-based interactive and hypermedia can be especially effective in teaching culture and professional language. Online resources are particularly rich in specific-purpose and cultural content. The language laboratory can also provide remedial or intensive language practice for those students "dropping into" the language program after an absence of months or years.

Language Labs Today

Although language laboratories exist in many forms, most are an eclectic mix of technologies ranging from overhead projectors to interactive videodisc workstations. Their broad technological base is seen in a comparison of two lab surveys. In 1976, 53.9 percent of the respondents said their labs were audio only; this was true of only 17.8 percent of the 1988 respondents. The number of labs with videotape facilities doubled between 1976 and 1988. Significant numbers of labs also had access to computers (57.2 percent) (Lawrason 1990:21). These two surveys also indicate the decline of the term *language lab.* In 1976, 79.8 percent of the respondents used *language lab* to describe their facility; in 1988, only 59.3 percent used it. A significant increase was seen in the use of *language center* (4.5 percent to 16 percent) and *media/ resource center* (7.9 percent to 16.5 percent) (Lawrason 1990:20). Current terms are *Learning Resource Center, Language Learning Resource Center,* and *Language Media Center.* These changes undoubtedly reflect a desire to eliminate the negative perceptions of faculty members who remember the old audiolingual labs as well as an attempt to convey the increased emphasis on video and computing technologies.

Typical of many recent language laboratory renovations at the university level are those of Notre Dame and the Massachusetts Institute of Technology (MIT). Determined to replace three aging audio labs that were becoming unusable and inspired by the adoption of the *French in Action* video-based course, Notre Dame's lab director designed a new Language Resource Center that would not only support but also promote the use of technology-based language instruction. One room in the Center is a media classroom equipped with the traditional console and student audio decks, a video/data projector, white boards, and multiple audio and video sources. A larger space provides facilities for individual and small-group practice. In addition to individual audio-video booths, there are video clusters, in which up to four students can view simultaneously the same videotape, and workstations for interactive video. VCRs are available to record satellite television broadcasts. Finally, the center is equipped with a video camera and editor so that students and faculty can produce their own materials (Williams 1992).

The renovation of the Language Learning and Resource Center (LLRC) at MIT yielded similar facilities but, because technology was already being used, planning was done with a more concrete understanding of the current instructional needs of the faculty. Although the LLRC was designed as a library facility, faculty expressed a need for classrooms near the technology so that they could use media without the difficulties of transporting equipment and materials. There was also a need to accommodate small-group work in both the classroom and the library setting. Two other decisions were made by the language lab director as she looked toward the future: (1) the renovated facilities had to be flexible enough to adapt to the demands of emerging technologies, and (2) the LLRC had to have access to foreign language television and electronic communications even though these had not yet been used in the instructional program. The new MIT language lab was designed with two media classrooms in close proximity to both the library-study labs and three study rooms for small groups. The classrooms and the study rooms have movable furniture so that groups can be formed at will. One study room is equipped with interactive video, the other two with a multistandard VCR and monitor. Flexibility is built into both the classrooms and the library facility through the use of movable and adjustable storage shelving and the installation of wiring to support future needs. Dividers separating the various areas can also be moved as the configuration of the lab's space changes to meet new needs. The video/computing area was placed next to the audio facility so that the former can grow if the implementation of digital audio decreases the need for student cassette decks. The success of this renovation resulted in the addition of four more media classrooms two years after the initial renovation (Trometer 1994).

Beyond the inclusion of computers and/or computer-controlled videodisc, neither of these lab renovations attempted to rethink the lab in terms of the digital convergence of all media. Two other renovations exemplify current moves in this direction. Both the Center for Foreign Languages and Cultures (CFLAC) at Smith College and the Language Learning Lab at the University of Otago in New Zealand were developed to incorporate the advantages of digital technology without sacrificing the beneficial features of traditional analog technology (Parker and Davis 1989; Tamblyn 1995). Digital technology allows the integration of audio, video, and text on one platform—no more paper workbook pages for use with audiotape and videotape. Both the Smith and the Otago facilities depend on the personal computer and networking technology. At Smith, the use of digital technology was not only a technical but also a pedagogical choice: the integration of media reinforces the pedagogical integration of the four traditional components of language instruction: reading, writing, listening, and speaking. The creation of a digital lab at Otago was motivated by a more mundane motive: the cost of replacing the aging audio facility would eliminate the possibility of also acquiring computers, leaving the university with a long-term investment in an obsolescent technology with no equipment for the future. The planners of both these labs realized that they would have to adapt hardware and create software to meet their needs. The audio component of these labs is fully digital; however, perhaps because of the six years between their development, different choices were made for video. Unable to predict how and when digital video would become a viable language learning tool, the designers of Smith's CFLAC decided to buy computer systems that could expand to meet the memory and storage requirements of digital video while they equipped the center with computer-controlled videotape and videodisc players. The lab at Otago provides the ability to digitize video source materials and incorporate them into the multimedia lessons distributed to the workstations.

Despite their leap to digital technology, the labs at both Smith and Otago serve the same functions as the more traditional labs at Notre Dame and MIT. All provide facilities and equipment for the development and use of media in foreign language instruction. All assume that students and faculty will come to the lab to work, either as individuals or with their classes. They are physical spaces in which machines, materials, students, and faculty come together. Will this be true of the language lab of the future?

Language Labs in the Schools

The nature of school schedules dictates that most precollege labs be classroom facilities that support not only media use in large-group instruction but also in-class individualized practice. The latter is especially important when class sizes are large. Classroom labs, particularly when they provide facilities for small-group activities, can also effectively aid the teacher who is expected to teach multilevel classes. Koerner (1988) proposes that the classroom lab be redefined as a Language Resource Center that serves as a focus for language instruction in a school. Such a lab includes audio, video, and computing technology. If a typical class needs thirty carrels, the lab should have an additional ten that can be used by individuals coming in to work independently while another class is taking place.

"Electronic classrooms" designed for both presentation and small-group activities provide another option for the integration of technology and classroom activities. These typically include a teacher console with a networked computer and a set of controls for playing audio and video from analog sources. Several multimedia workstations are available for small-group and individual activities. These classrooms do not provide the same opportunities for individual oral practice as a traditional lab, but they are less expensive. Because they also meet the needs of disciplines other than languages, administrators are willing to equip many classrooms. While schools with many language classes and only one classroom lab must carefully allocate time in the lab, teachers in schools with electronic classrooms can plan for the daily use of technology.

Language labs and electronic classrooms may assume even more importance in the schools as they adopt block scheduling. Although there are many variants of this model, in general students take fewer classes each semester but each class meets for a longer period of time each day. Students can complete the equivalent of a four-year language sequence in two years. This model creates two difficulties for language instruction that technology can help resolve: (1) the teacher must help students stay involved and learning for a much longer period each day, and (2) there may be long gaps in the students' language learning sequence as they fulfill other requirements. Multiple activities in the classroom lab combined with periods of individual practice can vary the pace of long classes. Opportunities for individual use of lab facilities can help motivated students maintain their skills when they are not enrolled in a language class.

Language Labs in the Digital Age

It is impossible to predict the future of technology. In 1989 Tandberg Educational asked a number of language lab professionals to imagine language-teaching methods and instructional technology in the year 2000 (Kennedy 1990). Few imagined the distributed environment made possible by fiber-optic networks. One who did wrote that "the expense of networking a school or campus with coaxial cable or fiber optics will probably keep these particular solutions from being tried in all but the best funded and most self-consciously modernistic installations" (Borchardt 1990:10). No one imagined easy access to the Internet, the development of the World Wide Web, or desktop videoconferencing.

Admitting that we may well be wrong, it is still useful to describe what a language lab might be in the digital age. On networked campuses some trends are already clear, although academic politics, funding, and other issues may influence their course. At Case Western Reserve University, the "library of the future" just opened. With network connections at every seat, it is the center of what has been named the "electronic learning environment." Students and faculty, all of whom have personal computers and network connections in their offices, classrooms, and dormitories, may access digital information resources managed by the library whenever they wish. If they prefer to work in the library, perhaps because they actually need to consult a book, they may bring a laptop or borrow one at the service desk in order to have network access. The library also includes "electronic classrooms" similar to the media classrooms of a language lab but based on the networked distribution of audio, video, and text from a centralized media center. More of these classrooms are located in other buildings on campus. The assumptions of this environment are that: (1) all information resources for research and teaching will be managed and distributed by Information Services through the library system; (2) all computers within this environment will have access to all information; and (3) all computing will be personal. In other words, the university will not support media and computing labs. The small lab that provides commuter students access to services not yet available through their dial-in accounts will be eliminated as the university begins to provide direct network access through wiring currently being installed in the Cleveland suburbs by the telephone and cable companies. Departments, including the language lab, that maintain a few computers configured to meet special needs or to control interactive videodiscs will be served by the expected implementation of digital video. Within several years only engineers and information systems specialists, who need to practice network troubleshooting and management, will maintain computer labs.

The centralization of all information seems extreme but is a logical result of current trends. Because of the cost of the installation and maintenance of the infrastructure—the wiring, the servers, the hardware and software support—centralized supervision and authority is needed to attain maximum efficiency. The costs of creating effective digitized materials, including the costs of obtaining rights, are also enormous; it is only reasonable that these materials should be made available as widely as possible. Finally, the effective use of networking requires that standardized protocols be used at all levels. If a laboratory, department, or school establishes its own standards, it may hear complaints from students, faculty, and staff unable to access information readily available elsewhere. And centralization offers a number of benefits, especially to the small department or lab: (1) servers are purchased and maintained by the central administration, eliminating the need for specialized technical support; (2) software is licensed and maintained by the central authority, usually at its expense; (3) the central authority provides training in the use of networked computing in teaching and research; and (4) the central authority provides support for the creation and distribution of networked materials.

Will a language laboratory exist in this kind of environment? If all classrooms provide media support and all individual media use is distributed, the need for a lab that provides physical space for machines, materials, teachers, and students will end. If all information resources are managed through a central authority, the lab as media library may no longer be needed. The language lab will survive in the digital age only by redefining itself.

The "virtual language lab" may well be a staff of specialists in the applications of technology in foreign language instruction. Descriptions of successful lab renovations always emphasize the human element of language lab use—the need for people who help faculty and students use technology effectively. This need becomes more pressing with the rapid evolution of technology and information. The physical space of the lab may be a small number of offices and conference rooms with network access. The staff will use the conference rooms to confer with faculty about their needs, to demonstrate new materials, and to work on development projects. Staff members will travel to offices, classrooms, and residence halls to provide subject-specific orientation to networked resources. They will work with the central authority to assess the special needs of language teachers and learners and ensure that these needs are met as the digital environment evolves. In other words, the language lab in the digital age will be a collection of human resources responsible for the development and distribution of technology-based materials for language learning. As Herren has said, "The language lab has withered. Long live the lab director." (Dvorak et al. 1995:39)

Of course, this concept of the "virtual" lab does not fulfill other stated goals of most current language-learning centers. A lab without a physical location cannot easily serve as the focal point for language-learning activities. It cannot entice students to enroll in language classes by its attractive and friendly design. And it cannot prevent students and faculty from becoming isolated from each other. Departments desiring to fulfill these goals might well add student-faculty lounges and study rooms to the conference rooms of the "virtual" lab.

Designing Today's Lab to Meet Tomorrow's Needs

Few schools will be willing or able to implement this or a similar vision of the "virtual" lab in the near future. From a technical standpoint, networked multimedia still poses a number of difficulties (McCandless 1996). Schools at all levels, particularly large public institutions, find it difficult to require that all students own a computer or to provide computer access to everyone. Obtaining the rights to digitize all the materials currently used in language instruction is a daunting task that probably will never be accomplished. When rights can be obtained, some kind of coordinated effort to realize the digitization will have to be organized among publishers and institutions to avoid needless duplication and to maximize the efficiency of the limited numbers of staff available for such efforts. Finally, and perhaps most important, it is usually easier to find funds for lab renovation or expansion than it is to find funds to hire staff.

Assuming then that a school is planning to install or renovate a physical space in which to deliver the technology-based language instruction discussed elsewhere in this volume, what are the issues that need to be considered? How does one meet both current and future needs when the future is so difficult to predict?

First of all, anyone planning a language laboratory should create a group of potential users to participate in the process. If new lab personnel will work in the lab, those staff members should be hired before plans are made so that they can bring their experience and expertise to the planning process. All members of the advisory group must visit other labs, talk with as many lab professionals and technology-oriented faculty as possible, and constantly discuss the choices they are making. They should gather information from the International Association for Learning Laboratories (IALL) and other organizations[1] dedicated to the use of technology in instruction. Finally, the planners should consider hiring an experienced language lab professional as a consultant, particularly if they are not familiar with newer technologies. Consultants conduct needs assessments, help bring the lab planners together with other media and computing services units, and work with the planners on their dreams for the future. They are often useful not only in the drafting of a plan for the new lab but also in selling it to administrators and funding agencies. Some consultants will verify that a lab has been installed according to designated specifications.

Technology changes so quickly that plans for the lab may well change several times during the course of the planning process. This fact should not, however, prevent the group from making decisions. If choices are made based on a sound assessment of current and future needs, they will not be regretted.

Three steps are essential in language laboratory design. The first is defining precisely the role of media and the language lab within the language program. All other decisions should flow from this determination. Next, the functions of the language laboratory must be examined within the context of the institution to explore how it will mesh with other technology units and what future institutional needs it may serve. Finally, lab planners must contend with the selection of the hardware and software needed to make their plans a reality.

Defining the Role of the Lab

The general purpose of every language lab in existence is to bring teachers, learners, and technology together, but the specific meaning of this statement must be decided in the context of each language program. This planning stage is often called a "needs assessment," and it is imperative that faculty and students be asked what they expect from a language lab. What technology is currently used by faculty and students? Is there a demand for more audio, video, or computer capability? How do faculty members want to use technology in their courses? Do teachers use media in the classroom or are students expected to work with media as homework? Is there an expectation that groups of students will be working together while using these materials? Do faculty also expect the laboratory to support research or clerical needs? How do students expect to benefit from a language laboratory? Do they use audiocassettes at home but expect the language lab to help them use foreign language software?

Unfortunately, most students and teachers are not prepared to answer many of these questions. The answers should be based on the pedagogical assumptions of the language programs the lab serves, assumptions that may vary radically. Some teachers prefer to have students use technology-based materials to prepare for classroom activities, an extension of the use of drills as homework. Others expect to use not only media-based pedagogical materials but also computer-based presentation software in class. Allocation of space, acoustic design, and choice of furniture are all affected by the expectation that students will work in collaborative groups in both classroom and lab. But teachers cannot be expected to anticipate their use of unfamiliar technology. Members of the group planning the lab must educate their colleagues as they educate themselves.

They can also help faculty and students state their expectations in terms of functions rather than equipment. For example, if they are told "We need ten more VCRs for student use," the planners should explore whether these VCRs will be used to view short segments tied to specific activities. This kind of video work is ideal for the current capabilities of digital video and is already beginning to appear on CD-ROM; VCRs that support this function may soon be replaced by computers. On the other hand, the VCRs may be needed to view the foreign language films and television programs already owned by the institution. Even if these materials become available in digital form, funds to replace the current collection may be difficult to obtain. In this situation, the best choice might be to acquire a mix of VCRs and videodisc players and plan for the integration of new delivery platforms. New materials will be purchased on videodisc or in new digital formats as these become available. Although videodisc technology is also obsolescent, it is an attractive alternative to the VCR in the language lab. Not only are videodiscs more durable than videotapes, videodisc players can be easily controlled by computers. Setting up an interactive workstation is more expensive than buying a VCR, but it provides a great deal more flexibility—the computer can be used without the videodisc—and can motivate faculty and students to create multimedia lessons.

Language lab planners must also look beyond the stated needs of the users to their needs in the future. This is the most difficult step because it involves predicting changes in technology, language pedagogy, and institutional goals and structures. The important question in terms of pedagogy is whether the language faculty and students expect their curricula and programs to change based on their access to technology. Will the teaching of beginning and intermediate language courses be assigned to a language-teaching center of which the language laboratory is a part? Will more of the curriculum be based on independent study and/or distance learning? Will these developments increase the need for access to equipment, materials development, media classrooms, faculty training? Some of the pedagogical issues are tied to the goals and structures of the institution; for example, an increased emphasis on distance learning may be the result of an institutional decision to increase its outreach efforts in its community. Anticipated changes in technology may also be linked to institutional goals and structures. The convergence of all media within a digital environment does imply a merging of "media" and "computing" services, a development that has yet to take place in most schools. Will the language laboratory exist as a separate facility, as part of a merged unit, or be abolished completely? There will not be clear answers to any of these issues, but planners should talk to as many academic administrators as possible after thoroughly reading as many statements of institutional goals as they can find to assess plans for the future. They should be well aware of both pedagogical and technological trends outside the institution and be able to ask specific questions of the administrators responsible for these aspects of institutional planning.

Although the primary role of the language lab is to deliver media-based language-learning materials, most language programs expect the lab to fill other roles as well. Quinn (1994:81) encourages department chairs to use the lab both to encourage scholarly pursuits and to "promote the department to prospective students, visiting alumni, and administrators." He also points out that effective use of the lab to "enrich and enliven" courses can help retain students. The lab can also accomplish this promotional role by being an attractive meeting and study space.

Quinn's encouragement to have faculty see the lab as a locus for scholarly pursuits meshes with the idea that the language lab can be an ideal site for language-acquisition research. Garrett (1988; 1991) has written eloquently both of the research needs of language teachers and of the possible role of the language laboratory in these efforts. To fulfill this role, the lab must be designed so that data on its use can be easily collected. Although the tracking of student use of language-learning software is primarily a function of software design, planners may also want to include observation areas for faculty members who need to see how students interact with each other when using technology in pairs or small groups. They may also need to consider placing audio and video recording devices to archive student interaction in the lab.

A language lab may also be expected to serve as a materials development lab, although expectations in this area will certainly vary according to institutional culture. The expectations will determine both the equipment and the staffing of the lab. Institutions like Carnegie-Mellon expect their labs to be centers of innovation in the use of technology (Dvorak et al. 1995:35). A more realistic goal for most labs is supporting faculty and students who are moving from paper-based activities to multimedia ones. The creation of audio and video materials by faculty and students has been a traditional function of most labs, although capabilities have varied from hand-held microphones and cameras to professional studios. Planners need to know if this function is still considered important.

Finally, the language lab may be seen as a center for professional development, particularly if it is part of a language-teaching center. In this case, facilities that can be used to educate faculty in pedagogy and technology are important. The ability to videotape teachers in their classrooms and private viewing facilities are essential.

Putting the Language Lab in an Institutional Context

Language labs are usually expected to play most of the roles discussed above: they serve as centers for the acquisition, distribution, and use of equipment and materials, as attractive locations in which students and faculty work together, and as resources for training and materials development. Placing the language laboratory in its institutional context helps determine how the lab might best meet these needs in cooperation with other units of the institution and which future needs the lab may be asked to serve. Increased service to other disciplines and increased governance by other media units are issues that must be confronted by language laboratory professionals as they plan for the future. Whenever language laboratory directors meet, one topic of discussion is the relationship of the language laboratory to other units on campus.

Few labs serve all the current technology needs of language teachers and students. In a 1991 survey of IALL members, 65 percent of the respondents reported they provided less than 40 percent of the total computer and media support for their clients (Lawrason et al. 1994:8). Classroom equipment, computer services, and audio-video production are often handled by specialized units within the institution. Some labs are physically located within larger media units or within the library; this allows sharing of equipment, materials, and staff. In some cases, language labs have themselves expanded to become multidisciplinary media resource centers. Language lab directors collaborate with other units both to broaden the lab's support on campus and to fill needs that the lab alone cannot meet, usually for financial reasons. For example, the language lab may be the only unit on campus with expertise in satellite television or interactive videodisc technology. It can provide this expertise to the entire campus in return for use of the audio-visual unit's recording studio. Few labs can afford technicians trained to repair all the lab's equipment; they can work with other units on shared repair facilities or service contracts.

Historically, collaboration and cooperation have been discussed as choices that language labs can make for their own benefit. Labs are under increasing pressure, however, to work with or merge with other units. In part this is a result of the high costs of creating and maintaining networked computing environments, but it is also a function of the short replacement cycle of new equipment. Traditional audio labs, when carefully maintained, could easily be useful for ten to twenty years; this is certainly not true of computers. While Apple IIs and IBM 286s may still function, they cannot run today's software, and the older applications designed for them generally do not meet the needs of today's user. In fact, computing changes so rapidly that labs must plan small upgrades on a yearly basis and major upgrades or replacements every two to three years. Multidisciplinary resource centers that serve a number of academic departments can spread the costs. Herren notes that there is also a pedagogical benefit to a multipurpose center: it brings language learning together with the disciplines that teach about culture (Dvorak et al. 1995:39).

Planning for the digital environment also forces cooperation among all the technology units on campus. An effective campus network requires adherence to common standards and protocols. User support is far easier when operating system and software choices are restricted. Some institutions enforce conformity by requiring centralized purchasing of computing hardware and software; others offer technical support only for hardware and software that meet institutional standards. Language labs that operate in these environments must carefully assess how the supported standards meet language-learning needs. Will the lab need to provide and support specialized equipment and software? If the campus computing services provide and support two common word processors for American English, the lab can support the specialized dictionaries and fonts that enable these programs to be used for foreign language word processing. Must the lab advocate standards and protocols that meet foreign language needs, for example, for diacritical marks in E-mail? Even if the language lab is free from institutional constraints, planners should be aware of the standards used by other units on campus. Eventually there will be a move to connect all the computers to each other and to the outside world.

The most common issue involved in any collaboration among units is interdepartmental communication. Always difficult, this problem only increases as technology becomes more complex. No longer can the language laboratory contact only the directors of the library, audio-visual services, and academic computing; these areas may be divided into subspecialties, and other academic departments may well have their own technology specialists. This chaotic situation lessens the chances for cooperation by making it difficult to find those people and units with common goals and interests. While institutions often create "media resources" or "information resources" committees, the University of Michigan established another means of exchange, the University of Michigan Educational Communication and Technology Association (Lawrason et al. 1994:17). This group, which brings together technology specialists from the Ann Arbor, Flint, and Dearborn campuses, has been able to work out an exchange system for some media services and to discuss the need for both a common copyright policy and its consistent application at all three institutions. Most important for enhancing communication, it developed a guide listing the services, interests, and contact information of the individuals at the three locations. Although smaller schools may not need such a formal mechanism, it is essential that the language lab staff regularly exchange information about projects and plans with current and potential collaborators.

How the various media units on campus work together affects the planning of the lab. For example, the language media center at St. Norbert College in De Pere, Wisconsin, is equipped with networked computers. The faculty, which uses video extensively, did not believe that the problems of digital video had been solved. They knew instead that their lab had never been expected to provide video services; that function was assumed by another campus unit with satisfactory results. The language center does include a small classroom furnished with a large-screen television with VCR, but the videotape collection and facilities for individual viewing are not part of the language media center.

There are reasons, however, for the lab to offer some services that appear to duplicate those of other units. The focus of the language lab has always been the use of technology to enhance language learning. Language lab personnel usually focus on serving the instructional needs of the language programs. Other units on campus, despite their own interest in service, may be too large or too pressured to respond to the special needs of language teachers. If the language lab is a self-contained unit, it may be small enough to avoid procedural rigidity and fulfill program needs more quickly than centralized media centers. For example, even when a school's audio-visual service distributes equipment to classrooms, the lab may find itself responsible for mobile equipment. Potential users may note that the school's audio-visual service cannot or will not provide equipment without a week's notice and that the language faculty prefer to be more spontaneous. For example, one professor starts the day by reviewing the SCOLA news broadcast from the night before and reorganizes his class plans to incorporate interesting segments, but the audio-visual service will not deliver on short notice. The lab can provide video-equipped carts for immediate checkout.

As a lab develops within its institutional context, it expands not only its ability to serve its own clientele but also the likelihood that its clientele will increase. The original lab at the University of Wisconsin-Madison began as a part of the Spanish Department but evolved into the Learning and Support Services for the entire College of Letters and Science. The evolution began as people from other language departments and other disciplines asked to use the lab's media facilities; the lab—particularly its media collection—grew to meet these new needs. The lab recognized a need to catalog this collection efficiently and provide more effective access to it. Eventually, as the lab became the acknowledged college leader in the support of nonprint media, the college decided that the lab should become a centralized agency for the acquisition, processing, and use of its instructional materials. When the LSS added its catalog to that of the university's library system, it began not only to serve clients beyond the College of Letters and Science but also to play a crucial role in the library system (Bakker 1992).

Changes in the role of the lab can be seen in changes in the lab director's position in the institution's hierarchy. Labs have been achieving more independence from individual language departments. In 1976, 62.8 percent of the lab directors reported to a language department chairperson; by 1988 that figure had fallen to 37.5 percent, and lab directors were more often reporting to deans or other administrative units (Lawrason 1990:23). This trend may reflect any of three changes in the status of the language lab: (1) increased professional status for the language lab director, who now reports to a higher level of administration; (2) increased responsibilities for serving disciplines other than languages; or (3) the merging of all "media units" into one administrative structure. There are advantages and disadvantages to any hierarchical structure, and much will depend upon institutional culture. The language lab director who reports directly to the dean, perhaps because the lab serves not only languages but also other disciplines, may be cut off from a firm support base in any academic department. On the other hand, he or she probably has more authority over the lab's activities and budget. If the language lab is part of academic computing, media services, or the library, it may benefit from the expertise of these units; however, the special needs of language learning may be lost.

Selecting Hardware and Software

One of the most difficult tasks of lab planners and personnel is the selection of hardware and software. The rapid pace of technological change makes it impossible to list specific equipment here. The major decision is whether or not to support analog media and, if so, to what extent. The size of the materials collection, the preferences of the faculty and students, and the computing policies of the institution are important factors to consider. Most labs of the 1990s will mix conventional with digital technology. A deciding factor may be the willingness of the faculty to develop new materials and the support that will be given to them in this effort. Few ready-made digital materials exist for language learning. If the faculty prefer to adapt ready-made materials to their programs, they will be dissatisfied with an all-digital lab. Of course, it may be possible for the new lab to deliver analog media as cassettes for individual use at home or by putting videotapes on reserve at the library. In this case, the choice of digital may be logical.

Consultants and vendors are more than happy to help potential purchasers determine which equipment to buy and how to configure the space in which it will be used. Lab directors shopping for new equipment should look for durability and ease of use. Seek advice from other lab directors and media specialists. Consider how the equipment will be used in classroom or lab. It is extremely difficult for the average teacher to use the controls of a 26-inch monitor mounted on a 5-foot cart when the controls are above the screen.

Computers pose a much greater problem than tape recorders, VCRs, and overhead projectors. The purchaser must first accept that whatever he or she buys will be outdated when it arrives, even though this does not mean that it will be useless. Buying the fastest CPU, the most RAM, and the largest hard drive possible will help in this situation. A greater difficulty is posed by platform choice. The usual rule—to choose software first and then buy the hardware on which to run it—is no longer as useful as it was. Although some excellent software, for example, *À la rencontre de Philippe,* is available for the Macintosh only, this is now an exception. Unless the faculty is determined to use a specific package, platform choice need not be made based on software. If the institution, college, or department has not committed to a specific platform, how should one decide? First, find out from those responsible for network planning which machines are supported. With the emphasis on using the Internet in language instruction, teachers want to ensure that they will have networking support. If neither Wintel (the combination of the Windows operating system and the Intel microprocessor) nor Mac is preferred for the network, ask which platform is used by the most avid supporters of the lab. Ask if faculty and students will be using a specific authoring program and, if so, determine which platform is needed. Finally, make a choice that will be immediately useful to the language program, so that faculty and students will use the equipment. Remember that few computing environments require that everyone use the same platform; it is always good to provide as much flexibility as possible. Remember that there are hardware and software solutions that allow Macs to run Windows programs. Remember, too, that both platforms seem to be merging into one machine that will run any of a number of operating systems.

The choice of vendor is extremely important. As Quinn (1994:83) writes, "Relying totally on one source may make you dependent, block cooperation and sharing with other departments, lead to a dead end, or cost more than buying from several vendors; nevertheless, being able to rely on dependable service from an established company may prove valuable." The reliability of the vendor and the availability of service are vitally important to labs that do not have their own technicians. Any prospective customer should ask for references and check them. Machines that do not function are worse than no machines at all because they discourage faculty and students from using any kind of instructional technology.

Cassettes replaced reels, CDs replaced records, and now a number of mutually incompatible digital technologies may compete for our attention. How can faculty and lab directors choose what to buy so that they won't be left with the 1990s equivalent of eight-track audio and Sony Betamax? Unless the lab is an experimental one intended to be in the forefront of technological development, there is no need to rush into the purchase of any new equipment. If there is interest in experimenting with a new machine, buy only one until its worth to the language program is proven. Consider how much software is available and whether it will help the language program meet its goals. Read as much as possible, not only in technology publications but also in the business pages of newspapers. After all, marketing and not superior technology made VHS the dominant video format. Talk to as many technology specialists as possible from as many backgrounds as possible. The language market is too small to determine the fate of a new product, so others may be able to provide a different perspective.

The selection of materials should always be a collaboration between the language laboratory staff, who may be better informed about products, and the faculty and students who will be using them. One duty of a lab director is to teach faculty how to evaluate materials. Since nothing is perfect, part of any evaluation is a determination of whether the flaws outweigh the positive aspects. The best-designed program will sit on the shelf if it is not relevant to the learners' goals. Whenever possible, ask for preview copies of the materials selected for purchase and show them to the faculty. Ask how they would use the materials, then check to make sure that the intended use falls within the copyright restrictions accepted as part of the purchase. Finally, when buying software for a networked environment, make sure that it will function as needed.

Staff for the Language Lab

Quinn (1994:84) writes, "To capitalize on the potential of the media and facilitate the coordination of coursework and labwork, it is essential to have a reliable, experienced lab director." Unfortunately, there is no standard for the qualifications, duties, and status of this person. Tanner (1995) discusses the institutional differences that affect the director's duties, differences that reflect not only the size and structure of the language program but also the role of the lab itself. A large lab with a number of staff people will probably require a director with superb administrative abilities, but he or she may not need to diagnose equipment problems or assist students on a regular basis. The director of a lab in a smaller program may have only student assistants and be totally responsible for maintaining equipment and cataloguing the collection.

Working lab directors list the following important qualities in a lab director:

1. management skills,
2. technical knowledge,
3. instructional design expertise,
4. language teaching experience and expertise,
5. commitment to service,
6. commitment to research and development, and
7. knowledge of another language or experience with another culture (Dvorak et al. 1995:32).

Lab directors in this era also need an eighth skill: the ability to raise funds through grantsmanship and campus politics. Typical duties involve educating faculty and students about the lab's capabilities, training and managing staff, supervising the cataloging and storage of the materials collection, and managing equipment. The lab director is also a source of information about materials development, even if he or she is not expected to lead these efforts.

Although there is disagreement on how these qualifications should be ranked, experience in language teaching and with another culture are highly rated. The lab director is usually expected to promote the use of technology-enhanced language instruction; he or she may find it difficult to be respected by many language faculty if he or she has never taught. In many cases the lab director must be the "expert on language learning and language teaching," the person who is aware of developments in both language teaching and technology so that he or she can advise faculty on "effective use of the media for new methodologies" (Rivers 1991:26–27). Both Quinn and Rivers consider this activity crucial for the effective use of the lab. Yet if the primary qualification is expertise in language pedagogy and success in language learning, does this mean that the lab director should be a faculty member with research interests in this field? Will such a person have the organizational and technical skills needed? What qualifications are needed when the lab is a part of a larger unit or has expanded to serve other disciplines? Can instructional technology experts be effective language laboratory directors?

The answers depend once more upon institutional culture. The secondary school or small college may not have a tradition or a budget for academic support personnel; the lab director will have to be an active member of the faculty. Where it is possible to make a choice, the decision regarding faculty status and tenure must be carefully made. Unless this kind of administrative service and, where appropriate, materials development or research in pedagogy are accepted as qualifications for tenure, it is unfair to expect an untenured faculty member to devote the time and effort required to maintain technical expertise and fulfill his or her responsibilities as lab director. One problem has been the evaluation of the lab director's accomplishments, particularly by the outside reviewers used in the tenure process. The Modern Language Association's Committee on Computers and Emerging Technologies has now issued guidelines that should help departments and faculty members develop tenure criteria for this kind of work.

The truth is that the application of technology to language learning has become so complex—due to changing attitudes about methodologies and the rapid evolution from analog to digital materials—that it is no longer possible for an effective lab director to be a faculty member released from one or two courses. Staying informed, cultivating relationships with faculty and administrators, raising funds, and managing the lab are full-time tasks, but they are only preparations for working with teachers and students to use technology. That said, the role and context of the lab can determine the precise weight given to each qualification. The director of a multidisciplinary media center that serves many language learners may not have been a language teacher, but he or she should have knowledge of and experience with language learning. Greater weight should be given to instructional design expertise if the lab is expected to be a locus for materials development than if it serves primarily as a materials collection and distribution point. If the institution prides itself on research, the director should have an appropriate degree and a commitment to a research agenda.

Possible models for language lab staffing vary greatly. At the precollege level, there may be no "lab director" because technology is managed by a media specialist. In this case the specialist and the language faculty should meet together on a regular basis. A language teacher interested in technology may also work as a liaison between the faculty and the specialist, helping the latter understand and meet the specific needs of language instruction. This liaison system can also be effective at large institutions where the language laboratory serves a number of departments. The Anderson Language Technology Center (ALTEC) at the University of Colorado at Boulder hires several liaisons each year to help lab staff communicate with the faculty and stay informed about developments in the language programs. The liaisons, who must have teaching experience, are chosen by the faculty of the departments with the approval of ALTEC. They are perceived as colleagues by both faculty members and lab staff, a status symbolized by their access to keys and shared office space at ALTEC. Liaisons, who work approximately ten hours per week, report on ALTEC activities to their departments and vice versa, but they also carry out a number of other tasks designed to facilitate the use of language-learning technology. Supervised by the ALTEC director, the liaisons are an essential part of ALTEC's projects (Sheppard and McClanahan 1995). An instructional technology or academic computing specialist may direct a large, multidisciplinary learning center with a language specialist as an assistant. Some labs have a manager supervised by a faculty member serving as "academic director."

Every lab needs a director, but other staff needs are determined by the role of the lab and the size of the budget. If the lab is to create computer-based multimedia, it needs production personnel and programmers. It may, however, swap the services of its programmer to audio-visual services in return for recording engineers and editing services. Maintaining a large materials collection in cooperation with the campus library may require that the lab hire a full-time librarian. Other staff might be needed to coordinate educational activities, write grants, or schedule facilities.

When the director's evangelizing efforts are successful, faculty begin to plan technology-based projects that require more time than they have. In particular, they often wish to incorporate audio, video, and text materials into multimedia lessons and quickly discover that they need help. The lab staff that supports these activities may be able to provide advice and guidance but not the time required to actually assemble the lessons. The University of Michigan's Graduate Media Assistant Project provides one solution to this problem. When a faculty member has designed a project with specific learning objectives, he or she is assigned a graduate student who is paid by the language lab to help. The GMAs do not need to be foreign language students; the skills demanded may vary from language expertise to video editing capability. Faculty members applying for GMAs must explain the instructional goal of the project and how it will be achieved. Because one goal of the language lab is to promote the creation of interesting materials for language learning, all projects must involve technology. Another language lab goal is to promote cross-departmental communication and innovation, so GMAs meet monthly and present their projects annually to language faculty (Crandall 1991).

Both ALTEC's liaison program and the GMA Project are designed to accomplish the most difficult task of language laboratory personnel: persuading faculty and students to use the resources available. Communicating with current and potential clients, educating faculty and students, and supporting the integration of technology into the curriculum require a level of staffing most labs cannot attain. Yet all these tasks are necessary if the language lab is to be effective. Creativity in finding and using appropriate staff is perhaps one of the most important traits demanded of an effective lab director.

Copyright and Other Issues

Gilgen has said that "probably the legal issues have been one of the greatest impacts on my life as a lab director" (Dvorak et al. 1995:30). Whether a language laboratory duplicates audiotapes or creates multimedia software, its personnel are faced with the multiple interpretations of copyright law as it applies to media. The lab director, without legal training, must establish and enforce a copyright policy even though there are no definitive rules that govern what a language lab does. Does viewing a film designated "for home use only" in the language laboratory constitute a public performance and therefore violate copyright or do the exceptions for "face-to-face instruction" apply when the film is a class assignment? Is there really an exception for instructional use? While he or she can seek the advice of the school's attorneys, read the endless copyright articles in professional journals, and attend workshops in order to create a copyright policy, the director is still faced with enforcement decisions on a daily basis. And often these decisions make the lab director appear to be an obstacle to rather than a facilitator of technology-based instruction. Asking faculty and students to participate in the drafting of the lab's copyright policy is a possible solution to this problem; educating all users is certainly a necessity. The lab personnel should also make every attempt to secure permission for teachers and students to use materials as they wish.

Staffing the lab requires the director to consider the institution's personnel policies as well. Violations may well subject the director to legal action. An institution's human resources department can help the director understand what is required for the hiring, evaluation, and dismissal of staff members. However, there may be no equivalent policies and regulations for student lab assistants. Job descriptions and statements of expectations should be developed for every employee, including students.

The language lab staff must also cope with the legal issues surrounding the Americans with Disabilities Act. Lab designers have always had to deal with building codes, and accessibility for all has been a goal. However, the scope of disabilities defined in the law and the accommodations that must be made, although valuable, complicate efforts to plan renovations, often because of the costs involved.

Fundraising is another issue that must be faced by the language lab. Institutional budgets are usually tight and technology is expensive. Purchasing equipment is only the beginning, a fact often forgotten when language laboratory grants are written. Equipment needs to be maintained, upgraded, and replaced on a regular basis; in addition, it is useless without materials. Dollars spent on equipment should be matched by dollars spent on software. And, of course, after faculty and students are educated about the technology, funds must be found to give faculty the time and support needed to revise their teaching to include technology use. Although most lab directors become adept at writing proposals for administrators and grants to outside agencies, it is impossible to budget without the assurance of a steady income. Some schools have begun to collect user fees to support technology on campus, but others resist. After all, if access to the Internet is intended to be seen as the equivalent of access to electricity and running water, it is difficult to charge students a fee for it.

The constant necessity to promote the use of technology is the most frustrating issue confronting language lab professionals. After all, those working in language labs believe that technology enhances learning when used effectively. It is very difficult to defend this belief on a daily basis, particularly when the opposition does not come from a competing belief but from indifference or a lack of interest. For this reason, lab directors are constantly trying to involve faculty members in the use of the lab. ALTEC's liaisons and Michigan's GMAs are two means of enticing faculty members to use technology. Other strategies are newsletters and workshops. Smolnik (1992:32) puts lab news on the back of the student attendance reports sent to faculty members. Quinn (1994:82) seems to attribute the lack of faculty interest to a lack of faculty training efforts, but all lab professionals have announced workshops to enthusiastic audiences who then failed to attend. The commitment to establish or renovate a language laboratory in any form cannot be the end of the institutional commitment to technology-enhanced language learning. The reward system must be restructured so that faculty members who make the time to learn and to reinvent their ways of teaching will be appropriately compensated for their efforts. Merit raises, points toward promotion and tenure, and public recognition are three important incentives. Until a commitment is made to this kind of restructuring, the language laboratory will not realize its full potential.

Conclusion

Otto (1989:38) wrote in the last ACTFL volume devoted to technology, "In the mid-80s, language laboratories have been redefined as multimedia learning centers that deliver computer and video services to faculty and students in addition to familiar audio resources. These expanded laboratories provide a variety of services to a broader segment of the academic community, including foreign language departments, international studies programs, and independent learners." In the 1990s, this redefinition and expansion continues to take place as familiar analog resources are replaced by new digital technologies and television cable companies connect us to the Internet.

It is an exciting yet frightening era for the designers and users of laboratories. The new technologies promise enhanced learning and new research into language acquisition. Telecommunications allow us to use many languages every day to gather information and communicate with people around the world. But while these developments bring new enthusiasm, they also create fear. How does a language teacher evaluate increasingly complex technological developments? Can teachers and students effectively use technology without understanding it? How do school administrators and language laboratory directors make decisions in an environment where today's "hot" technology will be forgotten tomorrow?

The key, of course, is remembering that any technology is only a tool to help teachers and students reach a goal—language learning. Faculty, language laboratory personnel, and students must work together to define how technology-based materials can be used most effectively in a particular curriculum. The language laboratory staff, collaborating with technical experts, can then select the most effective way of delivering those materials in a particular environment. The means of delivering audio materials for listening comprehension, for example, may vary from the mass distribution of cassettes through the creation and sale of a CD-ROM to the archiving of digitized audio and linked activities on a file server. Garrett (1991:75) wrote that "the use of the computer does not constitute a method." The learning activity the machine helps deliver is the important aspect of technology-enhanced education, not the machine itself. In other words, if those ancient clay tablets are still effective tools, use them.

It is clear that teachers and learners need to be aware of new technological resources but that the rapidity and complexity of change have made it nearly impossible for them to educate themselves while continuing to study and teach. Even worse, these same factors have made it nearly impossible for an individual language laboratory director to stay current in both the technical and pedagogical aspects of technology use. The future of the language lab lies in the growth of its role as the meeting place of teachers, learners, and machines—even if the machines belong to individuals and the lab location is "virtual." The language lab director will be the link between the technical and pedagogical specialists on the lab staff or in other campus units, faculty, and students. The essential role of the laboratory will not have changed—it will help language teachers and learners use technology effectively—but its role as an equipment provider will diminish as its role as information resource expands. One fear, promoted in many cases by administrators who are trying to cut costs by cutting staff, is that technology-enhanced language learning will replace teachers. Anyone experienced in the new technologies knows that the truth is the opposite: technology use is personnel intensive. Books and blackboards function for years with little technical support; machines and networks require technicians. Overhead projectors and VCRs require little technical expertise to use; computer users must be "trained." Information management specialists are needed simply to find and evaluate the foreign language resources that appear every day. Individuals can write textbooks, but media materials are created by teams. Finally, many teachers and students need to consult with specialists in pedagogy in order to decide how to use media effectively. Language labs will enter the next century defined as collaboratives of human beings working to help learners reach their goals with the assistance of technology.

NOTE

1. The International Association for Learning Laboratories (IALL) produces resources for the planning and use of language labs in both print and other forms. Particularly noteworthy is its recent *Management Manual*; a revised *Lab Design Kit* should be ready in 1997. Many of IALL's regional groups meet regularly to discuss new technology and other lab-related issues. More information can be obtained by sending E-mail to browne@macalstr.edu. Two other important organizations are: the Association for Educational Communications and Technology (AECT), 1025 Vermont Ave., N.W.,

Suite 820, Washington, DC 20005; and the Computer Assisted Language Instruction Consortium (CALICO, calico@acpub.duke.edu). *The CALICO Resource Guide for Computing and Language Learning,* edited by Frank L. Borchardt and Eleanor M. T. Johnson and published in 1995, is a lengthy listing of companies, organizations, products, courseware, consultants, and programs related to computer-assisted language learning. It also includes a bibliography. The Agora Language Marketplace <http:// www.agoralang.com:2410/index.html>, created and maintained by Carolyn Fidelman and the Network Technology corporation, provides both information about and links to organizations and companies involved in language=learning technology.

REFERENCES

Aoki, Paul. 1990. "Using Technology in Future Foreign Language Education," pp. 3–8 in Ann Kennedy, ed., *Designing the Learning Center of the Future: Language Laboratories: Today and Tomorrow* np: International Association for Learning Laboratories.

Bakker, Connie. 1992. "The Language Lab as Library: The University of Wisconsin-Madison Experience." *IALL Journal of Language Learning Technologies* 25,3:7–12.

Borchardt, Frank. 1990. "The Ideal Learning Center of the Future," pp. 9–13 in Ann Kennedy, ed., *Designing the Learning Center of the Future: Language Laboratories: Today and Tomorrow.* np: International Association for Learning Laboratories.

Crandall, Lynne. 1991. "Partners in Instruction: The Graduate Media Assistant Program." *IALL Journal of Language Learning Technologies* 24,1:31–34.

Dakin, Julian. 1973. *The Language Laboratory and Language Learning.* Longman Handbooks for Language Teachers, edited by Donn Byrne. London: Longman.

Dvorak, Trisha, Brigitte Charlotteaux, Read Gilgen, David Herren, Chris Jones, and Ruth Trometer. 1995. "Whither the Language Lab?" *IALL Journal of Language Learning Technologies* 28,2:13–45.

Garrett, Nina. 1988. "Computers in Foreign Language Education: Teaching, Learning, and Language-Acquisition Research." *ADFL Bulletin* 19:6–12.

———. 1991. "Technology in the Service of Language Learning: Trends and Issues." *The Modern Language Journal* 75:74–101.

Kennedy, Ann, ed. 1990. *Designing the Learning Center of the Future: Language Laboratories: Today and Tomorrow.* np: International Association for Learning Laboratories.

Koerner, Richard J. 1988 "Language Laboratory in the High School: Dinosaur or Valuable Tool for the Teaching of Foreign Languages?" *CALICO Journal* 6:82–85.

Lawrason, Robin E. 1990. "The Changing State of the Language Lab: Results of 1988 IALL Member Survey." *IALL Journal of Language Learning Technologies* 23,2:19–24.

Lawrason, Robin, Susan Clabaugh, Trisha Dvorak, Carmen Greenlee, and Jackie Tanner. 1994. "Cooperation Among Language Learning Centers and Campus Media Services." *IALL Journal of Language Learning Technologies* 27,1:7–20.

McCandless, Glen. 1996. "Networked Multimedia: Not Quite Ready for Prime Time."*Syllabus* 9,3:33–35.

Negroponte, Nicholas. 1995. *Being Digital.* New York: Alfred A. Knopf.

Otto, Sue E. K. 1989. "The Language Laboratory in the Computer Age," pp. 13–41 in William Flint Smith, ed., *Modern Technology in Foreign Language Education: Applications and Projects.* The ACTFL Foreign Language Education Series. Lincolnwood, IL: National Textbook Company.

Parker, Richard E., and Robert C. Davis. 1989. "Digital Audio, Networks, and Foreign Language Instruction." *CALICO Journal* 7:71–82.

Quinn, Robert A. 1994. "Opening the Doors of the Language Laboratory: New Perspectives and Opportunities," in Ann Bugliani, ed., *Chairing the Foreign Language and Literature Department, a Special Issue of the ADFL Bulletin* 25,3:81–86.

Rivers, Wilga M. 1991. "Understanding the Learner in the Language Laboratory." *IALL Journal of Language Learning Technologies* 24,1:23–29.

Sheppard, Marie, and Robin McClanahan. 1995. "ALTEC's Liaison Program." *IALL Journal of Language Learning Technologies* 28,2:54–57.

Smolnik, Steve. 1992. "The Lab Director: Minister of Foreign Affairs." *IALL Journal of Language Learning Technologies.* 25,2:31–37.

Stack, Edward M. 1971. *The Language Laboratory and Modern Language Teaching.* 3rd ed. New York: Oxford University Press.

Tamblyn, Rodney. 1995. "Creating a Digital Language Learning Lab," p. 178 in Frank L. Borchardt and Eleanor M. T. Johnson, eds., *Proceedings of the Computer Assisted Language Instruction Consortium 1995 Annual Symposium: "Computers and Collaborative Learning."* Durham, NC: CALICO.

Tanner, Jackie. 1995. "The Role and Job Description of the Learning Resource Center Director," pp. 1-1–1-16 in Robin E. Lawrason, ed., *Administering the Learning Resource Center: The IALL Management Manual.* Saint Paul, MN: International Association for Learning Laboratories.

Trometer, Ruth. 1994. "Making the Connection II: Designing the Language Lab to Meet Educational Objectives." *IALL Journal of Language Learning Technologies* 27,1:50–54.

Williams, Ursula. 1992. "Some Dinosaurs Don't Die, They Evolve." *IALL Journal of Language Learning Technologies* 25,3:75–78.

7

Learning Language and Culture with Internet Technologies

Peter A. Lafford
Barbara A. Lafford
Arizona State University

Introduction

The field of foreign language education has always been in the forefront of the use of technology to facilitate the language-acquisition process. This dates to the early use of tape recorders and traditional language labs in the 1960s and 1970s, when students would go to listen to tapes of the target language and might record their own voice for playback and self-correction.

In the 1980s, computers were hailed as the tireless taskmasters, allowing the foreign language student endless access to patient and nonjudgmental drill and practice. More recently, multimedia capabilities have broadened the scope and enhanced the potential application of computers in foreign language education by providing useful student-centered learning environments with cultural presentations and interaction tailored to the needs and interests of the individual learner.

Peter A. Lafford is Director of the Language Computing Laboratory in the Department of Languages and Literatures at Arizona State University. He taught French, Spanish, and English as a Second Language before becoming involved with CALL as coordinator of the VESL Curriculum Project at Mesa Community College in 1984. Since that time, he has been involved in software development and language-learning technology and has been at ASU since 1989. He has published articles and reviews on computer-assisted language learning and CALL software and made numerous presentations on CALL and technology.

Barbara A. Lafford is Associate Professor of Spanish and Linguistics at Arizona State University and was recently appointed Associate Dean of the College of Extended Education at ASU. She has served as President of the Arizona Foreign Language Association (AFLA) and the Rocky Mountain Modern Language Association (RMMLA) and was elected to the Board of SWCOLT in 1988. She is the recipient of teaching and service awards from AFLA and the RMMLA and was designated Outstanding Teacher in the College of Liberal Arts and Sciences at ASU in 1987. She is editor of the Applied Linguistics section of *Hispania,* has published on Hispanic linguistics, second language acquisition, and pedagogical issues, and has edited two monographs on culture.

Today's online technologies, however, afford opportunities for enhancing student access to up-to-date and even up-to-the-minute cultural materials and realia. The use of these online authentic materials can help provide students with a level of cultural awareness most often acquired only through experience abroad. In addition, communicative activities using these materials can provide engaging opportunities for students to acquire the target language.

In this chapter, the authors will discuss the types of activities that students at various proficiency levels can perform as individuals or small groups, using these online technologies. These range from individual/small-group exercises based on online text, audio, and video clips to interactive multimedia activities. The individual/small-group activities include summarizing online news reports (text- or video-based), listening to songs in the target language, and writing travel guides based on geographic and cultural information found on the World Wide Web. Interactive activities consist of E-mail, electronic conferencing, multi-user activities such as MOOs (where users log in and interact with each other), voice-based chatting with Internet-based telephone applications, and interactive video using *CUSeeMe* technology.

In addition, in order to take advantage of the interactive potential of the Internet, there will be frequent references to a companion *ACTFL Volume World Wide Web Page* created by the authors, with demo links to self-contained sample activities, and live links to appropriate sites and activities. The reader is invited to point his or her WWW browser to the Web site (URL) <http://www.asu.edu/clas/dll/actfl-it>, either now as a prelude to reading the chapter, or in the course of reading the chapter, for hands-on experience. On the page are instructions on how to download parts of the Web site for off-line use, as well as how to download a browser "bookmark" or "hot list" file and import it into the reader's own browser.

The Use of Content-Based Materials to Acquire the Target Language and Culture

Many scholars in the field of second-language pedagogy believe that a second language is acquired more effectively when it is used as a tool to teach content than when the acquisition of its structure is considered the primary goal (Genesee 1987; Terrell 1986; Guntermann 1993). Brinton, Snow, and Wesche (1989) define content-based instruction as "the integration of content learning with language teaching aims" (vii), and they characterize such instruction in the following ways:

• The content-based language curriculum takes into account the interests and needs of the learner.

- It incorporates the eventual uses the learner will make of the target language.
- It builds on the students' previous learning experience.
- It allows a focus on use as well as usage.
- It offers learners the necessary conditions for second-language learning by exposing them to meaningful language in use (1989:vii ff).

The access to contemporary authentic materials makes it easier for the foreign language instructor to use these content-rich texts as input and as a basis for activities to facilitate language acquisition. For instance, once the students are engaged in reading a text dealing with contemporary issues in the target culture (e.g., popular music groups among the youth of that culture) they become motivated to read more and investigate a topic further. As they read for content they will hone their skimming and scanning skills as well as practice extensive reading[1] of the available texts.

Although, unfortunately, research has shown (Robinson 1993) that while target language proficiency will not necessarily improve students' views of the target culture, studies have shown that a "positive attitude toward the culture"—or "integrative orientation"—does facilitate language acquisition (Robinson 1993:6).

Robinson (1993) suggests that one way of encouraging this type of "integrative orientation" would be to have the students focus on the similarities between the two cultures first, as a way of avoiding the formation of cultural stereotypes. Access to daily newspapers containing photographs of people in ordinary situations in the target culture would help foreign language students recognize the similarities between themselves and the inhabitants of the target culture and would counter tendencies toward the formation of negative stereotypes based on intercultural differences.

Robinson (1993) also states that a search for similarities that underlie differences through the use of analogies is crucial to the creation of a positive image of the target culture in the minds of the learners. "For example, if one is presenting the different forms of housing in Spanish-speaking countries, or the role of family unit, and how they differ from our own, it is also important to focus on how they are similar, e.g., how they serve similar functions" (7).

This article will show how access to up-to-date authentic content-based materials, needed to facilitate the process of second-language acquisition and the appreciation of the target culture, can be gained through use of online technologies.

The Acquisition of Cultural Competence, Using Online Technologies

Cultural competence is "the ability to relate a second language to the psycho-socio-cultural reality in which it functions" (Trescases 1981 cited in Hammerly 1986:513). Access to online technologies such as the World Wide Web facilitates the learner's understanding of the various social and psychological forces at work today in the target culture and provides a context in which students can interpret the behavior of the target culture's inhabitants.

Guntermann (1993) paraphrases Kramsch (1991) by saying "To understand an isolated cultural phenomenon, it is necessary to take into account all relevant contextual information, but this task is further complicated by the fact that the context itself evolves from moment to moment as the players interact" (p. 2). The immediate access to daily changes in the target culture that online technologies afford the foreign language student helps him or her to interpret more accurately the behavior of target culture inhabitants as changes affect their society.

Although Hammerly gives a broad definition of culture as "the total way of life of a people" (1986:513), he also proposes three subcategories of culture that embody the most important aspects of any culture: informational (or factual), behavioral, and achievement (or accomplishment) culture.

- Informational culture includes information on the geography, history, heroes, and villains and how they have made their mark on the fabric of the target culture society.
- Behavioral culture encompasses the routines of everyday life (customs, conversation formulas, kinesics, etc.) carried out by the inhabitants of the culture to be studied.
- Achievement culture consists of the artistic and literary accomplishments of a society.

The use of online technologies can facilitate the understanding of all three types of culture. This issue will be addressed as this article touches on the various types of non-interactive and interactive online technologies available to the foreign language student.

Invaluable resources for this are the Internet and the World Wide Web. These concepts will now be clarified before proceeding with our discussion.

The Internet and the World Wide Web

The Internet is the system of data communication links around the world (phone lines, fiber-optic cables, satellite data links) and the related electronics and software protocols that allow someone at one computer connected to the Internet to exchange files and data with another computer connected to the Internet. The data exchanged can consist of text files, data files, graphics, or other types of information sent as electronic mail relayed from one system to another using an E-mail address (such as <PLafford@ASU.edu>) or transferred directly from one computer to another via FTP (file transfer protocol).

The World Wide Web, hereafter referred to as "the Web," or "WWW" (most easily pronounced "dub-dub-dub") and sometimes referred to W3, is defined by the W3 Consortium[2] as a "universe of network-accessible information, an embodiment of human knowledge." The Consortium's Web-based documentation goes on to say that the Web "has a body of software, and a set of protocols and conventions. W3 uses hypertext and multimedia techniques to make the Web easy for anyone to roam, browse, and contribute to" (<http://www.w3.org/pub/WWW/WWW/>).

Basically this means that it is a system that operates within the framework of the Internet that is intended for public access where individuals and companies can make information and files available to anyone around the world who has access to the Internet. A defining characteristic of the Web is the hyperlinked nature of information. That is, on a "page" of information, the creator can define links to other pages of information, maintained at the same basic location and computer, or linked to pages at another computer across the campus, the continent, or the world. Each page (or "site") is identified by a unique address called a URL (for Uniform Resource Locator), such as <http://www.asu.edu> or <http://www.microsoft.com>. Information on the Web can be presented as text, as graphic images, or as sound, video, and animated graphics. You use a browser to view data on the Web and to visit the Web sites.

Graphical browser software (such as *Netscape Navigator* and Microsoft's *Internet Explorer)* and text browsers (such as *Lynx*) interpret the Web documents, which are written in HTML (hypertext markup language). Whether you see the Web pages graphically or only as text is determined by the hardware and software you are using to access the Web. After connecting to the first URL (identified by the software or entered by the user), the browser downloads the data from the site and displays it on the screen. The hyperlinks defined by the Web page creator are set off by highlighting or underlining or appear within brackets. By selecting or clicking on the link, the user's computer is connected to the new computer and page indicated by the link, without the user having to know where the page is located.

When using a browser without graphics capabilities or a computer or terminal without a mouse, the Web pages appear as text. In *Lynx,* for example, you move the highlighted selection point (functioning as a cursor) with the up and down cursor keys, and go *to* a link or return *from* a link with the right and left cursor keys.

When using a graphical browser like *Netscape Navigator,* the page appears in a window on your screen; if the page is longer or wider than the window, you use the mouse and scroll bars to see more of the page. When moving the mouse around the screen, the pointer changes from an arrow to a hand with the index finger ready to "push" on a link or button. Once you have gone to a new page, to move back to the previous page, click on the left arrow or "Back" icon at the upper left of most browsers.

When You Start Your Browser

When you start the browser software, if your computer has an active Internet connection (either through a local area network or through a dial-up Internet connection), the browser will connect with a *home page* or *start page,* which should have links to other pages. There may be a button or icon at the top of the browser screen (on the software, not the Web page) that makes it easy to return to that starting home page. Clicking on another button or icon causes the software to reload the current page, which might be necessary if there was a problem downloading it the first time. Another button brings up a dialogue box prompting for the URL of the next page to go to; you use that if you want to type in the address of a page that does not have a link on the page you are looking at.

Some browsers have *plug-in* or *helper* applications ("applets") built into the software that enable the browser to handle special files, such as sound files or video files, without any user intervention. It is also possible to install additional applets and plug-ins as new technologies are developed. Sometimes you will be offered an opportunity to connect to a site to have the plug-in added to your browser. Other times, you will have to look for instructions on how to add it to your browser. One thing is certain: technology is advancing at such a pace that no publication can hope to keep up with the latest developments. It is up to you to follow the scene and keep your browsers up to date.

Concerning the automatic connection and installation of new plug-ins, a word of caution is in order. In general, if a connection is to the official browser or plug-in site (for example, <http://www.netscape.com> or <http://www.realaudio.com> home page, as indicated at the bottom of the browser screen when pointing to the link), it should be safe to proceed. If, however, you are not sure where the link is going or what it is doing, because you cannot decipher the URL of the target link, you might prefer to decline any automatic upgrade or modification of your software, just in case it is a malicious link to a hacker's site, intended to install a virus rather than a valid browser plug-in or helper app.

Non-interactive vs. Interactive Technologies

Online technologies can be used to teach culture by either non-interactive or interactive means. Non-interactive technologies basically serve as reference tools that provide target language input—online newspapers, Web sites, and databases—while interactive technologies provide the student the opportunity to receive input and produce output in the target language: E-mail, chat, MOOs, and so forth. While even the newspapers and databases on the Web are "interactive" in that the user decides where to go and what to see, in this context we are reserving the term *interactive* for activities where the users provide more information than just selecting an option or clicking on a link. Our definition of *interactive* refers to an interactivity that requires oral or written production in the target language.

Non-interactive Technologies on the World Wide Web

A noninteractive use of the Web would be to utilize the cultural content material found in target country sites for reference. This use of the Web can facilitate the understanding of all three types of culture mentioned by Robinson (1993):

- *Informational:* Web sites are full of reference information about the culture (e.g., encyclopedias, daily newspapers).
- *Behavioral:* Web sites include newspaper editorials on cultural behavior, video and audio clips of interviews with leaders of the target culture society in which appropriate conversational and kinesic behavior is modeled (e.g., discourse strategies used to open, maintain, and close a conversation, appropriate gestures).
- *Achievement:* Web sites offer virtual tours of art museums, music clips, poems, literary works, and the like—elements of culture that may be hard to access without actually visiting the target culture.

Thus, a major advantage of the Web is its repertoire of authentic materials that contain important cultural content about aspects of the target culture society.

When students have control over what they read on the Web, they will focus on topics of interest to them and will probably want to read more articles related to that subject. The problem with traditional readers is that often the texts are only literary or are not of interest to the age group of most university students (18 to 24). The advantage of having the freedom to choose the online texts they will use as the basis for a report on the target culture is that it allows students of whatever age and social background to focus on topics of interest to them. Of course, the instructor should have a certain core cultural curriculum in mind, but allowing students to surf the Web on occasion to find articles of interest to them is a wonderful motivating technique.

The Use of the Web to Teach Foreign Languages

Bush (1996) gives a valuable overview of issues that arise when teaching foreign languages via the Web. In his review of the current status of the Internet, he recognizes two fundamental shortcomings: organization and bandwidth. However, Bush notes that more powerful search engines now help organize material more efficiently for the learner and that "increased bandwidth is supposedly just around the corner, . . . to follow on the heels of the deregulation made possible by the *Telecommunications Act of 1996*" (1996:1).

Two other difficulties with the use of online technologies mentioned by Bush (1996) are the problems involved with distributing materials on the Web and limitations of the type of interaction currently available with this technology. Regarding the first matter, Bush suggests that a way must be found to balance the interests of publishers and authors to protect intellectual property rights with those of individuals who believe in humanity's right to "freely access anything on the net" (1996:1). He summarizes his discussion of this issue as follows:

> The challenge, therefore, is to create a system that uses the payment mechanisms that are being put into place, all the while remaining something less than overly restrictive in how the system deals with intellectual property. While it is necessary to protect the efforts of content developers, it is also crucial not to stymie creativity in other quarters through the use of unnecessarily prohibitive copyright rules and regulations, problems that perhaps dwarf technical issues (1996:2).

The limitations on interaction using Web technology mentioned by Bush (1996) are important to understand for those students who are accustomed to using interactive videodisc or CD-ROM materials. These latter technologies have the advantage of providing the learner with full-motion video and audio input of a higher quality than most .MOV or .AVI files on the Web can produce at the moment. Another limitation of Web technology as compared to use of the videodisc or CD-ROM involves the speed of the interaction. "Even when materials are designed for some semblance of flow in a question/feedback instructional strategy, delays between a learner's click and the subsequent response (the system latency) can be disconcerting, due to the delays often encountered on our present Web-based system" (1996:2).

Bush (1996) finishes his paper by describing several modes of interaction based on the Internet and Web technologies: computer-mediated communication (synchronous [occurring at the same time] and asynchronous [taking place over time]), traditional browsing, guided browsing, Web-based tutorials, tutorial-based browsing, "dump and run" (what he calls the process of wholesale downloading of Web materials to be run off the local system), and distributed interactive multimedia. The entire paper is available at <http://moliere.byu.edu/calico/calico96.html>.

Sample Activities.   Assuming you are equipped with a browser and a knowledge of basic browser commands, here are some representative sites and related activities to enhance student access to cultural materials and realia. We have broken them down into *text-based* (which could be used without any special multimedia equipment [since most commercial sites have text-only versions of their pages, for those without a graphic browser]), *audio-based* (which require audio hardware and software), and *video-based* (which, for non-interactive activities, simply require the same audio hardware and a graphic browser). Within each category, we have further divided the activities into *Beginning-, Intermediate-,* and *Advanced-level* activities.

Text-Based Activities.   There are hundreds of newspapers and magazines around the world that have electronic editions accessible on the Web. While some are completely free, others require you to have a no-cost account available simply by submitting a name and password on the newspaper's Web page. Still others charge a fee for an online subscription that allows access to customized databases of current and archived information.

Any foreign language newspaper offering Internet access would lend itself to the activities discussed below, but we will concentrate on some representative sites that have open access (or at least free-account access) to their rich cultural resources. Since the World Wide Web is by nature a dynamic environment, there is always the possibility a link will have changed or disappeared by the time you try to access it. For that reason, we encourage you visit the *ACTFL-IT* Web site for up-to-date links. In the meantime, we have selected some German-, Spanish-, French-, Italian-, and Japanese-language Web sites to highlight that we feel are likely to be available on an ongoing basis (Figure 7.1).

Beginning-Level Activities: Germany's *Hamburger Morgenpost* <http://www.mopo.de/> (known colloquially as the *MOPO*) offers a graphics-rich page with many interesting links, including news, sports, entertainment, and more. The *MOPO Online* has a good example of an online flea market <http://www.mopo.de/, then FLOH MARKT>, where students

Figure 7.1.
The Home Page of the *Hamburger Morgenpost Online*

of German could be assigned to look for items for sale to furnish a student apartment for a semester abroad. The students could cut and paste the text of the want ads into a word processor (since most browsers allow you to select and copy text to the clipboard), and then print out a shopping list. The students could then add up the cost, and convert the amount to dollars by going to current currency data (located elsewhere on the Web, i.e., <gopher://una.hh.lib.umich.edu/00/ebb/monetary/noonfx.frb>). There is also an interactive currency converter on the Olsen & Associates Web site in Zurich at <http://www.olsen.ch/cgi-bin/exmenu/>. That site also has historical data on exchange rates and, with a mouse-click, can flip the exchange from dollars per Deutschmark to Deutschmarks per dollar, a useful tool for getting a handle on the target currency.

Still at the *MOPO,* beginning-level students can work in small groups to decide on an evening's entertainment. One group can be told they are sports enthusiasts looking for a game to attend or watch on TV, while another group is told that its members are interested in a classical music concert, for example. Each group can skim and scan the section of the paper that will give them the information they need to plan their evening, e.g., the sports, movie, TV, and concert listings. To make it more challenging, each group can be given a maximum amount of money each person is allowed to spend on the entertainment.

The *MOPO* also has a section called "SurfTips," with more links going beyond the newspaper's home page, for example, to the *Deutsches Bundesbahn* <http://www.bahn.de/>. From there, you can explore Web page information about almost every railway in Europe. Beginning students could be asked to plan an itinerary for trains across Europe, checking the departure and arrival times, fares, and the like, as a springboard for a discussion of transportation in the target culture.

From Buenos Aires, Argentina, the *Clarín Digital* <http://www.clarin. com/> is an electronic edition of "the largest-selling Spanish-language paper in the world." It is very colorful, with lots of interesting multimedia links, and beginning-level students can scan the headlines of the electronic edition or click on the picture of the paper edition to report on the headlines there.

With the sports news from any electronic newspaper, beginning-level students can adopt a "local" soccer (or other sports) team, and follow its progress through the season without much difficulty. (The *ACTFL-IT* Web page has links to other newspapers, as well as to the Yahoo! Search site <http://www.yahoo. com>, which has hundreds of links categorized by Region and Country, and subcategories such as News, Entertainment, Business, and so on. Yahoo! is definitely a site to have in your bookmarks.)

Intermediate-Level Activities: Let's go to the movies! It is always interesting to look over the movie listings in a foreign paper to see what title a movie has been given in another country, but given the time lag between the release of a movie in Hollywood and its release in a foreign country, added to the delay in getting the foreign newspaper in the States, students normally might have to wait a year for this information. However, many of the online foreign language newspapers have movie listings and reviews. By going to the *MOPO*'s current movie listing online <http:// www.mopo.de/, then EXTRABLATT, then KINO>, your students can be looking at translated movie titles only a few months old. Then they can write or talk about the movie from having seen it in English, but using vocabulary from the title or reviews they have just read. Having seen a movie is a wonderful advanced organizer for reading an ad or a review of it.

Buenos Aires' *Clarín Digital* <http://www.clarin.com/> does not have current movie listings, but it does have the movies on TV in the *cine en televisión* section, with times, channels, and links to the original review from their archives. Again, intermediate-level students could be given the task of choosing *one* movie to watch. The discussion would involve puzzling out the English movie titles and deciding on the winning movie.

Advertising by sponsors of foreign language online newspapers can also provide useful materials for students to use as a basis for language practice. One of the sponsors of Barcelona's *La Vanguardia Electrónica* <http://vangu.sei.es/> (requires free account) is a real estate firm with online classified ads offering houses and condos, arranged by section of the city. Intermediate-level students could be challenged to find appropriate lodging near the university for a summer or semester and to prepare a list of questions not answered in the ad (Figure 7.2).

La Vanguardia includes a *crucigramma* (crossword) in Catalan and Spanish, with the answers available by clicking on the clue. This paper also contains an interesting feature, *La Encuesta de La Vanguardia,* an interactive "Question of the Week." One week, the question was "Would you be in favor of Cataluña receiving a status similar to that of Quebec?" Of the 235 who participated, 53 percent said "Sí," 43 percent said "No," and 4 percent said "NS/NC" (*no sabe, no contesta*). This could serve as

Figure 7.2.

a topic for intermediate- or advanced-level discussion or research. Intermediate-level students could simply discuss the question on the surface, while advanced-level students could investigate background or related stories and present their findings to the class.

Madrid's *ABC Electrónico* <http://www.abc.es/> is a well-known daily paper in Spain, and once you have registered a log-in name (a requirement that may soon be eliminated), you have free access to the current edition and those of the last week. As with most electronic newspapers, the ABC menu offers you the various sections *(Cultura/Deportes/ Economía/Internacional/Nacional/Sociedad/Opinión/Portada)*. From there, the introductory paragraph of an article appears, which is linked then to the full text of the article. The intermediate-level student could read the introduction or summary of an article and then restate the main ideas in complete sentences in his or her own words.

Many of the electronic edition newspapers have comics and political cartoons, and other Web sites have extensive humor sections. *Gardel,* the Network of Argentinos <http://vishnu.nirvana.phys.psu.edu/argentina/ argentina.html> has a lot of interesting information, including a page for *Mafalda,* the Argentinian comic strip combining the youthful characters of a "Peanuts" strip with the witty political satire of "Doonesbury." Intermediate-level students can look at the cartoons, print out several examples, guess what is being said, describe the characters, and write another dialogue for those characters, using the same drawings.

While it is useful to expose students to the pop culture characters of the target culture, students will probably have more to say about characters and comic strips that are familiar to them. It is true that American comic strip characters do get translated into foreign languages (*Carlitos* ["Peanuts"], *Pepita* ["Blondie"], and so on), but it is not always easy to find them on the Web. There is, however, an American comic site <http:// www.unitedmedia.com/comics/> with strips from "Peanuts," "Dilbert," "Nancy," and others, whose strips can be printed out from the browser, their text whited out, and then used for the same purpose, that is, creating dialogue for the characters, and discussing the comic situations depicted in the strips.

Advanced-Level Activities: The political cartoons that appear in the editorial section of the online newspapers as well as the *Mafalda* strips can also be used with advanced students since these strips are full of political satire. The instructor should give the class some background on the sociopolitical situation in Argentina or the target culture over the last few decades so that the language students understand the cultural framework in which the cartoon is produced.

Advanced-level students can also write essays analyzing the political humor found on the editorial pages. However, advanced organizers with information regarding the characters portrayed in the political cartoons should always be given to the students beforehand. In addition, they should have to read an article about the incident portrayed in the political cartoon before having to comment on it.

From Mexico City, *La Jornada* (primary site: <http://serpiente.dgsca. unam.mx/jornada>, mirror sites at other locations) is one of Mexico's largest daily newspapers. *La Jornada*'s electronic edition has the standard sections (front page, sports, editorial pages, political cartoons, etc.), but distinguishes itself by offering not only archives of previous editions back through March 1995, but also a full-text searchable index (at least on the main site). This allows the user to peruse the current or previous editions of the newspaper by date and section, in addition to searching the archives by topic keyword or simply by searching for a word that occurs in the body of the text. As will probably frequently be the case, the index search is susceptible to overload, resulting in a textual busy signal but still has potential for allowing the advanced student to research interesting topics.

Even without using the index, advanced-level students could pick a date six months ago, identify a particular story, and search for follow-up stories in more recent editions. Then, armed with the whole story, the students could write a report or cut and paste the headlines for a quick summary of the whole event. There are usually photographs with captions that accompany the story that the students could print out and summarize to supplement the report.

Other newspapers from around the world have similar potential at the various levels. From Italy, *L'Unità* <http://www.mclink.it/unita/index. html> has an *Edizione sperimentale Internet,* which, without as much of a graphical interface as the *MOPO,* does have archives and full-text search. Another text site <http://www.bilink.it/bilink/comemai/> has headlines from three newspapers available all the way back through 1989. The *Alto Adige* <http://altea.dnet.it/aadige/testa_t.htm> is another text-oriented online paper, with an interesting twist: on the page titled *In Lingua Tedesca* all the stories in this Italian newspaper are in German! (Figure 7.3)

From Paris, there is *Le Monde en Ligne* (primary site: <http:// www.lemonde.fr/> (US Mirror: <http://lemonde.globeonline.com/>). The front page *("la Une")* of *Le Monde* is available online as a .PDF file. (.PDF files are electronic documents in the Adobe Portable Document Format, which are viewable with the *Adobe Acrobat Reader* available free of charge from Adobe <http://www.adobe.com/>. With files in the .PDF

Figure 7.3.
The Front Page of *Le Monde en Ligne* as a PDF File

format, the text and graphics of the document can be viewed online on the computer. *Netscape Navigator* and other browsers can be configured to launch the *Acrobat Reader* and other helper apps to deal with .PDF files and special file types such as sound and video files.) Once you download the 300 K .PDF file, you are able to zoom in on and follow a story or even print out the page. (Incidentally, Barcelona's *El Periódico* <http://www.elperiodico.es/>, in addition to regular online pages, has the whole paper in Adobe Acrobat .PDF files.)

Turning to a newspaper environment with particular graphical challenges, from Japan, *The Japan Times Online* <http://shrine.cyber.ad.jp/~jtinter/home.html> allows you to consult the standard range of online newspaper features translated into English. In order to display nonromanized Japanese text (kanji, hiragana, and katakana) on the screen in Windows, you need to install special font-support software. Union Way <http://www.unionway.com/> offers a package to do this for Japanese, Chinese, and Korean, and Pacific Software Publishing, Inc. <http://www.pspinc.com/> has a KanjiKit that uses some of the Union Way software to make a Windows machine Japanese-capable. (The Macintosh, inherently better at dealing with non-Roman character sets, still needs special tweaking to display writing systems other than the Roman alphabet, but poses less of a challenge.) (For more information on this topic, see Lunde 1993, *Understanding Japanese Information Processing.*)

However, until you add Japanese capabilities to your own browser, there is a Web site called *Shodouka* (which means "calligrapher") <http://www.lfw.org/shodouka/> offering a sort of "graphic translation" service. This site allows your non-Japanese-enabled browser to connect to a site that normally requires a Japanese-enabled browser. You are then able to view the Japanese site with all of its original graphics (including the nonromanized writing systems). It is really quite an accomplishment. In addition, the *Shodouka* home page has good links to Japanese pages, including *Yomiuri Online* <http://www.yomiuri.co.jp/>, an interesting, graphics-rich electronic newspaper site. The *Shodouka* page has links to these sites both through the graphics translator and direct to the page for those who are using Japanese-enabled browsers.

Audio-Based Activities.   If your hardware and software support audio, you will have access to other online resources. If you are using a Macintosh, your system probably has audio support enabled by default. In Microsoft Windows, you will need a Multimedia PC, that is, with a sound card or sound chip, speakers, microphone, and CD-ROM drive, though the CD-ROM is not absolutely necessary for the online activities.

In the early days, most sound coming out of computers consisted of beeps, boops, tones, and buzzes. That contributed to the "drill and kill" aspect of early CALL (computer-assisted language learning) software, in which the response to a wrong answer was a "Buzz" and "Wrong. Try Again!" on the screen. Computers today use audio technology capable of reproducing crystal-clear audio CD-quality voice and music by playing digitized sound files. These files are created by converting the analog sound *waves* (what we hear through the air) into sound *files* (digital data that can be saved, modified, transferred, and played back by a computer with audio capabilities). In Windows, the digitized sounds are usually saved as .WAV files, such as the "Ta-daa" and "Chimes" that can be heard at the start and end of a Windows 3.x session, and "The Microsoft Sound" that starts Windows 95.

These sounds can be incorporated into software, saved on diskette or on CD-ROM, and be transferred over the Internet. This is what allows Web-based activities to include sound, either included in the information available on the page or in two-way audio applications where one user can send voice and sounds to another.

One problem with sending .WAV or .AU (another digital sound format) files over the Internet, though, is that it is a two-step process to (1) download the file, and then (2) play the file. The time it takes to download the file depends upon two variables: the size of the file and the speed of the connection. The size of the file is directly related to the length of the sound and the quality with which it was recorded, called the *sampling rate*. The Windows 95 Sound Recorder software rates the qualities as "telephone quality" (11 Mhz), "radio quality" (22 Mhz), and "CD quality" (44 Mhz). At radio quality, a minute of audio might be a 1 mb .WAV file. As a more efficient .AU file, the same minute of audio would be less than half of that, but even so, that can take five, ten, or twenty minutes or more to download. Once it has been downloaded to your hard disk, it can be played and replayed with fidelity as high as the quality with which it was recorded. Some sites have news available in .WAV and .AU file formats, which could be downloaded by the teacher at the beginning of the day and played locally off the network without repeating the download each time.

Another way to avoid the download time involves a new sound technology that is becoming a standard on the Web, called *RealAudio* <http://www.realaudio.com>. Sounds stored in *RealAudio* format can be downloaded and played all in one step, without having to first download the sound, since the *RealAudio* player starts playing the sound file while it continues to download the rest of the sound file. This makes it possible to have short news briefs, 30-minute recorded programs, and even live, off-the-air radio. There are already English <http://www.abcradionet.com>, French <http://www.radio-france.fr/france-info/>, and German <http://www.dmc.net/dw/dw.html> news sites available, a number of foreign radio stations online, and certainly more to come. In addition to the *ACTFL-IT* site, the *RealAudio* Timecast site <http://www.realaudio.com/timecast/search.html> has a listing searchable by keyword and offers the most complete listing of *RealAudio* sites available.

Even though it is accessed by computer, it is possible to record on tape news briefs or music off the Web by connecting the output of the sound card to the input of a cassette recorder. If the connections are available, it would be best to take the "line out" signal from the sound card or computer and connect it to the "line in" on the recorder. If the hardware does not have the right jacks, it is still possible to do it with the signal from the headphone jack and the microphone input, but you would need to experiment with volume and recording levels and "attenuating patchcords" (which allow you to plug a "line-level" signal into a microphone input). With a little experimentation and some help from your A/V tech support, it should be possible to come up with a convenient setup to download news and sound off the Web with very little effort.

Beginning-Level Activities: While it is true that most radio and TV programs broadcast in a given country are too advanced for the beginning-level student to understand, they can still provide a useful motivating resource to introduce modern culture into the classroom. Once you have access to the news headlines or news briefs for the whole class to hear, you can play the news headlines once through for the students and then ask *choice* questions: "Was the top story about *the economy* or *a foreign visitor?*" You can also prime the students to be listening for information: "Listen for the reason the French Open Tennis Championships were postponed today." Then when they see the news that night at home or read the sports pages the next morning, they can say, "I heard on the French news that it was raining most of the day, and that caused the postponement!"

Intermediate-Level Activities: Students can be expected to pick out a little more information from a news brief on which they can prepare *true/false* or *choice* questions. If they have access to the news in a lab setting, they can work in pairs or groups to help figure out the headlines or stories and challenge the other groups to explain or restate the stories presented. Some sites offer transcripts of the stories to be heard online: TVI Online (the audio from Portuguese TV News) <http://www. cibertribe. pt/tvi/> and the CNN San Francisco Home Page <http://www.cnnsf. com/> both have sites with transcripted audio. The CNN page also has activities and various versions of featured stories for those whose target language is English.

Advanced-Level Activities: Students at the advanced level could be charged with preparing news reports in simplified language for the other class members. If they were good enough, they could be played for the lower-level classes as follow-up to the original news briefs off the Web. They could also compare the coverage of major world news events as covered on the foreign radio news to the coverage on the ABC World News Briefs off the Web and gain insight into world politics, which plays a more important role in advanced classes. Some sites maintain archives of past news, which could be accessed later as part of an assignment targeting one particular event. Advanced classes could also spend time listening to the live foreign language radio stations. Live radio has the disadvantage of not offering a second chance to understand a segment, but the immediacy of the medium would be an effective stimulus for discussion of what the people listening to this broadcast are doing *at that moment,* if it is half-way around the world. Of course, the live radio could be recorded for off-air study as well, using the patchcord procedure described above.

Video-Based Activities. If your computer supports audio, you probably also have support for Web-based video, since most video on the Web does not need special hardware, aside from 256-color or more video capability. However, the instructor should not assume that use of Web video is feasible for a class until he or she checks out the actual quality of the video that comes over the Web on the equipment available.

It is basically a question of how much data can be delivered over the wire, which again is determined by the speed of the modem or Internet connection. As big as digitized audio files get, digitized video files can be ten times as big, carrying ten times the data for what is still going to be a small, jerky picture.

While digitized audio can be reproduced fairly smoothly, the normal full-motion video picture on TV flashes by at the rate of 30 frames per second (fps). Anything less that that will appear jerky or in slow motion. Currently, most digitized video on computers is reproduced in small, 2- to 4-inch windows at about 15 to 20 fps. Some systems with "hardware-assisted video" make use of special "MPEG" circuitry and chips to achieve higher frame rates with larger screens of video, but it is still a technology in development.

Though *VDOLive* <http://www.vdolive.com> is video technology similar to the RealAudio technology that provides an ongoing stream of video while it is being downloaded, at the moment its performance may fall short of the demands of students who are quick to become frustrated with the trade-offs inherent with "bleeding-edge"[3] technology. The audio quality is quite good, but the frame rate over a 28.8 modem was about 2 to 3 fps in the experience of the authors for the version available at the time of this writing.

The French TV network *France 3* <http://www.sv.vtcom.fr/ftv/> is already putting their national and regional news online *(Breton, anyone?)*! The one-inch image is very slow to update, but there is something magical about *watching* today's news from France, even if the video is a series of single frames every second or two. You are invited to check out the most current version on the *ACTFL-IT* Web page.

If *VDOLive* requires too fast a connection, there is still a lot of *QuickTime* (.MOV) and *Video for Windows* (.AVI) video available for downloading and playback, which, as with the *VDOLive*, is viewable by means of viewers or plug-ins in your browser software. Once your browser is configured correctly, these videos can either be loaded into memory and played or with a RIGHT- or HELD-CLICK, can be downloaded to disk and stored locally to be played off-line (as with the audio .WAV and .AU files).

While the sound track can be recorded as described above, it is more complicated to record video from the computer, requiring a scan converter to take the computer's video signal and convert it to regular NTSC video (the video standard in North America), which can be recorded by a videocassette recorder in the United States. The video image would still be so small that it probably would not be satisfactory. There are better means of getting current foreign language video tape, such as SCOLA or the International Channel or the PBS Satellite broadcasts of FRANCE-TV Magazine and SPANISH-TV Magazine, and so on. Nevertheless, the audio could be borrowed from the video for audio activities.

The CNN site <http://www.cnn.com> includes a video vault with video clips available arranged by month and category; in the International category, stories are arranged alphabetically by country. It is therefore possible to find downloadable clips from which to save single frames from almost any culture—a great resource. (CNN is also quite good about granting rights for educational use—an issue of ever-increasing importance as technology provides new ways to distribute and adapt intellectual property.)

Beginning-Level Activities: These video activities echo those of the audio sources, with the added benefit of having pictorial support of the audio message, though limited to on-computer access. When dealing with foreign language clips, beginning-level students can be primed to listen for certain vocabulary or presented with specific questions whose simple answers are found by skimming and scanning the segment presented. If the story is visually clear, the student can pick up key vocabulary from the visual context. One could also look for clips where native gestures could be spotted and taught.

Although the stories are presented in English, clips from the CNN video vault can be utilized for their culturally rich information, images, and background sounds. A 15-second clip about harvesting olives in Spain followed by another 15 seconds about turning it into olive oil could be the introduction for a lesson on Spanish agriculture or culinary specialties. (Those files are <http://cnn.com/video_vault/WORLD/9604.html>; in that archive, the files <http://cnn.com/WORLD/9604/25/olive.oil/ooilharv.mov> and <http://cnn.com/WORLD/9604/25/olive.oil/ooilproc.mov>).

Intermediate-Level Activities: The intermediate students could record their own narration for video clips that have none. Since some sites have transcripts of the text being read, the text could be made available for further study. With the downloaded videos, still frames can be saved as bitmap images to be incorporated in on-screen documents or printed in word-processed reports. In addition, students in small groups can ask and answer simple questions about the video clip segment.

Advanced-Level Activities: These students could do research on the TV reports on current and recent events. The *France 3* site has extensive coverage of the 10-year anniversary of Chernobyl, for example. Advanced-level students could create their own Web site, compiling graphics and sound bites from various sources. The archives for *France 3* include stories such as the reopening of the renovated Paris Opera, the death of François Mitterand, and coverage of the Granada-Dakar automobile rally.

Other sites offer still frames from live video cameras around the world <http://www.ts.umu.se/~spaceman/camera.html>. These are usually updated every five minutes; taking a live peek at the progress of a bridge under construction in Sweden as the sun is setting at 4:00 P.M. in the winter or not yet down at 10:00 P.M. in the summer can bring to life a discussion of cultural differences brought about by "a whole new (l)attitude!" (with apologies to a Mexican beer company).

Tying It All Together.   Once your students have collected the latest news headlines or researched the archives for a past news story that took place over a period of time or have followed the progress of a soccer team adopted by the class or checked the European weather on the Web, what more can be done with it? If lab facilities permit, the students could videotape a mock news brief for the class. If video is not available, then tape record a radio news brief with authentic theme music from the target culture radio news, downloaded as .AU or .WAV audio files or with *RealAudio.* If the technology available does not allow for recording the news, a simple presentation to the class still gives the students formal speaking practice in the target language.

Arizona State Universitiy's Applications and Reactions to the Use of the World Wide Web.   Several language classes at Arizona State University (ASU) have given students a chance to explore the World Wide Web in search of cultural information. This section will report on the results of the use of the Web and student reaction to it from two elementary-level French classes, three Spanish language classes (two second-semester and one sixth-semester), one Portuguese language class (third semester), a Spanish-American 400-level civilization course and a Portuguese/Brazilian 400-level civilization course.[4] The use of the Web in the language classes was obligatory, while it was optional in the civilization courses.

Browsing the Web for cultural information was incorporated as an activity in some lower-division French courses during the 1995–96 academic year. The students were given a few training sessions on the use of the Web and its search engines and were provided with a written sheet of instructions on how to surf the Web. The students then wrote a three- to four-page summary (in English) of the information they found.

Students in FRE 101 were given an assignment to browse the Web for French language sites in search of information on any aspect of Francophone culture that interested them (e.g., music, food, tourist sites), while FRE 102 students were asked to find out specific cultural information (e.g., population, economy) on any of the forty-seven francophone countries.

Students in both classes had a very positive reaction to using the Web to learn about francophone culture. However, some students were also frustrated by the fact that the Web pages often took a long time to display graphics-intensive pages on the computer screens in the Language Computing Lab.

The SPA 102 classes were given one day of training and another three or four sessions to browse the Web, using prearranged sites. The response of these classes to the exploration of the Web was overwhelmingly positive (twenty-nine in favor to three against). Students appreciated having access to a great deal of knowledge about Hispanic culture. However, they complained that it took a lot of time to learn to use and little time was left for browsing. They requested more training and practice time in the future.

Students complained particularly about the poor sound quality of audio segments on the Web. This suggests that the "wow" factor is of limited value, and students will demand a certain level of performance before offering total acceptance of the use of that technology. If the level of technology available does not provide adequate audio or video performance, it would be important to omit activities relying on those technologies until adequate performance is available, either through upgraded hardware or improved software.

The POR 201 class's response to the Web was unanimously positive (ten evaluations received). Students considered the Web to be an "interesting source of topics" for compositions. They enjoyed the freedom they had to browse the Web for information on Brazilian culture and liked learning about this culture through nontraditional means. They considered the Yahoo Search Engine to be quite valuable in their use of the Web; they noted that they could access "massive amounts of information" on Brazilian topics.

Nevertheless, many were impatient with having to wait for graphics to download, and some considered the information they found of superficial value to their understanding of the target culture (e.g., tabloid items). Given time to incorporate such items into a lesson plan, a teacher could undoubtedly help students pick out important cultural icons and values in seemingly superficial materials.

The SPA 314 class was required to "surf" the Web for two assignments. The first task they were required to perform was to search the Web for an interesting Spanish site (with some help from links on the Language Computing Lab home page already established). They then had to write seventy-five words in Spanish about the cultural information they gleaned from that site (e.g., information on the Aztecs, travel information, news from Spanish-speaking countries).

The second assignment on the Web was to work with a partner to find a Web site with enough interesting information to form the basis for a final oral report. Most students were very enthusiastic about this assignment and worked hard to polish their final presentations, which were videotaped by the instructor. In addition, students were trained in the use of the TECH Commander in the Language Computing Lab, a system that allows the instructor to assume control of the computer screens of students for demonstration purposes. The students doing their final oral report had to learn to manipulate the TECH Commander in order to demonstrate the Web site in question during their presentation.

Students' reactions to the use of the Web were mostly positive. They noted liking the color graphics and audio and video segments on the Web. They also enjoyed being able to read cultural information in Spanish and to "travel" to different parts of the world without leaving Arizona. Some students downloaded lyrics to songs and recipes and actually made the dishes described.

However, some students reported frustration with the time needed to download graphics. One group found itself in trouble when the pages on which they based their oral report were actually taken off the target Web site without warning the day before their presentation. This suggests that if students are going to base presentations on evanescent Web material, downloading the site to local storage space for uninterrupted student access is recommended. (Special tools like *WebWhacker* from The ForeFront Group, Inc., <http://www.ffg.com>, and *Web Buddy* from Data Viz, <http://www.dataviz.com>, allow you to download a complete Web site for local storage and quicker access, pointing your browser to the local files rather than the actual URL. This would solve both the disappearing Web site problem and the problem of students getting too far out on the Web into inappropriate Web sites. Of course you cannot download the whole Web, but a desirable site could be preserved, with the second- and third-level links included, for example, to provide good off-line access to useful Web-based data.)

Students in the POR 472 Brazilian Civilization and SPA 472 Spanish-American Civilization courses were allowed to use the Internet as an optional source for information as they did research for their final paper on an aspect of the respective target culture.

Once again, the student response to the Web was very positive (POR 472: all ten in favor; SPA 472: nineteen in favor, two against)—

- "The Internet allowed us to explore history in a different light."
- "There was excellent information on very modern topics."
- "I liked the added information and it was a good break from the text."

Students complained mostly about technical issues—

- "I would get knocked off the Web."
- "The computers were slow to respond."
- "They take too long to download graphics."

Students thought the Web was a good source for general information but not for in-depth study of a topic—"I found many interesting articles . . . none of these articles contained enough information to write a paper." This underscores the fact that instructors need to browse the Web themselves in order to give students a realistic view of what they can find there when doing research for reports.

While it is true that many topics do have limited, superficial coverage, more training on the effective use of the search engines and databases would probably alleviate that problem. Alternatively, the instructor could ascertain which topics do have sufficient information available and steer students in those directions.

As a general rule, after completing their Web assignments, the students in the advanced classes just discussed reported feeling very empowered for having learned how to manipulate the various online technologies to which they were exposed during the course. Their evaluations of the use of these technologies seem to indicate that their attitude toward the use of Spanish or Portuguese as a medium for communication for content-based learning about the target culture was positively affected by their experiences with the World Wide Web.

Interactive Online Technologies

The way in which learners process and internalize linguistic input has been an important topic of discussion in the second language acquisition literature (Krashen 1985; Larsen-Freeman and Long 1991; VanPatten and Cadierno

1993). However, earlier "input models" of language acquisition (Krashen 1985) proposed that a second language is acquired by a learner as a result of just being exposed to "comprehensible input" (language at a level just beyond the competence of the individual, $i + 1$). On the other hand, Pica (1987, 1991) has noted the advantage of giving language learners the opportunity to negotiate meaning with native speakers so that both understand the intended message. "Linguistic input is thus made comprehensible to the learner and may be available for subsequent assimilation or internalization, known as intake" (Call and Sotillo 1995:15).

Moreover, more recent interactionist models of language acquisition (Hatch 1978; Swain 1985) propose that language is acquired through the negotiation of meaning and that new syntactic structures are developed when learners construct discourse collaboratively with an interlocutor. (See Collentine 1995 for a discussion of the presyntactic and syntactic stages in interlanguage development.)

Interactive technologies such as E-mail and electronic conferencing can give students the opportunity to interact with each other and with native speakers in order to help develop their second-language proficiency through the sharing of cultural knowledge.

This can occur either in real time, that is, when all participants are online and involved in the activity at the same time, as in a chat mode, where everyone's comments appear as they type them, or in nonreal time, where the participants post and read the messages when they log on to the system, as with E-mail.

Asynchronous (Not Real-Time)

E-mail. Electronic mail can be easily understood by comparing it with the U.S. Postal Service. Basically, you write someone's P.O. box address on the front of a postcard. You write a message on the postcard and put it into the mail system in a mailbox. The Postal Service picks it up, reads the city address, and transports it to the receiving post office, where they look at the P.O. box number, and put it in the appropriate P.O. box, where it remains until the intended recipient comes to the Post Office and retrieves it. That is just about what happens with electronic mail, except for a few minor computer-related details.

How to Use E-mail. To use E-mail, you need an E-mail account. At universities and colleges, this will probably be on your institution's E-mail system. It is also possible to have Internet E-mail access through one of the "Internet service providers," the companies who provide Internet access to the general public. Some electronic conferencing systems provide E-mail access, and Web browsers like *Netscape Navigator* now incorporate E-mail capabilities as long as there is access to an E-mail POP server somewhere. The details of setting up an E-mail account depend on the system you are actually using, and your local computer support people should be able to help you out.

Each E-mail account has an address on an E-mail server or system some-where, which has temporary storage space for electronic messages and files. When you want to send an E-mail message to someone, you need to know their E-mail address, which consists of the account name, and the Internet "node" at which that account receives mail. For example, the authors receive mail as <PLafford@asu.edu> and <BLafford@asu.edu>. In your software, you select the option to create or send a new message. The software prompts you to enter (or choose from an address book list, if you have one) the E-mail address of the intended recipient.

Next, you usually enter a brief "subject": *entry,* which makes it easy to identify messages that appear in your in-box or folder. Some systems allow you to specify a file to be sent with the mail, called an "Attachment." Unless you are sure that the recipient is using a system that deals with attachments though, it is better to limit your E-mail to text within the E-mail message itself, which is what you enter next, being careful not to use CAPITAL LETTERS, which gives the appearance of shouting.

If you are replying to another E-mail message, it is helpful to restate briefly the question being answered, since the asynchronous nature of E-mail means that even though you might be replying to a question one minute after seeing it, the person who wrote it may have forgotten what was in the original message, if it was written a day or a week ago. That is also why it is useful to have meaningful subjects, since a message generated "in reply to" an E-mail message lists the subject of the original message. In any case, once you finish your message, you select the SEND option (or press CTRL + Z in some systems) to actually send the message.

The E-mail you send off gets relayed through the system and, based on the E-mail address, ends up in the recipient's E-mail account, where it remains until he or she logs in and looks to see if he or she has any mail. There are some systems that will notify you when you have new mail, but it will still be up to the recipient to retrieve and open the E-mail message, usually by selecting the "READ NEW MAIL" option or an equivalent. If there is a problem delivering the mail—"No Such User" or "Server Down," for ex-ample—the mail will usually be bounced back, so you know about it and have a chance to figure out the mistake, correct it, and resend the message.

When the recipient reads the mail, he or she can REPLY to it (which opens up a new message automatically addressed to the sender), SAVE it (perhaps in a special folder, by topic, for future reference), or DELETE it. Be careful when responding to messages you receive from a LISTSERV (essentially a special interest group mailing list, which automatically resends a message to all E-mail addresses on the list), however, since many listservs are set up to distribute replies to the whole list, not just the person who wrote the message. In that case, you would need to copy the E-mail address of the sender and start a new message. A trick here (and in graphical browsers while on the Web) is to try using the mouse to "select" the text, and then select EDIT/ COPY from the menu, or press CTRL + C to COPY the address or URL, and then PASTE the address or URL in the destination field with CTRL + V (to make it VISIBLE, as I think of it). This also avoids the pitfalls of mistyping the address.

The Use of E-mail in Foreign Language Classes. Barson, Frommer, and Schwartz (1993) reported on a cooperative elaboration of research projects carried out among intermediate-level French classes at Stanford, Pittsburgh, and Harvard via E-mail. As a result of this experiment students reported more confidence in their use of the target language and a positive attitude toward the use of E-mail as an instructional tool. In addition, negotiation of meaning, an essential ingredient for interlanguage development, was carried out between instructors and students through their E-mail interchanges as students asked for clarification of various messages they received.

Despite the advantages of L2 student-peer interaction through the use of online technologies, research has shown that focused interaction with native speakers of the language provides opportunities for students to develop their internal grammars to a greater extent than through normal classroom activities.

For instance, Call and Sotillo's (1995) study showed that students who were required to spend an hour each week in face-to-face interaction with native speakers of Spanish made significantly more progress in their use of the preterit/imperfect distinction than the control group who spent that hour in the language lab. Although the interaction in Call and Sotillo's study was oral, it supports the notion that written focused interaction with native speakers on a regular basis might also have the same positive effect on the students' interlanguage.

Oliva and Pollastrini's (1995) study of the use of the Internet in Italian language classes at the University of Utah lends credence to this idea. In this study students in advanced-level Italian courses communicated with native speakers of Italian on cultural issues through E-mail, NEWS (newsgroups), and IRC (Internet Relay Chat), the last two of which are discussed below.

The results of this research were based on questionnaires that asked the students to assess their progress in four language skills and the helpfulness of the various Internet and computer tools for the development of those skills.

Not surprisingly, the students noted the most improvement in their writing skills. They also found E-mail to have been the most helpful technology of those used in the experiment. Oliva and Pollastrini suggest that the reason for the less positive assessment of NEWS and IRC by these students may be the level of computer skill needed to access them.

The notion of "ease of use" as an important factor in the creation of a positive impression of a given technology on the language learner was corroborated by the ASU SPA 102 students who had a more positive impression of E-mail (characterized by them as very easy to use) than of the Electronic Forum (which involved more intricate steps for its use). Instructors should keep this in mind at all times when planning to integrate various types of online activities into a course curriculum. Sufficient time should be dedicated to training students in the use of technologies that require higher-level computer skills for their implementation. In addition, clearly written instructions on their use should be handed out to students so they can access these technologies on their own time without extensive hand-holding by either the instructor or a lab assistant.

Sample Activities.   Since in E-mail, you can read and reply to only one message at a time, E-mail can be used more efficiently for pair work than for small-group work, where electronic conferencing (below) may be more appropriate.

Beginning-Level Activities: Students should be encouraged to communicate with the instructor (in their native language if necessary) from the first week of the semester in order to have questions on grammar or homework clarified. With their E-mail partners, students can use the target language to ask and answer simple questions that they have practiced in class. Novice-level speakers can also share personal information with their E-mail partners; this requires listing objects or activities, for example, describing the things in their room at home or listing their activities on a typical school day.

Most E-mail software has the capability to include the text of the original message in the body of the reply message, usually set off with angle brackets on the left margin of the quoted text. In some software such as *PINE* and *Eudora,* it is offered by default; on the IBM VMS mainframe, the command is "REPLY TEXT." This "quoted text" function can be used at the beginning level to have students practice filling out forms they might encounter in the target culture such as a visa application or a hotel registration form. The student would receive the message containing the form with blanks, and would insert the answers online.

Intermediate-Level Activities: E-mail can be used in a similar fashion to that described below for the Electronic Forum, for example, to ask and answer simple questions and describe themselves and their family, talk about their daily routine in complete sentences, and so forth. Students can also use E-mail to describe for their partner a cultural monument seen on a target language Web site, for example, the pyramids at Teotihuacan in Mexico.

The "quoted text" function (above) can be used at the intermediate level to have students respond to more-involved tasks, such as filling out an application for a semester abroad: "Why do you want to learn French?" "Where have you studied French before?" "What do you want to do when you graduate?" This helps prepare the student for real-world tasks in the electronic environment that more and more will be the norm.

Advanced-Level Activities: With some advanced planning by instructors of both classes, foreign language students in the United States can use E-mail with inhabitants of the target culture who are studying English as a foreign language. Students from the two cultures can be paired as E-mail pals based on a brief survey of likes and dislikes administered during the first week of class to both groups.

Once these pairs are established they will be assigned weekly cultural topics (informational, behavioral, or achievement) to explore together, alternating between the use of each group's native and target languages, for example, how each society views marriage, family, the importance of arriving on time to meetings, popular sports, music, famous artists or writers in both cultures, how different holidays that commemorate historical events are celebrated (e.g., Independence Day). Each group will be told to search more for similarities than differences in their discussions (Robinson 1993).

If it is feasible for the two groups to meet for a meal at the end of the semester (e.g., on the Arizona-Mexico border for students in Arizona and Sonora, Mexico) such a meeting should be arranged. If not, the two groups may try to connect visually using *CUSeeMe* (see below).

One of the greatest challenges posed by promoting E-mail contact between students from two or more countries is obtaining access to the names of target culture instructors and students who would like to communicate with American students. See <http://www.stolaf.edu/network/iecc/> for information on finding an electronic pen pal.

Arizona State University Applications and Reactions to the Use of E-Mail.   The first use of E-mail by ASU students in foreign language classes involved two classes of SPA 313 (fifth-semester college Spanish concentrating on conversation/composition).

The SPA 313 students were given the option of keeping a journal or using E-mail to communicate with students from the other class on topics of their choosing. Students were not given corrective feedback from the teacher or from their peers; they were told simply to write to their E-mail pal.

Student reactions to E-mail technology were mixed (nine in favor, six against). Many thought the use of E-mail was a new and exciting way to practice their writing skills and this motivated some to write messages to each other. "Getting messages from a variety of students helped expose me to a greater vocabulary. It was also fun to have several 'pen pals' in Spanish. I was constantly looking for an opportunity to seek out new people to communicate with."

However, this experiment took place before the renovation of the Arizona State University Language Lab into the Language Learning Laboratories, so students were forced to find remote sites on campus or to log in from home in order to do the E-mail assignments. Students were very critical of the lack of easy access to E-mail and this colored their view of the activities. "It was a good idea but it was hard for me to find time to go to the computer sites."

This lack of easy access to remote sites is an especially critical problem for students in large metropolitan universities (such as ASU) who commute to school and hold down part- or full-time jobs in addition to going to school. In cases where the student has a computer and a modem at home, access to E-mail is not difficult. However, for less economically advantaged students such lack of time and access may prevent them from keeping up with E-mail assignments if they are made obligatory. "The idea of being able to communicate with fellow students appealed to me. Because of my work schedule, however, I found it extremely difficult to go to the computer lab three or more times per week. Had it not been for this conflict, I believe I would have benefited from the experience." It is obvious that professors need to understand the logistical realities that their students face regarding computer/E-mail access and be realistic about what they can expect from them in the way of E-mail and any online assignments.

In addition, given too much free rein in the E-mail assignments, the students were at a loss for something to say: "I did not feel that I had a large variety of topics to write about." Students had mixed reactions about the lack of correction of their writing in this mode. Some students enjoyed the freedom of not having to worry about their grammar: "The E-mail exercise helped to coordinate my thoughts in Spanish without pressure of correction from teacher within class situations." However, others bemoaned the lack of corrective feedback.

Although this E-mail exercise did not require students to discuss Hispanic culture *per se,* it did motivate them to write more and to use Spanish as a communicative medium.

The use of E-mail solely to communicate with the instructor and others in the class on any topic (e.g., homework, reactions to assignments, plans) was judged very favorably by two SPA 102 (second-semester) classes during the Spring 1996 semester. The students enjoyed being able to use E-mail to ask questions about assignments and get extra help on grammar (online tutorials).[5] These students considered E-mail easy to use (editable), and those who had never been introduced to the technology considered this a valuable tool to use in their daily activities (writing to friends in or out of Spanish class). The students were adamant, however, that the training session on E-mail be done at the very beginning of the term so that they could take more advantage of it throughout the semester.

This points out the need for planned articulation of the use of E-mail technology. If facilities allow for it, all students in first-year classes should be introduced to this technology and be encouraged to use it to communicate with their instructors and with their classmates throughout their language-course sequence (100 to 400 level). If it is not automatically issued upon registration, students should be required to get an E-mail account as part of their enrollment procedures for the beginning language classes. Once they have this account established in the first year, they can keep using it as they progress through their courses at the university, foreign language classes, and others. Those students entering at higher levels from other institutions would be required to get an account in order to be able to communicate with the instructor.

Electronic Conferencing and Newsgroups.   Electronic conferencing and Usenet newsgroups are similar, in that an online structure is created

- to organize topics,
- to allow participants to post messages on these topics for everyone to read,
- for other readers to post replies, and
- for these messages to be accessed at the convenience of the user.

Newsgroups are maintained on servers on the Internet where anyone on the Internet can log in and participate. There are so many newsgroups (14,000 by some estimates) that there are whole books discussing them and how to use them. (For more information, see Williams, *The Internet for Teachers,* 1995, IDG Books, <http://www.idgbooks.com/>.) Here we will limit our remarks to suggesting that some newsgroups with a socio-cultural-linguistic orientation may lend themselves to use in the language classroom, providing access to real people with first-person accounts from the target cultures. As always, it is important to approach the public areas of the Internet with supervision and common sense. Some news reader software allows you to limit the newsgroups available for access. You would probably feel more comfortable with a controlled list of newsgroups when working with students.

As for electronic conferencing, *Electronic Forum* (EF) is an example of conferencing software developed at Glendale (Arizona) Community College (one of the Maricopa Community Colleges) as a virtual classroom-oriented closed conferencing system, similar to *VAX Notes* or *CoSy*, or the new Web-oriented *WebNotes* <http://www.ostech.com>, where access to reading and posting messages is usually limited to a particular group of students in a particular class or to students who are collaborating on a project.

How to Use Electronic Conferencing.   In general, to use an electronic conferencing system like EF, each student has an account that allows him or her to log on either on site or via remote (Internet or dial-up) terminal. The student has permission to join certain groups or discussions based on membership and can view topics posted by the leader or other members, who can also read the follow-up responses during subsequent log-on sessions. Like other asynchronous systems, EF is a bit cumbersome to use, since you can only see/read one message at a time.

Even though the EF is set up as an asynchronous communication system, training sessions on EF could involve a certain synchronicity in which students learn to post messages, read others' messages, and respond to them during the hour-long training session (see description of ASU SPA 314 class below). In this way, they will be better prepared and know what to expect the next time they log on to the EF for their assignments.

The systems also usually provide for private messaging between members and sometimes E-mail to the outside world as well. The activities described here for the Electronic Forum can be adapted to whatever conferencing or E-mail system is available.

Sample Activities.   The use of EF to teach informational, behavioral, and achievement culture can be very effective, as shown in the sample activities described below.

Beginning-Level Activities: Prior to the *Electronic Forum* activity the instructor can assign a different reading assignment containing basic information on a target culture country to each student. The instructor would then post basic questions on the forum to be answered by each student, using the information given to him or her on a specific country, e.g., naming the capital of the country, the monetary unit, the main mountain ranges or rivers. The EF activity would entail each student's answering these basic questions about his or her assigned country. Each student can then read the answers of another student and write a few simple sentences summarizing the information gathered on another country, e.g., The capital of France is Paris.

Intermediate-Level Activities: After reading a sheet with relevant background material (prepared by the instructor) to get the information needed for this exercise, students can describe themselves physically, taking on the identity of a persona (fictitious or real) from the target culture. Later, other students can comment on the description and ask questions to gather other information (suggested by the professor) on these personae. For instance, one student could pretend to be Don Quijote and another student could ask him or her the name of his horse (Rocinante) or favorite lady (Dulcinea) or any other question that might come to mind. Students should be encouraged to be creative if the answers to their colleagues' questions are not contained in the bio sheet.

Advanced-Level Activities: Students can be shown a video segment in class of two members of the target culture conversing on a "hot" topic, e.g., two citizens of Quebec arguing in French for and against secession from Canada. Students are randomly given one of five different things to notice about the conversation, e.g., the arguments (points for or against) made by speakers 1 and 2 (informational culture); their respective body language (behavioral culture); the way in which each interrupts the other, holds the floor, gives up his or her turn in the conversation; regional accent or vocabulary; the architectural characteristics of the setting of the debate (e.g., the Château Frontenac) (achievement culture).

The students then carry out a follow-up EF assignment in which five subforums have been set up to receive commentary in each of the five areas. Students post their observations to the appropriate subforum corresponding to the topic they have been assigned. After posting their statement they must also read the statements made by other students addressing the same question and comment on their statements. Discussion should continue until some sort of consensus is reached within the group regarding the most important points to bring up in class the next day for oral discussion.

If anonymity is to be kept for EF users, the instructor could lead the discussion in class based on one group's work, but he or she would expect all students to participate orally to some degree in the overall discussion, since they had all seen the video. If anonymity is not important, all students working on a given EF question outside of class would get together and discuss their EF session orally (with printouts of their statements in hand) before the entire class addresses all five issues.

Thus, by using the *Electronic Forum*, written small-group work is accomplished outside of class to complement the type of oral small-group and class discussions that take place in class. In this way, collaborative/ cooperative learning is extended beyond the classroom even for students at large metropolitan universities who do not reside geographically close to each other (such as in a dormitory in small liberal arts residential colleges).

Arizona State University's Applications and Reactions to the Use of the Electronic Forum: The use of the *Electronic Forum* (EF) in three ASU Spanish classes (two sections of SPA 102 and one section of SPA 314) and two Japanese classes (JPN 102) will be reported in this section. (The *Electronic Forum* does have chat capability, but in these classes, chat was not implemented.)

In the SPA 102 classes, homework assignments (short compositions) were given on the EF by the instructor and all students turned in their assignments online by posting them to the EF, where other students could read them.

SPA 102 student reactions to this technology were mixed (twenty-eight in favor, ten against). Some were excited about the use of EF since they enjoyed reading others' assignments; others disliked the fact that their peers had access to what they wrote. However, several felt less inhibited about letting others read their work since pseudonyms were used.

Some students preferred the EF over E-mail, since the EF assignment they were given gave them some structure while their E-mail task forced them to initiate topics on their own. This problem, of course, could be remedied by giving more structure to the E-mail assignment. Conversely, more freedom could be given to an EF assignment since not all students enjoyed having a prescribed topic to discuss. Other students preferred E-mail over EF since it was more private (they could correspond with one person at a time) and editing and indicating accent marks was easier than on EF. They also felt that E-mail was easier to use than EF (less training time required) and noted that they could use E-mail for other purposes (communicating with friends not in the Spanish class). (As mentioned earlier, later versions of EF and other conferencing systems provide external E-mail capabilities.)

Many students noted a great deal of disappointment when they got online and found they had no messages waiting for them. This could easily be remedied by having the instructor pair different sets of students (using pseudonyms or anonymously assigned numbers) for interactive assignments on a regular basis.

Many problems with the use of the *Electronic Forum* were noted by two Japanese 102 classes who were encouraged to use this technology to communicate with each other. A few students noted how new and unconventional the technology was and said they enjoyed talking to classmates in Japanese. In addition, some students appreciated being able to communicate with the instructor this way: "We can get help in more than one place."

However, many students were frustrated by the complexity involved in its use. Others complained that they were only able to use the romanized alphabet (romanji) on the *Electronic Forum* when they would have liked to have used katakana, hiragana, or kanji (the other three writing systems of Japanese)—"[I want] on screen kanji—make it more fun!" In all, only sixteen out of twenty-nine JPN 102 students said the use of the *Electronic Forum* was worthwhile.

The only use of the *Electronic Forum* to teach culture in an ASU Spanish language class was made by a sixth-semester Spanish class (SPA 314) Conversation/Composition during the Spring 1995 semester. One issue complicated the use of EF for these third-year students from the beginning—the problem of access.

The complication involved with assigning tasks on the EF or on E-mail to third-year classes stems from the fact that at ASU, only lower-division classes have regular access to the computing lab and its technology as a result of the lab fee they pay each semester. In order for upper-division classes to make use of the Language Computing Lab, they have to be scheduled for special training sessions in the lab at the beginning of the semester. During very busy morning hours, this scheduling can cause problems since often there are other lower-division classes already assigned to the lab during those times.

As a result, the SPA 314 class was able to visit the Language Computing Lab only four times during the semester to be trained and to practice the use of online technologies. During the first training session they were told to take on an assumed name, which they would keep throughout the semester. Only the instructor knew the real names of the students who posted the messages (in order to be able to give credit for assignments). All entries to the EF had to be at least seventy-five words; students were graded for completing the assignment but no feedback was given on form, just on content.

Students were given five EF assignments in Spanish during the semester:

1. describe themselves (physical aspects and their character). They were allowed to invent a new physical being and personality for this assignment; some took on the characteristics of the pseudonyms they chose, e.g., Fat Albert, Smurfette, and Lorena Bobbit.

2. respond to someone else's entry (commenting on what was said). Other students were intrigued by their colleagues' creativity and responded to

these "personalities" as though they were communicating with the real characters portrayed by the pseudonyms. For example, "Smurfette" lamented that no one would ask her out because she was short and "blue," and a kind response came back from another classmate: "Don't worry, someone will see the beauty of your personality."

3. give an opinion about Proposition 187 (California), which was related to their viewing of the movie "El Norte." Students were very excited about responding to this issue, which was in the news at the time they did this assignment. They felt uninhibited as they railed against the proposition and made such statements as "My grandparents came to this country and were given a chance. I wouldn't be here if this law had been in effect at that time."

4. give an opinion about censorship, which was related to their viewing of the movie *La Historia Oficial.* Students also felt free to express their opinions on this issue and actually related it to Watergate and Whitewater in American history.

5. evaluate the pros and cons of the four types of technology used in the teaching of the SPA 314 class. This feedback was invaluable in deciding what types of technology to use in future classes.

In addition to these required assignments, students were told that they could also use EF to communicate with the professor privately, and they were encouraged to bring up discussion topics of their own to which the class would respond. However, since only extra credit was offered for these non-assignments, there were very few students who responded to this initiative. The instructor even found a lack of enthusiastic response to a question put out about the Simpson trial being considered the trial of the century. It was obvious that the students used the EF only when it was assigned, not when it was used simply as an extra-credit activity.

These third-year Spanish students basically had the same responses to the EF as the first-year students: they felt free to write what they really thought due to the anonymity of the EF entries, they considered EF to be interesting, but they also noted that it was hard to edit and was time consuming. However, students in this third-year class were more enthusiastic about the assignment questions based on cultural aspects of the films they saw rather than just using EF for regular homework assignments.

A New Twist to Electronic Conferencing. WebNotes (from OS Technologies-SpyGlass, <http://www.ostech.com>) has been mentioned as a Web-based electronic conferencing system. Though not originally developed as an educational tool (as opposed to *Electronic Forum*), *WebNotes* is becoming popular in educational institutions due to its flexible access (anyone with a Web browser and the right permissions can connect and log in) and impressive capabilities for dealing with graphic and even sound files.

While offering the same basic structure of open-access or restricted forums, students can be assigned a user ID and password. The instructor establishes main topics and subtopics; students read the main topics and respond. Point-and-click access to the posts and easy access to the previous and follow-up replies makes it easy to follow the threads (complete discussions consisting of the original post and all the related responses). The Web-based HTML nature of *WebNotes* makes it possible to include accented characters, graphics, HTML links to Web sites, and even *RealAudio* or other sound files in the *WebNotes* posts (provided you are working with multimedia-capable computers). Imagine posting a short audio clip as a discussion topic. Technically, it should be possible to allow replies to include audio too, although the size of the files and the network traffic probably impose practical limits with the current technology. Check back to the *ACTFL-IT* page for ongoing feedback on the experimental installation planned here at Arizona State.

Synchronous Communication (Real Time)

Synchronous communication among second-language learners or between learners and native speakers is one of the most useful tools for the development of interlanguage skills that online technologies have to offer.

Chat.   The use of the chat capability in any of its online varieties allows for real-time negotiation of meaning (asking for clarification, getting immediate feedback, adjusting one's hypotheses about the target language's structure, etc.) normally only available in face-to-face conversations.

How Does Chat Work?   In order to do interactive text-based chat in real time, an individual uses chat client software on his or her own computer to connect to an IRC chat server computer somewhere on the Internet. (IRC stands for "Internet Relay Chat.") At the same time, other users from elsewhere on the Internet log on to the same IRC chat server.

The IRC chat server has various chat rooms or channels set up, usually identified by topic of conversation, interest, or age group, and each individual joins a chat room to participate in the discussion. Each user logs on with a nickname by which he or she will be identified, but the user can also make more information available in the user profile that can be configured in the software.

When you join a room, most IRC client software will show a window down one side listing the nicknames of all of the people who are in that room. A command window across the bottom provides a place to type in the text you want to contribute to the conversation, and the rest of the window is where the conversation scrolls by, one line at a time. Each line is preceded by the nickname of the person who contributed it. Look at this simulated chat session transcript:

\<BigBill\>	Did anyone see the latest Arnold Schwarzenegger movie?
\<SuzyQ\>	Yes. It was quite exciting.
\<JohnBoy\>	I prefer the high tech James Bond movies to the terrorist films.
\<DavyJones\>	BigBill: what was it called?
\<Jennifer\>	SuzyQ, I thought it had too much violence. :-(
\<BigBill\>	DJ: "Terminator Twelve" or "Thirteen."
\<DavyJones\>	The last James Bond film was kind of silly, though.
\<SuzyQ\>	JohnBoy, PIERCE BROSNAN RULES!

First notice the nickname of the speaker at the beginning of each message. Then, since there may be more than one conversation taking place at once in the same room, the speakers often start off their message with the nickname of the person being answered. (Notice where DavyJones starts off with "BigBill," who responds with "DJ.") At the end of Jennifer's message is the frowning "smiley," :-(. (A "smiley" or "emoticon" [for "emotion icon"] is a combination of punctuation intended to convey some of the extralinguistic information normally part of a face-to-face conversation that is missing in chat. If you tilt your head to the left, you see that the colon-hyphen-closing parenthesis :-) looks like a smiling face, ;-) is a wink, and so on.)

Once you join or enter a room, what you type in the command window will be sent when you press **\<ENTER\>**. To issue a command rather than text, start with a forward slash (/). To change your nickname to JoeCool, for example, type /nick JoeCool **\<ENTER\>**. To leave the the room, type /leave **\<ENTER\>**. To logoff the IRC server, type /quit **\<ENTER\>**. To see what other rooms are available, type /list **\<ENTER\>**, or press a button in the software offering to list the rooms or topics available. To join another room, type /join **#ROOM NAME**. The room name can be an existing room whose name you know, or you can display a list of all the available rooms.

Be forewarned, however, that many IRC chat rooms are for mature audiences, and the names of the rooms make it very clear. If you venture onto public IRC servers, you will want to closely supervise the rooms involved in your class activity. The Netscape Chat client allows you to configure an address book of only the rooms you want the students to visit. It would not preclude entering other rooms, but it would simplify finding the rooms you want your students to be in.

It is also possible to create a new room on a server, simply by typing "/join #MyNewRoom <**ENTER**>" (for example). You, as creator, could then moderate the channel and silence or kick out interlopers.

Variations on Chat.   There are a number of variations on the chat theme. Some exist on the commercial services like America Online (as Chat Rooms and Lounges) and CompuServe (with its CB Simulator). Time spent online with a commercial service, though, costs perhaps $2 to $4/hour, after your base monthly allotment of ten or twenty hours (or whatever) is used up. In addition, their gateways to the Internet and the WWW are often slow. Once you have learned the basics of the online world, you might consider casting off the training wheels of the commercial service and go with an Internet service provider, where hourly access rates are usually lower, and you will be able to use the wide range of Internet software from E-mail to special chat programs, to fancy browsers, to online video—even using a Minitel emulator (available from <http://www.minitel.fr>) to log on to France's pioneering national information service and search for the phone number of that exchange student who was here a few years ago. Other software allows you to run your own chat environment.

PowWow.   One of these chat-like applications requiring an Internet connection, called *PowWow* (available from <http://www.tribal.com/>), allows you to establish your own conference. *PowWow* also has some audio capabilities with which, if you have a sound card and microphone, you can send voice and sound effects along with your text. The default (and original) *PowWow* display mode is a multipanel chat where each of up to seven people can type and see the other messages as they go along. For a small group, it is easy enough to maintain separate discussions in separate windows. For discussions with many participants, however, it is easier to have the one chat window with all the text in one place.

CUSeeMe.   *CUSeeMe*, developed at Cornell University, <http://goliath. wpine.com/cu-seeme.html> and now marketed commercially by White Pine Software, is primarily technology for transmitting video images via a server like IRC (which for *CUSeeMe* is called a "reflector"). Sound is also a possibility, but because the audio quality is not always good enough to understand, there is also a chat window available in *CUSeeMe* that works like IRC. To send video, you need some way of getting a live video image into your computer, so a video camera connected to a video capture board can usually be set up with the software. Connectix (<http://www.connectix. com>) has a QuickCam (about $100 for black and white, $200 for color) that plugs right into the serial port on the Mac or the parallel port on the PC, so it does not use a special video capture board.

Since *CUSeeMe* does not require that you send video (if you do not have a camera or your connection is too slow, that is, slower than 14,400 bps), it is possible to use *CUSeeMe* software as a "lurker," that is, someone just looking on, but not sending video. You can see the others online sending video and can use the chat window to communicate with them. *CUSeeMe* is popular in the Internet coffee shops around the world, where people go to get on the Internet and have fun over coffee. Another warning, however: as elsewhere on the Internet, there are people who take advantage of the anonymity and are out looking for shock value, so you will want to be ready to close a window that comes up with unwanted images.

In a controlled classroom environment, *CUSeeMe* could be used to give E-mail pals (foreign or domestic) a glimpse of their fellow correspondents and converse with them orally or in the chat window face to face in the target language.

Internet-Based Telephony.   An audio technology corresponding to the one-to-one chat function of *PowWow* is direct audio connection from one computer to another over the Internet with "telephone" software. Two popular commercial packages are *InternetPhone* <http://www.vocaltec.com> and *WebPhone* <http://www.quarterdeck.com>, but there is also free software called *SpeakFreely* <http://www.fourmilab.ch/#speakfree> and *FreeTel* <http://www.freetel.com>. For these applications, like *PowWow,* each user has matching software on his or her machine and can connect to other users who are using the software. Users may register with a directory maintained by the software company and can then be sought out for cold-calling (being called by someone you do not yet know) and communication by voice, if your computer has sound capabilities and a microphone. Like IRC, there are all kinds of topic groups available, but it is easier to find foreign language and country-related users with whom to verbally chat than on IRC. It can be quite engaging and not too risky with prearranged class-to-class linkups.

Real-time chat and its slower cousins, the E-mail exchange and electronic conferencing, all have similar potential. The basic link is providing an environment in which communicative exchanges take place, generally in the target language, either with other students or with "real people" having "real communication."

The Use of Synchronous Communication via Networked Computers to Teach Foreign Languages.   Kern (1995) reports on the use of networked computers for synchronous written communication in the target language by instructors and students. In his study the class used the *Daedalus InterChange,* a local-area computer network application, to discuss a topic that the teacher had posted. The amount and type of written language produced was then compared with oral discussion data on the same topic. [Editor's Note: For a complete discussion of this topic, see Chapter 5 in this volume.]

The results of Kern's study support those of other studies regarding the benefits of using networked computers to facilitate classroom discussion (Beauvois 1992; Chun 1994; Kelm 1992). Compared to the oral discussion data, the written discussions using *InterChange* offered more opportunity for individual student expression and evidenced a higher level of morphosyntactic sophistication with a broader range of discourse functions. According to the results of an attitude survey toward the use of this technology, students became interested in getting to know the opinions of their peers, and they felt less anxiety expressing their ideas in written form than they would have felt in a class discussion.

However, Kern (1995) does report results that may make some instructors wary of this type of student interaction. Since students were free to communicate with each other without instructor interference, teacher control over the interchanges was diminished, and the coherence and continuity of the discussion was often lost. The fast pace of the written discussion can be a problem for students who do not read quickly in the target language. In addition, students were exposed to other students' written output, which contained errors.

Kern concludes his discussion with a realistic view of the use of such synchronous technologies: "Formal accuracy, stylistic improvement, global coherence, consensus, and reinforcement of canonical discourse conventions are goals not well served by InterChange. Conversely, unfettered self-expression, increased student initiative and responsiveness, generation of multiple perspectives on an issue, voicing of differences, and status equalization are supported by InterChange" (470). Therefore, teachers must weigh the pros and cons of this type of discussion group and have realistic expectations about its outcomes before implementing it into the curriculum.

Other studies that have demonstrated positive effects on students' interlanguage and attitudes toward the target culture through the use of online communication with native and nonnative speakers include Cohen and Miyake (1986), Cohen and Riel (1989), Barson, Frommer, and Schwartz (1993), Cononelos and Oliva (1993), and Sayers (1994).

Sample Activities.

Beginning-Level Activities: In order not to pressure students to produce output more sophisticated than their abilities allow, they should not be encouraged to use synchronous communication on open-ended topics for long periods of time until they can form simple sentences consistently. However, pairs of beginning-level students using this function on the computer can be prompted by the instructor to ask and answer simple *WH*-questions about each other ("Where do you live?" "What is your favorite sport?") or on a cultural reading discussed in class ("Where is the Eiffel Tower?").

Yes/no questions can be practiced by the use of the game "Twenty Questions," in which all students in the class are given the same list of famous real or fictional personalities. One student assumes the identity of one of them and entertains yes/no questions from other students logged into the chat session about his or her character: "Are you a man?" "Are you a woman?" The game continues until the identity is guessed, or until twenty questions have been asked, whichever comes first. This could be done in small-group work by using multiple chat rooms or *PowWow* software (above).

Intermediate-Level Activities: Students in the same class can be told to find out specific pieces of information about three other people in the class (e.g., descriptions of their house or family, daily activities, pastimes) and write up the results for homework. Instead of merely asking and answering questions practiced several times in class, intermediate-level students have to figure out what questions to ask to get the information they need from their conversation partners.

In order to carry out this assignment between two classes that are not at the same school, arrangements would have to be made to assure that all students have access to IRC and that they could be available for the task at the same hour of the day. Students at one school would be paired with students from another in order to foster communication with new foreign language E-mail pals. Once these pairs are established, several different kinds of simple target-language cultural assignments in pre-established chat rooms could be carried out, for example, sharing facts about a given target-culture country in order to prepare a joint report.

Advanced-Level Activities: Students could inform themselves, through use of the Web or other materials, about how various holidays in the target culture, for example, *El Grito* (Mexican Independence Day) or the New Year are celebrated. Then students could be assigned to pairs in which one student plays the part of a member of the target culture and the other student gives the American culture point of view. Their task would be to discuss (real-time) in the target language the similarities (cf. Robinson 1993) and differences in the way these holidays are celebrated in the target and home cultures. The next day in class the pair would orally present these similarities and differences regarding the celebration of a particular holiday in both cultures.

With advanced planning, second-language learners may communicate directly with students their own age in the target culture, using the target language (again, see <http://www.stolaf.edu/network/iecc/> about creating classroom links.) After the students have established E-mail pals and have gotten to know something about each other, prearranged cultural topics for discussion could be assigned by both instructors. Both the local and IRC interchanges could involve informational, behavioral, or achievement culture, for example, discussion of holidays, customs, real events.

One more point: the IRC sessions can also be captured or logged (that is, saved as a text file) and then distributed for later analysis. The instructor could study a sample of the transcript with the class to point out vernacular language and grammatical aberrations not usually used in the written language, but common in speech. Chat then becomes a source of meaningful, useful, productive vocabulary, and those who shy away because of unchecked errors can still participate with a chance to help students learn from the mistakes captured online.

MOOs/MUDs

A MOO is a real-time, text-based virtual reality environment where users log in, assume an identity, and interact with each other and the objects and spaces that are there. Developed from the MUD (referring to the Multi-User Domain, or to many aficionados of the genre, the Multi-User Dungeon) online Dungeons & Dragons games in the eighties, MOO stands for *MUD*, Object-Oriented. MOOs are a fairly complicated environment; the interested reader is referred to <http://www.cs.unca.edu/~davidson/du-about.html> to read about the Diversity University MOO.

How Do You MOO?   You log in to MOO using a TELNET command (from a mainframe) or a TELNET program on a PC or Mac. You specify the computer running the MOO by name or IP number and a port number and then furnish a log-in name and password. Most MOOs allow you to log in as GUEST, to look around, and then have some provision for creating a real account on the MOO. Once you are in, using commands like GO NORTH; LOOK; PICKUP BOOK, etc., you are presented with descriptions of the rooms, sights, and objects that have been "created" by the other users. If you are ready to jump in and experience it, TELNET to 128.18.101.106 port 8888. (If your browser has a TELNET helper application defined, in the space where you usually enter a URL, enter telnet://128.18.101.106:8888 and press <ENTER>.) Diversity University's MOO site is designed to help the new user become familiar with MOOs and commands. As always, check the *ACTFL-IT* page for updates.

Sample Activities.

Beginning-Level Activities: Simple problem-solving activities can easily be carried out with the use of MOOs and MUDs. A "Mystery Guest House" game could be constructed in which the students work collaboratively to identify the mystery guest in that room. The students could be furnished with a list of possible guests on a virtual sheet of paper in the lobby and a list of rooms to visit. "George Bush, Shirley Temple, Mario Andretti, Barbara Walters, John Wayne; Rooms 1, 2 3, 4, and 5." The objects in each room constitute a list of hints. If "REGARDER TABLE" in Room 1 yields "Sur la table, il y a des gants, une casque, des clés, et une carte d'identité pour la course 'Les 500 Milles d'Indianapolis,' " the student might guess that the mystery guest in that room is Mario Andretti. To help with the unfamiliar vocabulary among the objects, the student could go into the equivalent room in the parallel universe where the language is English and repeat the process: "LOOK TABLE." "On the table, there are some gloves, a helmet, some keys, and an Indianapolis 500 ID card." Then, returning to the French room, the student could ask to "shake hands with Mario Andretti." If that is right, they shake hands virtually (in cyberspace) *Mario vous félicite!* ["Mario congratulates you!"]; if not, *Il n'est pas là* ["He isn't there."]. More rooms could be added during the semester, and the Mystery Guest House would be completely built for the next semester's classes.

Intermediate-Level Activities: In addition to playing their own games based on "Clue" or other "whodunit" scenarios, intermediate-level students could contribute to building the "Mystery Guest House" used by the beginning-level students, providing new mystery guests and hints.

Advanced-Level Activities: A more involved activity for advanced students could have a class project involved in creating a virtual city (similar to Maxis's "SimCity 2000" civilization planning simulation <http://www.maxis.com/>, although without graphics). To add a cultural-historical twist, it could be set in a particular time in history: Paris at the time of the French Revolution, for example. The students would need to research historical maps and facts and could learn about the history and create the MOO in English and then use it in French. The art class could contribute museum and art rooms. The MOO could then be recreated graphically in a Web site. A truly integrated MOO could have involvement across the curriculum, with each department represented.

As we said, the MOO can become quite involved. We are not giving MOOs too much attention here because we feel that an instructor's time may be more efficiently used setting up class activities in less complicated environments. *Electronic Forum* or a good chat session, for example, can provide more interaction with less overhead.

The Value of Online Technologies/Conclusions

It should be kept in mind that these activities are using online technologies that are not necessarily focused on one grammar point, but rather provide an engaging environment for real use of the language. In the progression from reading and fact-finding to real communication (both in writing and speaking to others) and in writing up one's experiences with these activities, the students are using the language.

If students work in groups (either with students in their class or with other learners), there is oral or written communication in problem solving. If language learners present what they have found to the rest of the class, they practice speaking in formal registers of the target language. If students prepare reports based on the up-to-the-minute news from abroad (either from the Web or from native speaker E-mail pals), there is real-time interest and meaningful information to share. This last factor is a key motivating element for a student of a foreign language to acquire the target language and learn about the target culture.

Interest in using online technologies with foreign language classes at ASU has been gathering momentum since the recent renovation of our Language Learning Laboratories. For the last three years the Department of Languages and Literatures has received university funding to put on a year-end two-week workshop for departmental faculty on the use of these technologies. Faculty who have attended the workshops have voiced interest in incorporating these online resources into the fabric of lower- and upper-division courses in various languages taught in the department. For instance, according to the Supervisor of the French teaching assistants,[6] the use of the Web, electronic conferencing, and chat functions will be an integral part of the curriculum for next year's French language courses at the lower- and upper-division levels. We are confident that other language sections will follow the French section's lead and begin to incorporate systematically the use of online technologies in their language and culture classes' curriculum.

In summary, the online technologies of the Internet and the World Wide Web are excellent tools to support language learning and exposure to foreign cultures. Every day a new potential source of information appears and another opportunity is created for individual educators to share their findings with others, both educators and students alike. So, wait no longer—go explore these new communication tools for enhancing your foreign language classes. Remember, a journey of a thousand miles may begin with a single "click"!

NOTES

1. Richards, Platt, and Platt (1992) define extensive reading as "reading in quantity and in order to gain a general understanding of what is read. It is intended to develop good reading habits to build up knowledge of vocabulary and structure, and to encourage a liking for reading" (133).
2. The W3 Consortium is an international industry consortium supported by governments, universities, research institutes, and companies that "develop common standards for the evolution of the Web." See <http://www.w3.org/>.
3. A combination of the terms "leading-edge technology" and "cutting-edge technology," with emphasis on the fact that it is not always easy to accomplish. This term was used by Ray Smith, Chairman and CEO, Bell Atlantic, in an interview on "The Site," MSNBC, Friday, 19 July 1996. Also at <http://www.thesite.com/0796w3/work/aud_vid/work48_0719audio_14.ram>.
4. We would like to thank the following instructors for their cooperation in gathering feedback from their students on the use of these online technologies: Julie Nicole (FRE 101/102), Debora Cristo (SPA 102), Mark Curran (POR 472, SPA 472), Fumiko Foard (JPN 102), Gail Guntermann (SPA 313), Barbara A. Lafford (SPA 314), and Emi Ochiai (JPN 102).
5. Blake (1995) discusses the use of Remote Technical Assistance (RTA) software—a network-based software package that allows synchronous and asynchronous communication with instructors and foreign language students at other institutions.
6. Dr. Suzanne Hendrickson.

REFERENCES

Barson, J., J. Frommer, and M. Schwartz. 1993. "Foreign Language Learning Using E-mail in a Task-Oriented Perspective: Interuniversity Experiments in Communication and Collaboration." *Journal of Science Education and Technology* 2,4:565–84.
Beauvois, Margaret H. 1992. "Computer-Assisted Classroom Discussion in the Foreign Language Classroom: Conversation in Slow Motion." *Foreign Language Annals* 25:455–64.
Blake, Robert. 1995. "Remote TA: Speaking Spanish on the AATSP San Diego, CA Internet." Paper given at the Annual Meeting of the American Association of Teachers of Spanish and Portuguese, San Diego, August 1995.
Brinton, Donna M., Marguerite Ann Snow, and Marjorie Bingham Wesche. 1989. *Content-Based Second Language Instruction.* Boston: Heinle and Heinle Publishing.

Bush, Michael. 1996. "Language Learning via the Web." Paper given at the 1996 Symposium of the Computer-Aided Language Instruction Consortium (CALICO), Albuquerque, NM, 29 May 1996.

Call, M. E., and S. M. Sotillo. 1995. "Is Talk Cheap? The Role of Conversation in the Acquisition of Language." *Hispania* 78:114–21.

Chun, D. 1994. "Using Computer Networking to Facilitate the Acquisition of Interactive Competence." *System* 22:17–31.

Cohen, M., and N. Miyake. 1986. "A Worldwide Intercultural Network: Exploring Electronic Messaging for Instruction." *Instructional Science* 15:257–73.

Cohen, M., and M. Riel. 1989. "The Effect of Distant Audiences on Students' Writing." *American Educational Research Journal* 26,2:143–59.

Collentine, Joseph. 1995. "The Development of Complex Syntax and Mood-Selection Abilities by Intermediate-Level Learners of Spanish." *Hispania* 78:122–35.

Cononelos, Terry, and Maurizio Oliva. 1993. "Using Computer Networks to Enhance Foreign Language Culture/Education." *Foreign Language Annals* 26:527–34.

Genesee, Fred. 1987. *Learning through Two Languages.* New York: Newbury House.

Guntermann, Gail. 1993. "Foreign Language Teachers and the Challenge of Cultural Competence." *Culture and Content: Perspectives on the Acquisition of Cultural Competence in the Foreign Language Classroom,* Monograph Series #4. Tempe, AZ: Southwest Conference on Language Teaching.

Hatch, E. 1978. "Discourse Analysis and Second Language Acquisition," in Evelyn Hatch, ed., *Second Language Acquisition.* Rowley, MA: Newbury House.

Hammerly, Hector. 1986. "Toward Cultural Competence," pp. 513–37 in *Synthesis in Language Teaching.* Blaine, WA: Second Language Publications.

Kelm, O. R. 1992. "The Use of Synchronous Computer Networks in Second Language Instruction: A Preliminary Report." *Foreign Language Annals* 25:441–54.

Kern, R. G. 1995. "Restructuring Classroom Interaction with Networked Computers: Effects on Quantity and Characteristics of Language Production." *Modern Language Journal* 79,4:457–76.

Kramsch, Claire. 1991. "The Order of Discourse in Language Teaching," pp. 191–204 in Barbara F. Freed, ed., *Foreign Language Research and the Classroom.* Lexington, MA: D. C. Heath.

Krashen, Stephen. 1985. *The Input Hypothesis: Issues and Implications.* London: Longman.

Larsen-Freeman, Diane, and Michael Long. 1991. *An Introduction to Second Language Acquisition Research.* London: Longman.

Lunde, Ken. 1993. *Understanding Japanese Information Processing.* Sebastapol, CA: O'Reilly & Associates.

Oliva, Maurizio, and Yvette Pollastrini. 1995. "Internet Resources and Second Language Acquisition: An Evaluation of Virtual Immersion." *Foreign Language Annals* 28,4:551–63.

Pica, T. 1987. "Interlanguage Adjustments as an Outcome of NS-NNS Negotiation Interaction." *Language Learning* 38:45–73.

———. 1991. "Do Second Language Learners Need Negotiation?" *WPIEL* 77:1–35. Philadelphia: University of Pennsylvania.

Richards, Jack C., John Platt, and Heidi Platt. 1992. Dictionary of Language Teaching and Applied Linguistics. Essex, England: Longman.

Robinson, Gail. 1993. "Culture Learning in the Foreign Language Classroom: A Model for Second Culture Acquisition." *Culture and Content: Perspectives on the Acquisition of Cultural Competence in the Foreign Language Classroom,* Monograph Series #4. Tempe, AZ: Southwest Conference on Language Teaching.

Sayers, D. 1994. "Bilingual Team-Teaching Partnerships over Long Distances: A Technology-Mediated Context for Intragroup Language Attitude Change," pp. 299–332 in R. A. Devillar, C. J. Faltis, and J. P. Cummins, eds., *Cultural Diversity in Schools*. New York: State University of New York Press.

Swain, Merrill. 1985. "Communicative Competence: Some Roles of Comprehensible Input and Comprehensible Output in Its Development," in S. Gass and C. Madden, eds., *Input in Second Language Acquisition*. Rowley, MA: Newbury House.

Terrell, Tracy. 1986. "Acquisition in the Natural Approach: The Binding/Access Framework." *Modern Language Journal* 70,iii: 213–27.

Williams, Bard. 1995. *The Internet for Teachers*. Foster City, CA: IDG Books Worldwide.

Van Patten, Bill, and T. Cadierno. 1993. "Explicit Instruction and Input Processing." *Studies in Second Language Acquisition* 15:225–43.

8

Meeting the Technology Challenge: *Introducing Teachers to Language-Learning Technology*

Margaret Ann Kassen
The Catholic University of America
Christopher J. Higgins
University of Maryland, College Park

In our schools, every classroom in America must be connected to the information superhighway with computers and good software and well-trained teachers.

President Bill Clinton
1996 State of the Union address

Introduction

In his 1996 State of the Union address, President Clinton challenged the country to help American students become technologically literate for the twenty-first century. This presidential vision is partly in response to the rapid changes in technology we see around us on a daily basis: faster and more

Margaret Ann Kassen (Ph.D., the University of Texas at Austin) is Associate Professor in the Department of Modern Languages at the Catholic University of America. She coordinates the language program, works with graduate and undergraduate teacher preparation, and teaches language courses. Her research interests include technology-enhanced language learning, L2 writing, portfolio assessment, and TA development. She is a member of the Board of Directors of the Northeast Conference on the Teaching of Foreign Languages.

Christopher J. Higgins became involved in teacher technology training in 1991 while a graduate student at Georgetown University and working for the National Foreign Language Resource Center, jointly sponsored by Georgetown and the Center for Applied Linguistics. He taught at Gallaudet University as a Spanish teacher and then went to the Catholic University of America as Media Director. He is currently the Coordinator of Foreign Language Instructional Technology at the University of Maryland, College Park.

powerful computer systems, ever-increasing selections of software packages and CD-ROMs, the exponential expansion of communication networks. The President also recognizes that our global society's increased reliance on technology underlies our need to prepare our youth to be competitive in the future. He calls for collaboration among federal agencies, private business and industry, nonprofit groups, states, and local communities to provide not only the needed software and hardware but also "well-trained teachers."

In this climate of increased technological demands, the education profession is forced to face the fundamental question raised by Clinton's challenge: How can teachers gain the skills necessary to make effective use of technology to enhance their students' learning? The answer seems clear: pre- and in-service opportunities for technology education. Spurred on by states that have added the technology to their requirements for teacher certification,[1] a growing number of universities offer courses that introduce pre-service teachers to computers and their use in the classroom. All fifty states have initiated technology projects that include professional development, such as Florida's School Year 2000, California's Technology Information Project (CalTIP), and Texas's Long-Range Plan for Technology. Specifically within the foreign language (FL) field, professional organizations such as ACTFL, CALICO, and the AATs hold sessions and workshops on technology topics at their national, state, and local conferences. While opportunities for technology training are flourishing, a survey conducted by the U.S. Department of Education found that in 1993–1994, only 14 percent of teachers had more than eight hours of such training. More than 50 percent had little or no preparation for using technology in the classroom (US DOE 1995). Clearly, much remains to be done to help prepare teachers to meet the President's challenge.

In addition to the need pre- and in-service teachers have for greater access to technology education, there is a need to bring into focus the lessons learned from past initiatives to improve the design of future training opportunities. In this chapter, we address technology education by identifying three key issues that emerge in the literature on technology development:

- establishing a comfort level with technology;
- integrating technology into the curriculum; and
- developing the critical skills to use technology effectively.

We highlight two sample computer-based technology initiatives, one from a pre-service and one from an in-service context, that deal with these concerns. The reflective model of professional development provides a useful framework for addressing these concerns. In this model, familiar to many FL educators, professional growth occurs as a result of repeated cycles of practice and informed critical reflection. Specifically in the FL context, we will describe a computer-based instructional module designed to introduce graduate teaching assistants (TAs) to language-learning technology (LLT) and its effective use in foreign language education. Finally, we offer suggestions for adapting our LLT module to meet the particular needs of pre-service and in-service teachers.

Background of the Issues

In a recent review of the research on professional development, Guskey (n.d.) concludes that because of the complexity and diversity of contexts in educational settings, there is no "one best way" to design and implement effective professional development programs. In technology training, contexts—facilities, personnel and financial resources, organizational and individual goals—vary widely, and successful programs must be structured to take them into consideration. However, across the diversity of contexts, some common themes are identified in the recommendations and lessons learned reported by leaders in the field. Drawing on government and foundation reports as well as FL educational research, three issues emerge as central to preparing teachers in the use of educational technology: (1) the establishment of a comfort level with technology, (2) the integration of technology into the curriculum, and (3) the development of critical skills to evaluate it and its uses.

In the Edison Project's three Cs of technology literacy (Harvey and Purnell 1995), comfort is singled out as the foundation on which *confidence* and *creativity* are progressively built. Establishing a comfort level involves both *comfort* with the use of computers and comfort with the broader notion of using technology in education. Three of the five characteristics of successful technology professional development identified in the 1995 Department of Education report "Making It Happen" focus on this crucial concern. According to this report, technology training is most effective when it (1) offers teachers ample time to practice and experiment with technology and to share ideas; (2) provides sustained support rather than a one-shot training session; and (3) receives institutional commitment, thus clearly demonstrating to teachers that technology is not just another bandwagon. Other reports also recognize the value of long-term technical and instructional support (PBS Mathline project cited in Harvey and Purnell 1995; US DOE 1996; NCREL n.d.). Furthermore, helping teachers see practical applications for technology is cited as an additional way to counter teacher anxiety (Harvey and Purnell 1995).

Foreign language educators remind us of the centrality of the second issue, integration (Armstrong and Yetter-Vassot 1994; Furstenberg and Morgenstern 1992; Garrett 1991). Integration entails not only the use of the computer in the classroom but also its use to support curriculum goals. Training teachers on the specific hardware and software they will be using helps to facilitate their use in the classroom (NCREL n.d.; US DOE 1995). Garrett (1991) and Russell, Sorge, and Brickner (1994) also note that it is helpful for teachers to try out what they are learning with their students, a benefit of training that is offered concurrently with teaching. Teacher preparation should also help educators see the potential that technology offers in addressing the whole range of curricular objectives, from the low-level to the higher-level goals of their discipline. In the foreign language context, Schrier (1993) challenges language teachers to use software programs that help students learn discrete skills such as grammar and vocabulary and also to find ways of using computers to address communicative goals that allow learners to use the language creatively.

Citing previous disappointments with computer-aided instruction (CAI) from the 1960s, Schwartz (1995:534) warns that "teachers must not make CALL programs available to their students indiscriminately. Instead, these materials must be thoroughly evaluated to determine their efficacy and soundness for pedagogical purposes." Recent research has begun to investigate efficacy issues (Beauvois 1992; Chun 1994; Kern 1995), but there are still many unanswered questions regarding how technology can best help teachers and learners achieve their goals. The lack of research-based guidelines in combination with the expanding market of hardware and software titles places teachers increasingly in the position of needing to select appropriate media to meet their instructional objectives. While software reviews can help them sort through the vast array of materials, educators must remember that because users' needs vary widely, they should not rely implicitly on one reviewer's evaluation (Garrett 1991). Teachers must develop the critical skills to evaluate for themselves the usefulness and effectiveness of different media (NCREL n.d.).

Sample Pre- and In-Service Programs

The following two examples of technology initiatives from pre- and in-service contexts include concern for comfort, integration, and evaluation.

Online Pre-Service Course

The first initiative is an innovative online course[2] on Computers in Education offered by Arizona State University on a pass/fail basis as a requirement for K–12 certification. Weekly class sessions cover five major topic areas including hardware and software, network communication and resources, and classroom integration. By means of online assignments, students send and receive E-mail, locate materials on the WWW, use and critique software, and develop materials for classroom use.

As stated in the online description, this course is designed to help students become familiar with technology and how they will be using it in teaching. It thus emphasizes two of the three key issues, comfort and integration. To minimize student anxiety, topics are ordered from basic to more complex, many help links (background information, glossary, diagrams, etc.) are available, and class sessions allow for questions and ongoing support. Throughout the course, students work with their particular content area and ultimately create a thematic unit on a web page. Though not explicitly mentioned as a goal, evaluation is also addressed in the software assignment, where students read sample reviews and evaluate software on a teacher-provided form.

In-Service Workshop Series

Russell et al. (1994) describe a state- and grant-funded in-service program for math/science teachers in grades 5 through 12 that consists of six day-long workshops spread out over the academic year. Through presentations, demonstrations, and discussions, the participants learn to incorporate computers into their classrooms for presentations, as management tools, and in various student configurations (cooperative learning and individualized activities). The ASSURE model (Heinrich, Molena, and Russell 1994, cited in Russell et al. 1994) guides the integration of technology into the classroom, as it leads the participants to *A*nalyze learners, *S*tate objectives, *S*elect media and materials, *U*tilize media and materials, *R*equire learner participation, and *E*valuate and revise.

The stated goals of these workshops highlight integration and evaluation. The facilitators guide the participants through the process of selecting software to meet their specific needs and integrating it into their unique classroom setting. Concern for teacher comfort is evident in the structure of this in-service. The number of participants is limited to twelve, the participant-facilitator ratio is low (six or four to one), and the facilitators are available for consultation between the workshops. In addition to providing opportunities for learning about computers and for putting that knowledge into practice, the workshop sessions are organized to explicitly provide time for reflection and discussion of the teachers' experiences.

A Reflective Framework

In a recent study, NCREL researchers recommended designing professional development experiences according to a research-based framework. Their framework includes five components:

1. building a knowledge base,
2. observing models and examples,
3. reflecting on practice,
4. changing practice,
5. gaining and sharing expertise.

These components have much in common with reflective models of professional growth that have been at the center of recent discussions on improving FL teacher education (Bartlett 1990; Ellis 1990; Herschensohn 1992; Joiner 1993; Pennington 1990; Richards and Lockhart 1994; Tedick and Walker 1995; Wing 1993). In the reflective model advanced by Wallace (1991), professional growth is seen as the result of the interaction of received knowledge, a field's collective body of information from research, theory and conventional wisdom, and experiential knowledge, which includes both practice and conscious reflection on that practice. While many different definitions of reflection have been advanced by theorists and teacher educators (Bartlett 1990; Lange 1990; Valli 1992), their common focus is on high-level cognitive abilities such as the ability to problem-solve, to search for alternatives, to view from multiple perspectives, to support opinions, to relate theory to practice and practice to theory. According to these models, opportunities for reflection must be explicitly and systematically infused (Richards and Lockhart 1994; Wallace 1991).

What sets reflective models apart from earlier models is the increased importance placed on the practitioner who, individually and in collaboration with others, is seen as a contributor to the growing knowledge base of the field. This is particularly significant in the technology arena where the received knowledge base is extremely limited and the work of the teacher as guide/innovator (Avots 1991:125) is fundamental to increasing our understandings of LLT and to refining our research paradigms (Garrett 1991).

Background of the LLT Module

In our respective roles as language coordinator/methods instructor and media director in the Department of Modern Languages at the Catholic University of America, we found that increased access to computer technology required us to rethink our previous strategies for preparing graduate teaching assistants for using technology. Once-a-semester workshops and one- or two-week segments in the methods class were not sufficient to introduce our TAs to the broad range of possibilities of computer-assisted language learning (CALL) or even to the specific uses we had found for it in our classes. Furthermore, though many of the TAs typically had experience teaching, their background with computers was often limited and a number of them had no computer experience at all. With the support of the department chair, we determined that technology education was a priority for the preparation of our TAs, both for their present teaching assignments and for their future in the profession.

In 1993, the media director offered a one-day workshop that has gradually evolved over three years into our Language Learning Technology (LLT) module. Patterned after a workshop offered by the National Foreign Language Resource Center sponsored by the Center for Applied Linguistics (CAL) and Georgetown University, the LLT module now incorporates emerging technologies, the evaluations of past participants, and input from a brief informal survey of methods instructors posted on *FLTEACH*.[3] The current design, a four- to six-week module taught collaboratively by the methods instructor and media director, includes two four-hour computer sessions integrated into the classwork and assignments of the methods class, a three-hour credit course that is required of all new graduate teaching assistants. The module fits well with the theory to practice orientation of the methods course and with its fundamental reflective orientation. The extended time needed in the computer classroom and the multimedia language center is somewhat compensated for by released time from class, with the remainder falling within the range that could be reasonably expected of a graduate-level course.

The LLT Module

The Language Learning Technology (LLT) Module is designed to address the three key issues identified in the professional literature (Figure 8.1): building comfort level, integrating technology into teaching practice, and developing critical skills to select and evaluate software. These key issues and the basic components of the reflective framework—knowledge, practice, and reflection—form the foundation of the instructional goals established for the module (Figure 8.2). The module leads participants to learn about technology and its

Three Key Issues for an LLT Module

1. establishing a familiarity and comfort with the computer
2. integrating technology in the classroom
3. developing critical skills in the selection and evaluation of courseware for use in the classroom

Figure 8.1

Instructional Goals of the LLT Module

- to become familiar with the role of computers in language learning and education
- to use the software required in the courses you teach
- to explore the software and network resources available at your university
- to demonstrate your ability to integrate technology into your teaching
- to develop your ability to critically evaluate LLT
- to reflect on your experiences with technology and the role it plays in language learning and teaching

Figure 8.2

uses, to use and explore various media, and to think critically and creatively about technology and its integration into the classroom. This critical orientation is supported by the systematic inclusion of tasks such as those recommended by Ellis (1990:30) to raise awareness and develop understanding through reflection: comparing, improving, adapting, listing, selecting, ranking, and rearranging.

The LLT Module is divided into five phases:

1. *The Preparation Phase*—introduces language-learning technology, its background, and theoretical underpinnings, drawing on participant experiences to form a common frame of reference.
2. *The Familiarization Phase*—familiarizes the participants with CALL, FL software, and the Internet through hands-on activities, presentations, and demonstrations.
3. *The Exploration Phase*—gives the participants time to practice what they have learned through computer-based assignments and projects.

4. *The Integration Phase*—reinforces and deepens the participants' knowledge of CALL and its use in the FL classroom while simultaneously developing their critical and creative skills.

5. *The Synthesis Phase*—helps the participants put to use the knowledge, experience, and critical skills developed and honed throughout the module.

Each phase includes a mix of readings, classroom discussions, hands-on computer sessions, presentations, demonstrations, and computer-based assignments and projects. All of these activities work together in the reflective framework to address the three instructional objectives, as seen in Figure 8.1. The description of each phase includes a table that summarizes its contents, indicating as well the reflective framework components and the key issue addressed by each activity.

The Preparation Phase

The preparation phase of the module is designed to introduce the TAs to the topic of language-learning technology. It begins with a series of outside readings that focus on FL technology and its uses in FL education and learning. The readings, which are updated as needed, include "Technology in the Service of Language Learning: Trends and Issues" (Garrett 1991), "Using Technology to Support Contextualized Language Instruction" (Shrum and Glisan 1994), and "The Electronic Language Learning Environment" (Noblitt 1995). The articles present the TAs with some background on the topic and often look into current trends.

To familiarize module participants with the campus computing facilities, they are required to open an E-mail account with the university's computing services. Once they have their E-mail accounts, they are given a basic assignment that includes sending and receiving E-mail and signing on to a listserv such as *FLTEACH* (see Appendix 1) or *LLTI*. Joining a listserv allows the TAs to experience the rapid flow of communication on current topics among practitioners in the field. The TAs are asked to monitor the listserv messages and to send the methods instructor a weekly summary of a topic strand of their choosing. For these network activities the TAs are given explicit written step-by-step instructions.

In the classroom, this initial phase of the technology module continues with directed discussion of the assigned readings, drawing upon the previous experiences of the TAs and establishing links to concepts studied previously in the methods class (such as communicative testing). The TAs are asked to talk about their own background with computers and their feelings toward using computers in the classroom. The discussion brings out a wide range

Table 8.1.
The Preparation Phase at a glance
(1–2 week period)

Activity	Element—Issue #
Outside readings	Knowledge—#1
E-mail account	Practice—#1
In-class discussion	Reflection—#1 & #2
E-mail communication	Practice—#1
Listserv project	Practice—#1

of experience with and understanding of technology and its potential. This preparatory stage of the module serves to establish a common context from which to proceed to the next phase (Table 8.1).

The Familiarization Phase

The second phase is a four-hour computer session providing the participants with an introduction to the computer, CALL, FL software, and the Internet. Through a mix of presentation, demonstration, hands-on practice, and discussion, the participants see and use a range of software types and learn about their uses in different instructional settings in and out of the classroom.

After a brief introduction to the session's activities and to help allay any anticipatory anxiety, the module participants immediately begin a hands-on activity with the computer. They begin using a selected software program by following the step-by-step guidance of the facilitator and, as they gain confidence, they continue exploring it on their own. While any program that all the participants can work on together is acceptable, our experience suggests that the software used for this initial experience be more than drill and practice and that it have some intriguing aspects such as a story line or a problem to solve. We have used a program called *Junior Year Abroad,* a study-abroad simulation written in English. The exercise helps introduce the TAs to the machines they will be using during the session and may include some basic introduction to the computer itself (i.e., the mouse, windows, folders, etc.). In the discussion following the activity, the TAs are asked for their reaction to the program—how they see it being used for their students and what they liked and/or disliked about it.

Next the TAs become familiar with the basic hardware necessary for CALL and multimedia applications, from CPUs to videodiscs to different types of networks (LAN, WAN). They are also introduced to the Internet and its vast array of foreign language resources. In a hands-on activity, the TAs are guided through various Internet resources such as gopher, WWW, and MOOs. After a demonstration of search functions, the students are given a task such as a short scavenger hunt, a topical search, or a personal search. While they are exploring the Internet, the participants are encouraged to share their reactions to what they find. The ensuing discussion is geared toward eliciting participant opinions and brainstorming ideas for class use. After their trip on the information highway, the participants are introduced to assorted types of software (Figure 8.3), such as generic ("off-the-shelf") and text-based as well as numerous types of programs (Figure 8.4), such as drill and practice

Types of Software

- **Generic**—supplemental software not based on a text (*Triple Play Plus*).
- **Text-based**—textbook-specific software easily integrated into curriculum.
- **Course-based**—software that serves as the basis of a course (*Éxito*).
- **Course-adapted**—software adapted from various sources to serve a specific course (authoring: i.e., *Libra* lessons).

Figure 8.3.

Types of Programs

- **Drill & Practice** use word-level exercises like fill-in-the-blank and multiple-choice to focus on discrete grammar skills.
- **Simulations** make the users' responses have specific consequences to the character or story line of the program.
- **Tutorials** offer users pre- and post-tests, exercises, and explanations for improving linguistic skills.
- **Games** utilize the elements of competition, challenge, and problem solving to teach and/or reinforce learning.
- **Writing Assistants** are word processing programs that provide learners with on-line aids for writing.
- **Authoring Programs** provide the teacher with the ability to alter or create lessons for specific classes or commercial use.
- **Information Resources** are collections of information such as dictionaries, atlases, galleries, and encyclopedias.
- **Information Management** are database and spreadsheet software packages used to track student grades, progress, and more.

Figure 8.4.

(textbook software, Hyperglot *Lingua-ROM* with language tutors), simulations (*À la rencontre de Philippe*), games (*Carmen Sandiego, Triple Play Plus*), writing assistants (*système-D/Quelle/Atajo, WP Language Modules*), and others.

The TAs are then given thirty minutes to examine language-specific programs, particularly the ones that are used in the courses they are teaching. This hands-on time is followed by a demonstration of interactive video programs (*Libra* lessons, *Philippe*), CD-ROM programs (*Triple Play Plus, Astérix, Learn to Speak* series), and Web-based class projects, which provides the participants a brief but expansive taste of the possibilities of CALL. Again, the participants are asked what they liked or disliked about particular programs, how they could be used, how they think their students would react, how they could be improved, and so on. As the session winds down, the TAs are also asked to compare their new experiences with previous ones and reflect upon how they relate (Table 8.2).

The Exploration Phase

The exploration phase gives the TAs the opportunity to pursue what they have learned and to consider its potential uses. They are encouraged to continue developing the skills learned in the previous computer session through computer-based assignments that include an Internet search, listserv participation,

Table 8.2.
Familiarization Phase at a glance
(4-hour session in computer lab)

Activity	Element/Issue #
Introduction to ed. tech. (hardware & configurations)	Knowledge—#1
Step-by-step hands-on computer activity	Practice—#1
Guided discussion about program	Reflection—#2
Internet resources intro & hands-on	Knowledge & Practice—#1
Internet applications discussion	Reflection—#2
Software types introduction & hands-on	Knowledge & Practice—#1
Brainstorming uses	Reflection—#3
Language specific courseware hands-on	Practice—#1
Demonstration of multimedia programs	Knowledge—#1
Discussion of reactions to demonstrated programs	Reflection—#3

Table 8.3.
The Exploration Phase at a glance
(1–2 week period)

Activity	Element/Issue #
Software exploration	Practice—#1
Software review project	Knowledge—#3
Internet (WWW) search	Practice—#1
Lesson plan integrating technology (begin)	Practice—#1 & #2

and a software review summary (see Appendix 2). The participants also begin working on a long-range project: writing a technology-integrated lesson plan or syllabus in which they demonstrate their ability to apply technology to a specific instructional context (Table 8.3).

The Integration Phase

The fourth phase concentrates on deepening the TAs' knowledge of CALL and its uses for language education, and on developing their critical and creative skills. The participants go through a series of activities designed to elicit their reactions to software, devise their own list of evaluation criteria, and compare their criteria with sample lists collected from other institutions. The presentations in this session focus on the thoughtful application of software to language teaching and the evaluation of educational software.

The integration phase begins with a discussion in which the TAs are asked to summarize what was presented in the computer session, comment on the exploration phase projects, and then explain how the two are linked. Subsequently, the TAs learn about and discuss how CALL relates to the four modalities of language learning and culture. For example, reading can be facilitated by the use of hypertext annotations, as found in *Transparent Language*. Likewise, listening comprehension is strengthened by using interactive video lessons and computer exercises incorporating digitized video.

During the first hands-on segment of this phase, the TAs are able to explore assorted programs of various languages, skill levels, and complexity, including drill and practice programs, interactive video programs, simulations, multimedia CD-ROMs, and games. They spend about ten minutes with each type of program to get a taste of the great variety of software available.

In an open discussion, the facilitator elicits the participants' opinions of the software they have just used and pushes them to refine their judgments by identifying specific characteristics of the software that led them to their opinions. The TAs also brainstorm ideas for improving programs and for integrating them into language courses. To further hone their critical skills, the TAs are asked to generate a list of criteria that, from their perspective, seem important in analyzing software. They then compare their individual lists with others in small groups and come to a consensus on a group list, which they present to the class. In the resulting discussion, criteria lists developed at other institutions are distributed, and the TAs compare their lists with the sample lists. It is during this discussion that the TAs begin refining their views of their criteria to see the connections among them and to become sensitive to the relative contribution of such features as instructional objectives, cultural authenticity, and technical quality to their overall evaluation. They are encouraged to group criteria under broader headings (*graphics,* for example, may be grouped under *screen design*) and to weight evaluation criteria according to relative importance.

After discussion of the criteria for evaluation of software, the TAs are given sample evaluation forms used at other institutions. Participants spend twenty minutes evaluating a software program of their choosing, using an assigned form. This evaluation exercise is followed by time to reflect on and share their observations about the process of evaluation with the whole group (Table 8.4).

Table 8.4.

The Integration Phase at a glance
(4-hour session in computer lab)

Activity	Element/Issue #
Discussion review with individual reactions	Reflection—#1 & #3
Types of technology-assisted activities	Knowledge—#2
Hands-on with multimedia programs	Practice—#1
Open discussion on a. reactions to multimedia b. likes & dislikes c. uses in the classroom d. how to improve programs	Reflection—#2 & #3
Creation of individual and small-group criteria lists	Practice—#3
Discussion of evaluation elements and sample forms	Reflection—#3
Evaluation by participant of one program	Practice—#3
Discussion of activity and follow-up projects	Reflection—#2 & #3

The Synthesis Phase

In the final phase, students are given an evaluation project in which they create their own software evaluation form and use it and one developed by a colleague to critique a piece of software (see Appendix 2). The process of creating a form forces students to synthesize their previous experiences and knowledge, to select salient criteria, to organize them in a coherent fashion, and to weight them in terms of their overall importance. In a modified think-pair-share approach, the students prepare a draft of their form outside of class, work collaboratively with a partner in class to revise it, and then give a copy of the final version to each class member. This project also offers the students the opportunity to explore yet another software program of their own choosing. When the final evaluations are turned in, class discussion includes comparisons of the two evaluation forms used, reactions to the software evaluated, and ideas for using it with students.

In this final phase of the module, the TAs also complete the technology-integrated lesson plan that they began in the Exploration Phase. With input from the methods instructor, the participants modify their lesson plan and use it in their classes. A follow-up discussion in class focuses on the TAs' experiences using technology in their classes. The discussion will highlight the time and effort needed to integrate technology in their lesson plan, its effectiveness, and what can be done to improve it. Given the ongoing support of the methods instructor/language coordinator and the media director, the TAs are encouraged to continue their efforts toward integrating various computer-based activities into their syllabi (Table 8.5).

Table 8.5.
The Synthesis Phase at a glance
(1–2 week period)

Activity	Element/Issue #
Lesson plan integrating technology (complete & use)	Practice—#2

Evaluation project
  a. create evaluation form
  b. in-class peer review of forms
  c. evaluate 1 program with 2 peer forms
	Practice & Reflection—#2 & #3

Participant Response

The written evaluations of the module have been quite positive over the last three years, with the few negative comments generally dealing with the choice of day or time for the computer sessions. Written evaluations are valuable and have impacted the design of the module as it now stands, but they do not really tell the whole story. An even more concrete way of evaluating the success of such a training program is to look at what the participants have actually done with the knowledge and experience they gained. Most of the past participants continued to use E-mail and word processing for their personal and school-related needs. As can be expected, a few of the TAs did not develop their ability to use technology in their classes beyond the minimum required by their course descriptions and supervisors. Four individual cases of TAs who have participated in the module demonstrate a range of responses among those who continued to grow in their ability to use LLT.

One international TA, who came to the university with some knowledge of computers and E-mail, used what she learned in the module to more effectively integrate the first-year textbook's software into her classes. Rather than simply sending her students to the Multimedia Language Center, she previewed the software and assigned the exercises most appropriate to her class and her instructional objectives. As a follow-up to the exercises, she linked them to classroom activities and quizzes, thus holding her students accountable for their learning.

Another participant, who was working to complete her certification requirements while teaching in a local middle school, became the first foreign language teacher in her school to join the science and mathematics faculty in the use of computers in the classroom. She reports that as a result of the evaluation component of the module she has "gone on to install Spanish software in [her] school library's computers" and has "used computer activities as a tutorial."

In what we see as a remarkable transformation, another international TA arrived with virtually no technology experience at all, without even a typewriter, much less a computer or word processor. During the module she struggled with some of the basic functions but has gone on to regularly use word processing and E-mail. In the semester immediately following the module, she creatively integrated a multimedia CD-ROM into the intermediate-level conversation course she was teaching.

The final case is of a TA, one of the rare few, who quickly embraced a wide spectrum of technology and integrated it into his first-year language classes. Almost immediately after his introduction to the World Wide Web during the LLT module, he used the Internet as a basis for class activities and assignments. With his new knowledge of technology he stepped his students through their first required interactive video (IAV) lessons and helped them take full advantage of the learning potential of this medium. He proceeded to take a more proactive role in the development process of IAV lessons at CUA by enrolling in a *Libra* authoring workshop during the summer.

Adaptability

We designed the LLT module to address the specific needs of TAs. By considering the characteristics of in-service and pre-service teachers, particularly their experience and their teaching/learning contexts, the module can be modified to meet their needs.

Because pre-service teachers do not know what their ultimate teaching context will be, they naturally tend to focus less on the realities of implementation and more on getting a basic working knowledge of the software and hardware. While the latter is valuable, it is also important for the module to help these students build up their teaching experience as much as possible in order to make integration a more realistic task. Some techniques for accomplishing this include the use of case studies to simulate teaching situations, micro-teach lessons, and journal entries on observations of classes that incorporate technology. By collaborating with education department faculty, the methods class instructor may be able to arrange for students to teach a mini lesson, using some aspect of LLT in a class they are observing. While outside assignments and projects work well with this group, we have found the out-of-class computer sessions to be more problematic. Extending the module throughout the semester with periodic sessions in a computer classroom allows the methods instructor to incorporate the computer activities into class time.

For in-service teachers, the computer sessions of the LLT module are similar in format to professional development workshops. Facilitators need to consult with a site representative during the planning stages of the module to find out about available hardware and software, instructional settings, and so on. Because teacher-participants have considerable experience to draw on, the theoretical focus needed for the TA module can play a lesser role in the in-service module, and the time saved can be redirected to highlight one main concern: the immediate use of technology in their particular teaching context. This group of teachers can rely on their expertise to generate ideas for implementing software in the instructional situations they encounter: different levels of student proficiency; individualized, small- and large-group instruction; specific computer availability; and so forth. Because these teachers are accustomed to selecting materials for their classes, the facilitator can direct these evaluative skills to the context of CALL. In-service teachers are more likely to be interested in software evaluation, because they are often in a position to purchase or recommend materials for their schools.

To avoid the "hit and run" approach so common to workshops, the two computer sessions of the LLT module can be expanded, as Russell et al. (1994) did, in a series of four to six sessions. Additionally, collaboration can be facilitated by means of on-site visits by the workshop facilitator, E-mail communication among the participants and facilitators, and technology newsletters with updates on participants' projects.

Conclusion

Preparing teachers to use educational technology is a pressing concern for educators today. While the variety of professional development initiatives is at first overwhelming, closer examination reveals three key issues that they have in common. The first of these concerns—establishing a comfort level with technology—is a starting point for building technology literacy. Integrating technology into the curriculum, the second issue, is fundamental to improving teaching and learning with computers. The third issue focuses on the need to develop the critical skills to evaluate technology and its use in education. We have cited two examples from the professional literature that demonstrate how these issues can be incorporated into two specific contexts.

In looking to structure technology education in a way that is consistent with research on professional growth, we have elected to employ a reflective model as the theoretical framework for our module. Foreign language educators often use this model in teacher development due to its portrayal of growth as the dynamic interrelation of knowledge, practice, and reflection. These three components of the reflective model in conjunction with the three key issues that emerge from the technology education literature form the basis of the LLT Module and are tightly woven throughout each of its five phases.

The module we propose has been successfully used to introduce the CUA teaching assistants to language-learning technology. Although it is designed for a specific situation, the module remains flexible, allowing for adaptations to participant needs, instructional contexts, and emerging technology. Designed as an introduction, it prepares educators to continue their exploration of technology and its use in FL education.

With all the resources that technology brings to language education—authentic materials on the Web, voice recognition, digitized video—we have the potential to transform the way teachers teach and the way learners learn.

As we prepare to enter a new millennium teachers will open the doors to new realms of possibilities and provide students with the tools to reach beyond the limits of our imaginations. Professional development initiatives like the ones we have described here are evidence that America's educators are on the way to realizing the President's vision for education in the twenty-first century.

NOTES

1. According to a 1995 report by the U.S. Congress, Office of Technology Assessment, eighteen states require technology training for teacher certification (cited in US DOE 1996).
2. The syllabus for this course is accessible on the WWW at <http://seamonkey.ed.asu.edu/emc300/syllabus.html>.
3. During the summer of 1995, we posted a brief questionnaire for methods instructors. The responses, though limited in number, revealed many similarities across programs and lent support to the contents of our module while at the same time introducing some innovative ideas. We would like to thank the respondents for their input.

REFERENCES

Armstrong, Kimberly M., and Cindy Yetter-Vassot. 1994. "Transforming Teaching Through Technology." *Foreign Language Annals* 27:475–85.

Avots, Juliette. 1991. "Networking: Linking the Foreign Language Classroom to the World," pp. 122–53 in June K. Phillips, ed., *Building Bridges, Making Connections.* Northeast Conference on the Teaching of Foreign Languages Reports. Lincolnwood, IL: National Textbook Company.

Bartlett, Leo. 1990. "Teacher Development Through Reflective Teaching," pp. 202–14 in Jack C. Richards and David Nunan, eds., *Second Language Teacher Education.* Cambridge: Cambridge University Press.

Beauvois, Margaret H. 1992. "Computer-Assisted Classroom Discussion in the Foreign Language Classroom: Conversation in Slow Motion." *Foreign Language Annals* 25:455–64.

Chun, Dorothy M. 1994. "Using Computer Networking to Facilitate the Acquisition of Interactive Competence." *System* 22:17–31.

Ellis, Rod. 1990. "Activities and Procedures for Teacher Preparation," pp. 26–36 in Jack C. Richards and David Nunan, eds., *Second Language Teacher Education.* Cambridge: Cambridge University Press.

Furstenberg, Gilberte, and Douglas Morgenstern. 1992. "Technology for Language Learning and Teaching: Designs, Projects, Perspectives," pp. 117–40 in Wilga Rivers, ed., *Teaching Languages in College.* Lincolnwood, IL: National Textbook Company.

Garrett, Nina. 1991. "Technology in the Service of Language Learning: Trends and Issues." *The Modern Language Journal* 75:74–101.

Guskey, Thomas R. (n.d.) *Results Oriented Professional Development: in Search of an Optimal Mix of Effective Practices.* Oak Brook, IL: North Central Regional Educational Laboratory.

Harvey, James, and Susannah Purnell, eds. 1995. *Technology and Teacher Professional Development.* Santa Monica, CA: RAND Critical Technologies Institute.

Herschensohn, Julia. 1992. "Teaching Assistant Development: A Case Study," pp. 25–45 in Joel C. Walz, ed., *Development and Supervision of Teaching Assistants in Foreign Languages*. AAUSC Issues in Language Program Direction. Boston: Heinle & Heinle Publishers.

Joiner, Elizabeth G. 1993. "Reflecting on Teacher Development," pp. 187–212 in Gail Guntermann, ed., *Developing Language Teachers for a Changing World*. The ACTFL Foreign Language Education Series. Lincolnwood, IL: National Textbook Company.

Kern, Richard G. 1995. "Restructuring Classroom Interaction with Networked Computers: Effects on Quantity and Characteristics of Language Production." *The Modern Language Journal* 79:457–76.

Lange, Dale L. 1990. "A Blueprint for a Teacher Development Program," pp. 245–68 in Jack C. Richards and David Nunan, eds., *Second Language Teacher Education*. Cambridge: Cambridge University Press.

North Central Regional Education Laboratory (NCREL). (n.d.). *Learning Through Technology: A Planning and Implementation Guide*. <http://www.ncrel.org/tandl/>.

Noblitt, James S. 1995. "The Electronic Language Learning Environment," pp. 263–92 in Claire Kramsch, ed., *Redefining the Boundaries of Language Study*. AAUSC Issues in Language Program Direction. Boston: Heinle & Heinle Publishers.

Pennington, Martha C. 1990. "A Professional Development Focus for the Language Teaching Practicum," pp. 132–51 in Jack C. Richards and David Nunan, eds., *Second Language Teacher Education*. Cambridge: Cambridge University Press.

Richards, Jack C., and Charles Lockhart. 1994. *Reflective Teaching in Second Language Classrooms*. Cambridge: Cambridge University Press.

Russell, James, Dennis Sorge, and Dianna Brickner. 1994. "Improving Technology Implementation in Grades 5–12 with the ASSURE Model." *Technological Horizons in Education (THE) Journal* 21:9,66–70.

Schrier, Leslie L. 1993. "Prospects for the Professionalization of Foreign Language Teaching," pp. 159–86 in Gail Guntermann, ed., *Developing Language Teachers for a Changing World*. The ACTFL Foreign Language Education Series. Lincolnwood, IL: National Textbook Company.

Shrum, Judith L., and Eileen W. Glisan. 1994. *Teacher's Handbook*. Boston: Heinle & Heinle Publishers.

Schwartz, Michael. 1995. "Computers and the Language Laboratory: Learning from History." *Foreign Language Annals* 28:527–35.

Tedick, Diane J., and Constance L. Walker. 1995. "From Theory to Practice: How Do We Prepare Teachers for Second Language Classrooms?" *Foreign Language Annals* 28:499–517.

United States Department of Education (US DOE). 1996. *Getting America's Students Ready for the Twenty-first Century: Meeting the Technology Literacy Challenge: A Report to the Nation on Technology and Education*. Washington, DC: Office of Educational Technology.

———. 1995. *Making It Happen: Report of the Secretary's Conference on Educational Technology*. Washington, DC: Office of Educational Technology.

Valli, Linda. 1992. *Reflective Teacher Education*. Albany: State University of New York Press.

Wallace, Michael J. 1991. *Training Foreign Language Teachers: A Reflective Approach*. Cambridge: Cambridge University Press.

Wing, Barbara. 1993. "The Pedagogical Imperative in Foreign Language Teacher Education," in Gail Guntermann, ed., *Developing Language Teachers for a Changing World*, pp. 159–86. The ACTFL Foreign Language Education Series. Lincolnwood, IL: National Textbook Company.

Appendices

Appendix 1: Annotated List of FL Technology Resources

Journals

The IALL Journal of Language Learning Technologies is a professional journal that promotes effective uses of media centers for language teaching, learning, and research.

WWW address: <http://langlab.uta.edu/iall/journal/JournalHome.html>

Calico Journal is a journal dedicated to the intersection of modern language learning and high technology.

WWW address: <http://agoralang.com/calico.html>

Listservs

FLTEACH is a listserv for FL educators interested in foreign language teaching methods, training of student teachers, classroom activities, curriculum, and syllabus design.

WWW address: <http://www.cortland.edu/www/flteach/welcome...htmlx flteach/welcome..html>

To subscribe to *FLTEACH* send a message to listserv@ubvm.cc. buffalo.edu

In the body of the message type: *subscribe flteach* <your name>

A message will be returned to you, confirming your subscription and describing how to post messages to the list.

LLTI (Language Learning Technology International) is a listserv for people interested in language-learning technology.

WWW address: <http://eleazar.dartmouth.edu/IALL/LLTI.html>

To subscribe to LLTI, send a message to listserv@listserv.dartmouth.edu

In the body of the message, type: *sub LLTI* <your name>

A message will be returned to you, confirming your subscription and describing how to post messages to the list.

Software

À la rencontre de Philippe lets users step into the life of a young Frenchman and live his life, bearing all benefits and consequences of the choices they make.

Astérix combines pictures, sound, and laughter in an exciting story starring the world-famous Astérix.

Learn to Speak Series uses digitized video and sound to present students with conversation-based situations for language learning.

Lingua-ROM contains thirty-eight of HyperGlot's Macintosh foreign language products, including the Learn to Speak Series and Pronunciation Tutors.

Rosetta Stone Powerpac is a four-language CD-ROM intended for beginning students that uses groups of pictures in thematic relationships to foster language learning.

système-D, Quelle, and *Atajo* are software programs that facilitate the process of writing in French, German, and Spanish so that students and teachers can interact with a written text in new and useful ways.

Transparent Language is a hyper-text program that uses authentic texts with annotations of grammar, culture, and translations to help improve reading comprehension. The CD-ROM version integrates sound for listening comprehension.

Triple Play Plus uses a game-based immersion approach for students eight years and older. It can be played in listening, reading, and speech recognition modes.

Where in the World Is Carmen Sandiego? is a game in English and Spanish. The user becomes a detective in search of thieves.

Appendix 2: Module Projects

Software Review Project—Exploration Phase

Read an FL software review in a professional journal such as *The French Review, The IALL Journal,* or *The CALICO Journal* or a newsletter like the *Northeast Conference Newsletter* or the *Athelstan Newsletter*. In an E-mail message that you send to me and to another student in the class, summarize the review, comment on your reaction to the program, and indicate how you might be able to use it in a language class.

Technology-Integrated Lesson Plan, Part I—Exploration Phase

• Using what you have learned so far in the module as well as the course, create a lesson plan that uses a foreign language software program or the Internet as an integral part of your daily objectives. It must be a part of the assigned homework as well as part of your in-class activities or discussion.

• Turn in your lesson plan two days before the Integration Phase begins.

• The instructor will comment on the lesson plan and return it to you during the Integration Phase.

Technology-Integrated Lesson Plan, Part II—Synthesis Phase

• Using the instructor's comments as a guide, modify your lesson plan and use it in your class(es).

• After the class, note:

   a. the students' reaction to the use of technology in the class,

   b. the effectiveness of the activity in relation to the daily objectives,

   c. your own feelings on planning and integrating technology into your classes.

• Write out your findings, evaluating the integration process and commenting on changes you would make to improve the process.

• During class discussion, share your findings and turn in your evaluation.

Final Project—Synthesis Phase

Step #1 (*due one week after the Integration Phase*): Using the evaluation criteria discussed in the workshop, create an evaluation form. You may use other evaluation forms as a model but do *not* duplicate them. Keep in mind the following:

• prioritizing and grouping criteria (hierarchy)

• indicating relative importance of criteria, i.e., scores, grades, ratings

• limiting your form to one or two pages in length

Bring blank copies of your evaluation form to class for each student.

Step #2 (*due one week after completion of Step #1*): Select and become acquainted with one program available on the network (NET) or in the Multimedia Language Center (MLC). Evaluate this program, using *two* of the evaluation forms created by you and your classmates in #1 above. Turn in a copy of the two completed evaluations of your chosen software.

9

Implementing Technology for Language Learning

Michael D. Bush

Brigham Young University

Introduction

Society in general and the foreign language education profession in particular are in the midst of incredible advances in digital technology, with the most obvious manifestations being the incorporation of microcomputers and communications technologies into our daily lives in ways never before imagined. Permeated by a technological revolution unlike any other the world has seen, society is seeking to understand the impact of this revolution and how it can help people better learn, work, and even play. Many foreign language educators are no exception, seeking to discover ways these technologies can improve how they do their job.

In fact, over the years language-teaching professionals have not been strangers to technology in general. From the language labs of the 1950s and 1960s to the microcomputers of the 1970s and 1980s to today's new digital technology-based language labs, the language-teaching profession has looked to technology to provide useful tools to help teachers teach and students learn.

Furthermore, for some time now interactive technologies have been capturing the imaginations of a few language teachers and in turn energizing the minds of their learners. Benefiting from new developments that bring easily

Michael D. Bush, Ph.D. in Foreign Language Education and Computer Science from The Ohio State University, has been involved in programming different computers in various ways and using them to solve diverse problems over the past twenty-seven years. From 1980 to 1984 and from 1986 to 1992 he served as Director of Research in the Department of Foreign Languages at the United States Air Force Academy, where he played an instrumental role in the installation of what was probably the first operational interactive videodisc-based language-learning center of its kind and size on any college campus. Since his retirement as a lieutenant colonel in the United States Air Force in August 1992, he has served as an Associate Professor of French and Instructional Science at Brigham Young University, Provo, UT. He is also a partner in a multimedia development company, Alpine Media of Orem, UT. He served a three-year term on the Executive Board of CALICO.

accessible video to the learning setting, students are not only able to see and hear "real people" speak "real language," but they also receive a target language experience that is made comprehensible for them in a way never before possible. The use of these new technologies in this fashion creates experiences that are extremely compelling and motivational for those language learners fortunate enough to have the experience.

Resonating with this apparent potential, increasing numbers of researchers have been investigating ways to harness various forms of digital technology to make such experiences possible. For example, seven years ago two volumes of the ACTFL Foreign Language Education Series were devoted to the application of technology to the language-learning process (Smith 1987, 1989). Furthermore, such interest is spreading and is beginning to have its impact on publishers, a group often conservative with respect to new trends in foreign language methodology. One only has to walk through the exhibit area of any major language conference to see evidence of intense publisher interest in these new developments as reflected in their new technology-based product offerings.

Yet despite this intense interest, there is little evidence that technology is having any significant impact on the way most students learn languages in today's classrooms. A West Coast think-tank organization, the RAND Corporation, recently completed a study commissioned by the White House Office of Science and Technology Policy and the Office of Technology of the U.S. Department of Education (Glennan and Melmed 1996). The study took an in-depth look at the role that technology is playing and probably should be playing in public schools today. The authors of the final report cited Becker (1994), who found that 31.2 percent of the time high school students spent using computers was spent pursuing academic subjects, as shown in Table 9.1.

As shown in Table 9.2, of the time spent on academic subjects, students spent 2.7 percent of their computer time studying foreign languages, the lowest of all the percentages for the other subjects shown in the table.

Technology's low impact in foreign language learning is also illustrated by the fact that none of the "technology-rich" schools that served as exemplars for technology implementation in the RAND study mentioned that foreign language study was part of their technology-based curriculum. In a similar vein, a recent informal survey of subscribers to the 850-member, Internet-based LISTSERV, Language Learning Technology International (LLTI), found few examples of language-education programs where students spend at least 10 percent of their time using technology to help in their learning.

This low level of implementation could have several possible explanations. The implementation of technology for language learning has at times

Table 9.1.

Percentage of student computer time spent in various areas

Computer education	45.5 %
Academic subjects	31.2
Vocational subjects	17.3
Recreation and other	6.3

Table 9.2.

Percentage of student computer time spent on various academic subjects

Mathematics	7.7 %
English	7.4
Science	6.2
Social studies	4.1
Fine arts	3.0
Foreign languages	2.7

brought critics to admonish the profession "to avoid the mistakes of wasting money on costly equipment when the key to effective language instruction lies in good teachers using better methods toward clear goals" (Otto 1989, citing Grittner 1977). Among other complaints, some faculty also perhaps respond to fears that technology will replace them in their jobs or that instruction will be dehumanized through its use (Olsen 1980). For many others expense has been a deterrent. Still others have perhaps been discouraged by the low availability of quality software combined with the difficulty of creating software for use in one's own classes.

The point is that it has been easy to find reasons not to implement technology, despite the excitement on the part of many professionals regarding its potential, with which we began this discussion. Thus the overall and subsuming purpose of this volume is to address these apparent contradictions:

- Many language-teaching professionals are extremely enthusiastic about the use of technology for language learning.
- Most students go through their language courses without the sort of experience on which this enthusiasm is based.

On the one hand we see increasingly capable technology used by committed researchers who are working hard to make its potential available to language students, and on the other we see large numbers of students whose learning experiences remain untouched by its capabilities. To address this paradox and to explore the potential for foreign language education derived from the ongoing technological revolution, we need answers to three fundamental questions relative to the use of technology in the foreign language curriculum:

- Should technology be used in foreign language learning?
- If it makes sense to use it, what is the best role it can fill in the instructional equation?
- Once we have decided to use it and know what we want to do with it, how should it be implemented so students will benefit?

With respect to the first question, the authors of the previous chapters in this volume have provided many reasons that technology should be useful. Moreover, they have thoroughly addressed important pedagogical issues, showing many ways that technology can be useful for language teachers and learners. Although this present chapter will at least briefly address these two areas as well, making points on certain issues not necessarily made by the other authors, we will pay particular attention to logistics and practical issues involved not only at the program level but also on a broader scale. Thus, its main objective is to focus on the third question, examining topics related to technology implementation.

To provide context to the search for answers, we will examine the experience at one university, the United States Air Force Academy, where technology plays a significant role in the language instruction program. Using this particular instance of successful implementation as a backdrop, an excellent setting for our examination of these crucial areas, we will seek out those issues most likely to help us answer these questions.

This is important because language programs do not exist in isolation. Because they function within the context of the schools where they operate and even within society itself, it is crucial to consider technology implementation issues at those levels as well as issues involved with the language-learning problem itself. Underlying this discussion is the assumption that it will be necessary to implement technology on a much broader scale than that undertaken in almost every program where it exists today, a scale more significant than many might think. It is only through this increase in scope that technology can have more than incidental impact on student learning. On such a scale the technology's affordability is an overriding issue.

Integrating Technology into the Language-Learning Curriculum: A Case Study

Overview

In considering questions of such a practical nature as technology implementation for language learning, an example should be quite helpful. No better example exists than one where technology implementation efforts have been successful in changing the way students learn languages. Just such a successful instance exists at the United States Air Force Academy (USAFA), where students in the basic courses in French, German, and Spanish spend 50 percent of class contact time working with video materials in the interactive videodisc-based language-learning center. Furthermore, research conducted there has produced significant results pertaining to the use of technology for language learning.

Background

The effort to implement technology in language instruction at USAFA had its beginning in the mid-1970s with an investigation into the potential of time-shared PLATO lessons. PLATO was a large mainframe-based system developed at the University of Illinois, later commercialized by Control Data Corporation, to which users attached interactive terminals via modem and standard telephone lines. The academy's investigation into PLATO revealed interesting potential but also showed that its costs were prohibitive, amounting to about $1,200 month per terminal for the terminal itself, connect time on the mainframe, and telephone charges.

Nevertheless, encouraged by the potential illustrated by the department's investigation, the faculty undertook the creation of grammar review lessons that ran on the academy's mainframe computer. These lessons were created by the faculty in addition to their regular teaching duties and were used for about two years before hardware and software changes made them obsolete.

Beginning in 1977, the foreign language department became the first academic department at USAFA to document a requirement for support for computer-assisted instruction (CAI) (Bush 1988). These requirements were filled by the purchase in 1981 of a Digital Equipment VAX 11/780 to which were attached Terak graphics terminals to support various instructional needs of the computer science curriculum as well as the foreign language department's documented requirement for software containing non-Roman orthographies. Lesson creation was prohibitively difficult on this mainframe system, so other than a few new grammar review lessons in a couple of languages, the development of interactive lesson materials stagnated somewhat.

During the development process for this system, department personnel entered into a collaborative development agreement with Texas Instruments (TI), which was looking for ways to produce language-learning materials for its home computer, the TI 99/4. The company's marketing surveys had identified a surprising interest among the people they surveyed. It seemed that one of the things consumers wanted to do with a home computer was to learn a foreign language. This interest led TI in 1982 to lend for an indefinite period of time about twenty TI 99/4A microcomputers (each containing 16K of main memory with a 32K memory expansion unit!) for the development of lessons for use by the Academy's language students. Using this early hardware and the very rudimentary authoring system provided by TI (rudimentary by today's standards in that it could handle only text-based interactions), faculty members produced a number of interactive videotape lessons that were delivered using Sony $^3/4$" U-Matic videotape machines controlled by proprietary TI hardware added to the microcomputers. The success of this incredibly slow delivery system was remarkable in the reaction it generated among teachers and students, and it paved the way for further development with the significantly more capable technology, interactive videodisc.

In the early 1980s, the Academy's Board of Visitors (roughly equivalent to a typical university's Board of Trustees or Board of Regents and appointed by the president of the United States) made a strong recommendation that the Cadet Education Program needed to be brought more in line with the technology-rich environments in which academy graduates would serve during their careers as officers in the United States Air Force. The plan that resulted from the this group's recommendation paved the way for congressional funding ($300,000) and provided the means to implement interactive videodisc technology in the Language Learning Center (LLC) of the Department of Foreign Languages. Furthermore, the board's guidance gave rise to an additional academy-wide initiative that led to the requirement that each student purchase upon arrival at the academy a microcomputer to support his or her education during his or her four years at the academy, a development that still today continues to have a profound effect on the way education is conducted there.

Learning Center Design

Following numerous budgetary programming and planning efforts that began in 1982, the first full-scale implementation of the Language Learning Center came online in 1988. The culmination of these planning efforts followed an extensive remodeling effort on the facility that previously accommodated the foreign language department's sophisticated but outdated audio lab.

Within the unique, functional, and aesthetic design of the new language-learning center, each of the thirty-five two-person workstations was equipped with a Sony View 3000 videodisc-based, interactive workstation consisting of an IBM PC-AT compatible microcomputer combined with a Sony LDP 2000 videodisc player. The Academy's staff modified each unit with the addition of an Ethernet networking card and a 20 megabyte (MB) hard disk drive and connected these stations to a central file server for the delivery of lesson materials over the internal network in the LLC.

Since the initial installation in 1988, the LLC has acquired ten Apple Macintosh computers and undergone two additional system upgrades, bringing the total number of interactive workstations to 104 (ninety-four PC compatibles and ten Apple Macintoshes) (Geiss 1996). As part of these upgrades, three years ago LLC personnel acquired thirty-four Everex 386-based microcomputers running at 33 megahertz (MHz) with 8MB of memory and 100MB hard drives. These machines were subsequently upgraded to 486 machines using a Cyrix microprocessor upgrade package that runs at 66MHz. Two years ago the LLC added an additional sixty machines that contained 486 microprocessors also running at 66MHz, 280MB hard drives, and 16MB of memory. All of the machines are equipped with Sony LDP 1550 videodisc players and the ninety-four PC compatibles contain video overlay cards from either Videologic or New Media Graphics. Each of these machines is networked to the file server in the LLC, using Banyan Vines networking software.

Current Technology Setting

The LLC's initially independent Ethernet-based network has been integrated into the Academy's optical fiber-based Ethernet network, now known as USAFANet, the system installed in the mid-1980s after the initial academy-wide system. The LLC's file server is connected to the main fiber backbone, and each of the workstations is attached to the file server using twisted-pair connections.

The early coaxial-based network was designed not only to carry data but also to serve as an internal, closed-circuit video system. Although the network functionality for delivering digital data has been transferred to the new fiber-based network, the old coaxial cable system is still used for transmitting television programs to classrooms and to students in their dorm rooms.

The LLC thus exists within the Academy's extensive local area network, which is probably one of the largest on a college campus anywhere, especially for a university the size of the Academy. There are about 8,500 machines networked within a university that serves a little more than 4,000 students.

It is quite interesting to note that the capability envisioned in the 1977 planning document for the CAI system was far surpassed by the time the LLC was completed eleven years later. Where the 1977 plan called for a mini-computer with terminals, the center that grew out of the early planning and research was equipped upon installation in 1988 with networked microcomputers attached to a file server that served all the machines in the center.

As an additional example of the technological evolution that is taking place so quickly, the class of 2000, which entered the Academy during the summer of 1996, purchased CD-ROM-equipped, Pentium-based, microcomputers with 16 megabytes of memory and running at 100MHz. These machines are significantly more powerful than the computer described in the 1977 planning document and are even capable of displaying video from the CD-ROM using the native capabilities of the computer combined with appropriate video decoding software. The follow-on machines to this type of configuration will ultimately obviate the need for a videodisc player and video overlay card as are required for the software running in the LLC today.

This evolution will once again drastically change how technology is used, as we will see below. Moreover, the backdrop of massive implementation of microcomputer technology we see here provides an interesting perspective for future efforts of technology utilization in education. Although such a system is prohibitively expensive for many institutions today, it will continue to provide a pattern that is worthy of consideration for the future, given the solid evidence that prices for digital technology will inevitably continue to drop.

Empirical Research

Beginning with the investigation into PLATO that took place in the 1970s, research was a vital ingredient of preparation from the earliest stages of thinking and planning for the Academy's Language Learning Center. A crucial study was conducted, using lessons based on the French grammar series *En Français* that were prepared to run on the microcomputer systems lent to the academy by Texas Instruments. Students and teachers alike responded very favorably to the use of this approach, despite the slowness of system response inherent in the videotape delivery system used for this study.

The TI system was also used to create and deliver listening-comprehension exercises with the videodisc *Klavier im Haus,* which was produced by the Goethe Institute of San Francisco and the New Technology Division of the Defense Language Institute in Monterey. These exercises were the basis for an experiment designed to test interactive technology for teaching listening comprehension (Schrupp, Bush, and Mueller 1983). The results of that experiment clearly demonstrated a decided advantage in listening comprehension for the students in the experimental group. This group had access to the interactivity provided by the computer and videodisc player; the control group watched the video in a passive, linear fashion.

The Department of Foreign Languages at USAFA also produced a videodisc version of the slide/tape audiovisual teaching materials, *De Vive Voix* (Moget and Neveu 1972). Crotty (1984) used this videodisc in her research designed to test the effectiveness of the use of interactive videodisc technology in language teaching. Her study demonstrated that students who received instruction via the interactive videodisc system performed as well on the multiple-choice portion of the posttest as those who received the teacher-based classroom presentation. On the writing portion of the posttest, the students using the interactive videodisc system outperformed the classroom-based group at a level that was determined to be statistically significant.

Also as part of the extensive planning and development process that the language department carried out, Sony Corporation loaned several SMC 70 microcomputer and videodisc systems that were used by Verano (1987) to test the effectiveness of levels of interactivity using interactive videodisc-based materials. His experiment involved three treatments and one control group. Group 1 watched passively and in linear fashion. Group 2 saw the video in a form that had been segmented and interrupted with the presentation of true/false and multiple-choice questions. The only feedback this group received was in the form of "Correct" or "Wrong." Group 3 (the experimental group) saw the video similarly to Group 2, but in addition, these students had access to feedback on incorrect choices, vocabulary lists, the capability to replay the video, and hints that provided remediation. The control group (Group 4) received material in English that was completely unrelated to the video, permitting an evaluation of whether the results were prejudiced by using the same pretest as the posttest.

Students who received the passive videodisc presentation preferred learning foreign language from an instructor. Students in the experimental group showed the least preference for learning from an instructor. Furthermore, they were more interested in learning Spanish and felt a stronger desire to visit a Spanish-speaking country. Students who received true/false and multiple-choice questions with limited feedback (indication of the correctness of answers) at selected breakpoints in the story line performed better on the posttest than those who watched passively. Students who had the most interaction had results that were "dramatically better" than students in the other groups (Verano 1987:97).

Recent research corroborates these earlier findings and continues to support the use of technology for language learning. For example, Moraco (1996) conducted an experiment that concluded that interactivity is a definite boon for learning outcome. The experiment involved the presentation of three video clips to the students, one per day for three days. Students in the first experimental groups received access to key vocabulary glosses by clicking on words, while another group received contextual clues such as having their attention focused on gestures, background, facial expressions, and setting. A third group received both glossary and guided listening clues. The control group had an instruction booklet that took the students step by step through an overview of the video segments and allowed them to work through the video phrase by phrase, listening as many times as they wanted, with the text for each phrase displayed on the screen upon request as the phrase was accessed. Having access to key vocabulary glosses proved to be a significant factor on an immediate-recall protocol as well as on a multiple-choice exam measuring listening comprehension. The guided listening treatment and the combined treatment were both significant on the first day's measures of recall and comprehension.

These various research efforts motivated, informed, and guided the design of the technology-based LLC from the very beginning. Conceived during the earliest moments of the research presented here, the LLC has continued to grow and undergo improvements as additional research has been conducted.

Technology Transfer

The experience at USAFA is of course in many ways unique to that institution. As a result, from the beginning, Academy personnel have looked for ways to share their experience with anyone who could benefit from the exchange of ideas. Thus, other organizations over the years have sought information and support from the Academy as they have gone about their own efforts of technology implementation.

The Department of Foreign Languages at USAFA has undertaken this transfer of technology in two ways. First, it has made its software available to external organizations through a technology transfer partner. And second, each summer since 1991 it has made the LLC available for language camps for high school students.

Foreign Language Interactive Videodisc Project: Yorktown High School

One of the institutions that sought and received help from the Academy was Yorktown High School in a small town adjacent to Muncie, Indiana (Underwood et al. 1992). As part of their evaluation and revision of the foreign language curriculum during the 1989–90 school year, individuals from the Mount Pleasant School District and from the high school were looking for creative ways to improve their foreign language program. After having decided to explore videodisc technology, they responded to a technology-oriented Request for Proposals from the state, subsequently receiving a grant. During their search for ways to proceed in their research, school district personnel were having trouble locating information regarding the implementation of interactive videodisc technology. After coming across an article that mentioned the LLC at the Air Force Academy, individuals from the Yorktown project contacted the LLC's director and arranged a visit during May of 1990.

Following their initial work with the Academy and system acquisition and installation, the Yorktown project team solved all of their technical problems, bringing their laboratory to operational status in February of 1991 with ten Sony VIW 5000 foreign language interactive videodisc workstations. Their lesson materials were based on the Random House Spanish Video Program for Beginning Spanish and the German Velvet series developed by Brigham Young University for the Defense Language Institute in the 1980s. Some of the materials were locally developed, and some were obtained from USAFA.

The Yorktown project participants measured their success in several ways—from the experience of the teachers, by the reactions and success of the students, and by the interest from other schools. Furthermore, they actually received awards for their innovation.

The teachers liked using the technology for several reasons:

- the value of authentic video
- active student learning
- student self-pacing and sequencing
- the teacher's ability to deal with various learning styles and modalities
- the development of complex skills
- the cooperative learning environment.

In addition to their own positive attitudes, the teachers felt that they could document improvements in student language proficiency as well as changes in student attitudes. They were able to show that more students continued into second-year study once the technology had been integrated into the language program. The students also responded favorably to the instruction and completed questionnaires in which they cited why they liked the technology. They

- liked working at their own pace and controlling the instructional process;
- found the lessons to be interesting;
- liked hearing native speakers in authentic situations;
- remarked, often with surprise, that they could actually understand the conversations in the video.

The Yorktown team members also received additional grants from the state to take their program into other schools. Following training workshops, forty-two foreign language teachers at twelve additional schools adopted the approach that Yorktown had put together. They presented their results at a state conference and did training for teachers from other schools. These efforts led to additional grants that in turn enabled the project team to provide various schools with on-site training, using Yorktown teachers, videodiscs, and software (Underwood 1996).

In 1992 the Yorktown group received a Pioneering Partners Award from a program sponsored by a public-private partnership between the Council of Great Lakes Governors and GTE Telephone Operations [See <http://www.macomb.k12.mi.us/pionpart/ind/ppmtpl.htm>]. This award brought the project an initial prize of $3,000 combined with professional development training at GTE Headquarters, "the best in-service training experience I have ever received," according to the project director, Barbara Underwood (Underwood 1996). GTE added the promise of another $2,000 based on the project getting matching funding from the state, which it did.

Among the lessons the Yorktown project gained from the experience was that the technology was a definite enhancement to their language program. They found that they could easily train teachers, but that due to the costs of hardware and software development or purchase, full-scale implementation would be very expensive. As Underwood et al. (1992:31) summarized, "The Yorktown High School project team is even more convinced that interactive videodisc technology has the potential to transform the teaching of foreign language."

High School Language Camp

In 1991, in another effort to make the capabilities at the LLC accessible to more students, the Department of Foreign Languages at the Academy decided to undertake a language camp for students from around the country. Still today, each summer, anywhere from forty to sixty high school language students assemble at the Academy for a two-and-a-half-week intensive lan-guage-learning experience. After declaring their intention to speak only in the target language during their time at camp, the students embark on an experience that moves most of them at least one year forward in their language skill level as measured by the academy.

This summer camp includes intensive small-group instruction, hands-on work in the interactive videodisc (IVD) learning center, and target-language cultural activities. While living in cadet dormitories, the students speak the language they are learning as they enjoy afternoon, evening, and weekend social and recreational activities such as films, sports, games, picnics, and dances [See <http://www.usafa.af.mil/dff/langcamp.htm>]. The language instruction program, modeled after the academy's basic language courses, places the students in the Language Learning Center for about 50 percent of the total instruction time and in the classroom with the specially trained teachers for the other 50 percent of their time. Teachers are normally state-certificated high school teachers who have been trained by the camp leadership.

The success of the language-camp program can be measured in several ways. Using the same placement test that the department of foreign languages administers to incoming first-year students each year, it has been possible to establish that the average language-camp participant moves forward in his or her language skill level the equivalent of at least one year of high school language study. In other words, the average students with no prior language-learning experience are typically placed at least in second-year classes when they return to their various schools in the fall. Each year there are students who move up the equivalent of two years of high school, usually when the student follows up the camp experience with a home stay in the country where the target language is spoken. After reporting their experience to their language teachers in the fall, and following an interview and/or placement test, these students were then placed in third-year language courses, going on to succeed quite ably in their study.

Lessons to Be Learned

It is possible to glean from this experience three points that summarize important lessons pertaining to technology-based language learning:

- Technology can help students learn a foreign language.
- Students like using technology for language learning.
- It is possible to resolve technical and practical issues related to implementing technology.

The research conducted at the Academy, and the experience of the team that worked on the Foreign Language Interactive Videodisc Project at Yorktown High School confirm that technology can be a useful component of a forward-looking language education program. Not all of the evidence is experimental, but as the amount of anecdotal evidence mounts, it nevertheless strengthens the case for having students use technology as an integral part of their learning programs.

Not only does technology contribute to learning, but the efforts cited here show that students like having access to it. Indeed, an internal survey of

USAFA students who were using the LLC at USAFA (1996) shows the extent to which students felt they benefited from the experience gained there. For instance, 60 percent of the students said they "strongly agree" that the "LLC language learning activities are well integrated into the target language curriculum" and another 34 percent said they "agree." Their responses indicated that they like the environment and the mix of LLC and classroom activities. Also, 76 percent said they would like access to the learning center outside of the classroom. Several beginning-level language students added comments to the end of their questionnaires that indicated their degree of satisfaction with the experience provided by the LLC. Asked what changes they would recommend, several responded:

- "I don't think any changes should be made."
- "It's an excellent learning environment, enjoyable, so I learn more."
- "The LLC is a great place to learn French."

One student with couple of years' study in high school commented:

- "I think the LLC is the way a language should be taught. It is much easier to learn a language by being immersed in it instead of memorizing."

One with even more experience in high school wrote:

- "I like it a lot. It helped make the class exciting and not get boring. It was a good addition to the classroom instruction and helped give variety to the classroom."

There were other comments to the effect that students wanted to see even more utilization:

- "I also like the idea of watching French movies, TV shows, or commercials."
- "We should have soap operas and films."
- "I would definitely like to see more non-FIA [*French in Action*] programs on disc after we have finished FIA."
- "There should be lessons including actual French TV programs. There should also be more options available to the students than just the *French in Action* series."

With respect to implementation issues, the group at Yorktown benefited from its association with USAFA, but its efforts were not without problems.

The group was quick to pick up on a phrase often used at the academy to describe what it was like to be among the first to go beyond research and actually implement technology for supporting language learning in regular classes on a fully operational scale: "Life on the bleeding edge!" they called it (Underwood et al. 1992). But despite the difficulties encountered in the LLC and by the team at Yorktown, both groups met with success. With respect to technical problems, implementation will only get easier from this point on as technology gets cheaper, more available, and more powerful. The biggest challenges probably pertain to organization and personnel issues, as shown below.

Finally, lessons to be learned at the Air Force Academy go beyond those associated with the LLC itself. Given that each student is required to purchase his or her own microcomputer and given that the power of these machines increases with each incoming class, the future should prove interesting as the Department of Foreign Languages takes this into account in their technology implementation efforts. How will instruction be affected as students are able to use materials on their own machines that previously required the specialized configurations of the LLC? Needless to say, this will be an interesting development to follow as time passes.

Justifying Technology for the Language-Learning Curriculum

It makes sense to use technology in language-learning instruction for several reasons. Educational technology

- is effective for delivering instruction;
- has unique pedagogical value;
- enables teachers to better address students' need for individualization;
- will help students better relate to life in the Information Age;
- can potentially inform the foreign language education profession about the nature of language and how it is learned.

Technology's Effectiveness

It is normal that anyone interested in using educational technology would want to know if it works. Research presented earlier that was conducted at the U.S. Air Force Academy illustrates the value that technology can have in foreign language education. This evidence is corroborated by other sources.

For years now researchers have studied the impact and effectiveness of various technologies on learning outcomes. Primarily addressing technology for distance learning, one extensive overview looked at 218 "Research Reports, Summaries, and Papers," all of which found "no significant difference" between teacher-based and technology-based instruction [See <http://tenb. mta.ca/phenom/phenom.html>]. This study overview was compiled by Thomas Russell, the Director of the Office of Instructional Telecommunications at North Carolina State University, who indicated in an E-mail correspondence that the study was used by proponents as well as opponents of technology for educational delivery (Russell 1996). One side of the argument maintains that since it is no better, we should not be considering its use; the other side says that since it works just as well, we should be increasing its use as its affordability increases. A simple conclusion from this evidence is that because good instruction is good instruction, regardless of the delivery system, we need to make instructional design decisions based on what each system does best.

One examination of costs and effectiveness (Melmed 1995), which was referenced as part of the extensive RAND study cited earlier (Glennan and Melmed 1996), looked at extensive research conducted in education as well as within the military training setting. This report concluded from a wide assortment of studies of specific applications of technology that these implementations brought about improvements in student performance, student motivation, and teacher satisfaction, as well as in other important educational outcomes. Not only did the writers conclude that technology could be an effective component of education, but also that its expanded use would be cost effective.

A landmark study that began in 1979 specifically examined videodisc use for teaching freshmen at a community college as well as at a four-year university and found that students learned more, in less time, and with significantly better attitudes toward the study of biology (Bunderson et al. 1981; Bunderson et al. 1984). Another less-cited study looked at technology for foreign language learning. Bunderson and Abboud (1971) found that students in an experimental program at the University of Texas at Austin learned the fundamentals of the Arabic writing system in a total of eight to twelve hours compared with twenty-four to thirty hours before the implementation of computer-based exercises. For comparison purposes the researchers looked at student learning outcomes at two other universities that used the same text. Students at one university took twenty-two to thirty hours in the writing fundamentals course, and at another university students completed the course in twenty-six to thirty hours. Interestingly, the students who used the computer outperformed the others at a statistically significant level.

Technology's Unique Pedagogical Strengths

Other chapters in this volume have shown that there are many ways that technology can be used in virtually any foreign language learning setting. The authors have thus provided excellent justification with respect to ways that methodology can motivate the use of technology in foreign language classrooms. In so doing, they respond very well to an important concern held by some members of the language-teaching profession. These individuals fear that proponents of applying technology to instruction support such efforts chiefly as a response to technological push rather than from a desire to enhance the learning process for language students. But as illustrated by these other authors and by evidence provided here, there is strong evidence of a fundamental motivation that amounts to what we might call pedagogical pull.

In her book *Mind and Media* (1984), Greenfield cites research that she and others conducted that is quite relevant to the efficacy of the use of technology for certain types of learning (Beagles-Roos and Greenfield 1982; Beagles-Roos and Gat 1983). Although the research was conducted in a field other than language learning, researchers discovered that the addition of dynamic visual images makes verbally presented information easier to remember. For example, Beagles-Roos and Gat (1983) compared students' recall of explicit story content between radio and television and found that elementary students' recall of explicit story content was equivalent across the two media. When the television presentation was added, however, the students' recall of details was improved. They also found that the recognition of expressive language was facilitated by presentation of the story via radio, whereas the students' ability to sequence pictures was improved by a television story. In a later summary of their research Greenfield and Beagles-Roos (1988) also found that radio was more stimulating to the imagination than television, but that television led to greater overall recall of information.

Today's technology goes far beyond what is possible with simple television and radio and thus can do things to enhance learning in a way that would have been inconceivable a few years ago. It can present video and audio segments that illustrate a wide variety of speakers of the target language, providing exciting access to many speaking styles, voices, and accents. This sort of capability can provide a realistic and even in-depth look at the target culture that is not possible through conventional means—teachers speaking to classrooms. Furthermore, students have complete control over their viewing and listening in a way never before possible. Finally, the interactive nature of the technology makes it possible to have a tireless drillmaster ready to respond repetitively for as long as the student is willing to lend his or her attention. This application, limited only by the instructional design that it embodies, will of course reflect principles based on whichever learning theories are espoused and implemented by developers of materials.

Technology and Individualization

In an era when supermarkets have innumerable shelves full of every variety of soft drinks imaginable, drinks that are designed to best suit the individual tastes of every consumer possible, our students come into our classrooms and get what amounts to one flavor. It is a bit like the joke about army uniforms for new recruits that says the outfits come in two sizes—too large and too small.

Although we pay lip service to individualization, education today seems to assume the universality of simple instructional approaches. More often than not, the demands of typical classrooms everywhere prevent teachers from carrying through on the best of intentions. We go through period after period with some students sitting in our classes bored because our activities are too easy, while others are struggling to keep up. As expressed by Mueller, "when one considers the disparity of student ability, it seems quite clear that individualized learning is necessary" (1971:122).

Our unbridled optimism for technology in the late 1970s and early 1980s, which we perhaps possessed even to the point of naïveté, gave rise to the notion that computers would be able to effectively address individual differences as it adapted its instructional sequences to suit the needs of each learner.

> For example, it is quite feasible that a computer used to aid instruction could assess the personality and attitudinal profile of the student about to receive the instruction and adapt its teaching to that student accordingly. A student high in anxiety and ethnocentrism would not receive the same instructional presentation as would a more well-adjusted student (Bush 1983:283).

Another author (Garrett 1987:183) wrote of the difficulties of applying the processing approach to grammar instruction and went on to show how the computer can help in the process:

> The computer, on the other hand, can be programmed not only to present instructional material but also to elicit student response to it, collect information about student performance, analyze that information for evidence of idiosyncratic processing, and give feedback based on that analysis to the learners. Finally, the computer can, if teachers desire, use the analysis to control the choice of the next instructional material offered to help the learner reshape the processing.

Although these applications are indeed both feasible, they are not practically available today, nine and thirteen years after the descriptions were written. As unfortunate as this may be and despite extraordinary increases in computer power since that time, today's hardware and software combinations are not yet at the point that such individualization is a practical reality. Nevertheless, this does not mean that all individualization is impossible.

One way that technology can indeed tailor instruction is by varying the time spent on various elements of instruction. Consider, for example, John Carroll's nicely optimistic view (1963) of learning that asserted that any student can learn a language given enough time. Stated another way, he theorized that language-learning aptitude could be defined in terms of the length of time it takes learners to learn a given amount of material rather than as a statement of how much they can learn.

A simple actualization of this principle of aptitude defined as time required to learn can be seen in various software applications described throughout this volume. In these programs, students can use simple capabilities provided by the technology such as a "Repeat" or "Replay" function to easily hear or see a particular phrase or passage as many times as necessary to understand what is being said. Although not very complex on the one hand and perhaps trivialized by at least one author on the other (Garrett 1987), such capability goes a long way in making materials more useful to a wider range of students. Although such control does not represent the ultimate contribution we can expect from technology-enhanced language learning in the future, such control is a practical reality today and responds nicely to a very basic individual difference, the need for some students to see or hear some material more than others.

Another form of individualization has to do with modalities of learning. Some individuals have a difficult time understanding new words in context when they hear them the first time. Being able to see the text allows these people to bring to the comprehension problem significantly more brain power or different skills for learning than they would ordinarily be able to. For this group and others, cognates are much more easily understood when they are written than when they are heard. Furthermore, since seeing the word breaks for a new language is an important tool for improving comprehension as well as recall, the text helps significantly in the storage and retrieval of the new information. Access to the written form helps in this case, because it provides an extra index for the words as they are stored in memory.

This individualization exists at what we can consider to be the "micro" level—students controlling materials according to their individual needs. It is possible to consider individualization at the "macro" level, where instruction itself is primarily under the control of the learner. Under this model students progress on schedules that they set for themselves and that are monitored by the computer and its software. Such a scenario harks back to individualized instruction as it was practiced before educational technology had the capabilities that it currently has (Ervin 1980).

Some individuals feel that technology will soon usher in a new era of individualized instruction as illustrated by Patrikis (1995). He stated that language instruction via technology will give students more control over what and how they learn. He went so far as to conclude that it will even expand the study of foreign languages.

At the rate technology is progressing, this scenario is increasingly plausible. Certain additional developments, however, are absolutely crucial. First on the list is assessment. Without the means to determine student progress, truly individualized instruction will not be possible. It will also be necessary to develop cost-effective means to produce the necessary software. Current products do not pretend to allow individualization beyond the "micro" level as discussed above and are already limited in quantity as well as being expensive to produce. There is every reason to project that such developments will be forthcoming.

The Imperatives of Life in the Information Age

Changes wrought upon society by the advent of the Information Age are more fundamental and far-reaching than any societal transformation of ages past. Naisbitt writes that changes are at least getting faster (1982). It is perhaps possible to go even further and say that neither the agricultural nor the industrial revolutions changed things in daily life to the degree they are changing today. When our ancestors began to raise their food rather than hunting and gathering, they changed their work and eating habits. When their descendants moved from their farm-based cottage industry to the factory, working and eating were once again affected. In contrast with these previous two revolutions, the transformations of the Information Age will go far beyond just affecting how we work and eat. We will most likely change the way we work, learn, and play and how we communicate during all of these activities. Eating might be the only activity previously affected that will remain unchanged in the future.

Putting this transformation into the general context of education, we observe, however, that as the world is changing around us, education remains immutable. Teachers teach and students learn pretty much the way things were done hundreds of years ago. Given the role that education plays in preparing students to go into the world, it seems clear that there should be a connection between the world and the classroom. Unless education reflects the world in which it exists, it has no relevance for the students.

In short, technology must be implemented in classrooms because of and with regard to two critical aspects of life today as we rapidly enter the Information Age:

- The Information Explosion
- The contrast between a student's world as it exists inside and outside the walls of the school.

The Information Explosion

A general motivation for using technology in education has to do with the extent to which knowledge is exploding in the world, a natural fact of the Information Age mentioned above. As Ong (1968:3) stated:

> We can be fairly certain that there was a time toward the beginning of man's history when knowledge took 10,000 years—perhaps even 100,000 years—to double, and that at a later period it doubled in 1,000 years, and still later in 500 years. It has been estimated that today man's knowledge doubles every 15 years.

To test Ong's assertion, let us assume for a moment that the number of books published in a given year in science, technology, and medicine is an adequate measure of knowledge. The Statistical Abstract of the United States began recording the number of books published in a given year in 1950, a year when 1,645 new books were published in those three categories. By 1965 the number had increased to 4,933 and to 8,738 by 1980, yielding an annual growth rate that effectively doubled twice in less than thirty years, a trend that would certainly support Ong's assertion. Extrapolating somewhat from these data, we see that there were roughly 42,000 books published during the period from 1950 through 1964 and over 97,000 published from 1965 through 1979, another way to consider these same data (U.S. Bureau of the Census 1950, 1952, 1970, 1984, 1994). These data are confirmed by Naisbitt (1982), who stated that scientific and technical information was increasing 13 percent per year when he wrote *Megatrends,* a rate that would cause information to double every five and a half years. In fact, he wrote that "We are drowning in information but starved for knowledge" (1982:24).

Given such an increase in information availability, it is logical to assume that information technology has played a large part in this explosion. It seems only reasonable that this same technology should also be the source of a solution. There is an important step that needs to take place that information technology can facilitate: the conversion of information into knowledge. This process will require human intervention by people using technology as a tool, and such use will come only through practice, much of which must come through education. As students become more and more accustomed to using technology in their pursuit of learning, they will come to expect its use in all areas of their educational experience. Their foreign language courses should be no different.

The Student's World: Inside and Outside the School

Years before Sesame Street and MTV began appearing on the televisions of North America, Marshall McLuhan, the prophet of modern media, commented on the contrast that exists between students' worlds in and out of the classroom. He referred to the information-rich world in which we live as one of a boundless or "marginless" nature (to paraphrase his terms). He drew a sharp contrast between what we might call the "all-at-onceness" of electronic culture and the fragmented and classified world of the classroom: "Our children are born into a total electric environment of information only to find themselves inserted into a very different kind of environment at school" (1968:119). This contrast creates an incongruity for many students as they attend school, an incongruity that in some measure can certainly only be addressed through an increased use of technology in the classroom. Today's technology can indeed be seen as devices capable of transporting students' imaginations beyond the confines of the schoolhouse, creating an effect not unlike the environment to which students are normally accustomed.

Mary Alice White spoke in similar terms, stating that "for 10,000 years, humans learned from images and speech" (1986:43). The relatively "modern" technology that is the printed page itself has been the medium of choice for only 500 years. Is there any wonder that television has the attraction that it does? Given the affinity that students have for TV, it does not seem out of line to assume that the audiovisually poor environment of the typical classroom is not one that today's students find stimulating. Not only are they accustomed to something radically different outside the classroom, their brains (our brains!) might perhaps in fact be wired in such a way as to have created organisms better capable of receiving presentations rich in sounds and pictures than we can yet imagine. In any case, White's ideas seem to call into question the sacred role typically assigned to text in education. The primacy of text might indeed by a principle of a past era that is quickly being overtaken by new technologies. It will most certainly never be replaced; hardly any new technologies ever completely supplant the old. But the role that text plays is most certainly changing.

The contrast between the classroom and the student's home is no more striking than that between the classroom and the workplace. The crucial needs of the workplace are such that students need to be competent in the use of the tools they will encounter there. Despite the fact that students with all varieties of academic backgrounds will face this situation in whatever jobs they take in their lives, there is a marked difference between the exposure students get in some fields and that received by others. A study by Juska and Paris (1993) showed that some differences in exposure occurred in some fields of study where they would probably be expected but others did not. For example, there were expected differences between students in engineering and natural and physical sciences on the one hand and the humanities and social sciences on the other. But this particular study showed that there were classes of users and nonusers within the humanities and social science group they considered. Furthermore, these differences widened as the students advanced in their academic careers.

Such differences do our students a disservice. Given the increases in information technology use that characterize the Information Age, today's students can expect to have more and more demands placed on them. The profile of computer users in the workplace is quickly expanding to include all workers, not just those in science and engineering positions. As today's managers increasingly rely on these technologies, the number of students who can expect to use such tools in the workplace will only increase. In 1993 for example, 45.8 percent of all workers used computers in their jobs (U.S. Bureau of the Census 1995). Why should their efforts in school not reflect what they will be doing on the job, any job? Would the use of technology as a tool in the foreign language classroom not be an excellent preparation to use technology as a tool in other settings that our students will encounter?

Technology and Research on Language Learning

Foreign language teaching professionals have at times lamented the lack of research into appropriate ways to relate language-learning theory to classroom practice (Jarvis 1983). Others have discussed the need for technology-based learning to be well grounded in language acquisition theory (Doughty 1987). Doughty also discussed an exciting application for technology to bring both of these concerns together, stating that technology-based learning materials

> may contribute to this effort by providing rich sources of input and interaction data captured through learner and session logs. Such data is likely to contribute substantially to the theory building—research—theory cycle that will eventually lead to a more complete understanding of the process of second language acquisition (1991:13).

In another vein pertaining to the process for conducting research, Clark and Davidson (1993), for example, propose that the computer can be a useful tool that would be an important part of a large-scale "Research Consolidation Project" to aid in the collection, storage, and dissemination of data collected during studies conducted within many institutions and agencies. Their application seems to be more directed toward the concept of using the computer in such tasks as test administration and data collection, but would be greatly useful in helping extend the empirical research base upon which language-teaching practice can be built.

Using Technology in the Language-Learning Curriculum

Technology in Education

It is possible to classify the uses of digital technology for education in general in four fundamental ways. It can be used as

- a means to deliver or to support the delivery of instruction;
- a tool to facilitate the educational process;
- a medium to access information;
- a medium to facilitate communication.

As a tool for delivering instruction, technology can be used by the classroom teacher or by students working alone or in small groups. A teacher can use a computer to present outlines of lecture notes using presentation software, graphics, digital audio from files or from compact disc, digital video clips, or computer-controlled videodisc.

Students spend an enormous amount of time typing papers and doing various types of analyses involving numbers. In both of these instances, software for word processing or for manipulating spreadsheets can be quite useful in facilitating education. Such use mirrors very closely the type of work graduates will most likely be expected to do as they enter the workplace, a very positive contribution to their general education.

The impact of using the computer to access information has been well publicized. Much of the coverage in the press and in media of all types has amounted mostly to hype regarding the Internet and the World Wide Web (Bush 1996a). This telecommunications phenomenon is a natural step in the evolution of a process that began in the late 1970s with the initiation of online services from CompuServe. Using Web technology, users can access in a matter of seconds materials (text and even audio and video, albeit in a degraded form at present) that are located on computers anywhere in the world. Education is already feeling a significant impact from this technology, the extent of which is yet to be determined.

Closely related to this concept of information access is that of employing the computer for communications purposes. This application consists mainly of electronic mail, or E-mail, a technology that preceded the World Wide Web on the Internet and continues today, already involving millions of people worldwide.

Technology in Foreign Language Education

When considering how to use technology in foreign language education, it is not hard to conclude that the receptive skills of reading and listening lend themselves quite well. Indeed, the first uses of the computer were limited to text-based interactions, creating the situation where exercises were oriented toward reading and grammar.

The productive skills are more difficult, but Beauvois provides an overview in Chapter 5 of how technology can play a role in promoting the speaking and writing skills. In the application she discusses, the computer facilitates exchanges among students, but there are other applications that are possible.

Speaking to the computer, other than in the form of single-word answers and pronunciation drills, is quite difficult. To obtain the best results for accuracy in speech recognition, it is necessary for the user to "train" the software that handles this function. The evaluation by a computer of speech that is natural (as we normally speak) and that is speaker independent (the computer requires no training) is entering the realm of the possible today. Although these applications require hardware and software platforms that surpass what is commonly available today, this situation is rapidly changing. Nevertheless, software applications exist that allow learners to record their voice for comparison to an utterance by a native speaker. Such applications are finding their way into the marketplace in increasing numbers.

Many researchers involved with developing and testing technology applications for foreign language learning have been saying over the years that technology will not replace teachers, but teachers who use technology will replace teachers who do not. It should be clear to anyone who knows anything at all about technology that teachers can do things that technology will not be able to do for the foreseeable future. Given this realization, teachers should not be afraid to give up such tasks to the technology. If technology can do something worthwhile in instruction, then it is of questionable value to waste human effort on those activities. Teacher time can be more useful for those things the human element does best—interestingly, the things that teachers enjoy the most. Thus, we should leave to the technology those things that it can do and concentrate our time on the rest. As technology continues to get cheaper, an issue we will examine in detail below, it will be much easier for people to benefit from its use.

The type of activity that can be most easily relegated to technology are those things that are static, predictable, or convergent (easily predictable correct answers). This has often translated into exercises based on measuring comprehension of a passage, either written or spoken, using fill-in-the-blank, multiple-choice, or true/false types of questions. Consider the now-classic reading or listening comprehension exercises that employ activities in three phases:

- Pre-,
- During-, and
- Post-.

It is possible to find elements of any of the three phases that would lend themselves to implementation of technology. On the other hand, those activities that are dynamic, unpredictable, or divergent (no particular correct answer) are probably best left to the teacher in the classroom.

Information collected from students at the Air Force Academy shows that video is an important part of the success of the instructional program Academy personnel have put together. Students report that they love it and that they enjoy the way it is presented in the Language Learning Center (LLC) (USAFA 1996). The basic aspects of the instructional strategy are described by Bright, Verano, and Cubero (1991) and involve the teacher accompanying students to the LLC where the class can get an initial familiarization with the video. Following the students' return to the classroom, the teacher can exploit the LLC experience to the fullest extent possible by talking with the students in the target language about what they have seen. As the students move from the video to their own lives, it becomes possible for them to use many different communicative exercises among themselves in the classroom.

An interesting aspect of this experience is the leveling effect that the technology has on the students in any given class. Prior to using the LLC in this way, using video would involve some students understanding the material right away while other students would have a very difficult time. With the LLC, students watch the video as many times as necessary to get what is going on. They can see the text they are hearing and click on words to get definitions. Following this initial presentation of the material, they complete a mastery check, using a simple fill-in-the-blank exercise to see how they are doing before returning to the classroom. This capability of students to deal with the video at their individual level prompted a certain excitement for teachers during the earliest research efforts at the academy. Teachers were amazed at the quality of interaction they could have with the whole class following the students' experience with the materials presented using the technology.

Requirements for Implementation

There are several requirements for implementing technology in any language instruction program. Those responsible for putting the total program together must have

- a suitable model of language to guide implementation;
- an appropriate instructional design strategy to implement the total program;
- a system implementation strategy for the technology.

A Suitable Model of Language

It is not possible to implement technology-enhanced language learning materials without some form of a theory base, be it informal or formal, widespread or idiosyncratic. Stated another way, by definition, all materials implement some particular model of what language is and how it is learned. The technology itself, like most other tools, is theory-neutral. It stands ready to be employed in consonance with the particular theory sustained by the instructional designer who is responsible for the materials development process. Making the necessary instructional design decisions is dependent upon having a suitable model of what language is and how language learning works. No doubt some theories lend themselves to implementation via technology, as discussed by Pusack and Otto in Chapter 1 of this volume.

Yet an interesting juxtaposition of phenomena exists within the field of second-language education. Frequent changes in trends and fads in language-teaching pedagogy are well known throughout the profession. On the other hand, many learners become proficient in a second language despite significant discomfort inflicted by well-meaning language teachers. Because such a condition exists, there is no reason to think that the field is close to widely accepting any single model of what language is and how it should be learned. Indeed, as stated by Grittner (1990:38),

> there is no single agreed-upon theory to explain how one best learns (or acquires) a second language. Thus, since there is no "one true theory" upon which to base instruction, the practitioner must either select from among conflicting theories or else become "eclectic" and choose whatever seems to work in a given situation. In fact, if we consider the variables that confront teachers throughout the profession, it becomes almost ludicrous to contemplate a single set of teaching strategies that will be appropriate for every age group, proficiency level, learning

style, class size, socioeconomic background, motivational mindset, ethnic background, teaching style, teacher preparation level, and administrative support system, to name but a few of the most common teacher-learner variables.

Basically therefore, technology implementation is very much program-specific. There is no "one size fits all" for all programs. Teachers need to select materials very much the way they choose textbooks—they pick something that fits into their current setting.

Developers at the Air Force Academy based their software implementation on some simple assumptions, the most important of which was that video is a powerful yet flexible medium of instruction. Krashen's Input Hypothesis played an important part in the instructional strategy that was implemented, although its impact was informed by consideration of other theorists such as Bialystok, McLaughlin, Chaudron, Long, and Oller (Bright, Verano, and Cubero 1991).

Other choices for organizing principles from language-learning theory would be possible as well. The key is for technology implementation efforts to have system planning and execution components that are based on solid language-learning principles, whatever their theoretical underpinnings.

Instructional Design Strategy

Related to the selection of a suitable model of language is the need to subscribe to an appropriate instructional design strategy and to have that strategy guide planning and implementation. This strategy must at a minimum be sufficiently detailed to provide answers to two specific questions:

- Will technology be integrated into the instructional program as a supplement or as the core of the program?
- Which elements of the instructional equation will be relegated to the technology?

Hubbard points out related details that are crucial to program planners. He says that it is important to "determine to what extent the orientation and content of the software is compatible with the orientation, content, and sequencing of an institution-specific syllabus" (1987:240). This determination is not possible without an instructional design that underlies the entire program.

For example, some language-teaching professionals maintain that there is significant evidence that language cannot be learned in isolation and offer as evidence the fact that years of grammar teaching around the world have not produced people who can communicate in the languages learned this way.

After recognizing the debate regarding whether the explicit learning of grammar rules contributes to spontaneous communication, Garrett has argued for considering grammar from a psycholinguistic rather than a linguistic perspective. She concluded that "the computer is ideally—perhaps uniquely—suited to assist learning in that effort" (1987:169).

Whether language programs include the teaching of grammar overtly or assume that it will happen implicitly, the technology component must reflect the principles that guide the other aspects of the program.

System Implementation Strategy

Within any given language-learning theory and instructional design strategy, it is possible to implement technology in any one of a myriad of ways. For example, it is possible to address ways to support the teacher in the classroom or to support individual learning. Individual learning can be supported in class or out of class. Technology can be implemented in numerous ways. Lyman-Hager (1994), for example, talks about class members being seated at tables in groups of seven or so students with sufficient computers for them to work in pairs or in groups of three. The Air Force Academy model places students in the LLC for a little less than half of each class period, followed (or preceded) by work with the teacher in the classroom.

Given that technology prices are dropping, there is another implementation model that is quickly entering the realm of the possible for some settings. In this situation, students would enter class with their personal notebook computers and plug them into power and network outlets at their desks. Once the machines were booted, they would have easy access to E-mail, file-servers, and software to facilitate the integrated use of the systems in the classroom.

As the student machines come online, the teacher's machine would connect to each of the student machines to allow easy exchange of information. Because the teacher's machine would be connected to a large-screen projector, it would be possible for the teacher to display student screens as desired during each lesson, permitting the sharing of information at appropriate times from one student to the others in the class.

The purchasing of personal machines by the students would reduce the investment that their institution would have to make in hardware. Given that the student machines would be constantly updated each year, this would also solve the obsolescence problem faced by schools that install large-scale learning centers. This obsolescence issue was one of the earliest lessons learned at the Air Force Academy. Initial recommendations there involved having the government purchase each computer as had traditionally been the case for regular computer-based implementations. Management quickly saw that such a plan would not work.

Another model would involve the placement of technology to support teacher presentations in the classroom. In one such implementation that has been taking place at Ball State, about 200 classrooms have been wired with fiber optics to create what the school and their cooperating partner, AT&T, call their Video Information System (VIS). This installation is the result of a partnership between Ball State and AT&T, which developed the Teaching Environment Model of the Campus of the Future. The system enables teachers to tap into the library's inventory of videos, films, videodiscs, and other media and have ready access in the classroom (Cirtin 1996).

Finally, it is possible to support the classroom teacher with a large screen monitor, videodisc player, and barcode reader—one of the approaches we have been investigating in the Department of French and Italian at Brigham Young University. Initial findings support using a configuration with a large-screen monitor (31") rather than a projection system that is quite expensive and requires the room to be darkened. Lessons consist of printed materials that have bar codes interspersed throughout to control the videodisc presentation. Videodiscs consist of movies that are commercially available in videodisc format as well as write-once videodiscs (meaning one-off or single copies) created specially for this project, using pedagogical materials for French that are normally only available on videotape. Another part of the project is the placement of large numbers of still images (photographs) on the videodisc as well as on CD-ROM to provide easy access to large quantities of materials for the teacher in the classroom.

The system has been used to date in French 201 courses (third-semester college) at BYU and in special courses taught by BYU professors for linguists from the U.S. Army's Forces Command. Initial reactions by teachers and students alike are quite positive. Students enjoy the use of video in the classroom and have very favorable comments. Teachers who had not previously used video in the classroom in this manner were convinced of its value following the very first lesson taught.

Despite its demonstrated value, videodisc is a technology that probably has a limited remaining life span, due to a newer technology, Digital Videodisc (DVD), that is to be available supposedly very soon, as is discussed in the next section. Nevertheless, videodisc is a technology that is available today, and it is not clear how long it will take for DVD to reach videodisc's current level of functionality (Roberts 1996).

Achieving Technology Implementation for Students

Once it is accepted that it makes sense to implement technology in the language-learning curriculum, then it is necessary to focus on the logistics or practical issues involved with getting the technology in front of the students. So, just how can schools at all levels go about infusing enough technology into the instructional setting to have any significant influence on the language-learning process? What conditions must be met if administrators and teachers are to bring about any positive benefit for the students for whom they are responsible?

The answers can be derived from a correct understanding of two basic areas that impact the implementation of technology in the language-learning curriculum:

- powerful, affordable, and available technology, hardware as well as software;
- the human factor.

There are ample reasons to project that hardware and software costs will continue to drop, yet two primary questions will remain for some time: "Can sufficiently powerful technology be made cheap enough so that it will be affordable for all students?" and "Can sufficiently interesting software be created that is not only plentiful but also affordable?" The good news is that current trends seem to indicate that the answers to both questions will soon be a solid "Yes!"

The bad news is that budgets are going through rough times at all levels of education. Many public schools are quite literally crumbling and will require a massive infusion of funds to return to a minimal level of functionality (Applebome 1995). Institutions of higher education are enduring challenging budget limitations and even cutbacks. It will be hard for schools at any level to show commitment to implementing technology as long as technology is seen as something beyond the other requirements that are currently levied. The challenge of course is to show administrators how they can use technology to help schools reach the goals they already have.

In addition to schools addressing budgetary problems, there remain the challenges of implementation within the context of current societal and institutional demands. There are cases where schools have received an infusion of funds for investing in technology programs, such as in the Yorktown example cited earlier, only to have the programs fade as a result of low commitment as measured by continued funding.

Powerful, Affordable, and Available Technology

Technology Projections: The Perspective of History

Implementation requires planning, which in turn requires at least some level of anticipation of what the future may hold. As someone once said, however, "Forecasting is very difficult, especially when it involves the future!" Nevertheless, there is one thing that seems to be clear when looking back over the early years of the digital revolution with respect to the advances in digital technology—experience shows that anyone given to prognostication has a tendency to overestimate the near term and underestimate the long term. It is therefore not uncommon to project that things will happen before they actually do, but when they do happen, the impact is very often greater than any knowledgeable person would have predicted at the outset.

The past is the first place to which we turn when trying to anticipate the future. Unfortunately, it is often an unreliable source of useful information. Consider the story of Thomas Watson, Sr., the person most responsible for the formation of the company that immediately preceded today's IBM. *Time* magazine quotes Watson from 1943, "I think there's a world market for about five computers" ("The Past, Imperfect" 1996). This was a source of serious conflict between him and his son, Thomas Jr., who became president of IBM in 1952 and bet the company on a scientific mainframe that he debuted that same year (Majumder 1994). As demonstrated by the events that followed, his gamble paid off. Based on his significant break with the past, Watson Jr. went on to build IBM into one of the largest corporations in the world, certainly by far the largest company in the information industry.

For its July 15, 1996, issue, *Time* used the World Wide Web as its source for a few other technologically oriented, landmark forecasts that illustrate the difficulty of making projections based on one's experience from the past:

- "This 'telephone' has too many shortcomings to be seriously considered as a means of communication. The device is inherently of no value to us." —Western Union internal memo, 1876.

- "Everything that can be invented has been invented." —Charles H. Duell, commissioner, U.S. Office of Patents, 1899

- "The wireless music box has no imaginable commercial value. Who would pay for a message sent to nobody in particular?" —David Sarnoff's associates, in response to his urgings for investment in the radio in the 1920s [Sarnoff was at the time an engineer at Marconi Wireless and went on to become an important figure at the Radio Corporation of America (RCA).]

- "There is no reason for any individuals to have a computer in their home."
  —Ken Olsen, president, chairman and founder of Digital Equipment Corp.,
  1977 [For many years DEC was the second largest computer company after
  IBM. In 1994 there were more microcomputers sold than televisions, with
  a majority of those units going into homes.]

Such predictions were of course based on what the people knew, on knowledge strongly influenced by the past they had experienced.

Perhaps the past is not always a perfect predictor of what will happen in the future, but given that we need to make guesses that are as informed as possible, we can assume for the sake of our discussion that digital technology will continue to advance on the same evolutionary path on which it has found itself since the mid-1970s. We are ignoring the fact that there is high likelihood that something paradigmatic will certainly come to pass, but paradigm shifts are difficult, if not impossible, to predict.

Also, for the purpose of simplicity in this discussion, when we speak of digital technology, we should assume that we mean microcomputers. Anyone at all familiar with the digital revolution will recognize this oversimplification, for digital technology with its ubiquitous microprocessors is finding its way into even the most unlikely of places. In fact, it is highly improbable that anyone will develop an exhaustive list of the things that will be affected by their implementation. The important issue is that digital technology is very quickly now encompassing functionality that was previously handled by other technologies such as televisions, VCRs, and audio recording and playback systems, bringing about a convergence that makes microcomputers central to this evolution.

Given these two assumptions, history thus provides an important perspective pertaining to important developments in digital technology, which can be best understood within the context of four important areas of consideration:

- the price and performance of student workstations;
- the information types in which student workstations deal;
- the information infrastructure within which student workstations operate;
- software advances for the creation of interesting and useful materials.

Underlying this discussion is the important assumption that current computer-to-students ratios and the availability of hardware to support classroom instruction are both woefully inadequate. The 1994 edition of technology census information from Quality Education Data (QED) (1994a) shows dramatic improvements in these ratios. In 1983 there was one computer available for 125 students in public schools; by 1994 this ratio had dropped to one computer for twelve students, with that number projected to go to one for nine in 1995. QED reported that 23 percent of school districts had videodisc available, an increase from 3 percent in 1990. Even in those schools that have videodisc technology, it is not clear that they have them in many classes other than science classes. To have any significant impact on instruction, it seems safe to assume that improvements are necessary in technology penetration.

Workstation Price/Performance: The Inexorable Advance
of Digital Technology

Consider this advertisement for the North Star HORIZON Computer taken from a computer publication in 1978:

> The Z80A processor operates at 4MHZ—double the power of the 8080. And our 16K RAM board lets the Z80A execute at full speed. HORIZON can load or save a 10K byte program in less than 2 seconds. Each diskette can store 90K bytes (*Byte* magazine, July 1978).

To better understand just what has happened since that time, compare this with an advertisement in *Byte* magazine for a 166MHz Pentium-based Micron Millennia Plus P166. This machine contains 16 megabytes of main memory, one $3^{1}/2''$ floppy drive, an 8-times normal speed CD-ROM drive, a 15" color monitor, digital sound card, the Microsoft suite of personal productivity software, Microsoft Windows 95, and a hard drive that contains 1 gigabyte (1,000 megabytes) of storage space. The Horizon cost $1,899 with one $5^{1}/4''$ disk drive and $2,349 for a model with two. The Micron computer sells for $2,699. Considering inflation, this unit is actually cheaper than the 1978 unit, given that inflation would place the Horizon system at $3,288 in 1996 dollars! Of course, due to the fact that the Pentium is significantly more powerful, it is interesting to develop a way to analyze more carefully just how far things have come.

For example, these numbers reveal that the disk drive unit on the Horizon system cost $500. Considering that it held 90K[1] of data or programs, it is possible to compare this to a typical $3^{1}/2''$ drive today that holds 1,440K or about 16 times the data of just eighteen years ago. Instead of costing the predictable $8,000, a typical $3^{1}/2''$ drive today costs about $60.

The Horizon machine contained a second floppy drive; all new machines sold today probably contain a hard disk. Consider that the Pentium machine's hard drive contains about 11,111 times the storage of the Horizon. Using this number for a comparison calculation and once again ignoring the effects of inflation, a drive with this capacity would have cost about $5.5 million in 1978!

Turning to memory, the Horizon contained 16K or about 1/1000 of the memory of today's typical Pentium-based machine. Memory in 1978 cost about $360 for 16K; using this rate and assuming no technical progress in terms of price, 16 megabytes would cost $360,000 today!

To keep things simple for the price comparison, we will not consider the increased power of the Pentium in the final price we derive. Nevertheless, it is interesting to see how far things have come. Thus, consider that operations take place significantly faster in today's microprocessors, independent of clock speed. The Pentium is roughly the fifth generation beyond the chip to which the Horizon was compared, the 8080 (8080, 8086, 80186, 80286, 80386, 80486, and the Pentium). For the sake of discussion, the computer world often considers that each generation is twice as powerful as its immediate predecessor. This means that Pentium is 64 times as powerful as the first 8080 devices that appeared in some of the first microcomputers, but keep in mind that it runs at 41.5 times the speed of the Horizon, making the unit roughly 2,656 times as powerful as those first units!

Adding all of this up and ignoring the increases in power of the microprocessor, we arrive at total cost of just under $6 million, an amount probably not unlike that paid for the largest mainframes of 1978. In 1976 it was not unusual for college mainframe computers to contain 8 megabytes of main memory. Today, students or professors transport in satchels to and from school notebook computers that have 8 or even 16 megabytes of memory and have hard disk drives with well over 1,000 megabytes, rivaling today's desktop machines.

To understand just how significant these developments are, consider the change in price over time. While the cost per machine has remained notably constant, the performance of machines far surpasses those of the past, revealing the need for a way to combine cost and performance. This is best thought of as a ratio of cost to performance. Thus the incredible drop in the cost of computing power is illustrated rather remarkably in Figure 9.1.

Considering this demonstration, it seems to be a perfectly safe assumption that the penetration of computers within society is a function of cost. In other words, as prices of technology drop, more people will choose to purchase their own devices.

This concept was recognized early in the microcomputer era by people such as science fiction writer and columnist Jerry Pournelle (1983:242), who stated in a talk at the 1983 National Computer Conference:

Cost/performance

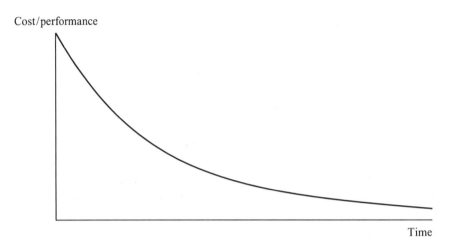

Time

Figure 9.1.
Cost of digital technology over time

> A few years ago, those of us who like peering into the future said that the trend was toward "one user, one CPU." We believed that multiuser systems were swimming against the current. Now I think it's clear: we're headed not just for "one user, one CPU," but several CPUs for each user.

Indeed, in addition to the main central processor (CPU), today's systems as a minimum have at least one processor for audio and another for graphics. Furthermore, most printers have microprocessors in them that are significantly more powerful than the CPUs of the microcomputers that existed at the time Pournelle made his statement.

Information Types

In the early days of computer-aided language learning (CALL), lesson materials were by definition limited to text-based interactions. Lesson materials reflected this limitation and thus focused on developing the reading skill as well as grammatical accuracy. It was this limitation that caused many critics to dismiss the possibility that computers would ever be useful for learning language.

Without perhaps knowing how to express it, these critics were summing up language learning as they knew it—a truly multimedia phenomenon that should reflect human communication. Because of the multimedia nature of communication between people, any system designed to help students learn how to communicate must itself emulate reality. It is therefore only reasonable that the information that comprises instruction be multimedia in nature.

This means that lesson materials will be made up of graphics, audio, and video, as well as the ever-present medium of communication, text. Traditionally, these elements of instruction have been made available to students, using such technologies as textbooks, film strips, films, records, tapes, cassettes, pictures, and most recently, videos. Even a teacher in a classroom can provide something that more closely resembles reality, a multimedia experience unmatched by early computers.

A big part of the digital revolution is summarized under the term *media convergence*. In other words, all of the information types mentioned in the previous paragraph will be deliverable via digital technology and its most visible exemplification, the microcomputer. The capabilities brought about by this convergence will greatly enrich the experience that a computer will be able to mediate for the student.

A major difficulty exists, however, in the fact that in digital terms, graphics, audio, and video are bandwidth-intensive, meaning that it takes a lot of information storage and transmission capability to construct basic instructional interactions. To make them available to students requires a technology with a lot more capacity than the floppy disks that have been the mainstay of the digital revolution until only recently.

Infrastructure for Information Delivery

Because audio, graphics, and even video are the information types that will be indispensable to creating the interactions most useful for student learning, the instructional delivery system must have the means to make the necessary information available when needed. In the past, this has been done using a combination of videodisc and floppy disks. At present it is done with videodisc and/or CD-ROM, with an evolution to the Internet that is happening at mind-boggling speed. Whether these systems are based on mechanisms such as optical storage technologies or on telecommunications-based systems such as the Internet, the point is that information (i.e., lesson distribution) is a problem that demands a solution.

Whichever of these mechanisms is used to solve this problem, student workstations need to have an infrastructure in place that provides the lesson materials that students will be able to use at the workstation.

Optical Storage Technologies. Videodisc controlled by microcomputer was the system of choice for lesson delivery in the late 1970s through the 1980s and even into the 1990s. Moreover, this is still the system that is used in many language-learning centers such as the one at the Air Force Academy. There are also a significant number of schools where teachers use videodisc controlled with barcode technology. Videodisc is a versatile technology that makes high-quality video and audio available either in the classroom or at the workstation.

Unfortunately, the death knell for videodisc was sounded in 1984 when the *Wall Street Journal* and other elements of the news media announced RCA's abandonment of its particular proprietary videodisc system in April (Landro 1984) with the headline, "RCA Will Quit Making Players for Videodisks." Three months later it announced CBS's termination of manufacturing of the type of videodiscs used by the RCA system, "CBS Will End Its Production of Videodisks" (Abrams 1984). Overlooking the misspelling of the name of the technology (*videodisk* versus *videodisc*), these stories in no way provided sufficient context for readers to properly understand the impact of the announcements. The main thing that stuck in readers' minds was that RCA had lost $500 million over five years and that CBS posted a $15.7 million loss in one quarter due to declines in videodisc sales. The first story only mentioned that RCA's was "one of two incompatible technologies on the market" (Landro 1984:20). The other story said nothing of the competing laser videodisc technologies that were still making gains in the marketplace. It is quite reasonable to assume that many companies discounted the importance of videodisc as a viable medium for delivering training. Had laser videodisc made more and faster headway in that sector of society, costs would have dropped more quickly, creating additional opportunities for the education marketplace. As it stands now and despite these problems, videodisc usage in schools has increased from presence in 3 percent of schools in 1991 to 23 percent in 1994 (QED 1994a). Furthermore, there are over 3,000 educational videodisc titles available for purchase today.

The consumer electronics industry seems to have learned an important lesson from this videodisc experience as well as from the VCR format war where Beta lost out to VHS. This marketing battle took place about the same time as the videodisc shootout. The confusion that is wrought on the marketplace by such a conflict makes life difficult for everyone, producers and consumers alike. In this situation, consumers are at a disadvantage—they have to choose between the competing formats and risk picking the wrong one— and the manufacturing companies are at a disadvantage—they cannot make money in a market defined by such confusion. Finally, schools with their limited budgets suffer from an inability to benefit from the economies of scale that would result if the producers would decide on one format from the beginning. It appears that such a decision has been made and is about to yield positive results in the marketplace: the Digital Videodisc (DVD).

Progress for foreign language education is possible with such technologies as DVD, not only because of the lessons learned through past experience, but also because of where technology is in terms of its development. For example, five years ago we edited a volume on the use of videodisc in foreign language instruction (Bush, Slaton, Verano, and Slayden 1991). Five years before that time, it had been obvious to many that digital technology would eventually replace interactive videodisc as the delivery system of choice for foreign language instruction. It was of course impossible to predict exactly when the transformation would take place. In the five years since that publication, things have continued to progress at a steady pace.

A principal characteristic of the "media convergence" phase of the Information Age through which we are now passing will allow all information types (text, graphics, audio, or video) to be represented digitally—the information can be encoded using a fundamentally simple system of 1s and 0s or bits, binary digits that can be made to represent letters, sounds, or colors, in short, the fundamental elements of all of the data types described above. Given this digital reality, it is therefore now possible to deliver highly interactive materials that contain text, graphics, audio, and video from a wide variety of systems that are candidates for becoming part of the rapidly developing information distribution infrastructure. Digital information of any type can be distributed, using digital optical storage such as CD-ROM or even from a network under certain conditions. The problem is the amount of data, the number of 1s and 0s that are required to create a meaningful and interesting lesson. This is where DVD comes in.

DVD is an optical-based technology not unlike videodisc and CD-ROM. Where videodisc is an analog medium, CD-ROM and DVD are digital technologies. In each case, the discs each have smaller-than-microscopic pits on their reflective layers that are protected by a clear outer layer of plastic. These tiny pits break up the light from a miniature laser diode in each unit. The differences between the two technologies focus on how the pits are spaced on the discs' reflective layers. In videodisc technology, the pits are spaced in a pattern determined by an ordinary television signal that has been reasonably standard since the 1930s. For CD-ROM and DVD, the pits and the spaces between the pits represent 1s and 0s. As the laser reflects from the disc back into the player's pickup mechanism, the light is turned off and on to represent the digital signals.

The interesting feature that differentiates CD-ROM and DVD is the incredible increase in capacity that DVD provides. Where a typical CD-ROM holds about 650 megabytes of information, a first generation DVD will hold 4,700 megabytes (4.7 gigabytes) of information. This equates to about 73 minutes of less than optimum quality video on one of today's CD-ROMs and over two hours of higher quality video on DVD. Furthermore, the next generations of DVDs have already been demonstrated and will hold twice that amount of information, with a second, double-sided version that will hold four times the initial version. This amounts to about 18 gigabytes of data that the player will be able to read without the user having to turn over the disc! To understand this number, consider the contents of the manuscript for this article. One page of the original double-spaced version contains 2,795 characters of text. Using this as a basis for figuring the number of printed pages that one of these future generation discs would hold, we come up with 6,440,071 pages of information. Figuring that a typical book contains 300 pages, that would equate to 21,466 volumes of text. Stated another way, this would be equivalent to a stack of 12,500 typical floppy disks containing 1.44 MB of text each. Such a collection of disks would stack to about 150 feet high or half the length of a football field.

Such capacities have two very important sectors of our economy extremely excited. Hollywood is ready to distribute movies in this new format and the computer industry is ready to incorporate DVD as the successor to today's CD-ROM units (Roberts 1996). These two groups have already sorted through what appeared initially to be another format war about to happen, like the ones involving videodisc on the one hand and Beta vs. VHS on the other. The parties to the disputes made their way through that hang-up and now seem stalled on difficulties with finding a mutually agreeable scheme for solving copy-protection problems. Companies that represent Hollywood's interests want copy protection and the computer companies do not, but as *Newsweek* recently summarized:

> DVD's woes hardly seem fatal. Once factories get the OK, they could start turning out DVD players and DVD-compatible personal computers in a matter of weeks. But between here and there stand countless multi-industry meetings. Minor problems will create major headaches. Thinking DVD for Christmas? Maybe Christmas 1997 (Roberts 1996).

A positive outcome to this development will be an exciting technology that will go a long way in facilitating the affordable delivery of interesting, media-rich language-learning software.

Networking Technologies. An examination of books written in the 1980s on educational technology reveals that no one predicted the current rate of change or scope of the impact of what is quite literally a network of networks, the Internet. The closest approximation might well be a concept entitled "The Education Utility," documented by Gooler in a book of that same name and summarized as follows:

> The Education Utility is an electronic delivery and management system that will provide instantly, to the desks of educators and students located anywhere in the world, massive quantities of continually updated instructionally interactive

information (software programs, databases, sophisticated graphics capabilities, news services, electronic journals, electronic mail, and other instructional and administrative materials). All of the these materials will be stored or accessed through a main "host" computer. Individual educational sites (school buildings, etc.) will be connected via a state network to that main host or Network Control Center, through whatever communications channels are most easily and inexpensively available. Each education site will have a special site-based computer, permitting storage of any of the materials or services the local site wished to obtain from the control center. Those materials will be transmitted directly (and at off-hours when transmission costs are lowest) from the network center at the request of teachers and administrators at the local site (1986:11–12).

As astute as these predictions were in some respects, the designers of the Education Utility seem to have totally missed the possibility that communications costs would drop as drastically as they have, thus allowing virtually instantaneous access to information stored on appropriately configured servers located anywhere in the world. Gooler did say that "Eventually, each student in an elementary or secondary school might have a microcomputer terminal at his or her desk" (1986:16), but reality has taken a form that is very much in sharp contrast with the centralized, carefully controlled system he described. Such a vision is one typical of prevalent thinking during what was still very much the age of the mainframe computer.

Working in consultation with engineers from AT&T, the designers of the system Gooler describes came up with an overall system that was based on prevalent technology of the day, mainframe computers, UNIX-based mini-computers, and MS/DOS microcomputers.

Considering the hardware costs of the mid 80s, the total financial investment necessary to implement the system as described by Gooler would have staggered the imagination of even the most numbers-jaded congressman in Washington. Furthermore, at that time hardly anyone could have imagined today's World Wide Web with its total absence of centralized control and the access that is easily becoming available in offices, homes, and schools everywhere. Government funds have played a major part in the establishment of the infrastructure upon which the Internet and World Wide Web depend, but other components of the total system have come from every source imaginable, from individuals, companies, universities, and of course from government at all levels. The only limiting factors today remain the cost of connecting to the Internet and the speed at which data can be transmitted, but as time passes, it is clear that communications costs will drop at the same time that data transmission speeds up (Gilder 1994).

Many forces are lining up to help the Internet realize its potential. Telephone companies, cable companies, and ventures based on Hughes' Direct

Satellite System (DSS) are preparing to make high-capacity, affordable Internet connections available to all sectors of the economy (Bush 1996a). At least one satellite communications company that does not yet have its satellites in orbit is entering the fray, backed by $10 million from none other than Bill Gates of Microsoft (Kupfer and Davies 1996). Aided by legislation from the U.S. Congress that is making telecommunications deregulation a reality (Bush 1996b), these are just a few of the many plans to make extremely affordable global communications via the Internet a reality in the life of literally everyone on the planet who chooses to be connected. Data transmissions via satellite and compact, turbine-powered electrical generators will even allow many places in developing countries to avoid the huge investments in power grid and wire-based telephone infrastructures that have been installed for many years in developed nations. The braking forces are at present often more political than they are economic.

Software Advances

Over the past several years there have been significant advances in software capabilities that have moved forward the state of the art in language-learning software. Some efforts have had more success than others, but the areas of emphasis fall into four basic categories:

- general purpose authoring software;
- templates for creating language-learning software;
- artificial intelligence;
- speech recognition.

Progress in authoring software probably signals the most significant advance that is impacting interactive language-learning materials development. This is not meant to be an exhaustive list, but generally available authoring systems and tools such as HyperCard and Authorware on Apple's Macintosh and ToolBook and IconAuthor for systems running Microsoft Windows have all permitted a level of development effort that was impossible ten years ago. In the mid-1980s microcomputers were limited in power; the requirement to program software in BASIC and other languages at that level was also a severe limitation in producing interesting software.

These new and advanced authoring software systems have permitted the development of such tools as *Libra, Guided Reading Templates,* and *Language Tool* from the Air Force Academy, some of which along with several others are mentioned in other chapters of this volume. Such tools as these enable the creation of interesting interactive software without requiring each developer to actually resort to programming as was necessary a few years ago.

One area of pursuit that has not yet fulfilled initial expectations is the field of artificial intelligence (AI). The Athena Language-Learning Project at MIT (Murray, Morgenstern, and Furstenberg 1989) put a great deal of effort into developing "conversation-based programs" using artificial intelligence techniques. Underwood (1987) documented several other efforts that were looking at ways that AI could improve the nature of computer-based interactions with language learners. Unfortunately, very little (if any) of the software that is available for distribution makes use of AI techniques.

The Athena Language-Learning Project has created such exciting applications as *À la rencontre de Philippe* and *Quartier St Gervais,* two very interesting programs described elsewhere in this volume that are now commercially available. It is hoped that the AI aspect of that effort will soon yield practical results as well.

One capability that is starting to appear in commercially available language-learning software is speech recognition. This technology is indeed problematic, given that the ability to achieve truly speaker-independent speech recognition is quite a computationally intensive effort. We can expect to see continued progress in this area as hardware power and software capabilities continue to improve.

Crucial to the discussion of advances in software capability is the means to distribute the software that research efforts are revealing to be useful. For several years we were faced with a tremendous "chicken or egg" problem in that publishers could not justify producing software because schools had no machines on which to run it. Schools that were otherwise able to invest in technology could not justify the expense due to the low availability of software. A walk through the exhibit area of any major language conference will reveal that the Catch-22 is finally resolving itself. Technology is now becoming a part of the standard offerings of publishers.

The Human Factor

The discussion above is easily summarized with a single statement: For all practical purposes, technical problems no longer constitute a critical issue for implementing technology for language learning. Even the problem of cost does not seem insoluble, given the advances that have already occurred and that show no sign of abating. Remaining are the questions that make up the "human factor." For example, can we implement technology, given certain fundamental attributes of human nature, such as natural resistance to change? Answers to questions in this area lie in how people organize themselves within institutions and within society. We need answers to two specific questions. Is there sufficient commitment to implement technology for language learning to be found within

- society at large?
- institutions such as schools and policy-making bodies?

Societal Commitment: A Case for Equity

The good news, therefore, is that good software is becoming available and hardware is getting cheaper and more powerful. But along with this good news, there is some seriously bad news: many schools are crumbling around the heads of the students they were built to serve.

In three reports released last year, the General Accounting Office documented that $112 billion is needed to address pressing construction needs in the nation's schools, finding also that states spent less than $3.5 billion in 1994 addressing them (Applebome 1995). Providing examples, Applebome writes:

> A glance at some school districts around the country illustrates the scope of the problem. Century-old school buildings are crumbling in New York City, while schools in New Orleans are being eaten away by termites. A ceiling in a Montgomery County, Ala., school recently collapsed, 40 minutes after children left for the day. In Chicago, there is not enough electrical power and outlets for computers, which remain in their packing boxes. And in suburban Philadelphia, some schools are so crowded that students are not allowed to carry backpacks because there is no room in the halls and lunch starts at 9:22 A.M. so that all students get a chance to eat. (pp. A–1)

It is difficult to imagine the possibility of integration of very much technology in schools that have this level of problems with their basic infrastructure.

Requiring all students to purchase their own individual computers has made sense to administrators and educators at numerous institutions of higher education. This is evidence that whatever we do, we are going to have to look at the technology availability problem and related issues in ways different than most people have to date. For example, personnel responsible for computer operations at the Air Force Academy initially stated that policies dictated the necessity for the government to own the microcomputers that the students would use. A CAI Working Group comprised of interested faculty had already recommended that students be required to purchase microcomputers, but their recommendation had been dismissed immediately as impractical and against government policy. They were not authorized to connect "personal" devices to the "government" infrastructure. Upon further reflection, management recanted on this decision, stating that it would cost too much money and would raise other administrative issues, such as students' use of government-owned computers for leisure-time games.

Such a solution is perhaps suitable for many instances of higher education, but it is clear that it will not be very applicable to all public school settings. Considering the infrastructure problems in the schools mentioned above, it is probably fair to assume that students in the areas served by these schools will not have in their homes very much technology they can use to supplement their educational experience. Furthermore, the RAND study on developing a national strategy for technology in public schools cited personal ownership as the weak link in the distinctions made among children from various socioeconomic settings. They found that the differences between technology availability in schools in these diverse areas to be minimal. The authors went on to suggest that differences in availability at home, however, constitute a potentially serious problem that needs to be addressed (Glennan and Melmed 1996).

With findings that disagree somewhat with the RAND report, Rockman (1995) decries the inequity that he says is documented in many places throughout the United States. He concludes that poor, minority, and female students have less access to computers at school than others, contradicting Glennan and Melmed. As Rockman asserts, many of the students are "unlikely to have a computer at home and, in many cases, their schools don't have enough computers for students to use more than an hour or two per week" (1995:25). There are bright spots, he says, such as inner-city schools in Oakland where donated 286 PC compatibles are sent home for the semester, and in Indiana where fourth-grade students "receive a computer, printer, and modem to take home until they go on to middle school." He summarizes:

> Solutions to equity problems, whether gender-, race-, or economically related, will take time and money and, more importantly, a public moral commitment to reach this goal. People do not resist change, rather they resist the social and political consequences of change. We need to move the change effort to letting others move up the educational ladder—and use technology effectively to accomplish it (1995:29).

Just as public libraries provided books to the masses, so will public access to information technology be necessary to maintain the powerful democratic principle of equal access to education, the principle to which technology access is being tied. Education in most developed countries today has generally shown success in avoiding a situation where there are educational "haves" and "have-nots," and technology needs to be factored into the equation. As in the past, help can come from public or private sources.

Evoking this concept, House Speaker Newt Gingrich, testifying before the House Ways and Means Committee, proposed what he said might be a "nutty" idea:

> Maybe we need a tax credit for the poorest Americans to buy a laptop. Now maybe that's wrong, maybe it's expensive, maybe we can't do it, but I'll tell you, any signal we can send to the poorest Americans that says, 'We're going into a twenty-first century, third-wave information age, and so are you, and we are going to carry you with us,' begins to change the game (Andrews 1995:A–22).

Quick to point out that the poorest Americans do not pay taxes, critics accused Gingrich of gross insensitivity. For example:

> Regarding "Newt's Notion: Laptops for All" (Jan. 7): The new speaker of the U.S. House of Representatives, Newt Gingrich, has transformed Marie-Antoinette's historic "Let them eat cake" into the technologically smart, late-twentieth century, "Let them have laptops." As we all know, Marie-Antoinette lost her head for her phrase, and for the insensitivity it represented. Perhaps Mr. Gingrich should keep that in mind. LARRY LIPPA. Rome (Lippa 1995).

Another concerned citizen wrote to the *Los Angeles Times,* "The virtual unemployed can have virtual jobs" (Whittier 1995:M–4).

Undaunted by Mr. Gingrich's disclaimer of nuttiness and the perceived insensitivity that led to these criticisms, President Clinton embraced the idea, citing its soundness (Purdum 1995). Others agree as well. Referring to John F. Kennedy's 1960 inaugural pledge to place a man on the moon before the end of the decade, Frankel (1996:40) picks up on one type of technology use and states:

> But like conventional telephone and postal service, E-mail will never fulfill its social and commercial promise until it is universal. . . . And we, too, could use a great new enterprise. E-mail for all won't guarantee how well we speak to one another, but it can keep us talking and growing richer together.

Achieving equity on such issues in a democratic society is critical, so the question remains how to derive a solution. Some would propose, as did President Clinton, that the government should play a major role. Others would say the responsibility lies with individuals and within existing educational frameworks. These frameworks are so burdened already that it will most likely take a combination of both to implement any changes at all.

Another source of support is from individuals who are concerned about this equity issue and want to help address the problem. For example, Bill Gates, Chairman and CEO of Microsoft and by many accounts the person whom we might call the richest non-potentate in the world [the Sultan of Brunei is said to be the richest individual in the world], has evoked Andrew Carnegie's efforts with endowing communities all over the United States with libraries as a model worthy of emulation. Gates wondered in an interview with the *Washington Post* whether the technology will get cheap enough for such a program to be possible:

> Something I'm very interested in—but it'll take me many years to figure out if it's an opportunity—is like what Carnegie did with libraries. Will there be a point where the PC has come down in price enough—and its ability to be used for education is good enough—that it really makes sense to have it available on a widespread basis? I don't know the answer to that, but it's the kind of activity that would fit in pretty well for my declining years—if there's still money there to be given (Mind: 1995:1).

This is not so much about the potential for philanthropic[2] efforts by Bill Gates as it is contemplation of ways to implement technology. If education can benefit from technology, then we need to find a way to make it happen. The size of the investment is such that it will require efforts from individuals up through all levels of government. The effort to infuse our schools with an acceptable level of technology will most likely require anywhere from $8 billion to $20 billion over the next five to ten years (Hayes 1996). According to this same source, this amounts to three to six times the current spending levels on technology, but is only 6 percent to 7 percent of total current expenditures on education.

Institutional Commitment

There are several consequential ingredients at the institutional level that are necessary for new educational technology implementations to flourish:

- planning and budgeting,
- trained personnel,
- organizational integration, and
- properly specified instructional programs.

It is possible that some efforts can be successful to a point without the presence of all four elements from this list. In those cases where a single component is missing, it is likely that those new programs will be short-lived.

Planning and Budgeting.   Because hardware and software sophistication have increased, it is now easier to make a case for the cost effectiveness of technology. Unfortunately, even with falling costs, the budgets available to support language teaching are often considered inadequate, reflecting the lack of societal commitment mentioned above. There are at least two reasons that this is the case. First, the lack of interest in foreign language study in U.S. society is a well-known phenomenon that can easily cause language programs to get short shrift in public schools when program budgets are developed. Such a sentiment can be expected to manifest itself in technology efforts as well. Second, unless teachers undertake proper planning and budgeting, even language students in schools with above-average resources will not have the level of access to technology necessary to effect positive impact on learning outcome.

For example, initial planning efforts at the Air Force Academy began in 1977 and were updated in 1982 before coming to full fruition in 1988. Individuals who wish to effect change must be attuned to the procedures of their particular organization.

Innovators must also remember that one-time infusions of funds are not sufficient to ensure a long life for the program they wish to implement. There are maintenance costs over the life cycle of the system they implement, as well as upgrade costs when the system is outdated. Unless these are planned in advance and institutional support secured at the outset, even the most exciting innovations will be short-lived.

One issue that not many proponents of technology want to mention is the possibility of replacing teachers with technology. A recent visitor at Brigham Young University was on an errand commissioned by administrators at his home institution to find ways to use technology to reduce the number of instructor positions. It is to be expected that such demands will increase as technology becomes more capable and budgets continue to decrease. Planners must be able to differentiate between the tasks that technology can assume and those that require a teacher. Changing the instructional equation this drastically will certainly increase the need for teacher training, especially during the transition.

The Need for Trained Personnel.   The requirement to train personnel is important on two levels. First, there is the situation where teachers must integrate the technology into their teaching. If certain instructional tasks are assumed by the technology, the teacher's role will by definition be modified. The manner in which teachers plan and execute their lessons must change as the technology enters the instructional equation. Kassen and Higgins document a program in Chapter 8 that addresses these issues for TAs who are about to begin teaching for the first time.

Second, there is a serious requirement to train personnel in how to deal with the technology itself. In some situations teachers will be intimately involved with technology as it becomes part of their instructional program. To address this need, most teacher-training programs at universities probably have a course on technology for teachers. The challenge is to find an appropriate level of detail at which to instruct the future teachers. Technology is more robust today and thus less prone to problems, operating system software is more user-friendly, and application software is easier for students and teachers alike. There are nevertheless challenges that good training will help future teachers face when the time comes.

Consider an example that involved my integrating technology into the second of the two methods classes that French Teaching majors and minors at our institution are required to take. Most of the students had taken the required course on microcomputers from the College of Education. When I asked them to copy a file from the file server to a floppy disk using the File Manager in Windows 3.1, I might as well have been speaking Martian. This is not a criticism of the particular course or courses they had taken, rather it is a comment on the value of having technology use be an integral part of the students' overall program. Future teachers who have used technology as a tool in their own education will be more likely to be able to use it effectively in their own teaching.

The Importance of Organizational Integration.   It is a general assumption that advances in technology move at a quicker pace than most human beings are able to assimilate. The resulting changes are embraced by a few individuals, accepted reluctantly by others, and strongly opposed by yet others. Language teachers and their administrators are no exception. Organizations must be prepared to raise technology implementation from the level of the grass-roots innovator to the program level to ensure institutional support for the innovation. The efforts of even the most motivated teacher wanting to make change cannot succeed for very long without the incorporation of any new program into the appropriate organizational structure.

For the Air Force Academy, technology implementation took place not only with full institutional support but within the framework provided for programmatic innovations. The planning took into account the long-range impact on budgets and thus the system provided for proper maintenance and procedures for system upgrade at the appropriate moment in the life cycle of the technology that was implemented.

In the case of the Yorktown program, the team there was able to achieve excellent results with motivated personnel who learned what was necessary to get the job done. Through significant individual initiative they started an award-winning program. Unfortunately, the school district does not seem to have made a long-term institutional commitment to integrate this program into its regular organizational structure. As a result, the program has dwindled from its peak three years ago (Underwood 1996). Minus one of the four necessary elements for success, a once-exciting program is presently totally dependent on the teachers who were part of the initial development team and remain at the school.

With respect to such a case, the definition of "haves" and "have-nots" goes beyond the issue of socioeconomic status raised above. In responding to the issue of supplying the poor with laptops, Nicholas Negroponte, the director of the Media Lab at MIT, took the discussion in a direction quite related to the problem of organizations accepting or rejecting technological innovation:

> When Speaker Newt Gingrich spoke of buying laptop computers for needy Americans, critics promptly dismissed the idea as silly. But it is not silly at all. It raises a question that doesn't seem to have occurred to those who brushed aside his suggestion as a case of offering cake to the starving: Just who are the needy? Who are the have-nots?

Responding to his own question, he states that "most Americans over 30, rich or poor, have been left out of the digital world" (Negroponte 1995:19).

If people over 30 do not understand what is going on, then this specific group will have difficulty providing proper leadership to move things forward. It would appear then that the "digital homeless" with respect to education can be defined as the decision makers who must consider requests for innovation within our schools.

Properly Defined Instructional Programs.   Even when those in charge have a commitment to innovation, this does not guarantee the ability to convey the commitment to those under whose guidance implementation must take place, in this case the teachers. Good instructional programs depend on the successful interaction of committed administrators and teachers. Given adequate administrative support, it is ultimately up to teachers to incorporate innovation into well-defined instructional programs. Such programs will implement instruction consisting of a balanced mix of technology-based delivery of materials, teacher-led activities, and appropriate homework assignments that could be either "high tech" or "low tech" in nature.

The Status of Technology Implementation for Foreign Language Learning

Whether the reasons for the lack of technology implementation are budgetary or organizational, the term *digital homeless* appropriately describes foreign language students. This situation is illustrated in the RAND study cited earlier

(Glennan and Melmed 1996) in which, for example, we see a noticeable lack of attention to foreign language study in its findings. Other than the reference in the table the authors provided to illustrate how students spend the time they have available on the computer, the RAND report only mentioned foreign language study twice. In the first case the authors cited the value of distance learning in providing language instruction to small, remote schools. In the second case, the authors were discussing the availability of software and stated that teachers and students benefit from "a well-known and quite widely used class of content software" for foreign language instruction.

As further illustrated by a report from Quality Education Data (1994a), purchases in instructional software for teaching foreign language lag behind most other academic areas. Table 9.3 shows this trend expressed in percentages of school districts planning purchases over the next year.

It might be possible to rationalize this state of affairs with the argument that there is not much computer software for learning foreign languages—probably not an unfair assumption. We could perhaps also surmise that things would be different for video, a technology cited in 1989 by Richardson and Scinicariello (1989:44):

Table 9.3.
Instructional software purchase plans in school districts (Quality Education Data 1994:133).

Subject	89–90	90–91	91–92	92–93	93–94
Art	1 %	28 %	29 %	35 %	41 %
Business Education	6	52	57	56	63
Computer Education	22	44	43	41	53
Foreign Language	0	0	24	27	41
Home Economics	0	0	0	0	0
Industrial Arts	0	0	0	37	48
Language Arts/English	33	82	68	66	72
Math	44	85	83	82	85
Music	0	0	0	30	45
Reading	17	61	58	56	74
Science	29	76	70	75	83
Social Studies	14	60	64	65	78

The arguments for using television technology in the classroom are so convincing that perhaps those not using it should be asked why they have neglected this important aid to second language learning.

Considering purchase plans for videotape as a barometer for video use as shown in Table 9.4, the picture, however, does not improve much for this particular technology.

Finally, a similar situation exists for three very specific technologies, interactive videodisc (as defined primarily by videodisc players and bar-code readers), CD-ROM, and multimedia PCs (as defined by machines with sound and color and most likely CD-ROM). Table 9.5 shows the extent to which typical schools in the responding school districts used each of these three technologies during the 1993–1994 school year.

These figures parallel quite closely the findings by Becker (1994) as cited in the RAND study mentioned in the introduction (Glennan and Melmed 1996), which placed student time spent using the computer in foreign language study at 2.7 percent as compared to 7.7 percent for math, 7.4 percent for English, and 6.2 percent for science. Our students are clearly the "have-nots" whenever they are engaged in foreign language study.

Until language teachers themselves make a case for using technology with their students, it is unlikely that societal demands will move them in that

Table 9.4.

Videotape purchase plans in school districts (Quality Education Data 1994:146)

Subject	89–90	90–91	91–92	92–93	93–94
Art	0.0 %	0.0 %	52.9 %	43.8 %	41.0 %
Business	0.0	37.3	45.1	25.0	28.2
Computer Science	0.0	33.3	43.1	29.2	33.3
Foreign Language	0.0	15.7	49.0	37.5	38.5
Language Arts	16.7	72.5	56.9	52.1	51.3
Math	5.0	49.0	56.9	37.5	35.9
Music	0.0	47.1	0.0	33.3	35.9
Reading	3.3	51.0	0.0	50.0	46.2
Science	25.0	78.4	70.6	60.4	61.5
Social Studies	23.3	88.2	74.5	62.5	66.7

Table 9.5.
Technology use in typical schools (Quality Education Data 1994b:77, 85, 95).

Subject	CD-ROM	Videodisc	Multimedia
Art	14.8%	17.1%	24.3%
Business	13.7	3.0	3.5
Computer Education	27.3	19.8	44.6
Foreign Language	5.7	4.1	4.8
Industrial Arts	10.9	8.8	11.9
Language Arts	29.9	22.6	23.5
Library Reference	78.0	22.1	31.9
Math	23.9	11.7	11.9
Music	24.5	9.1	22.6
Reading	40.6	14.3	20.3
Science	49.8	73.2	47.0
Social Studies	64.1	64.5	47.6

direction. It is possible that society might make demands of schools to use technology to improve math and science learning due to the attention these subjects receive in the media and to the association often made between these subjects and the competitiveness in the international marketplace. It is unlikely that the same thing would happen for foreign language instruction. Pressure to change the status quo will probably have to come from language teachers themselves.

Conclusion

Three fundamental questions were provided at the outset to frame the discussion to consider the use of technology in foreign language instruction:

* Should technology be used in foreign language learning?
* If it makes sense to use it, what is the best role it can fill in the instructional equation?
* Once we have decided to use it and know what we want to do with it, how should it be implemented so students will benefit?

There are two sources of relevant information for answers to these questions. First, there is the empirical evidence gleaned from the cases of actual implementation such as the experience at the U.S. Air Force Academy and Yorktown High School. Second, two types of studies can provide guidance—those pertaining to foreign language learning and those pertaining to research within a broader range of academic subjects. Based on the evidence provided here, these three questions become two. First, given the capabilities for addressing the important pedagogical issues discussed here, a key question becomes not "Why?" but "How?"—stated another way, "How will technology implementation most likely unfold?"

Second, given the dramatic developments that are taking place in society today with digital technology and its extraordinary price decreases, a second question is not "Whether?" but "When?"—stated with more precision, "When will it be reasonable to expect technology implementation on a scale such that language learning will benefit?"

Implementation Scenario

How will technology implementation most likely unfold? Despite the low levels of current observed in schools today, there is reason for optimism.

Video Technologies

Videotape and videodisc are two technologies that hold significant promise for language learning. Unfortunately, as shown by Tables 9.4 and 9.5, the expected use of these technologies for foreign language learning falls significantly behind use in science classrooms. As useful as videotape can be in the classroom, it is not as flexible as videodisc. But as publishers continue to distribute videotape materials, it is safe to assume that the availability of this technology will increase.

Although the life span of videodisc will be shortened by the advent of DVD technology, schools wishing to upgrade their language instruction could benefit from its use in the very near term. It will probably take a couple of years for DVD players and compatible discs to become available for purchase by schools. Furthermore, there is evidence that purchasers of videodisc materials will be able to continue to use into the future any discs purchased now.

Video in the Classroom

It is not likely that prices on technologies for individual workstations will fall sufficiently in the next two years to permit very many schools to implement the level of student technology use attained with the learning center model employed, for example, at the Air Force Academy. Thus, video technologies will probably have their impact during the near term in support of the classroom teacher, initially with videotapes and videodisc and later with DVD.

Given the similarities between DVD and videodisc technologies, it is quite reasonable to assume that companies such as Pioneer and Sony will produce players that are compatible with both formats for distribution to schools. Pioneer has announced that it will begin producing a videodisc-DVD combination player this fall (Kasten 1996). Although this initial player is intended for the consumer marketplace, the past interest of this company in the school market would seem to indicate that it will have a presence there in the future as well. If a school purchases videodisc and associated materials, therefore, the investment in videodisc software will most likely be useful into the foreseeable future.

New Marketing Channels for Publishers

Technology implementation will advance only as fast as publishers are able to supply teachers and students with new materials. Moreover, the costs associated with developing materials for new technologies will probably dictate a change in the development and marketing strategies of traditional textbook publishers. For example, their conventional model of distributing language-learning video has been to make it part of the ancillary materials that accompany textbooks. Traditionally, they have sold their textbooks and given the video resources to schools for free. This model will break down as the role of video increases in the future. Not only will video be an independent component as it is today, it is already becoming an important element in the materials produced for the various interactive technologies mentioned here. Given the expense of producing video with high production value, however, publishers who wish to increase the quality and variety of their video offerings will need to develop new pricing and marketing models.

Furthermore, the first place that interactive multimedia systems that implement the converged technologies of text, graphics, audio, and video impact will probably not be the schools. It is a safe guess that the strongest initial impact of this system will be felt in the consumer marketplace, where the installed base is sufficiently large to justify the investment required for materials development. For this reason, it makes sense for publishers to consider distributing in this market sector materials that can be used in conjunction with textbooks that students are using in school. This would be a major departure from the way publishers have marketed their materials in the past, but it seems reasonable that they will welcome a change, given the cost of keeping up with the technological evolution that is under way.

Software Development

Because the availability of software has not been what some teachers expect, a fair number of them (primarily at the university level) have developed software for use with their students. As the market develops, however, it is unlikely this trend will continue. Just as most teachers do not typically develop their own textbooks, there will not be many who will insist on developing their own interactive materials. Instead, they will depend on the evolving role of publishers as described above.

Research and Development

Given the complexity of technology and rapid developments in its capabilities, there is a serious need for research and development (R&D) into the best ways to develop materials and to use interactive technologies. If publishers were to take the lead of high-technology segments of industry, such as computer software companies for example, they would assume this role. Because they must transform themselves from an old business model to a new one, it is not likely they will do so. Instead, researchers, most likely at universities, will need for the foreseeable future to continue to conduct the type of R&D that has been under way in the field of technology-enhanced language learning for some years now. In this process, there exists the possibility of publishers and academics working together in new ways that go beyond traditional textbook development.

Learning Centers over the Longer Term

As the price/performance ratio of hardware and software continues to improve, schools will most likely increase their investment in language-learning centers. Given the speed at which interactive technologies are developing at present, it is not unreasonable to assume that future implementation will surpass the pace of recent years. Systems will continue on their current path of implementing optical memory devices such as CD-ROM drives and their successors, DVD. As online capabilities increase and the infrastructure for providing communications bandwidth develops, however, we will perhaps eventually reach the point where online connections will be capable of delivering the sort of materials for which optical memory systems are useful today. Until this happens, CD-ROM and the not-too-distant future technology that is DVD will be essential components on the student learning workstation.

As developments continue and prices drop, certainly within ten years, any classroom will be a full, computer-based, multimedia classroom. Students will bring their notebook computers to class, as described earlier, and connect them to the network and power connections converting the classroom to a learning center every bit as powerful as any dedicated center today. Within this same time period, students will have the ability to look into their system and speak face to face with students from the culture of the target language they are studying.

Another possible model involves students working outside the classroom on their personal interactive devices. They will interact with video-based materials, respond to questions, and demonstrate their listening, reading, and writing proficiency. As they reach various levels, they will then schedule themselves into discussion sessions with the teacher and other students who have reached the same level to work on their speaking skill. Related to this model, Scinicariello wonders in Chapter 6 if dedicated labs will cease to exist and then goes on to describe the "virtual language lab" of the future. It seems reasonable to assume that centralized laboratories will continue, but will be more useful as testing centers to support this more flexible scheduling learning environment in which students work outside of class, test, and then come to class when they are ready for particular group-learning sessions.

Reasonable Expectations for the Future

The one thing we know for sure about technology is that it will only get more affordable with the passage of time. Negroponte predicts that by the year 2000 "as many homes will have a computer as have a TV; in fact, many Americans will be watching TV in the upper-right-hand corner of their P.C.s" (1995:19). After stating that 35 percent of American homes have at least one personal computer, he points out that the trend is already in place for his prediction to become a reality—computer sales surpassed television sales for the first time in 1994.

Just how realistic is this projection? For both technologies, it is hard to ascertain absolute dates to use in a comparison. In 1939 the American television industry settled on the fundamental broadcast and display technologies that are still in use today. Although perhaps not an essential feature, color display became a reality in the early 1950s. For microcomputer technology, it was 1975 when Bill Gates left his undergraduate studies at Harvard to create the BASIC programming language for Ed Roberts's Altair microcomputer, a major step toward making computers available for the masses (Wallace and Erickson 1993).

Television began to appear in American homes in noticeable numbers in the second half of the 1940s. During the period 1945 to 1952 penetration went from 0.02 percent to 36 percent, (calculated from data contained in U.S. Bureau of the Census 1952, Table 985). After reaching 90 percent of American homes eight years later in 1960, TV took another nine years to reach a level of 98 percent of homes in 1969 (Statistical Abstract 1970: Table 1098), only slightly under its peak of 98.3 percent where it remains today (Statistical Abstract 1995: Table 897).

Can microcomputers beat that? Television took thirty years to reach 98 percent of American homes. It will certainly be interesting to see if computers can do it over a period of twenty-five years, as Negroponte is predicting. Only time will tell, but such a milestone is not unthinkable. The exponential increases in capabilities combined with the incredible drops in price discussed earlier create a trend in cost effectiveness that is hard to fathom, certainly laying the groundwork for the advances that Negroponte and others predict.

If such a level of penetration becomes a reality, equity issues should no longer occupy a prominent position in the discussion of the implementation of technology in society in general. Education would also benefit from a significant carryover effect in the process.

Summary

The implementation of technology for foreign language learning must be considered within the larger context of technology in education in general. Hayes summarized several sources in addressing the need to develop a national strategy for instructional technology that she entitled "Our National Technology Goals" (1996):

- All teachers will have the training and support they need to help students learn how to use computers and the information highway.
- All teachers and students will have modern multimedia computers in their classrooms.
- Every classroom will be connected to the information superhighway.
- Effective software and online learning resources will be an integral part of every school's curriculum.

Hayes's points track very well with the discussion that we undertook for this chapter in particular and for this volume in general. In short, we can answer quite simply the three questions posed at the outset:

- Technology can indeed help in language learning, just as it can in education in general.
- There are elements of language instruction that can be handled quite ably by technology. This will save teachers' effort for those tasks best performed by teachers.

- Technology implementation is already practical in many settings and there is reason to believe that it is quickly becoming practical for many others as costs continue to drop and as quality language-learning software becomes available.

Any effort to use technology in foreign language education must focus primarily on one objective: the improvement of the language-learning experience. Anyone who has ever watched students' faces as they experience their first interactive video-based language-learning experience knows that it is worth what it takes to make it happen.

NOTES

1. A K of data is typically interpreted to be 1,000 bytes (or characters) of information. In reality it is 1,024 bytes, a number that is the integer power of 2 (2^{10}).
2. Bill Gates has been quoted as saying that he will not leave more than 5 percent of his vast wealth (from $15 billion to $18 billion, depending on Microsoft's stock price on any given day) to his children. He has already begun his philanthropic efforts at a low level by donating the proceeds of his book, *The Road Ahead,* to education. In addition, Microsoft has donated $10 million to educational technology efforts in community and technical colleges in the state of Washington, Microsoft's home state. [See <http://www.microsoft.com/corpinfo/press/1996/feb96/clintonpr.htm>] He said also in the *Washington Post* interview cited in this chapter that he gives from $10 to $20 million to United Way and other charitable causes each year.

REFERENCES

Abrams, Bill. 1984. "CBS Will End Its Production of Videodisks." *The Wall Street Journal,* July 10,6:7.

Applebome, Peter. 1995. "Record Cost Cited to Fix or Rebuild Nation's Schools." *The New York Times,* December 26, p. A–1.

Andrews, Edmund L. 1995. "Mr. Smith Goes to Cyberspace." *The New York Times,* January 6, p. A–22.

Beagles-Roos, Jessica, and Isabelle Gat. 1983. "Specific Impact of Radio and Television on Children's Story Comprehension." *Journal of Educational Psychology,* February, 75,1:128–37.

Beagles-Roos, Jessica, and Patricia Greenfield. 1982. "Radio and Television Experimentally Compared: Effects of the Medium on Imagination and Transmission of Content." Final report to the National Institute of Education, Teaching and Learning Program.

Becker, H. J. 1994. *Analysis of Trends of School Use of New Information Technology.* Prepared for the Office of Technology Assessment, March, University of California, Irvine.

Bright, Duane E., Miguel Verano, and Ruben A. Cubero. 1991. "From Theory to Practice: A Model for an Interactive Videodisc Lesson," pp. 17–23 in Michael D. Bush, Alice Slaton, Miguel Verano, and Martha E. Slayden, eds., *Interactive Videodisc: The Why and the How.* Provo, UT: CALICO. [EDRS: ED 386 942].

Bunderson, C. Victor. 1981. *Proof-of-Concept Demonstration and Comparative Evaluation of a Prototype Intelligent Videodisc System.* Orem, UT: WICAT, Inc. [EDRS: ED 228 989].

Bunderson, C. Victor, and Victorine C. Abboud. 1971. "A Computer-Assisted Introduction Program in the Arabic Writing System." NSF Grant GJ 509 X, Technical Report No. 4. [EDRS: ED 052 603].

Bunderson, C. Victor, James B. Olsen, Bruce Baillio, J. I. Lipson, and K. M. Fisher. 1984. "Instructional Effectiveness of an Intelligent Videodisc in Biology." *Machine-Mediated Learning* 1,2:175–215.

Bush, Michael D. 1983. *Selected Variables in the Mathematical Formulation of a Model of Second Language Learning.* Unpublished doctoral dissertation, The Ohio State University.

———. 1988. "De l'E.A.O. à l'E.A.V.O. des langues étrangères à l'école de l'air américaine," pp. 167–73 in Mylène Garrigues, ed., *Nouvelles Technologies et Apprentisage des Langues,* special issue of *Français dans le monde,* August–September.

———. 1991. "Hardware for Language Training." *Applied Language Learning.* 2,2:77–91.

———. 1996a. "World Wide Web Technology: What's Hot and What's Not." *Multimedia Monitor,* February, 14,2:15–19.

———. 1996b. "Language Learning via the Web," in Frank Borchardt and Eleanor Johnson, eds. *Proceedings of the CALICO '96 Symposium,* June 29, 1996, Albuquerque, NM.

Bush, Michael D., and Jill Crotty. 1989. "Interactive Videodisc in Language Teaching," pp. 75–95 in Wm. Flint Smith, ed., *Modern Technology in Foreign Language Education: Applications and Projects.* The ACTFL Foreign Language Education Series. Lincolnwood, IL: National Textbook Company.

Bush, Michael D., Alice Slaton, Miguel Verano, and Martha E. Slayden editors. 1991. *Interactive Videodisc: The Why and How.* Provo, UT: CALICO. [EDRS: ED 386 942]

Carroll, John B. 1963. "A Model of School Learning." *Teacher's College Record* 64:723–33.

Cirtin, Arnold. 1996. "The MBA Degree on Television: The Fusion of Teaching and Technology." *THE Journal,* June, 70–73.

Clark, John L. D., and Fred Davidson. 1993. "Language-Learning Research: Cottage Industry or Consolidated Enterprise," pp. 254–78 in Alice Omaggio Hadley, ed., *Research in Language Learning: Principles, Processes, and Prospects.* The ACTFL Foreign Language Education Series. Lincolnwood, IL: National Textbook Company.

Crotty, Jill. 1984. *Instruction via an Intelligent Videodisc System versus Classroom Instruction for Beginning College French Students: A Comparative Experiment.* Unpublished doctoral dissertation, University of Kansas.

Doughty, Catherine. 1987. "Relating Second-Language Acquisition Theory to CALL Research and Application," pp. 133–67 in Wm. Flint Smith, ed., *Modern Media in Foreign Language Education: Theory and Implementation.* The ACTFL Foreign Language Education Series. Lincolnwood, IL: National Textbook Company.

———. 1991. "Theoretical Motivations for IVD Software Research and Development," pp. 1–15 in Michael D. Bush, Alice Slaton, Miguel Verano, and Martha E. Slayden, eds. *Interactive Videodisc: The Why and How.* Provo, UT: CALICO. [EDRS: ED 386 942]

Ervin, Gerard L., ed. 1980. *Proceedings of the National Conference on Individualized Instruction in Foreign Languages.* The Ohio State University, October 24–25. [EDRS: ED 203 662]

Frankel, Max. 1996. "The Moon This Time Around." *The New York Times,* May 5, p. 6.40.

Garrett, Nina. 1987. "A Psycholinguistic Perspective on Grammar and CALL," pp. 169–96 in Wm. Flint Smith, ed., *Modern Media in Foreign Language Education: Theory and Implementation.* The ACTFL Foreign Language Education Series. Lincolnwood, IL: National Textbook Company.

Geiss, Bertold. 1996. Telephone interview, August 15.

Gilder, George. 1994. *Life After Television.* New York: Norton.

Glennan, Thomas K., and Arthur Melmed. 1996. *Fostering the Use of Educational Technology: Elements of a National Strategy.* MR-682-OSTP. Santa Monica, CA: RAND Corporation. Also available at <http://rand.org/publications/MR/MR682/contents.html>.

Gooler, Dennis D. 1986. *The Education Utility: The Power to Revitalize Education and Society.* Englewood Cliffs, NJ: Educational Technology Publications.

Greenfield, Patricia M. 1984. *Mind and Media.* Cambridge: Harvard University Press.

Greenfield, Patricia M., and Jessica Beagles-Roos. 1988. "Radio vs. Television: Their Cognitive Impact on Children of Different Socioeconomic and Ethnic Groups." *Journal of Communication,* Spring, 38,2:71–92.

Grittner, Frank M. 1977. *Teaching Foreign Languages.* 2nd ed. New York: Harper & Row.

———. 1990. "Bandwagons Revisited: A Perspective on Movements in Foreign Language Education," pp. 9–43 in Diane W. Birckbichler, ed., *New Perspectives and New Directions in Foreign Language Education.* The ACTFL Foreign Language Education Series. Lincolnwood, IL: National Textbook Company.

Hayes, Jeanne. 1996. "A First Look At QED Research Results: QED'S 1996–97 Technology Purchasing Forecast," a presentation at QED's Education Marketers' Forum, July 11, Quality Education Data, Inc., Denver, CO.

Hubbard, Philip L. 1987. "Language Teaching Approaches, the Evaluation of CALL Software, and Design Implications," pp. 227–54 in Wm. Flint Smith, ed., *Modern Media in Foreign Language Education: Theory and Implementation.* The ACTFL Foreign Language Education Series. Lincolnwood, IL: National Textbook Company.

Jarvis, Gilbert A. 1983. "The Psychology of Second Language Learning: A Declaration of Independence." *The Modern Language Journal* 67:393–402.

Juska, Arunas, and Arthur E. Paris. 1993. "Student Computer Use: Its Organizational Structure and Institutional Support." *Collegiate Microcomputer,* February, 11,1:42–50.

Kasten, Alex S. 1996. "1996 Winter Consumer Electronics Show." *Multimedia Monitor,* February, 14,2:12–13.

Kupfer, Andrew, and Erin M. Davies. 1996. "Craig McCaw Sees an Internet in the Sky." *Fortune,* May 27, 62–72.

Landro, Laura. 1984. "RCA Will Quit Making Players for Videodisks." *The Wall Street Journal,* April 5, 203.67:3,20.

Lippa, Larry. 1995. "Let Them Log On." *International Herald Tribune,* January 19, Letters to the Editor.

Lyman-Hager, Mary Ann. 1994. "Video and Interactive Multimedia Technologies in French for the 1990s." *The French Review* 68,2:209–28.

Majumder, Diganta. 1994. "Empire of the Son." *Information Week,* January 10, 58.

McLuhan, Marshall. 1968. "Environment as Programmed Happening," pp. 113–24 in Walter J. Ong, ed., *Knowledge and the Future of Man.* New York: Holt, Rinehart, and Winston.

Melmed, Arthur, ed. 1995. *The Costs and Effectiveness of Educational Technology: Proceedings of a Workshop,* November, DRU-1205-CTI, Santa Monica, CA: RAND Corporation. Initial draft available at <http://www.ed.gov/Technology/Plan/RAND/Costs/index.html>.

"Mind Behind the Microsoft Miracle: Gates Reflects on the Future of Software, Money and the World of Washington." 1995. *The Washington Post,* December 3, p. H–1.

Moget, Thérèse, and Philippe Neveu. 1972. *De Vive Voix.* Paris: Didier.

Moraco, Donna A. 1996. *Key Vocabulary and Guided Listening as Influences on the Listening Comprehension of Beginning Foreign Language Learners.* Unpublished doctoral dissertation, Utah State University.

Mueller, Theodore. H. 1971. "Student Attitudes in the Basic French Courses at the University Of Kentucky." *Modern Language Journal* 55:290–98.

Murray, Janet H., Douglas Morgenstern, and Gilberte Furstenberg. 1989. "The Athena Language-Learning Project: Design Issues for the Next Generation of Computer-Based Language Learning Tools," pp. 97–118 in Wm. Flint Smith, ed., *Modern Technology in Foreign Language Education: Applications and Projects.* The ACTFL Foreign Language Education Series. Lincolnwood, IL: National Textbook Company.

Naisbitt, John. 1982. *Megatrends.* New York: Warner Books, Inc.

Negroponte, Nicholas. 1995. "homeless@info.hwy.net." *The New York Times,* February 11, p. 19.

Olsen, Solveig. 1980. "Foreign Language Departments and Computer-Assisted Instruction: A Survey." *Modern Language Journal* 63,3:341–49.

Ong, Walter J. 1968. "Knowledge in Time," pp. 3–38 in Walter J. Ong, ed. *Knowledge and the Future of Man.* New York: Holt, Rinehart, and Winston.

Otto, Sue K. 1989. "The Language Laboratory in the Computer Age," pp. 13–41 in Wm. Flint Smith, ed., *Modern Technology in Foreign Language Education: Applications and Projects.* The ACTFL Foreign Language Education Series. Lincolnwood, IL: National Textbook Company.

"The Past, Imperfect." 1996. *Time,* July 15, Technology Section.

Patrikis, Peter C. 1995. "Where Is Computer Technology Taking Us?" *ADFL Bulletin,* Winter, 26.2:36–39.

Pournelle, Jerry. 1983. "The Next Five Years in Microcomputers." *BYTE,* September, 8,9:233–44.

Purdum, Todd S. 1995. "Defending Affirmative Action, Clinton Details Plan to Review It." *The New York Times,* March 24, p. A–23.

Quality Education Data, Inc. (QED). 1994a. *Technology in Public Schools, 1993–94.* Denver, CO.

———. 1994b. *Educational Technology Trends, 1993–94.* Denver, CO.

Richardson, Charles P., and Sharon Guinn Scinicariello. 1989. *Modern Technology in Foreign Language: Applications and Projects.* The ACTFL Foreign Language Series. Lincolnwood, IL: National Textbook Company.

Roberts, Johnnie L. 1996. "The Disc Wars." *Newsweek,* August 26, 128,9:42–43.

Rockman, Saul. 1995. "In School or Out: Technology, Equity, and the Future of Our Kids." Communications of the ACM, June, 38,6:25–29.

Russell, Thomas L. 1996. E-mail correspondence. <Tom_Russell@NCSU.EDU.>

Schrupp, David. M., Michael D. Bush, and Gunther A. Mueller. 1983. *"Klavier im Haus*—An Interactive Experiment in Foreign Language Instruction." *CALICO Journal* 1,2:17–21.

Smith, Wm. Flint, ed. 1987. *Modern Media in Foreign Language Education: Theory and Implementation.* The ACTFL Foreign Language Education Series. Lincolnwood, IL: National Textbook Company.

————. 1989. *Modern Technology in Foreign Language Education: Applications and Projects.* The ACTFL Foreign Language Education Series. Lincolnwood, IL: National Textbook Company.

Underwood, Barbara, Karen Brammer, Rocco Fuschetto, Sigrid Koehler, Jack Jorden, and James Mervilde. 1992. "The Yorktown High School Foreign Language Interactive Videodisc Project," in William Hatfield, ed., *Creative Approaches in Foreign Language Teaching. Selected Papers from the Central States Conference,* Dearborn, Michigan, 1992. [EDRS: ED 362 035]

Underwood, John H. 1987. "Artificial Intelligence and CALL," pp. 197–225 in Wm. Flint Smith, ed., *Modern Media in Foreign Language Education: Theory and Implementation.* The ACTFL Foreign Language Education Series. Lincolnwood, IL: National Textbook Company.

USAFA (Department of Foreign Languages, United States Air Force Academy). 1996. Internal Survey of Language Center Users. Colorado Springs, CO: Department of Foreign Languages, United States Air Force Academy.

U.S. Bureau of the Census. 1950. *Statistical Abstract of the United States: 1950,* 71st ed. Washington, DC: GPO.

————. 1952. *Statistical Abstract of the United States: 1952,* 72nd ed. Washington, DC: GPO.

————. 1970. *Statistical Abstract of the United States: 1970,* 91st ed. Washington, DC: GPO.

————. 1984. *Statistical Abstract of the United States: 1984,* 105th ed. Washington, DC: GPO.

————. 1994. *Statistical Abstract of the United States: 1995,* 115th ed. Washington, DC: GPO.

Verano, Miguel. 1987. *Achievement and Retention in Spanish Presented via Videodisc in Linear, Segmented, and Interactive Modes.* Unpublished doctoral dissertation, The University of Texas at Austin.

Wallace, James, and Jim Erickson. 1992. *Hard Drive.* New York: HarperCollins.

White, Mary Alice. 1987. "Information and Imagery Education," pp. 41–63 in Mary Alice White, ed., *What Curriculum for the Information Age?* Hillsdale, NJ: Lawrence Erlbaum.

Whittier, Laurel Hall. 1995. "Opinion: Laptops for Poor." *The Los Angeles Times,* January 15, p. M-4.

Epilogue

This volume represents the transformations brought about by the Information Age in two ways. First, it presents many different facets of the impact information technology has had and will continue to have on teaching and learning. Second, the collection of articles itself is a product of new ways of bringing about collaborative work within a community of teachers and scholars. It is this second point that we wish to document in this Epilogue, for the production of the publication is in itself a story worth telling. Procedures similar to those employed here are becoming integral to the functioning of collaborative work groups in all phases of society.

For centuries, text has been the mainstay of the process for disseminating knowledge, but we have to wonder if things are about to change. Text-based materials for education, which today primarily take the form of textbooks, remain an essential ingredient of the educational delivery system in virtually the same fashion in which it has functioned for hundreds of years. Moreover, despite predictions to the contrary, paper consumption in society as a whole has not dropped during the Information Age, but has increased drastically with the advent of the high-quality, high-speed laser printers that are mainstays of technology implementation efforts.

Of course, because no new technology ever totally displaces the old, yesterday's technology often continues to operate side by side with the new. Consider the horse-drawn buggies seen from time to time in streets today alongside automobiles and taxis. Although long since replaced for most practical endeavors by newer vehicles built around the internal combustion engine, these critical devices of transportation of yesteryear still take tourists through romantic visits to many of our modern cities.

We can see, therefore, how most new technologies come on the scene to complement the functionality of previous technologies, not to totally replace them. Television did not eliminate radio. VCRs and cable TV have not eliminated the television networks or movies.

And so it will be with the printed word. For example, the World Wide Web significantly reduces the need for printing and distributing a great deal of text material. Regardless, newspapers will not disappear.

Although text materials are not being replaced, the manner in which they are produced continues to change drastically. The publishing industry used lead type for centuries, gradually transforming that technology from a character-by-character assembly of the alphabet from a large inventory of letters in the appropriate font type, to the Linotype machines that assembled a full "line of type" from pots of molten lead, to today's "cold type" process that produces sheets of photoready copy from photocompositors that are basically powerful computers in disguise.

The story of this epilogue is about what happened prior to the creation of that copy, the intellectual process that assembles the words to be printed.

Determining Content

General volume content was determined for the most part at the outset by the editor in the initial proposal to ACTFL. The proposals that were submitted by potential authors also brought about some modifications to our initial direction. In several cases chapter proposals seemed to capture the volume's purpose better than the initial prospectus. In those cases, the initial prospectus was modified as necessary to respond to suggestions from the advisory committee.

As part of the discussions with ACTFL that led up to this volume, we decided to proceed slightly differently than most efforts of this sort. Rather than asking for contributions from specific individuals, we decided to ask for proposals for contribution, with final selections for authors to be made by an advisory committee. The thinking was two-fold. First, it seemed reasonable to assume that authors who volunteered would be willing to put forth the necessary effort to complete their chapter on time. Second, this was an effort to commission articles that would fit the volume's emphasis, all the while giving authors reasonable assurance that their writing effort for a chapter would be rewarded with publication.

Once the prospectus was accepted by ACTFL, we established a simple protocol for advertising the volume and collecting proposals. Authors were asked to write two-page proposals, with one page describing the contents of the proposed chapter and a second to describe why the proposed chapter would be an important contribution to the volume in particular and to foreign language education in general. Two topics that were part of the initial prospectus did not capture the attention of potential authors and thus were not included in the final list of chapters that make up the volume.

Finding Contributors

Once the commission was received from ACTFL to proceed, the first step of the content development process took place at Middlebury College in June 1995 at the Annual Symposium of the Computer-Aided Language Instruction Consortium (CALICO). As gatherings of researchers and scholars committed to making intelligent use of technology in language education, CALICO Symposia have existed since 1984 and have been the likely place to find people interested in collaborating in such an endeavor. Two groups of people pledged their support in response to a flyer distributed at that meeting—an initial group of individuals interested in serving as members of the volume advisory committee and several potential authors.

Following the CALICO meeting and prior to the ACTFL Annual Meeting, a call for participation was also posted on Language Learning Technology International. LLTI, a LISTSERV for scholars and practitioners moderated by Otmar Foelsch of Dartmouth College, exchanges information and discusses topics of interest pertaining to technology for language learning. Potential contributors were directed to the volume prospectus posted on ACTFL's Web server <http://www.infi.net/~actfl>, which provided an overview of the volume and instructions for submitting proposals for consideration for inclusion.

In addition to the announcements at the CALICO Symposium and on LLTI, we also used a mailing list that we had received from a couple of sources to send out a call for participation. This event led to the biggest technical glitch of the process. Although we looked over the list for obvious formatting errors, there was no way to verify the correctness of all of the addresses short of sending out a message, which we did. Several of the addresses were inaccurate, either out of date or just plain incorrectly typed by those who had initially created the list. The problems with the incorrect addresses caused the mailing software at several points along the routing via the Internet to generate error messages to some of the addressees as well as to us, the transmitters. We received responses alerting us to the problem. Some expressed irritation at being bothered in this "unnecessary" way and others just wanted to alert us to the problem. Where a few of our importuned correspondents received a dozen or so messages, we had to clear our in box of a couple of thousand! This experience confirmed the sentiment of many pioneers of the Information Age–technology is great as long as it works as we want it to, rather than how we tell it to!

The volume advisory committee was selected from among those individuals experienced in language-learning technology development and implementation. Its main purpose was to serve as reviewers for the proposals that potential authors submitted in response to the call for participation.

Selecting Authors

All authors submitted their proposals for the chapters to the editor in electronic form. To make reviews blind, we edited the proposals to remove references to the authors' institutions and placed them on a World Wide Web server that was accessible to all members of the advisory committee. In this way, committee members were able to submit proposals for chapters as well as serve as reviewers. Indeed, there were proposals submitted by members of the advisory committee, including one submitted by the editor, that were rejected during the selection process.

To be able to distinguish between submissions, we accepted a suggestion from one committee member to use a four-category evaluation: Accept, Maybe Accept, Probably Reject, and Reject. To derive a quantitative score, we converted the ratings received from the advisory committee for each proposal to numbers.

Of the twenty-three proposals received, only six were accepted outright. Other proposals were accepted based on significant revision of their direction and focus. In one case a potential author's proposal did not adequately fit the volume's thrust, and there was no suitable proposal received in another area. This author accepted to switch topics and finished by submitting an excellent contribution. Of all the authors initially accepted, only one did not fulfill the commitment to make a contribution. That topic was incorporated into other areas at the last minute.

Managing Content Production

It only makes sense that a volume on technology should be produced using technology. We managed every phase of content development from start to finish using tools such as E-mail, servers running World Wide Web software, and FTP (File Transfer Protocol), a mainstay of Internet functionality. We used technology for

- the solicitation for contributions;
- the coordination of advisory committee activities;
- the exchange of ideas for topic development;
- the selection of authors;
- the coordination of author efforts;
- editor coordination;
- draft submission and correction.

Once the authors were selected, they submitted their drafts to the editor either as an attachment to an E-mail message or as a file transfer, using FTP. After reviewing the submission for adherence to the volume and chapter outlines, the editor E-mailed suggestions back to the authors who then re-submitted their draft, once again electronically. The associate editor then picked up the revised document from the project's FTP server, using this version to make final edits prior to submitting the final draft to the publisher on diskette.

All of the document flow was handled electronically, with only two or three papers being shipped in paper format. Even these versions turned out to be superfluous, as technical problems were solved following their shipment. About 98 percent of document transfer during the editing process took place using the Internet. A couple of diskettes were sent via overnight courier during this phase of the project.

One author initially experienced difficulties converting and submitting files prepared with an MS-DOS-based word processor. Other than with this case, however, authors and editors freely exchanged files between Macintosh and Windows word processors, preserving formats and accented characters flawlessly.

This is not to say there were no problems. But the problems that came up were solved as they arose, with a few retransmissions of documents taking place along the way. There is a certain irony in the fact that the most resource-intensive glitch (i.e., it took the most time and money to fix) occurred during final production steps when "atoms" (pages of paper) were shipped instead of "bits" (electronic representations in the form of "binary digits" or 1s and 0s). Galleys were being sent to authors for final review and the editor's inadequate instructions caused packages to be jumbled, and packages were routed to the wrong authors. In a couple of cases the problem was fixed by the shipment of "bits" in the form of faxes. In others, the "atoms" were re-shipped via overnight courier. Things will significantly improve when this final review process can take place electronically, a distinct possibility in the very near future.

Interesting statistics for the project of developing the volume's content include

- almost 3,000 E-mail messages exchanged between the editor, associate editor, advisory committee members, and authors;
- over 40 file transfers using FTP;
- relatively few paper versions printed during the editing process.

When all is said and done, we are convinced that without the use of technology it would have been patently impossible to create a volume of this scope, with this many contributors, in what finally amounted to a very short time for a production phase.

Index to Authors Cited

Index to Topics Cited

grammar paradigms, 16

grammar practice, 15

grammar review, 291

graphical user interfaces, 2, 228

Guided Reading, 129

Guided Reading Templates, 328

H

Hamburger Morgenpost, 223

hardware costs, 327

hardware, computer, 10

harmonics, 81, 107

Hypercard, 38, 328

hyperlinks, 2, 219

hypermedia, 2, 121, 129, 131, 144, 147, 148, 149, 150, 189

HyperStudio, 33

hypertext, 2, 4, 219, 275

I

IconAuthor, 38, 328

Illustrator, 40

individualization, 304

information

background, 30, 104, 126, 127, 134, 142, 144, 267

cultural, 216, 235, 236, 237

digital, 4, 193

extratextual, 123, 132

multimedia, 41

textual, 129

video, 24

visual, 142

written, 102

information access, 194, 310

Information Age, 33, 77, 301, 306, 307, 309, 325, 332

information availability, 307

information exchange, 77, 111

information explosion, 307

information highway, 273, 344

information industry, 318

information providers, 187

information resources, 193, 194, 201, 211

information superhighway, 77, 263, 344

information technology, 307, 309, 331

information types, 6, 319, 323, 325

infrastructure

information, 319, 325

school, 330

student support, 323

technology, 40

instructional design strategy, 313–315

instructional strategy, 222, 312, 314

integration phase (Reflective Framework), 275

intellectual property rights, 37

interaction

classroom, 14, 20, 27, 168, 176, 180

face-to-face, 82, 241

interactional structure, 22

oral, 168, 171, 176

student-to-student, 25, 172, 175, 255

student-to-teacher, 22, 166, 172

interactions, pedagogical, 40

interactive video, *See video, interactive*

interactivity, 6, 10, 43, 79, 82, 87, 88, 173, 221, 295, 296